Principles of Digital Design

Daniel D. Gajski

UNIVERSITY OF CALIFORNIA

PRENTICE HALL
Upper Saddle River, New Jersey 07458

Library of Congress Cataloging-in-Publication Data

Gajski, Daniel D.
    Principles of digital design / Daniel D. Gajski.
      p. cm.
    Includes bibliographical references and index.
    ISBN 0-13-301144-5
    1. Integrated circuits—Design—Data processing. 2. Logic design
    —Data processing. 3. Computer-aided design. I. Title.
TK7874.O34 1997
621.39'5—dc20   96-1339
                CIP

Editor-in-Chief: **Marcia Horton**
Acquisitions editor: **Tom Robbins**
Managing editor: **Bayani Mendoza de Leon**
Production editor: **Irwin Zucker**
Copy editor: **Barbara Zeiders**
Art director: **Amy Rosen**
Assistant art director: **Rod Hernandez**

Creative director: **Paula Maylahn**
Cover idea: **Daniel D. Gajski**
Cover design: **Thomas Nery**
Cover illustration: **Patrice Van Acker**
Interior design: **Sheree Goodman**
Manufacturing buyer: **Donna Sullivan**
Editorial assistant: **Phyllis Morgan**

 ©1997 by Prentice-Hall, Inc.
Simon & Schuster / A Viacom Company
Upper Saddle River, New Jersey 07458

The author and publisher of this book have used their best efforts in preparing this book. These efforts include the
development, research, and testing of the theories and programs to determine their effectiveness. The author
and publisher make no warranty of any kind, expressed or implied, with regard to these programs or the documentation
contained in this book. The author and publisher shall not be liable in any event for incidental or consequential damages
in connection with, or arising out of, the furnishing, performance, or use of these programs.

Printed in the United States of America

10 9 8 7 6 5 4 3 2

ISBN 0-13-301144-5

Prentice-Hall International (UK) Limited, *London*
Prentice-Hall of Australia Pty. Limited, *Sidney*
Prentice-Hall Canada Inc., *Toronto*
Prentice-Hall Hispanoamericana, S.A., *Mexico*
Prentice-Hall of India Private Limited, *New Delhi*
Prentice-Hall of Japan, Inc., *Tokyo*
Simon & Schuster Asia Pte. Ltd., *Singapore*
Editoria Prentice-Hall do Brasil, Ltda., *Rio de Janeiro*

This book is dedicated to my wife
ANA
for her patience and unquestioned support
through easy and difficult times on this project.

Contents

Preface

RATIONALE

With advances in VLSI technology, we can now manufacture microchips containing several million transistors each. Since the manual design of such microchips is almost impossible, the CAD industry has emerged to provide software tools for the design of these large microchips. As a result, most of the digital design techniques we used to teach are now encapsulated in CAD tools, and designers are now free to concentrate on the design process as a whole, extending from product definition to manufacturing. Given this broader focus, the designers now have to master various techniques for requirements analysis, specification capture, design modeling, software/hardware codesign, microchip synthesis, verification, simulation, and testing. In this sense, the notion of design expertise has been redefined, shifting from a knowledge of all possible design techniques to a knowledge of the principles, and an ability to use CAD tools to explore various design alternatives and implementation techniques.

TEXT GOALS

DESIGN PRINCIPLES. This book is designed to provide a thorough understanding of design's fundamental principles without requiring students to memorize a lot of potentially confusing technological details. We have achieved this simplicity by introducing generic component libraries that reflect practical design constraints, such as cost and delay. We use this generic library to explain all the concepts we present and to implement all the examples that are worked out in the text.

DESIGN PROCESS. Taken as a whole, this book has been structured around a concern for the complete design process instead of addressing particular design techniques that are relevant to a particular phase of design. For this reason we explain the digital design process first and throughout the book, emphasize the role of each task within the context of the larger design process.

RELATION OF THEORY AND PRACTICE. Unfortunately, many texts on digital design tend to gloss over basic principles, or, conversely, discuss in great detail theory that will rarely be used. To counteract these deficiencies we have constructed this book such that from the beginning there is a clear relation between principles and practical design. Theoretical foundations are introduced only when they will help to simplify certain explanations of design techniques.

DETAILED EXAMPLES. In each chapter we present several comprehensive examples that demonstrate every step in the design process.

We have found that detailed examples are the best learning vehicle since students can trace all design steps, evaluate design alternatives, and question the reasons behind all design decisions. Students also prefer detailed examples over text since through examples they can easily grasp the meaning of new concepts. In this way we avoid the frequently encountered mistake of defining concepts through trivial examples and leaving students to combine them into a design process and deduce why and how to go from one design step to another.

REGISTER-TRANSFER DESIGN.   In addition to these general goals, this book has the more specific goal of extending students' knowledge of design methodology beyond the logic and sequential levels to encompass register-transfer design techniques for the design of general-purpose and application-specific processors and microchips. In presenting the register-transfer design, the text goal is to provide the missing link between logic and sequential design, covered in the first course in computer design, and computer organization, usually covered in the second course on computer design. This material is omitted in many textbooks, leaving the student guessing how to use adders, counters, and memories in the design of processors and other microchips.

TOPICAL HIGHLIGHTS

MODERN DESIGN PROCESS.   In the first chapter we introduce the discipline of system design defining the design process and its main tasks. This chapter serves as a foundation for the more detailed discussions that follow as well as providing a road map for the entire book. We also discuss modern design technology and the CAD tools that facilitate its use. A short overview of the manufacturing process is provided and the relation between design and manufacturing is discussed. The aim of Chapter 1 is to motivate students to learn system design by giving them a broad view of the role of design science in the real world.

BINARY NUMBERS AND DATA REPRESENTATIONS.   In Chapter 2 we present the data model used by digital systems. Since an understanding of binary representation is crucial for understanding the operation of digital systems, we thoroughly explain binary numbers (both fixed and floating point) as well as various algorithms for the arithmetic operations that use them. We also explain several of the other types of data models and how to use them efficiently.

IMPACT OF VLSI TECHNOLOGY.   Design techniques must always be able to accommodate certain trade-offs between the requirements of a given system and the technologies available for its implementation. For this reason we introduce the principles and constraints of VLSI technology very early and discuss their impact on various design techniques in almost every chapter. However, this book does not require a knowledge of electronics, nor does it deal with electrical circuits. Instead, we use components that represent standard Boolean and arithmetic operators as well as simple and complex data structures. The book does not use particular component libraries such as TTL or commercially available CMOS libraries, because it has been written under the assumption that understanding the principles of various components and knowing how to use them is much more important than knowing the exact names and packages of all circuits commercially available. For this reason we use generic components that remain independent of any proprietary technology.

CONTEMPORARY APPROACH TO LOGIC AND SEQUENTIAL DESIGN. Contemporary design libraries tend to be small in order to simplify their maintenance as well as design algorithms and CAD tools that use them. Throughout this book, we use a simple gate library and build all higher-level components that we require from this basic library. Chapters 5 and 7, for example, introduce all combinatorial and sequential components needed for design of processors and application-specific integrated circuits. At the same time, though, the fact that adequate CAD tools exist should not be overlooked, as these tools can relieve designers of the need to go through complex manual optimization techniques. For this reason, we emphasize the basic goals and principles of optimization and demonstrate modern design process.

FORMAL APPROACH TO REGISTER-TRANSFER DESIGN. In the past, the design techniques beyond the level of sequential synthesis have been considered an art and have received very little space in design texts. To fill this gap, in Chapter 8 we introduce the concept of a finite-state machine with a datapath. Having defined this concept, we show how to map arbitrary algorithms that have been expressed in terms of either a standard flowchart or register-transfer charts into hardware that consists of a datapath and a control unit containing given combinatorial and sequential components defined in Chapters 5 and 7.

PROCESSOR DESIGN. In Chapter 9 we show how a CPU can be designed using the formalism and methods of register-level design that were introduced in Chapter 8. In addition, this chapter provides an introduction to instruction sets, computer architecture, and processor design methodology. To demonstrate these concepts, Chapter 9 also features the design of 16-bit CISC and 32-bit RISC processors with data forwarding and branch prediction.

EDITORIAL FEATURES

ROAD MAPS. To help orient the student, we utilize a topical block diagram that summarizes the topics presented in the book, and defines their interrelationships. Each chapter opens with an introductory paragraph that summarizes that chapter's goals and the topics it covers. This overview will help students relate the concepts presented in earlier chapters with new concepts as they are introduced.

DESIGN PROCEDURES. Each design technique is presented as a step-by-step procedure, summarized in the form of a flowchart. The flowchart sallow students to solve problems in an orderly way as well as suggesting how to extend given techniques to new problems or new technologies that emerge in the future.

COMPREHENSIVE EXAMPLES. The book includes worked examples to illustrate the principles and design procedures that are relevant to certain applications. In each chapter we use a small number of these comprehensive examples to demonstrate various design alternatives, leading the reader through all the necessary design steps, from definition to the final schematic.

INSTRUCTOR'S MANUAL AND LECTURE TRANSPARENCIES. We have developed a solution manual that contains a completely worked out solution for each end-of-chapter problem. The manual also includes original problem statements for the convenience of the instructor. We also provide transparencies of lectures given by the author while using this book. The manual and a set of these transparencies will be made available to all instructors who adopt this text for course use.

COURSE OPTIONS

Based on its organization, this book should be equally effective in two different types of courses. In an introductory course on digital design, for example, the book can be used to emphasize the traditional combinatorial and sequential design covered in most computer science and computer engineering curricula in the United States and abroad. The material for such a course is presented in Chapters 1 through 7. In addition, we present material on register-transfer design of general-purpose and application-specific processors usually covered in a second course in digital design or in an introductory course in computer architecture.

In this course, students would first learn basic register-transfer components: combinatorial components in Chapter 5 and sequential components in Chapter 7. The major part of the course would consist of learning register-level design techniques and the design process for synthesis of arbitrary application specific processors, which is given in Chapter 8. Finally, in Chapter 9, the students would learn the design of modern instruction sets and general-purpose CISC and RISC processors.

In either case, we suggest supplementing the lecture series with a lab course in which students work through real design problems using modern CAD tools for design capture, modeling, simulation, verification, synthesis, timing analysis, floor planning, physical design, and other aspects of the design process. In our experience lab courses are very popular with students, as they allow them to relate the learned concepts to practical designs in a real working environment. As an aid for the instructor, we described several different lab settings and gave several examples of lab experiments in the Appendix.

Daniel Gajski
Irvine, California

Acknowledgments

First, I would like to thank all of the students who have taken my courses and asked hundreds of questions, making me aware of the learning process and forcing me to experiment with various methods of conversing knowledge about design science.

I would like to thank Nikil Dutt, Alex Orailoglu, Fadi Kurdahi, Youn-Long Steve Lin, and Allen C. H. Wu, who class-tested an early version of this book and provided many helpful suggestions as to how to improve the context and presentation of the material. I also appreciate very much helpful suggestions from anonymous referees on selected material and presentation quality.

I would also like to thank the people who helped with production of the book. Jon Kleinsmith generated all the drawings and entered and formatted all the text. Without his patience and dedication this book would never reached the publisher. I am also grateful to Sarah Wilde for dedicated and thorough editing of the manuscript. Thanks also go to the members of the CAD LAB who helped with corrections and proofreading of the final version of the text: Tedd Hadley, Jie Gong, Hsiao-Ping Juan, Smita Bakshi, Alfred Thordarson, David Kolson, Pradip Jha, Preeti Panda, Jianwen Zhu, Min Xu, Laurent Chouraki, Marie-Lise Flottes, Nong Fan, Joanna Kang, Wenwei Pan, Viraphol Chaiyakul, and Poonam Agrawal. I am also very grateful to Gerry Johnson and Don Fowley of Prentice Hall, who convinced me that writing this book would be an appropriate and interesting challenge at this point in my life. I would also like to acknowledge Tom Robbins, Barbara Cappucio, Irwin Zucker, and the staff at Prentice Hall for highly professional production of this book.

Design is not just a set of techniques or how-to-do-recipes, but a process in which many different people contribute to different aspects of the final product. Each of these people looks at the product from a different view, has different expertise, and uses different tools. Together, they turn a concept into a real product.

CHAPTER

Introduction

For any particular product, the design process extends all the way from conceptualizing its functions to developing a manufacturing blueprint. Many people are involved in this process, each performing a specific task.

The marketing department, for example, studies market needs and determines the requirements for a new product. Technologists select the technology, possible components and suppliers, while a support group acquires or develops software tools that can support the design of the product and of each of its parts. The product designers convert product requirements into blueprints for manufacturing. Test engineers develop test strategies to verify design correctness and to test manufactured products for malfunctioning, while manufacturing engineers develop manufacturing plans and develop production schedules.

1.1 DESIGN REPRESENTATIONS

Within the product definition, design, and manufacturing process, each person involved looks at the product from a slightly different point of view and requires specific information to support his or her work. For this reason, each product, and consequently each design, requires several different representations or views, which differ in the type of information that they emphasize. In addition, the same representation often requires different levels of detail in different phases of the design or manufacturing cycle. The three most common types of representation that are used are behavioral, structural, and physical representations.

A **behavioral** or **functional representation** is one that looks at the design as a black box and focuses on specifying its behavior as a function of its input values and expired time. In other words, a behavioral representation describes the functionality but not the implementation of a given design, defining the black box's response to any combination of input values but without describing a way to design or build the black box using the given components.

A **structural representation**, by contrast, is one that defines the black box as a set of components and their connections. Unlike a behavioral representation, it specifies the product's implementation without explicit reference to its functionality. In some cases, of course, the functionality could be derived from that of its interconnected components. However, deriving the functionality of a design this way is difficult and prone to error, since the functions of some components may not be used to their full potential, or they may be modified by encoding the component's inputs and outputs. Furthermore, in cases where the number of components is very large, say 10,000, it would be impossible to discover their functionality, especially since today's technology allows the manufacture of microchips with several million transistors.

Finally, a **physical representation** is one that specifies the physical characteristics of the black box, providing the dimensions and locations of each component and connection contained in the structural description. Note that while the structural representation provides the design's connectivity, only the physical representation describes the precise spatial relationships of the various components. In other words, the physical representation is used to describe the design after it has been manufactured, specifying its weight, size, heat dissipation, power consumption and the position of each input or output pin.

EXAMPLE 1.1   Simple alarm clock

PROBLEM   Develop behavioral, structural, and physical design representations of a simple alarm clock.

SOLUTION   The simple alarm clock consists of a liquid-crystal display (LCD) showing seconds, minutes, and hours, and five different switches used for time setting (S_1), alarm setting, (S_2), minute advance (S_3), hour advance (S_4), and alarm enabling (S_5). When S_1 is closed, we can set the time by pressing S_3 or S_4. Each time that S_3 or S_4 is pushed, the set minute or hour is advanced by 1 and the change in the set minutes or hours is displayed on the clock display. When S_2 is closed, the wake-up time can be set in a similar fashion, by pushing S_3 or S_4 to advance the wake-up minutes or hours. Whenever the wake-up time is being set, the wake-up hours and minutes are displayed by the LCD. Finally, when switch S_5 is closed, the alarm is enabled, so that a 5-second buzzing sound is generated when the clock reaches the wake-up time.

The behavior of this alarm clock can be represented by three concurrent tasks or processes: clock, setup, and alarm. Each of these processes, in turn, can be described by a simple **flowchart**, which consists of diamond-shaped boxes that indicate questions and rectangular boxes that indicate computations. The flowcharts that represent the behavior of these three processes are shown in Figures 1.1 to 1.3.

As you can see from Figure 1.1, the clock process has one input signal, *Pulse*, and six internal variables: *Seconds*, *Minutes*, *Hours*, *Sdisplay*, *Mdisplay* and *Hdisplay*. The *Pulse* signal, which is used for counting seconds within the alarm clock, lasts for 1 second, taking the value 1 for the first half of the second and 0 for the remainder. Three of the internal variables—*Seconds*, *Minutes*, and *Hours*—are used for counting seconds, minutes, and hours. The *Seconds* and *Minutes* are counted modulo 60—that is, they reset to 0 whenever they reach a count of 59. The *Hours* are counted modulo 12, starting with 1 and returning to 1 after a count of 12. In operation, *Seconds* are be incremented by 1 whenever the *Pulse* signal transitions from 0 to 1, as indicated by ↑ in the flowchart. Similarly, whenever *Seconds* reaches 0, *Minutes* is

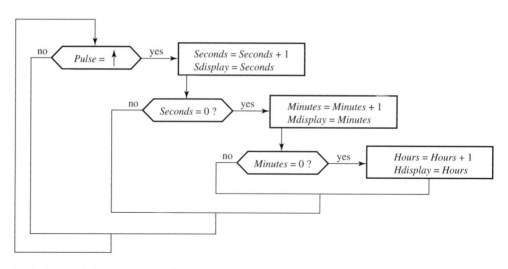

FIGURE 1.1
Alarm clock behavioral representation: clock process.

incremented by 1, and whenever *Minutes* reaches 0, *Hours* is incremented by 1.

The other three internal variables—*Sdisplay*, *Mdisplay*, and *Hdisplay*—are used to display the seconds, minutes, and hours. Note that each of these display variables is updated individually whenever there is a change in the corresponding clock variables—that is, in *Seconds*, *Minutes*, and *Hours*.

As distinct from the clock process, the setup process (Figure 1.2) describes how to set the clock time or wake-up time to any time we desire. We use two additional internal variables, *Mwakeup* and *Hwakeup*, to store the minutes and hours of the wake-up time. By closing switches S_3 and S_4, we can increment the wake-up minutes and hours that are stored in *Mwakeup* and *Hwakeup*, respectively. Thus we set the proper time by first closing switch S_1 or S_2, depending on whether we want to set the clock time or the wake-up time, and then repeatedly pressing switches S_3 and S_4. Note that we cannot close both S_1 and S_2 at the same time. Note also that the time we have set by closing S_3 or S_4 will be displayed immediately on the clock display.

The last of the three processes, the alarm process (Figure 1.3), is designed to set the alarm to "on" by setting the output variable, *Buzz*, to 1 at the precise moment when the clock time equals the wake-up time, assuming that the alarm switch, S_5, has been closed. In other words, whenever the *Minutes* = *Mwakeup*, *Hours* = *Hwakeup*, and S_5 is closed, *Buzz* gets the value 1.

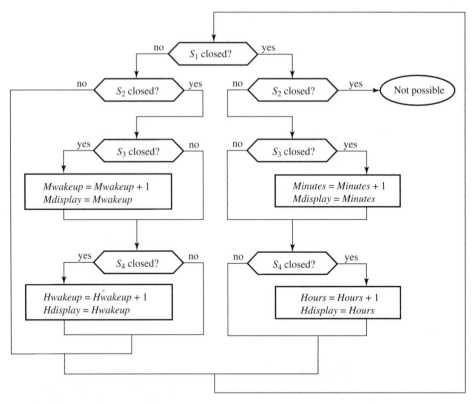

FIGURE 1.2

Alarm clock behavioral representation: setup process.

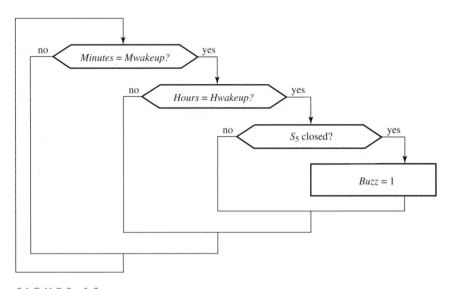

FIGURE 1.3

Alarm clock behavioral representation: alarm process.

For a behavioral description such as the one that we have just introduced for the alarm clock, there could be many different structural descriptions because a behavioral description does not specify the exact structure. Instead, it specifies a number of internal variables to be used for data storage and a number of assignment statements to be used for data transformation. Given this information, we proceed by converting the variables into memory components and inferring arithmetic components to perform the data transformations specified by the assignment statements. This conversion yields the most obvious, though nonoptimal structural representation, as shown in Figure 1.4.

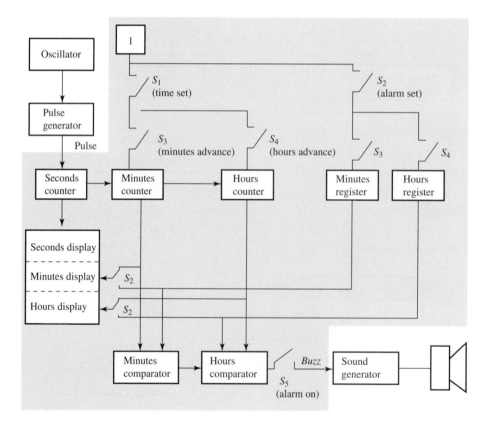

FIGURE 1.4
Alarm clock structural representation.

Note that according to Figure 1.4, the alarm clock is driven by the oscillator, which produces a sine wave with a frequency of one cycle per second, as shown in Figure 1.5(a). This sine wave is converted by the pulse generator into the

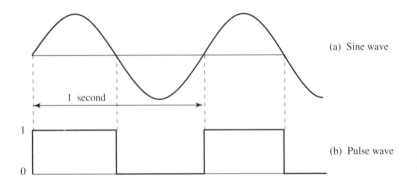

(a) Sine wave

1 second

(b) Pulse wave

FIGURE 1.5
Wave generators.

pulse signal, shown in Figure 1.5(b), which has the same frequency as the sine wave but takes only two values: 0 and 1.
Such a signal, which takes only two values, is called a **digital
signal**, and any system that processes digital signals is called
a **digital system**.

Returning to Figure 1.4, you can see that the rest of the
structural specification of the alarm clock consists of three
counters, a seconds counter, a minutes counter, and an hours
counter, which count seconds, minutes, and hours, and two
single-word memory components, minutes register and hours
register, used for storing the wake-up minutes and hours.
The display unit displays the seconds, minutes, and hours
for either the clock or the wake-up time, depending on the
position of the S_2 switch. In the minute comparator, the
clock and wake-up minutes are compared. If they are the
same, the value 1 is fed to the hour comparator. Similarly,
the hour comparator sets its output to 1 whenever the clock
hours and wake-up hours are the same and the input from
the minute comparator is equal to 1. Assuming that the S_5
switch is closed when the output of the hour comparator
becomes 1, the *Buzz* signal also becomes equal to 1. The
sound generator is used to convert the change from 0 to 1
in the *Buzz* signal into a 5-second buzz tone, which drives a
miniature speaker in the alarm clock.

Categorizing components in the structural representation of the alarm clock, the oscillator and the speaker are
considered **analog components**, since their input and outputs can take any value within a given range. For example,
during each second, the oscillator generates all the values
between -1.5 and $+1.5$ volts at its output. The pulse generator is what we call an **analog-to-digital (A/D) converter**,
since it takes an analog input and generates a digital output.
Conversely, the sound generator is a **digital-to-analog (D/A)**

converter, since it is designed to convert a digital signal into an analog signal. The rest of the system, contained within the dashed lines in Figure 1.4, is a digital system composed of digital components. The material in this book deals exclusively with the design techniques for digital systems.

In Figure 1.6 we present the physical representation of the alarm clock, giving the sizes and positions of the real components as they are assembled on a printed circuit board (PCB) inside the alarm clock chassis. Note that this PCB contains several microchips: the oscillator, the pulse generator, the sound generator, and all the digital parts of the alarm clock. It also contains the display, the switches, and the battery box, as well as the printed metal wires that connect all the components.

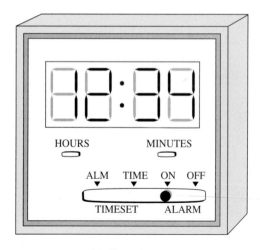

(a) Front view

(b) Printed circuit board

FIGURE 1.6
Alarm clock physical representation.

As we have indicated in Example 1.1, the design process of electronic products in general, and digital systems in particular, always consists of at least three phases centered around three main representations:

1. Deriving a behavioral representation to define the functionality of the product

2. Converting it to a structural representation consisting of components from a given component library

3. Producing a physical representation that specifies how to assemble and manufacture the product

Any digital design may go through these three phases on several differ-ent levels of abstraction, as we see in the next section.

1.2 LEVELS OF ABSTRACTIONS

In Section 1.1 we described behavioral, structural, and physical repre-sentations. In the design process of electronic systems, any one of these three representations might be used at several different levels of ab-straction or granularity, in which levels are defined by the type of ob-jects they use. In general, four different types of objects can be identi-fied in an electronic system: transistors, gates, registers, and processor components. These abstraction levels are summarized in Table 1.1. As the table indicates, the main components on the **transistor level** are tran-sistors, resistors, and capacitors, which are combined to form analog and digital circuits that can satisfy a given functionality. This functionality is usually described by a set of differential equations or by some type of current–voltage relationships. The physical representation of these analog and digital circuits, called cells, would consist of transistor-level components and the wires that connect them.

TABLE 1.1

Design Representations and Abstraction Levels

LEVEL	BEHAVIORAL FORMS	STRUCTURAL COMPONENTS	PHYSICAL OBJECTS
Transistor	Differential equations, current-voltage diagrams	Transistors, resistors, capacitors	Analog and digital cells
Gate	Boolean equations, finite-state machines	Gates, flip-flops	Modules, units
Register	Algorithms, flowcharts, instruction sets, generalized FSM	Adders, comparators, registers, counters, register files, queues, datapaths	Microchips
Processor	Executable specification, programs	Processors, controllers, memories, ASICs	Printed-circuit boards, multichip modules

In general, a **cell** is defined in terms of its transistor layout, com-prising a set of rectangles, usually depicted with different colors, that represent rectangular areas on the various material layers in a microchip.

From these layouts we then generate masks for the photolithographic process, which is the first step used during the fabrication of microchips. In this process a mask serves to expose certain areas of the silicon surface so that these open areas can be altered by chemicals, thus creating various distinct material layers on the silicon surface. Ultimately, the proper combination of materials creates a transistor effect, so that an electrical current can flow between two layers of different materials whenever a voltage is applied to their ends.

As indicated in Table 1.1, the main components on the **gate level** of abstraction are logic gates and flip-flops. Logic gates are special circuits that perform Boolean operations which are similar to conjunctions in the English language such as *or* and *and*. A flip-flop is a basic memory element that is capable of storing one bit of information which will be one of two values: 0 (false, no) or 1 (true, yes).

Gates and flip-flops are typical digital cells that have inputs and outputs on their boundaries. These cells can be grouped and placed on the silicon surface to form arithmetic and storage **modules** or **units** that are used as the basic components in the register level. These units are described behaviorally by means of Boolean equations and finite-state-machine (FSM) diagrams.

In Table 1.1 you can see also that the main components on the **register level** of abstraction are arithmetic and storage units, such as adders, comparators, multipliers, counters, registers, register files, queues, and datapaths. Each of these register components is a module or unit which has fixed dimensions, a fixed propagation time, and a fixed position for the inputs and outputs located on its boundary. These register components can be assembled and interconnected into microchips, which are used as the basic components on the next-higher level of abstraction. In general, these microchips are described by flowcharts, instruction sets, generalized FSM diagrams, or state tables.

The highest level of abstraction presented in Table 1.1 is called the **processor level**, since the basic components on this level are processors, memories, controllers, and interfaces, in addition to the custom microchips called application-specific integrated circuits (ASICs). Generally, one or more of these components are placed on a printed-circuit board and connected with wires that are printed on the board. In some cases we can reduce the dimensions of the board by using a silicon substrate instead of a printed-circuit board to connect the microchips, in which case the package is called a multichip module. The systems that are composed from these processor-level components are usually described behaviorally by either a natural language, an executable specification in a hardware description language, or an algorithm or program written in a programming language.

During the design process of an electronic digital system, any one of these levels of abstraction may be used one or more times, depending on how many different goals, technologies, components, libraries, and design alternatives we want to explore. Since this exploration could potentially be performed in several different ways, we must choose carefully an efficient **design methodology** which determines the proper subset of abstraction levels, synthesis tasks, the order in which they are executed, and the type of CAD tools used during the execution of each task in the design process.

The most popular methodology consists of building a library for a certain abstraction level, then using synthesis to convert a behavioral description into a structure that can be implemented with the components from this library. For the last 20 years, the most popular libraries have consisted of gate-level components, although register libraries have recently been gaining in popularity. In this book we also follow this methodology, first defining a gate-level library which can then be used to build a register library that will be used for register-transfer synthesis of general-purpose and application-specific processors.

1.3 DESIGN PROCESS

In very general terms, the **design process** can be defined as that sequence of steps which leads from a product concept to manufacturing drawings that show how to build that product. In real practice, of course, this process is always heavily influenced by which product is being designed, by how soon the product must be brought to market, by the particular technology used for its manufacture, and even by factors such as the company's organizational structure, the design team's experience, the availability of CAD tools, and adequate financing. In this sense the design process always varies from organization to organization, and even from product to product, within each organization. Despite these variations, though, we can safely assume that the following basic steps are always present, in one form or another, in every design process.

1.3.1 Design Specification

Once market requirements have been analyzed, the chief architect will write a **product specification** that defines the product's functionality and the interfaces to the environment in which that product is going to operate. On many occasions, this process of specification includes a very sketchy design of the product architecture, which is usually given as a high-level **block diagram**. Within the diagram, each block will have a well-understood functionality that can be specified by a mathematical formula or an algorithm, or just described in a natural language. Such a block diagram may also specify the type and format of the data passed among the blocks and input/output ports.

In general, this kind of specification tends to be vague in places and perhaps even incomplete, since the product has not yet been designed and evaluated. Such incompleteness is not necessarily a problem, since specification serves primarily as a starting point for the design team and is usually modified and refined as the design progresses. In most cases the specification is written in a natural language such as English, although executable specifications have been gaining popularity because they can be verified, analyzed, and synthesized more easily.

1.3.2 Library Development

Once the high-level block diagram has been developed in the specification phase, it must be iteratively refined or decomposed into smaller components. The goal of this process is to ensure that the product contains nothing but the predefined components from a **library of components** that has been characterized for a particular manufacturing technology. In some cases these libraries contain components from two or more abstraction levels. For example, it is not unusual to find some components from the register level included with gate-level components.

The components in the library must then be designed, tested, and fully documented so that designers can use them without having to analyze their structure. The characterization information should include the following:

1. The component's functionality, the names of inputs and outputs, and the typical application

2. The component's physical dimensions, the position of inputs and outputs, and the packaging information

3. The electrical constraints, the power supply requirements, the current and voltage ranges that are allowed at the inputs and outputs, and the heat dissipation

4. The voltage waveforms for inputs and outputs, the timing relationships between them, and the critical delays from inputs to outputs

5. The component models to be used by CAD tools for simulation, synthesis, physical design, and testing

1.3.3 Design Synthesis

In the design process, synthesis is the procedure by which we convert a specification or behavioral description of a component into a structural description, using components from lower levels of abstraction that are included in the given library. In those cases where we need components that are not contained in this library, we need to perform further synthesis.

Synthesis can usually be thought of as a process of refining the behavioral description, in which more structural detail is added at each step. In practice, this usually means that the behavioral description is partitioned into several blocks and then rewritten to reflect the result of the partitioning. This new refined description contains a structural description of partitioned blocks and their connections together with behavioral descriptions for each block. This process is continued until each block represents one of the components in the target library.

Following the levels of abstraction described in Table 1.1, we can identify several distinct synthesis tasks:

1. **System synthesis** converts a specification into a structure of processor-level components, such as processors, memories, and ASICs.

2. **Architecture synthesis** converts algorithms, flowcharts, or instruction sets into register-level components, such as counters, registers, stacks, queues, adders, and multipliers.

3. **Sequential synthesis** transforms a finite-state-machine description into gates and flip-flops.

4. **Logic synthesis** transforms Boolean expressions into gate-level components.

Below the gate level, synthesis techniques are divided according to specific application areas, because of the diversity of styles in circuit design. For example, different techniques are needed to synthesize circuits for different domains, such as A/D conversion, filtering, audio processing, or image enhancement. It is important to note that each of the synthesis steps described in this subsection can be further divided into several substeps or problems, which are discussed throughout the remainder of this book.

1.3.4 Design Analysis

Once a design has been synthesized, the next step is to evaluate that design, verifying that it actually satisfies the specification requirements, or in some cases, verifying that the design we have developed is really the best of several design alternatives. When we evaluate a design, we usually focus on one of several quality metrics, such as cost, performance, or testability. One of the most important of these metrics, for example, is the **cost of manufacturing** a particular product. This metric is usually approximated by the size or area metric, since the area of a microchip or PCB is proportional to the cost of its manufacture. The number of input and output pins is another important cost metric, since the cost of packaging is proportional to the number of input/output pins. Recently, power consumption has become an important metric because of the widespread use of portable equipment such as laptop computers and cordless telephones. Since power consumption determines the size of batteries, it also has a strong impact on the weight of the product.

The other important concern in the design process is **product performance**, which can be measured in several ways. The three most popular performance metrics are (1) the input/output delay, (2) the clock period, and (3) the time needed for a program, algorithm, flowchart, or a single instruction to complete its execution. In general, components with shorter delays, designs with shorter clock cycles, and products with shorter execution times are considered to have higher performance.

Finally, **testability metrics** are defined in terms of the number of detectable manufacturing faults and the number of test patterns that are needed to detect all these faults. Each test pattern or test vector contains a set of input values with a corresponding set of the output values we expect to obtain in a fault-free operation. In general, the number of potential faults is proportional to the number of test patterns we need, which is proportional to the time needed to test the manufactured product.

1.3.5 Documentation

The final step in the design process consists of preparing the documentation for the manufactured microchip or system. This documentation generally includes both the behavioral and physical representations of the product but omits detailed structural representations, which are considered to be proprietary information that will be disclosed only to the company's manufacturing divisions. The behavioral information is usually given in the form of a rough block diagram accompanied by a flowchart that describes the behavior of the complete system or of some of its parts. In addition, this behavioral documentation presents communication protocols, which specify how the system communicates with its environment, and are usually given in the form of timing diagrams for one or more of the inputs and outputs. The physical representation, on the other hand, contains the size, the packaging information, and the names and positions of all connectors. Finally, this documentation also specifies the minimal, normal and maximal ranges for the current, voltage, power, temperature, and time delays.

1.3.6 Manufacturing

Manufacturing is not really part of the design process; it is, rather, its goal, in the sense that the manufacturing process converts the final design drawings into a microchip or a printed-circuit board by assembling all the parts and connecting them properly. After manufacturing, we usually perform further testing to separate any faulty products from those that are functionally correct. This testing can be performed at normal operating speed or at speeds slower than those at which the product normally operates. In the case of high-performance products, testing at the normal speed is very difficult since the testers have to be much faster than the normal speed of the product under test.

1.4 CAD TOOLS

In Section 1.3, we discussed the basic steps of the design process, and in this section we discuss briefly computer-aided design (CAD) tools that are used by designers in various stages of this design process. These CAD tools can be divided into five different categories, corresponding to the way they are used in the design process.

1. Capture and modeling
2. Synthesis
3. Verification and simulation
4. Placement and routing
5. Test generation

These five categories correspond roughly to areas of specialization in CAD-tool research and development.

1.4.1 Design Capture and Modeling

At some point in every design process we need to transform a behavioral representation into a structural representation comprised of various components from a well-characterized library. At this point we could specify all of these components and their interconnections textually, although this can be a tedious and error-prone procedure. On the other hand, we can also capture the structural representation more easily and accurately by using a capture tool. Basically, such a tool allows the designer to select a component from the menu, position it on the screen, and connect it to other components with lines that represent wires. This kind of captured structural representation is called a **schematic**, and the capture tools we use are frequently called **schematic capture** tools.

Alternatively, this goal of capturing schematics can be accomplished equally well with a **hardware-description language** such as the IEEE-standard called VHDL. In addition to capturing schematics, however, these hardware-description languages also allow us to capture behavioral representations, so that a design can be described as a combination of its behavior and structure. The product description of the design usually begins with a behavioral description of each block within a high-level structural block diagram. As the design process progresses, each of these behaviors would be decomposed recursively into a structure of lower-level blocks until the design becomes a hierarchy of blocks, wherein the lowest-level represents specific components from the given library. Thus each design will have been described at several different levels of abstraction, each level containing a different type and amount of detail. Such a hierarchical set of descriptions is needed so that we can verify different design properties and design compliance with the imposed constraints. In addition, it simplifies design-project management, speeds up the communication between designers, allows for smooth design integration, reduces design errors, and supports design evolution and maintenance. Each of these descriptions is called a **model** of the real design, since it provides some but not all of the information about the design at hand. The design information provided by each model can be used by designers, or by other CAD tools, for further analysis or evaluation of the design's quality, or even for further synthesis. The process of developing these models is called modeling, and the guidelines which provide directions for writing models that include all the proper information required for use by other tools are called **modeling guidelines**.

1.4.2 Synthesis Tools

Synthesis techniques are used whenever we need to convert a behavioral description into a structural description that contains components from a given library. For example, **logic synthesis** tools enable us to convert Boolean expressions into gate-level structures, while minimizing the number of gates, the propagation delay, or the power consumption. Logic synthesis tools are very useful when we design combinatorial circuits such as arithmetic operators, data comparators, encoders, decoders, and control logic.

Sequential synthesis tools are needed to synthesize structures that contain memory elements. These synthesis tools are designed to minimize the number of memory elements to be used in the circuit, to generate an encoding of the states and inputs that will reduce its cost, to minimize input/output delay, and to simplify the Boolean expressions that will be required for its implementation.

Behavioral or **high-level synthesis** tools are used to convert arithmetic expressions, instruction sets, or algorithmic descriptions into register-level structures, while minimizing both the microchip size and execution time. Behavioral synthesis is very useful in the design of interface circuits, special-purpose accelerators, and digital-signal algorithms. We describe synthesis principles and techniques in Chapters 4, 6, 8, and 9.

1.4.3 Verification and Simulation

After a design has been captured by a schematic capture tool or specified as an HDL description, we need to verify that the design will perform as expected. This is difficult to achieve, since we do not know what design functionality was intended if it was not captured in one way or the other. On the other hand, what we can verify, by comparing its structural and behavioral descriptions, is the fact that the design structure was correctly synthesized. By using symbolic computation, theorem proving, or algebraic manipulation, we can prove that two different representations of the same design are equal for all possible sets of input values. In addition to proving representational equivalence, timing verifiers can generate all critical paths through a given behavioral or structural representation and guarantee that even the longest delay will satisfy the requirements. Since **equivalence verifiers** must prove equivalence of two designs for every set of input values, and **timing verifiers** must prove constraint satisfaction for every input/output path in the design, they may run for a long time. For this reason the most popular kind of verification is design **simulation**, in which a design is verified only for a given set of input values by generating the set of output values from a structural description and comparing it to the given set of expected output values obtained from the behavioral description.

Given a structural description consisting of components with known models, a simulator works in the following way. First, it computes the output value for every component whose inputs are connected to the input ports for which input values have been supplied. Then, having computed these output values, it advances the simulated time by the amount given in the models of these particular components. It then selects the next set of components, whose input values are now known, and computes their output values from these new input values, advancing the simulated time as before. This step is repeated until the operations of all the components have been simulated or until there is no longer any change in any output value. Finally, the output value generated is compared to the expected value and the input/output propagation delay to the given delay constraint. In this manner, a simulator can verify the functional and timing correctness of a design, although this verification will be valid only for that particular set of input data. For this reason, a designer who uses a simulator must attempt to develop the sets of input and expected output values in a way that exercises all the paths through the design. This development may not be an easy task in the case of designs that can contain 1 million gates or transistors.

1.4.4 Physical Design

The CAD tools available for physical design are **placement tools** that enable us to optimize the placement of components on a printed-circuit board or of cells and modules on a microchip. By taking into account the size, aspect ratio, and pin positions of each component, these placement tools allow us to position each component in the structural representation in a way that minimizes the area occupied by all the components. Once the position of each component has been determined, we use **routing tools** to determine the position for each of the wires that connect these components, in a way that minimizes the maximum wire length, or the sum of all wire lengths, and to optimize the use of all the connection layers on a printed-circuit board or a microchip. In applying these routing tools, special consideration is given to power-supply wires, which must be able to reach every component and supply enough current. Similarly, special consideration is given to the wires as for component clocking, since their excessive length can sometimes generate clock signal delays, which can be a source of intermittent or permanent failures.

1.4.5 Testing

Testing is performed after the product has been manufactured as a means to separate good units from faulty ones. In general, the testing procedure consists of applying certain test patterns to the unit being tested and comparing that unit's output with the responses can be expected from a unit that is working correctly. Within this testing process, CAD tools are used for test pattern generation and for fault grading. The purpose of **test-pattern generation** tools is to help us generate that set of test patterns that exercises as many paths through the design as possible.

It is very difficult, however, to create a set of test patterns that covers all the potential faults in every design. For this reason, we usually supplement tools for test-pattern generation with tools for **test grading**, which enable us to generate a list of all the faults covered by a particular set of test patterns.

1.5 TYPICAL DESIGN PROCESS

The typical design process, as practiced in industrial environments for the past 20 years, is one that starts with a market analysis and a definition of the product's requirement. From these requirements, the chief architects then conduct a feasibility study to determine the technology, the architecture, and the typical applications for the product. At this stage, they would develop a preliminary block diagram and write a specification for the product. The design team then takes over this preliminary block diagram, and refines it to a system-level, then a register-level, and finally, a gate-level structure. Then this gate-level structure is usually captured with a schematic-capture tool and simulated, to verify its functionality and its timing. If at this point, it is found that some design constraints have not been met or some quality metrics are not satisfactory, the design requirements, the specification, and the architecture have to be modified and the entire process repeated. Once a satisfactory result is achieved, the next step is the physical design, which specifies placement and routing of the design's structure. In the case of a microchip implementation, of course, each logic or storage component has to be laid out before placement and routing. Finally, after the physical design is completed, the testing team generates the appropriate test patterns for use in manufacturing, and the design team writes the documentation for the product.

In the past, most of these design tasks have to have been performed manually, since only a small part of the design process was automated. This began to change, however, with the availability of CAD tools for physical design that were developed to help designers with placement and routing. Later, additional tools for the capture of gate-level schematics and for gate-level simulation were developed, which made it possible for the design process to be automated further.

More recently, in the 1990s, this automation of the design process has been advanced significantly by the introduction of standard hardware-description languages and synthesis tools. With hardware-description languages we can now generate behavioral descriptions that are readily simulated, and with the new synthesis tools it has become much easier to translate from a behavioral to a structural representation.

Given these recent developments, a new design process has emerged which is heavily dependent upon describing the design behaviorally on higher abstraction levels and refining or synthesizing the behavioral description. The early success of the new synthesis tools has generated a demand for automating the design process on even higher levels, and eventually developing techniques for synthesizing entire systems from executable specifications. In this book we follow this new design process, with the exception of system synthesis, which is beyond the scope of this book.

1.6 ROAD MAP

In this book, we are concerned primarily with digital design techniques that are prerequisites for the design of computer systems. In its broadest scope, the design of computer systems could be said to start with solid-state physics and with the fabrication process for integrated circuits, which determines the types and properties of the most basic electronic components, such as transistors, resistors, and capacitors. These components can be connected into either digital or analog circuits, according to the basic laws of electronics. Digital circuits process signals that can take on only a small number of fixed values, usually two, which makes them very robust and easy to design. Because of these two features, all computation and information processing is performed with digital circuits.

On the other hand, analog circuits process signals that take on any number of values within a given range. Most of the signals generated or recognized by humans, such as text, voice, and video, are analog signals. Since all the processing is performed digitally, general electronic systems must convert these analog signals, which are generated by humans, into digital signals, then perform computations, transformations, and communications entirely within the digital domain, converting the results back into analog signals only for purposes of human consumption.

The analysis and synthesis of analog and digital circuits are taught in introductory courses in most engineering curricula and has been omitted in this book. We will not even require knowledge of electronics or circuit design for understanding the material in this book. With this in mind, we start our exploration of computer systems with logic gates and flip-flops, which are specific digital circuits that work with only two values and exhibit only two states. For convenience, we assume that our library of logic components has already been defined for us by a hypothetical silicon vendor. In this way, we do not need to get involved with circuit design and fabrication. This situation resembles present industrial practice, in which silicon vendors also supply their customers with logic libraries. Thus, system designers work with libraries and provide the system description in terms of library components, while silicon foundries insert the layout of each component before fabrication.

In this book we use the bottom-up strategy in learning the principles of digital design. As shown in Figure 1.7, we start in Chapter 2 by presenting the binary number system and the data representations that are used in all digital systems and computer-based products. All of the arithmetic and storage components we use will be based on the binary representation of numbers and alphabets. However, before we embark on the design of particular components, in Chapter 3 we introduce the theoretical foundation for digital design, which is called Boolean algebra. In the same chapter, we introduce our logic library, which is basically an implementation of the operators of this Boolean algebra. In Chapter 4 we cover the most basic logic design techniques that are used for the synthesis and optimization of arbitrary Boolean functions. Then, in Chapter 5, we use these techniques to build various arithmetic and logic components, including adders, comparators, selectors, encoders, and decoders which represent a combinatorial library for register-transfer designs.

In Chapter 6, we introduce the finite-state-machine model, which is necessary for the design of storage components such as registers, counters, and memories. These storage components are usually called sequential components because their behavior depends upon a sequence of input values instead of just the present input value. In addition to the finite-state-machine model we also introduce in Chapter 6 some of the sequential design techniques that use in Chapter 7 when we build basic sequential components, such as registers, counters, memories, stacks, queues, and datapaths.

Once our combinatorial and sequential libraries have been designed, we can proceed to the next level of abstraction. In Chapter 8 we introduce the model of the generalized finite-state machine and present the design techniques that are used for the synthesis of processor components, whose behavior is usually described by algorithms, flowcharts, or programs, or in the case of processors, by instruction sets. Finally, in Chapter 9, we use these techniques to design processors with both complex and reduced instruction sets.

Standard and custom processor components, presented in Chapters 8 and 9, together with interface components and electro-mechanical devices such as disks, tapes, and keyboards, are used in the design of many types of computer systems, including personal computers, engineering workstations, file servers, and communication controllers. The

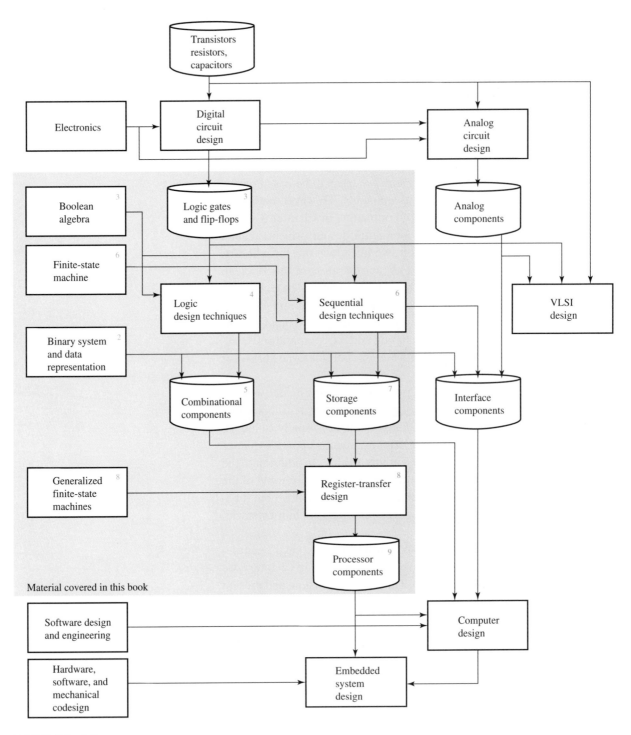

FIGURE 1.7
Road map of this book.

design of computer systems is studied in computer architecture courses whose material is beyond the scope of this book. In the case of computer systems, of course, the basic hardware would be supplemented with several layers of software programs, including assemblers, compilers, operating systems, and graphical user interfaces. They are studied in software design and engineering courses. The computer systems are used in the design of more complex embedded systems which are suitable for applications such as signal processing, mechatronics, robotics, communications, transportation, image processing, medical instrumentation, and multimedia, among others. In general, though, the techniques and applications of embedded-system design are studied only in advanced architecture and system courses, whose material is also beyond the scope of this book.

1.7 CHAPTER SUMMARY

In this chapter we introduced the three basic design representations, namely, the behavioral, structural, and physical representations. We described four different levels of abstraction: the transistor, the gate, the register, and the processor levels. We also explored the interrelations between design representations and abstractions levels by describing the design process of electronic digital systems, starting with a specification and ending with the manufacture of the product. We described very briefly some of the CAD tools used in the design process.

   In the rest of this book, we study those principles and techniques that are used in digital design on the gate, register, and processor levels. They enable us to convert a design specification or a behavioral description into a structure of components from a specific library based on present industrial libraries. Before we can introduce the design process, however, we need to learn the principles of binary systems and the algebras of logic.

1.8 FURTHER READINGS

Almasi, G. S., and A. Gottlieb. *Highly Parallel Computing*, 2nd ed. Redwood City, CA: Benjamin-Cummings, 1994.

   An overview of parallel processing which relates parallel applications and computational models to parallel software and architectures.

Dasgupta, S. *Computer Architecture: A Modern Synthesis*, Vol. 1. New York: Wiley, 1989.

   A well-written and clearly explained design process focusing on the architectural level of abstraction. This is an advanced text, best suited to students with some knowledge of basic computer architectures.

Gajski, D. D., F. Vahid, S. Narayan, and J. Gong. *Specification and Design of Embedded Systems*. Englewood Cliffs, NJ: Prentice Hall, 1994.

> An introduction to the problems and solutions of embedded-systems design, with an emphasis on design modeling, exploration, and refinement.

Geiger, R. L., P. E. Allen, and N. R. Strader. *VLSI Design Techniques for Analog and Digital Circuits*. New York: McGraw-Hill, 1990.

> An excellent survey of analog and digital circuit theory and design techniques, with an introduction to the physical design and fabrication of VLSI integrated circuits. Requires a basic knowledge of electronics.

Hayes, J. P. *Introduction to Digital Design*. Reading, MA: Addison-Wesley, 1993.

> A thorough introduction to digital design, relating electronics and logic through a set of simple, easy-to-understand models.

Hennesey, J. L., and D. A. Patterson. *Computer Architecture: A Quantitative Approach*. San Mateo, CA: Morgan Kaufmann, 1990.

> An introduction to computer design, connecting applications, and implementations written by two pioneers in the field of modern RISC technology.

Lauther, U. *Introduction to Synthesis*. Chapter 1: "The synthesis approach to digital system design." Boston: Kluwer, 1992.

> A very readable introduction to design representations and the design process.

Maly, W. *Atlas of IC Technologies: An Introduction to VLSI Processes*. Menlo Park, CA: Benjamin-Cummings, 1987.

> An excellent pictorial overview of the fabrication process for nonexperts.

McCluskey, E. J. *Logic Design Principles*. Englewood Cliffs, NJ: Prentice Hall, 1986.

> One of the pioneers of digital design explains the basic methods in digital design, with a very good overview of testing problems and solutions.

Sapiro, S., and R. J. Smith II. *Handbook of Design Automation*. Englewood Cliffs, NJ: Prentice Hall, 1986.

> An introductory treatment that provides a concise description of the design process, its basic tasks, and the role of CAD tools within it. Requires some basic knowledge of digital design.

Wolf, W. *Modern VLSI Design: A Systems Approach*. Englewood Cliffs, NJ: Prentice Hall, 1994.

> An easy-to-read text explaining the principles of VLSI design and covering the various phases of digital design, from layout to architecture.

1.9 PROBLEMS

1.1   (Design representation) Describe the differences between the behavioral, structural, and physical representations of an electronic product.

1.2   (Design representation) Add a new feature to the alarm clock described in Section 1.1 so that if we keep the minute or hour advance switches, S_3 and S_4, pressed for 4 seconds, the time will start advancing at the high speed of 1 minute or 1 hour for every 0.1 second. Modify the (a) behavioral, (b) structural, and (c) physical representations to reflect this specification change.

1.3   (Design representation) Add a new construct to the behavioral representation allowing us to specify that the *Buzz* signal will have a value of 1 for only 5 seconds after the clock becomes equal to the wake-up minutes and hours. Note that in the present description, the *Buzz* signal will have a value of 1 for the duration of 1 entire minute—that is, until *minutes counter* has advanced by 1 and the value in *minutes counter* is no longer equal to the value in *minutes register*.

1.4   (Design representation) Give the behavioral and structural representation for the traffic light controller described as follows: Four traffic lights will point in four directions, identified by the letters N, S, W, and E. Each light will go through the following sequence: green (45 seconds), yellow (15 seconds), and red (60 seconds). Furthermore, the N and S lights will always be the same color, as will the E and W lights, and the N-S lights will never be green or yellow at the same time as the E-W lights.

1.5 (Design process) Describe the difference between:
- **(a)** A specification and an executable specification
- **(b)** A custom library and a standard library
- **(c)** Synthesis and refinement
- **(d)** Representation and abstraction
- **(e)** Test patterns and a testability metric
- **(f)** Documentation and HDL description

1.6 (CAD tools) Describe the differences between:
- **(a)** Schematic capture and modeling
- **(b)** A block diagram and a specification
- **(c)** Verification and simulation
- **(d)** Optimization and technology mapping
- **(e)** Placement and floorplanning
- **(f)** Fault grading and test pattern generation

1.7 (Design process) Define a methodology in which the system library contains processors, memories, and ASICs, while the design process starts with an executable specification and ends with the manufacture of MCMs.

1.8 (Physical design) Given a structure of six microchips, as shown in Figure P1.8(a), place them onto a 3×3 MCM and connect the microchips by using the routing tracks indicated by the dotted lines in Figure P1.8(b). Further, connect I_1, I_2, O_1, and O_2 to the MCM ports. Note that vertical routing is on the first metal layer, while horizontal routing is on the second metal layer. Note also that each microchip has two ports on each side and that any connections to these ports cannot be reassigned to other ports.

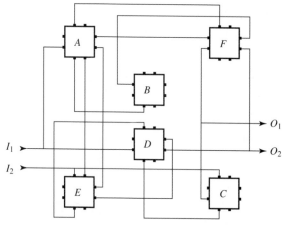

(a) Structural representation

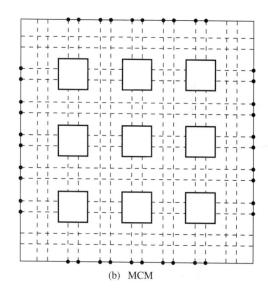

(b) MCM

F I G U R E   P1.8

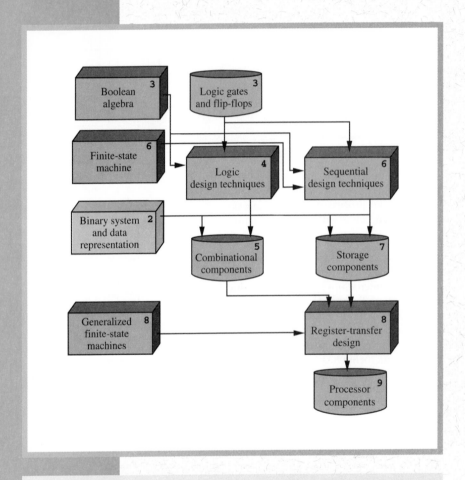

Since it is easy to construct digital circuits that recognize and manipulate only 0's and 1's, our goal in system design is to perform all the computations within a computer by using only those two symbols. Thus all numbers and data in a computer are to be represented in this binary form. In this chapter we discuss how to represent numbers and characters in binary form and how to perform arithmetic operations on these binary representation of numbers.

CHAPTER

2

Data Types
and
Representations

In this chapter we introduce the most common types of data found in digital systems and then show how they can be represented in binary-coded form. The data found in digital systems may be classified in three general categories, including (1) the numbers that we use in arithmetic computations, (2) the letters of the alphabet that we use in data processing, and (3) a range of discrete symbols that we use for a variety of purposes. All three of these types of data are represented in the computer in binary-coded form, which is the most natural for use in computers, simply because it is easy to construct electronic circuits that exhibit two alternative conditions that can conveniently be interpreted as values of 0 and 1 of a binary digit. Although all the information in digital systems is represented with these binary digits, whenever this information is made available for human consumption, it must be converted into decimal digits and letters of the alphabet.

2.1 POSITIONAL NUMBER SYSTEMS

To understand the binary number system used in computer design, we need to recognize that the number system we use every day is a **positional number system**. In such a system, any number is represented by a string of digits in which the position of each digit has an associated weight. The value of a given number, then, is equivalent to the weighted sum of all its digits, as, for example,

$$1234 = 1 \cdot 1000 + 2 \cdot 100 + 3 \cdot 10 + 4 \cdot 1$$

Note that in this example, each weight is a power of 10 that is equal to 10^i, where i corresponds to the digit's position counting from the right. A decimal point allows us to use negative as well as positive powers of 10 in the number representation. For example,

$$1234.56 = 1 \cdot 1000 + 2 \cdot 100 + 3 \cdot 10 + 4 \cdot 1 + 5 \cdot 0.1 + 6 \cdot 0.01$$

In general, any decimal number D of the form $d_1 d_0 d_{-1} d_{-2}$ has the value

$$D = d_1 \cdot 10^1 + d_0 \cdot 10^0 + d_{-1} \cdot 10^{-1} + d_{-2} \cdot 10^{-2}$$

Here 10 is called the **base** or **radix** of the number system. In a general positional number system, the radix may be any integer r, and a digit in position i then has the weight r^i. Therefore, we could describe the general form of a number in such a system as

$$d_{m-1} d_{m-2} \cdots d_1 d_0 . d_{-1} d_{-2} \cdots d_{-n}$$

where there are m digits to the left of the point, known as the **radix point**, and n digits to its right. Note that if there is no radix point, we should assume that it is to the right of the rightmost digit. The value of this number is the sum of products of each digit multiplied by the corresponding power of the radix:

$$D = \sum_{i=-n}^{m-1} d_i \cdot r^i \tag{2.1}$$

Within a positional number system, the representation of every number is unique, except for possible leading and trailing zeros. Note that the leftmost digit in such a number system is called the **most-significant digit** (MSD), and the rightmost is the **least-significant digit** (LSD). Since digital systems use binary digits, we use a **binary radix** to represent any given number in a digital system. The general form of such a binary number is

$$b_{m-1}b_{m-2}\cdots b_1 b_0 . b_{-1}b_{-2}\cdots b_{-n}$$

and its value is equivalent to

$$B = \sum_{i=-n}^{m-1} b_i \cdot 2^i$$

Similarly to a decimal point in a decimal number, the radix point in a binary number is called the **binary point**. Typically, whenever we are working with binary and other nondecimal numbers, we use a subscript to indicate the radix of each number, although the radix is often clear from the context. Here are some examples of binary numbers and their decimal equivalents:

$$10101_2 = 1 \cdot 16 + 0 \cdot 8 + 1 \cdot 4 + 0 \cdot 2 + 1 \cdot 1 = 21_{10}$$
$$110101_2 = 1 \cdot 32 + 1 \cdot 16 + 0 \cdot 8 + 1 \cdot 4 + 0 \cdot 2 + 1 \cdot 1 = 53_{10}$$
$$10.101_2 = 1 \cdot 2 + 0 \cdot 1 + 1 \cdot 0.5 + 0 \cdot 0.25 + 1 \cdot 0.125 = 2.625_{10}$$
$$.1111_2 = 1 \cdot 0.5 + 1 \cdot 0.25 + 1 \cdot 0.125 + 1 \cdot 0.0625 = 0.9375_{10}$$

2.2 OCTAL AND HEXADECIMAL NUMBERS

From our discussion of positional number systems, we can easily recognize the importance of radix 10, which we use in everyday life, and radix 2, which is used by digital systems to process numbers. There are, however, two additional radices that are also important for our purposes, since the radix 8 and especially, radix 16 are often used to provide convenient shorthand representations for binary numbers, reducing the need for lengthy, indecipherable strings.

The **octal number system** uses radix 8, while the **hexadecimal number system** uses radix 16. Since the octal system needs to express eight different values, it uses digits 0 through 7 of the decimal system. The hexadecimal system, however, needs to express 16 different values, so it supplements the decimal digits 0 through 9 with the letters A through F. In Table 2.1 we have shown the binary integers from 0 through 10001 with their octal, decimal, and hexadecimal equivalents. Note that the octal digits can be represented by three binary digits, while the hexadecimal and decimal digits can be represented by four binary digits. Table 2.2 shows the binary integers 0 through 10001 and their binary-coded octal, decimal, and hexadecimal equivalents.

TABLE 2.1

Different Representations of Numbers 0 Through 21

BINARY	OCTAL	DECIMAL	HEXA-DECIMAL
0	0	0	0
1	1	1	1
10	2	2	2
11	3	3	3
100	4	4	4
101	5	5	5
110	6	6	6
111	7	7	7
1000	10	8	8
1001	11	9	9
1010	12	10	A
1011	13	11	B
1100	14	12	C
1101	15	13	D
1110	16	14	E
1111	17	15	F
10000	20	16	10
10001	21	17	11

TABLE 2.2

Binary-Coded Representations

BINARY	BINARY-CODED OCTAL	BINARY-CODED DECIMAL	BINARY-CODED HEXA-DECIMAL
0	000	0000	0000
1	001	0001	0001
10	010	0010	0010
11	011	0011	0011
100	100	0100	0100
101	101	0101	0101
110	110	0110	0110
111	111	0111	0111
1000	001 000	1000	1000
1001	001 001	1001	1001
1010	001 010	0001 0000	1010
1011	001 011	0001 0001	1011
1100	001 100	0001 0010	1100
1101	001 101	0001 0011	1101
1110	001 110	0001 0100	1110
1111	001 111	0001 0101	1111
10000	010 000	0001 0101	0001 0000
10001	010 001	0001 0111	0001 0001

It is very easy to convert a binary number to octal form. Starting at the binary point and working left, we simply separate the bits into groups of 3 and replace each group with the corresponding octal digit, as shown in the following example:

$$1010011100_2 = 001\ 010\ 011\ 100 = 1234_8$$

Our approach for binary-to-hexadecimal conversions is similar, except that we use groups of 4 bits:

$$1010011100_2 = 0010\ 1001\ 1100 = 29C_{16}$$

Notice in these examples that we have added zeros on the left as required to make the total number of bits a multiple of 3 or 4.

Binary fractions would be converted to octal or hexadecimal form by starting at the binary point and grouping the binary digits that lie to the right. Again, we would add zeros to the rightmost group as needed to get multiples of 3 or 4 bits, as indicated in the following example.

$$.10111_2 = .101\ 110 = .56_8$$
$$= .1011\ 1000 = .B8_{16}$$

Converting in the reverse direction, from octal or hexadecimal to binary, is also quite simple. We replace each octal or hexadecimal digit with the corresponding 3- or 4-bit binary string from Table 2.1. For example,

$$765_8 = 111110101_2$$
$$765.432_8 = 111110101.100011010_2$$
$$FED_{16} = 111111101101_2$$
$$FED.CBA = 111111101101.110010111010_2$$

Although the octal number system is not much used today, the hexadecimal system is quite popular, because it can easily be converted to and from binary, and because standard 8-, 16-, 32-, and 64-bit data can be documented efficiently by 2, 4, 8, and 16 hexadecimal digits.

2.3 NUMBER SYSTEM CONVERSIONS

As a rule we cannot convert a number representation in one radix into representation in another radix simply by substituting numbers in one radix for their equivalents in another radix representation; this works only when both radices are powers of the same number. When this is not the case, we must use more complex conversion procedures that require arithmetic operations. In this section we show how to convert a number in any radix to radix 10, and vice versa, using radix-10 arithmetic.

As indicated in Section 2.1, the value of a number in any radix is represented by the formula

$$D = \sum_{i=-n}^{m-1} d_i r^i \tag{2.1}$$

where r is the radix of the number, m indicates the number of digits to the left of the radix point, and n indicates the number to the right. Thus the decimal value of a number in any radix would be determined by converting each digit of the number to its radix-10 equivalent, and then expanding the formula using radix-10 arithmetic. Two examples are:

$$12EF_{16} = 1 \cdot 16^3 + 2 \cdot 16^2 + 14 \cdot 16^1 + 15 \cdot 16^0 = 4847_{10}$$
$$436.5_8 = 4 \cdot 8^2 + 3 \cdot 8^1 + 6 \cdot 8^0 + 5 \cdot 8^{-1} = 286.625_{10}$$

On the other hand, as an alternative to using this formula, we can obtain a simple procedure for converting numbers in another radix to radix 10 by rewriting the integer part of Equation (2.1) as follows:

$$D = ((\cdots ((d_{m-1})r + d_{m-2})r + \cdots)r + d_1)r + d_0 \tag{2.2}$$

From Equation (2.2) we can devise an iterative procedure that would scan the number from the MSD to the LSD and accumulate a decimal sum, S. As shown in Figure 2.1, this procedure would first assigns 0 to S, and then in each step of the procedure, starting with the most significant digit, S is multiplied by radix r, and the next less significant digit (the next one to the right) is added to the product. This step is then repeated for each digit until the least significant digit has been added to S, which then represents the decimal equivalent of the number given in radix r.

Equation (2.2) is also a useful starting point for converting a decimal number D to a number in radix r. If we divide the number D in Equation (2.2) by r, the parenthesized part of Equation (2.2) represents the quotient

$$Q = (\cdots ((d_{m-1})r + d_{m-2})r \cdots)r + d_1 \tag{2.3}$$

while the rest is the remainder,

$$R = d_0$$

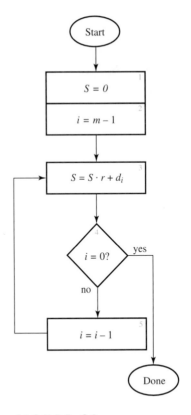

FIGURE 2.1

Procedure for conversion of whole radix-r numbers to decimal numbers.

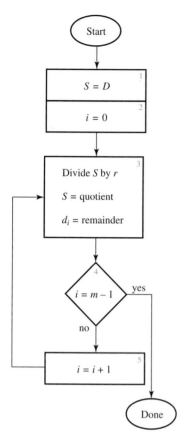

FIGURE 2.2
Procedure
for conversion of whole decimal
numbers to radix-r numbers.

In other words, d_0 is obtained as a remainder of the long division of D by r. Furthermore, since the quotient Q in Equation (2.3) has the same form as the original number, we know that successive divisions by r yields successive digits of D from right to left until all the digits of D have been derived. In the following example, we provide several applications of this procedure, which is summarized in Figure 2.2.

EXAMPLE 2.1   Binary conversion

PROBLEM   Convert (a) 179 to binary, (b) 467 to octal, and (c) 3417 to hexadecimal.

SOLUTION

(a)
$$179 \div 2 = 89 \quad \text{remainder 1 (LSD)}$$
$$89 \div 2 = 44 \quad \text{remainder 1}$$
$$44 \div 2 = 22 \quad \text{remainder 0}$$
$$22 \div 2 = 11 \quad \text{remainder 0}$$
$$11 \div 2 = 5 \quad \text{remainder 1}$$
$$5 \div 2 = 2 \quad \text{remainder 1}$$
$$2 \div 2 = 1 \quad \text{remainder 0}$$
$$1 \div 2 = 0 \quad \text{remainder 1 (MSD)}$$
Therefore, $179_{10} = 10110011_2$.

(b)
$$467 \div 8 = 58 \quad \text{remainder 3 (LSD)}$$
$$58 \div 8 = 7 \quad \text{remainder 2}$$
$$7 \div 8 = 0 \quad \text{remainder 7 (MSD)}$$
Therefore, $467_{10} = 723_8$.

(c)
$$3417 \div 16 = 213 \quad \text{remainder 9 (LSD)}$$
$$213 \div 16 = 13 \quad \text{remainder 5}$$
$$13 \div 16 = 0 \quad \text{remainder 13 (MSD)}$$
Therefore, $3417_{10} = D59_{16}$.

2.4 ADDITION AND SUBTRACTION OF BINARY NUMBERS

Adding and subtracting binary numbers by hand are simple procedures because they use familiar techniques that we also apply to decimal numbers; the only difference, in fact, is that, for binary numbers, the addition and subtraction tables contain only 1's and 0's instead of decimal digits.

As you know, we add two decimal numbers by adding one pair of digits at a time, starting with the least significant digit of each number. If the sum of a given pair is equal to or greater than 10, we carry the excess into the sum of the next more significant pair of digits. In adding two binary numbers, $x = x_{m-1} \cdots x_0$ and $y = y_{m-1} \cdots y_0$, for example, we use essentially the same procedure by adding together the least significant bits, x_0 and y_0, with an initial carry, c_0, equal to 0, which produces the output carry bit, c_1, and the sum bit, s_0, as indicated in Table 2.3, which shows the sum, s_i, and the carry bit, c_{i+1}, for every possible combination of x_i, y_i, and c_i. We then continue this process for every pair of bits, proceeding from right to left, and including the output carry from each column in the the sum of the next-most-significant column. The complete addition procedure is summarized in Figure 2.3. We demonstrate this procedure with the following example.

TABLE 2.3

Addition of Binary Digits

$x_i + y_i + c_i$			c_{i+1}	s_i
0	0	0	0	0
0	0	1	0	1
0	1	0	0	1
0	1	1	1	0
1	0	0	0	1
1	0	1	1	0
1	1	0	1	0
1	1	1	1	1

EXAMPLE 2.2   Binary addition

PROBLEM   Add the binary equivalents of decimal numbers 987 and 123.

SOLUTION   In Figure 2.4, we show the binary representations of 987 and 123. Note that 123 will be padded with zeros on the left during addition.

	512	256	128	64	32	16	8	4	2	1
x		1	1	1	1	0	1	1	0	1	1
y					1	1	1	1	0	1	1
Carries	1	1	1	1	1	1	1	0	1	1
$x + y$	1	0	0	0	1	0	1	0	1	1	0
	s_{10}	s_9	s_8	s_7	s_6	s_5	s_4	s_3	s_2	s_1	s_0

FIGURE 2.4
Example of binary addition when adding two binary numbers, x (987) and y (123).

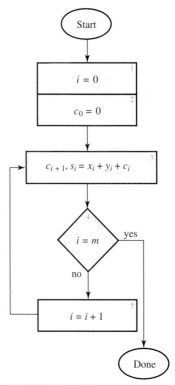

FIGURE 2.3
Procedure for the addition of binary numbers.

We first add $x_0 = 1$ and $y_0 = 1$, producing carry $c_1 = 1$ and sum $s_0 = 0$, as indicated by the dashed box in Figure 2.4. Next, we add $x_1 = 1$, $y_1 = 1$ and $c_1 = 1$, obtaining carry $c_2 = 1$ and sum $s_1 = 1$, as shown by the shaded box in Figure 2.4. This process continues until we generate $s_{10} = 1$ and carry $c_{11} = 0$.

Binary subtraction is performed in a similar manner, subtracting one pair of bits one at the time, although we produce a borrow bit in-

TABLE 2.4

Subtraction of Binary Digits

$x_i - y_i - b_i$	b_{i+1}	d_i
0 0 0	0	0
0 0 1	1	1
0 1 0	1	1
0 1 1	1	0
1 0 0	0	1
1 0 1	0	0
1 1 0	0	0
1 1 1	1	1

stead of the carry bit, and a difference bit instead of the sum bit in each step. Table 2.4 shows the difference d_i and borrow b_{i+1} for all possible combinations of x_i, y_i, and b_i. Given these differences, the procedure for binary subtraction shown in Figure 2.5 is the same as that used for binary addition: we start with the least significant bits, generating borrow bit b_1 and difference bit d_0, and continue from right to left until the most significant borrow bit, b_m, and the most significant difference bit, d_{m-1}, are generated.

■ **EXAMPLE 2.3** Binary subtraction

PROBLEM Perform binary subtraction of 123 from 987.

SOLUTION As in the addition procedure, we first pad the binary representation of 123 with zeros. Then we subtract each pair of binary digits, starting with the least significant bits and deriving results according to Table 2.4. Subtraction of y_0 from x_0 generates the difference bit $d_0 = 0$ and the borrow bit $b_1 = 0$, which is illustrated within the dashed lines in Figure 2.6. Similarly, the subtraction of y_1 and b_1 from x_1 generates $d_1 = 0$ and $b_2 = 0$, as shown in the shaded area in the figure. This process continues in the same manner until d_9 is generated.

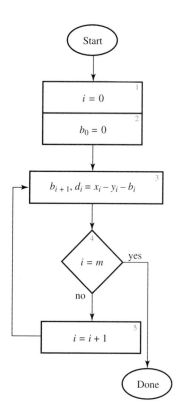

FIGURE 2.5

Procedure for the subtraction of binary numbers.

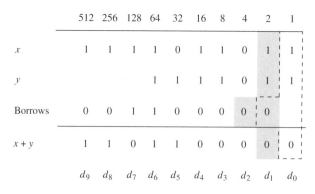

	512	256	128	64	32	16	8	4	2	1
x	1	1	1	1	0	1	1	0	1	1
y				1	1	1	1	0	1	1
Borrows	0	0	1	1	0	0	0	0	0	
$x + y$	1	1	0	1	1	0	0	0	0	0
	d_9	d_8	d_7	d_6	d_5	d_4	d_3	d_2	d_1	d_0

FIGURE 2.6

Example of decimal and binary subtraction.

Addition and subtraction tables can also be developed for octal and hexadecimal digits or for any other desired radix; however, most engineers find that it is easier to convert numbers to decimal, compute the results, and then convert the numbers back into their original form.

2.5 REPRESENTATION OF NEGATIVE NUMBERS

In previous sections we dealt only with positive numbers. Negative numbers can be represented in many different ways. In everyday business, for example, the system we use is the sign-magnitude system. However, most computers use the complement number system, to simplify the implementation of arithmetic circuits.

2.5.1 Sign-Magnitude Representation

In the **sign-magnitude system**, a number consists of two parts, the magnitude and the sign, which is + or − and indicates the positive or negative value of the magnitude. As you know, we assume that the sign is "+" whenever no sign symbol has been written. Within this system, there are two possible representations of zero, "+0" and "−0," which have the same value.

When the sign-magnitude system is used for binary numbers, the sign is represented by a single additional bit: whenever this sign bit equals 0, we assume that the number is positive, whereas a 1 signifies a negative number. In general, the most significant bit (MSB) of a number representation is used as the sign bit, and the lower-order bits signify the magnitude. Thus +123 and −123 differ only in their most significant bits, as follows:

$$01111011_2 = +123_{10}$$

$$11111011_2 = -123_{10}$$

Note that the sign-magnitude system contains an equal number of positive and negative integers. Any sign-magnitude integer with n bits lies within the range $-(2^{n-1} - 1)$ through $+(2^{n-1} - 1)$, noting that there are two possible representations of zero.

As shown in Figure 2.7, sign-magnitude arithmetic requires us to compare both the signs and the magnitudes of the operands. Assume, for example, that we want to add two sign-magnitude numbers, $D_1 = <s_1, m_1>$ and $D_2 = <s_2, m_2>$, which generate the result $D_r = <s_r, m_r>$. If the signs of both numbers are the same, we simply add their magnitudes and the result inherits the sign of the operands. If, however, the signs are different, we have to compare magnitudes: where the magnitudes are the same, the result is zero; where the magnitudes are not the same, we subtract the smaller magnitude from the larger and the result inherits the sign of the larger magnitude. As shown in Figure 2.7, a subtraction is performed by addition after reversing the sign of the subtrahend.

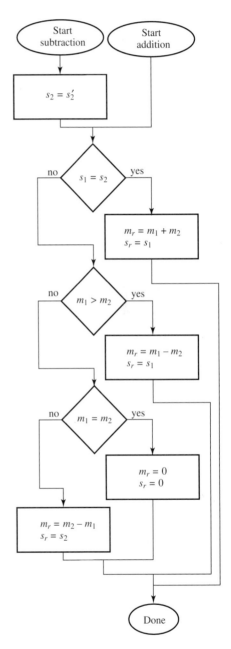

FIGURE 2.7
Procedure for addition and subtraction of sign-magnitude numbers.

To perform multiplication or division operations, all we need to do is to multiply or divide the magnitudes and make the result positive whenever both operands have the same sign and negative otherwise. Whenever the result is zero, a positive sign is inserted.

Since multiplication and division are usually performed by iterative addition and subtraction, the only arithmetic circuits we need will be adders and subtractors. On the other hand, since addition and subtraction of sign-magnitude numbers requires the comparison of signs and magnitudes, the sign-magnitude adders and subtractors tend to be slower than their counterparts that use the complement number system, which does not require this comparison.

2.5.2 Complement Number System

The complement number system was invented to make addition and subtraction faster and easier to implement, by omitting the need for sign and magnitude comparison. Instead, it requires complementation, which can be performed quite efficiently on binary numbers. Throughout this book we use the standard complement number system described below, called the **radix-complement system**. Although we explain this system only in relation to integers, the system can easily be extended to all real numbers by using a floating-point form.

As mentioned above, any integer can be represented as $D = \sum_{i=0}^{m-1} d_i r^i$. In this definition we assume that the number of digits is exactly m, and if any operation were to generate a result with more than m digits, we retain only low-order m digits. In the radix-complement system, the complement $\bar{D}$ of an m-digit number D is obtained by subtracting that number from r^m:

$$\bar{D} = r^m - D \qquad (2.4)$$

For example, the radix complement for the three-digit numbers 987 and 123 can be obtained by subtracting them from $10^3 = 1000$. Thus the radix complement, or the **10's complement** in this case, of 987 is 13 and the 10's complement of 123 is 877. In general, whenever D is between 1 and $r^m - 1$, this complement subtraction generates another number that lies between 1 and $r^m - 1$. If, however, D is 0, the result of the complementation will be r^m, which has a total of $m + 1$ digits, that is, the digit 1 followed by m 0's. Since we retain only m least-significant digits, the zero number is uniquely represented, by a string of m zeros.

Alternatively, we can also obtain the radix complement $\bar{D}$ described in Equation (2.4) without subtraction, by rewriting the equation as follows:

$$\bar{D} = r^m - D = ((r^m - 1) - D) + 1 \qquad (2.5)$$

The number $r^m - 1$ in Equation (2.5) consists of m digits whose value is $r - 1$. If we define the digit complement as $d' = (r - 1) - d$, then

$$(r^m - 1) - D = ((r-1)(r-1)\cdots(r-1)) - (d_{m-1}d_{m-2}\cdots d_0)$$
$$= ((r-1) - d_{m-1})((r-1) - d_{m-2})\cdots((r-1) - d_0)$$
$$= d'_{m-1}d'_{m-2}\cdots d'_0$$

Furthermore, if we define

$$D' = \sum_{i=0}^{m-1} d'_i$$

we can rewrite Equation (2.4) as

$$\bar{D} = D' + 1 \qquad\qquad (2.6)$$

According to this equation, the radix complement of a number D is obtained by complementing the individual digits of that number and then adding 1. For example, we determine that the 10's complement of 987 is 012 + 1, or 13, and the 10's complement of 123 is 876 + 1, or 877. In Table 2.5 we have listed the digit complements for binary, octal, decimal, and hexadecimal digits.

In contrast to sign-magnitude representations, the advantage of the radix-complement system is that negative numbers can simply be represented by the complement $\bar{D}$, since $D + \bar{D} = 0$ whenever we retain only m least significant digits. We now demonstrate this advantage in relation to binary numbers.

The radix complement for binary numbers is called the **two's complement**, and the number representation that we derive from it is called the two's-complement representation. For binary numbers, the sign of the number is represented by the MSB, which is 0 for positive numbers and 1 for negative numbers. Thus a negative number is obtained from a positive number by complementing each binary digit, including the sign bit, and then adding 1 to it—that is, we change all the 0's into 1's or 1's into 0's and then add one. The carry that occurs out of the MSB is discarded. Therefore, if we are complementing 0 and the MSB carry is discarded, we obtain 0 as the two's complement. Thus we conclude that in two's-complement system, 0 has a unique representation and represents its own complement. Furthermore, since 0 is a positive number, there will be one less nonzero positive number than there are negative numbers. Therefore, the range of representable numbers in the two's-complement system is $-(2^{m-1})$ through $+ (2^{m-1} - 1)$. For example, the range of 4-bit numbers extends from $-2^3 = -8$ to $2^3 - 1 = 7$. In Table 2.6 we show both the two's-complement and sign-magnitude representations of all 4-bit integers.

TABLE 2.5

Digit Complements

DIGIT	BINARY	OCTAL	DECIMAL	HEXA-DECIMAL
0	1	7	9	F
1	0	6	8	E
2	—	5	7	D
3	—	4	6	C
4	—	3	5	B
5	—	2	4	A
6	—	1	3	9
7	—	0	2	8
8	—	—	1	7
9	—	—	0	6
A	—	—	—	5
B	—	—	—	4
C	—	—	—	3
D	—	—	—	2
E	—	—	—	1
F	—	—	—	0

Occasionally, while performing arithmetic operations, we need to convert an m-bit number to an n-bit number. In such cases we first determine if $n > m$; if so, we then append $n - m$ 0's beyond the sign bit for every positive numbers. By definition of the complement, for negative numbers, we append $n - m$ 1's beyond the sign bit. Since we have inserted bits that are equal to the sign bit, this extension is called **sign extension**. Alternatively, whenever $n < m$, we perform a **sign truncation**, by discarding $m - n$ bits that follow the sign bit. This truncated number is valid, however, only when all the discarded bits are the same as the sign bit.

2.6 TWO'S-COMPLEMENT ADDITION AND SUBTRACTION

As mentioned above, two's-complement representation was invented to make the addition and subtraction of binary numbers simple by making it unnecessary to treat the sign bits separately. In other words, using this system enables us to add and subtract both signed and unsigned integers with the same logic circuit. As indicated in Table 2.6, we can obtain any number between the smallest (-8) and the largest ($+7$) simply by adding 1 to the previous number and ignoring any carry out of the sign bit.

2.6.1 Addition Rules

To add two's-complement numbers, we use the binary arithmetic rules shown in Figure 2.3, and ignore any carry beyond the sign bit. As long as the range of the number system is not exceeded, the result of this addition will always be correct, including the sign. For example, the addition of two positive numbers generates a correct positive result:

$$\begin{array}{r} 0010 \ (+2) \\ + \quad 0100 \ (+4) \\ \hline 0110 \ (+6) \end{array}$$

Similarly, adding two negative numbers will always generate a correct negative sum, as long as we ignore the carry beyond the sign bit:

$$\begin{array}{r} 1110 \ (-2) \\ + \quad 1100 \ (-4) \\ \hline \text{ignored carry} = 1 \quad 1010 \ (-6) \end{array}$$

TABLE 2.6

Two's Complement and Sign-Magnitude Representations

DECIMAL	TWO'S COMPLEMENT	SIGN-MAGNITUDE
−8	1000	—
−7	1001	1111
−6	1010	1110
−5	1011	1101
−4	1100	1100
−3	1101	1011
−2	1110	1010
−1	1111	1001
0	0000	1000 or 0000
1	0001	0001
2	0010	0010
3	0011	0011
4	0100	0100
5	0101	0101
6	0110	0110
7	0111	0111

There are cases, however, when an operation produces a result that exceeds the range of the number system, producing a condition known as **overflow**. As a rule, the addition of two numbers with different signs never produces an overflow. However, when we add two numbers with the same sign which produce a sum that is larger than the largest representable number, we can obtain an incorrect result, as for the case of 4-bit two's-complement numbers:

$$\begin{array}{r} 0100 \ (+4) \\ + \quad 0101 \ (+5) \\ \hline 1001 \ (-7) \end{array}$$

Similarly,

$$\begin{array}{r} 1100 \ (-4) \\ + \quad 1011 \ (-5) \\ \hline \text{ignored carry} = 1 \quad 0111 \ (+7) \end{array}$$

As these examples suggest, it is possible to establish a simple rule for detecting addition overflow: that is, an addition overflow occurs whenever the sign of the sum is different from the signs of both addends. Computer designers use a slightly different rule in the design of a two's-complement adder circuit. If both operands are positive, an overflow occurs whenever there is a carry into a sign bit. In this case there is no carry out of the sign bit, since both signs are equal to 0. On the other hand, if both operands are negative, an overflow occurs whenever there is no carry into the sign bit, since large negative numbers have small complements. In this case, there should be a carry out of the sign bit. Thus the overflow rule can be restated as follows: An addition overflow occurs whenever the carries into and out of the sign bit are different.

2.6.2 Subtraction Rules

Using the procedure outlined in Figure 2.5 we subtract two's-complement numbers as if they were ordinary unsigned binary numbers, in which case the rules for detecting subtraction overflow are the same as those we use for detecting addition overflow. However, most subtraction circuits for two's-complement numbers do not perform subtraction directly, but rather, negate the subtrahend by taking its two's complement and then add it to the minuend using the normal rules for addition. Fortunately, taking the two's complement of the subtrahend and adding it to the minuend can be accomplished using only a bit complementer, followed by an adder circuit: The bit complementer complements each bit in the subtrahend, and then the adder adds to it the minuend and an additional 1, to complete the two's complementation. The addition of 1 is achieved by setting the adder's input carry to 1 instead of 0.

To demonstrate the difference between direct subtraction and addition of the two's complement, let's consider subtraction of two small integers. For example, we can subtract +4 directly from +2 and obtain −2:

$$
\begin{array}{rcl}
 & 0010 & (+2) \\
- & 0100 & (+4) \\
\hline
 & \underline{1100} & \text{borrows} \\
\text{ignored borrow} = 1 & 1110 & (-2)
\end{array}
$$

Alternatively, we can obtain the same result by complementing the subtrahend (+4), and then adding it to the minuend (+2):

$$
\begin{array}{rcl}
 & 0010 & (+2) \\
+ & 1100 & \text{two's complement of } (+4) \\
 & \underline{000} & \text{carries} \\
 & 1110 & (-2)
\end{array}
$$

Since the second case of subtraction is performed by adding the two's complement, we can apply the same rules for overflow detection; that is, a subtraction overflow occurs whenever the sign of the difference is different from the signs of the minuend and the complemented subtrahend. The carry rule remains the same as before.

You should note that the most negative number in the range, -2^{m-1}, will not have a complement and that taking its two's complement results in an overflow. Nonetheless, its two's complement can still be used in addition and subtraction as long as the final result does not exceed the number range. For example, when we subtract −8 from −4, we generate the proper result of +4, even though the two's complement of −8 is out of range:

$$
\begin{array}{rcl}
 & 1100 & (-4) \\
+ & 1000 & \text{two's complement of } (-8) \\
\text{ignored carry} = 1 & \underline{0000} & \text{carries} \\
 & 0100 & (+4)
\end{array}
$$

In this example we first generated the complement of −8 by inverting each bit and setting the first carry bit to 1, thereby creating the two's complement of −8. Next we performed binary addition and discarded the carry out of the sign bit.

Since two's-complement numbers are added and subtracted by using the same procedure as with unsigned numbers of the same length, the same adder/subtractor circuit can be used for both as illustrated in Figure 2.8, where two binary numbers, B_1 and B_2, are added or subtracted to generate the result B_r. The subtraction is performed in Figure 2.8 by adding the two's complement of B_2, which is equal to $B_2' + 1$. Note that although the same circuit could be used for unsigned and signed numbers, different rules for overflow detection would have to be used in each case.

2.7 BINARY MULTIPLICATION

The familiar method of multiplying two numbers consists of adding the shifted partial products that are derived from multiplying the multiplicand and one of the multiplier digits. For example, when multiplying 14 by 13, we multiply 14×3 and add it to the shifted product of 14×1:

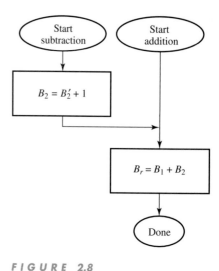

FIGURE 2.8

Procedure for addition and subtraction of radix-complement numbers.

$$
\begin{array}{rl}
14 & \text{multiplicand} \\
\times \quad 13 & \text{multiplier} \\
\hline
42 & 3 \times \text{multiplicand} \\
14 & 1 \times \text{multiplicand} \\
\hline
182 & \text{product}
\end{array}
$$

The same shift-and-add method can be used to obtain the product of two unsigned binary numbers:

$$
\begin{array}{rl}
1110 & \text{multiplicand (14)} \\
\times \quad 1101 & \text{multiplier (13)} \\
\hline
1110 & \\
0000 & \\
1110 & \\
1110 \quad\;\; & \\
\hline
10110110 & \text{product (182)}
\end{array}
$$

As you can see, forming shifted products in binary multiplication is a trivial operation, since the only possible values of the multiplier digits are 0 and 1. In other words, each shifted product is either the multiplicand or a string of zeros.

Many computer systems employ a more efficient algorithm to perform this multiplication: Rather than listing all the shifted multiplicands and then adding them together at once, we can simply create a partial product and add the shifted multiplicands to it one at a time. Initially, this partial product is set to 0. Next, we look at the LSB of the multiplier and, if it is 1, add the multiplicand to the partial product; if the

LSB is 0, we do nothing. We can then repeat this step for the next more significant bit, shifting the multiplicand one bit to the left, and continue adding these shifted multiplicands or zeros until all the multiplier bits have been used. Using this method, we need four additions and four partial products to multiply the 4-bit numbers 14 and 13:

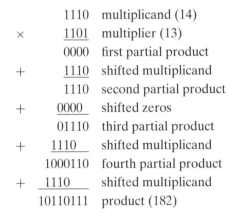

In Figure 2.9, we show this general procedure for multiplying an n-bit multiplicand MD with an m-bit multiplier MR, which has been represented by $b_{m-1}b_{m-2}\cdots b_1b_0$. The product is obtained by shifting the multiplicand i bits to the left and adding it to the partial product PP whenever the corresponding multiplier bit b_i does not equal zero. The shift of i bits to the left is obtained by multiplying the multiplicand by 2^i. As you can see, PP is equal to the final product after we have considered the most significant digit, b_{m-1}.

In general, multiplying an n-bit number by an m-bit number produces an $(n + m)$-bit product. Initially, the partial product has only n significant bits, but it gains one significant bit each time we add the shifted multiplicand. Since the shifted multiplicand is added m times, the product gains up to m additional bits.

To multiply two signed numbers, we simply multiply their magnitudes, making the product positive if the operands have the same sign and negative if they do not. In sign-magnitude systems, this is very easy to do, since signs and magnitudes are separate. Working with two's-complement representations is more difficult, however, since obtaining the magnitude of a negative number and, if necessary, negating the product requires complementation, and this, in turn, requires addition. For this reason we generally perform multiplication of two's-complement numbers by using two's-complement addition, with the slight modification explained below.

As you will recall, we have seen that in binary multiplication of signed numbers, the shift amount of the multiplicand equals the weight

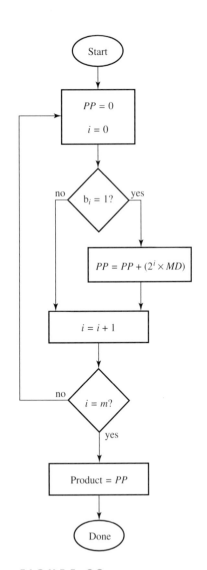

FIGURE 2.9

Procedure for multiplication of unsigned binary numbers.

of the corresponding multiplier bits. Therefore, since the bits in a positive two's-complement number representation have the same weight as the bits in a negative number, two's-complement multiplication can be accomplished through a sequence of two's-complement additions, adding the shifted multiplicands as in the case of unsigned numbers. The single exception in this procedure is the sign bit of a negative multiplier: Since this sign bit has a weight of -2^{m-1}, the multiplicand has to be negated before it can be added to the partial product.

In carrying out two's-complement multiplication, we must also remember to perform a sign extension before we add a shifted multiplicand to a partial product, since each new partial product will have an extra bit of precision. As before, we would ignore any carry out of the MSB during the addition. In the next example we demonstrate two's-complement multiplication.

EXAMPLE 2.4   Binary multiplication

PROBLEM   Perform the binary multiplication of -14 by -13.

SOLUTION

	10010	multiplicand (-14)
$\times$	10011	multiplier (-13)
	000000	extended partial product
$+$	110010	extended multiplicand
	1110010	extended partial product
$+$	110010	extended shifted multiplicand
ignore carry	11010110	extended partial product
$+$	000000	all zeros
	111010110	extended partial product
$+$	000000	all zeros
	1111010110	extended partial product
$+$	001110	extended, shifted, and
		negated multiplicand
ignore carry	0010110110	product (182)

In this multiplication example, note that the carries out of the MSB have been ignored in the third and fifth partial products, before the sign extension. Also note that the last shifted multiplicand was negated before addition. As you can see, the generated product has 10 bits of precision, although only 9 bits are needed to express 182. To obtain 9 bits of precision, we need to perform sign truncation.

2.8 BINARY DIVISION

As in multiplication, the algorithm for binary division uses the shift-and-subtract method. In this algorithm we first subtract the largest possible multiple of the divisor to determine the first digit of the quotient. Then we perform this task again with the diminished dividend and the shifted divisor. When dividing 186 by 14, for example, we first select 14 as the greatest multiple of 14 that is less than 18. This operation leaves us with 1 as the first digit of the quotient. Then we select 42 as the greatest multiple of 14 that is smaller than 46, which produces a quotient of 13 and a remainder of 4.

$$
\begin{array}{r}
13 \\
14)\overline{186} \\
14 \\
\hline
46 \\
42 \\
\hline
4
\end{array}
\quad
\begin{array}{l}
\text{quotient} \\
\text{dividend} \\
\text{shifted (divisor} \times 1) \\
\text{reduced dividend} \\
\text{shifted (divisor} \times 3) \\
\text{remainder}
\end{array}
$$

When working with binary numbers, we use a similar procedure. However, with binary numbers, there can be only two choices for the greatest multiple of the divisor: zero and the divisor itself. Consider, for example, the binary division of 186 by 14:

$$
\begin{array}{r}
1101 \\
1110)\overline{10111010} \\
1110 \\
\hline
1001010 \\
1110 \\
\hline
10010 \\
00000 \\
\hline
10010 \\
1110 \\
\hline
100
\end{array}
\quad
\begin{array}{l}
\text{quotient (13)} \\
\text{dividend (186)} \\
\text{shifted divisor} \\
\text{reduced dividend} \\
\text{shifted divisor} \\
\text{reduced dividend} \\
\text{shifted divisor} \\
\text{reduced dividend} \\
\text{shifted divisor} \\
\text{remainder (4)}
\end{array}
$$

As you can see, binary division is similar to binary multiplication, except in the size of the operands and the result, since it takes an $(n + m)$-bit dividend and an n-bit divisor to generate an m-bit quotient and an n-bit remainder. Whenever the divisor is zero, or when the quotient needs more than m bits, a division **overflow** will occur.

To divide signed numbers, we divide their magnitudes then make the quotient positive if the operands have the same sign and negative if they are different. If there is a remainder, it retains the sign of the dividend.

Division can also be performed directly on two's-complement numbers. However, these techniques, which are usually implemented by high-performance computers, are beyond the scope of this book.

2.9 FLOATING-POINT NUMBERS

So far in this chapter we have focused our discussion on fixed-point number representations, which assume that the radix point has a fixed position. In case of integers, for example, the radix point is assumed to be to the right of the least significant digit. Therefore, we can represent numbers 0 through 9999 with only four decimal digits. We cannot, however, represent 99,000 with the same representation, even though it requires only two nonzero decimal digits. In this case we say that 99,000 is not in the range of the four-digit integer representation.

In general terms, the **range** of a number system is defined as the interval of all representable numbers between the largest and the smallest. For the four-digit representation, for example, the range size is approximately 10^4. Unfortunately, many scientific computations need a much wider range than the one provided by this kind of fixed-point representation. To expand this range, we use what we call **floating-point numbers**, which have the form

$$\text{mantissa} \times (\text{radix})^{exponent}$$

We can think of a floating-point number as a fixed-point number, given by the mantissa, whose radix-point position is specified by the exponent.

Since the radix of a floating-point number is implicit, only the mantissa and the exponent must be represented explicitly. For example, one of the floating formats for the four-digit floating-point number representation could use positive two-digit integers between 0 and 99 for the exponent and mantissa. Then the smallest representable number is 0×10^0, whereas the largest representable number is 99×10^{99}. As you can see, the range size of this four-digit floating-point representation is 10^{101}, which is 10^{97} times larger than the size of the fixed-point range.

At the same time, though, the larger size of this floating-point range was obtained at the expense of the number of significant digits which determines the precision of floating-point numbers. In other words, within a given subrange, there are fewer floating-point numbers than fixed-point numbers. Consider, for example, the subrange between 1000 and 2000 in our four-digit representation. Using fixed-point numbers, we can represent 1001 numbers in this subrange, namely, 1000, 1001, 1002, 1003, . . . , 1999, 2000. By using floating-point numbers, on the other hand, we could represent only 11 different numbers: $1000, 1100, 1200, 1300, \ldots, 1900, 2000$, which are represented as $10 \times 10^2, 11 \times 10^2, 12 \times 10^2, 13 \times 10^2, \ldots, 19 \times 10^2, 20 \times 10^2$. Consequently, since all computers operate with a fixed number of bits, the floating-point representation always gives us more range and less precision than the fixed-point representation.

In its most general form, a floating-point number has a signed mantissa and exponent, so it can accommodate positive and negative integers and fractions. As shown in Figure 2.10(a), the mantissa sign is followed by a signed exponent, and finally by the mantissa magnitude. The exponent is usually encoded in the excess-code format that is called **characteristic**, which is obtained by adding a **bias** to the exponent. In this format, the bias is equal to half the largest representable integer in the exponent field when it has been decremented by 1. Therefore,

$$\text{bias} = \tfrac{1}{2}\text{radix}^s - 1$$

where s is equal to the number of bits in the exponent field. For this reason, this exponent is always a positive number.

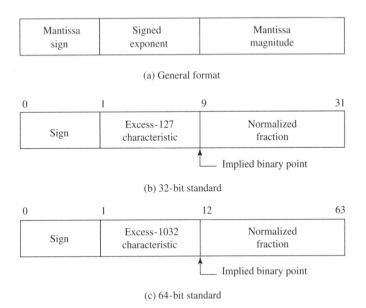

FIGURE 2.10

Floating-point representation.

The mantissa, however, is usually a fraction, within which the binary point is assumed to lie to the left of the most significant bit. The fraction will always be normalized, in the sense that the fraction always starts with a nonzero bit. Since the only nonzero bit is 1, however, it is frequently omitted, as in the standard floating-point representation used in all computers today. The 32-bit floating-point standard, shown in Figure 2.10(b), has a 1-bit sign, an 8-bit excess-127 characteristic, and a 23-bit normalized fraction, which in reality has 24 bits, since the most significant fraction bit is always 1. Similarly, the 64-bit format shown in Figure 2.10(c) consists of a 1-bit sign, an 11-bit excess-1023 characteristic, and a 52-bit fraction.

The addition and subtraction of floating-point numbers can be performed according to standard algebraic rules. However, since addition and subtraction both require that the exponents of the two operands are equal, we have to equalize them by shifting the mantissa of the smaller operand to the right and increasing its exponent proportionally until it is equal to the exponent of the larger number. After this alignment, the two mantissas can be added or subtracted as required and joined with the common exponent into a floating-point result.

In performing addition, there is a possibility that the result will overflow the mantissa field, in which case it must be corrected by shifting the mantissa a single space to the right and incrementing the exponent by 1. If the exponent overflows during incrementation, this floating-point overflow has to be recorded since it cannot be corrected. Furthermore, in performing subtraction, there is a possibility that the result will have one or more leading zeros in its mantissa, in which case it must be normalized by shifting the mantissa to the left and decrementing the exponent proportionally. The maximum possible shift required is always smaller than the number of bits in the mantissa. If the exponent underflows during decrementation, this underflow also has to be recorded.

Conceptually, the multiplication of floating-point numbers is easier than their addition and subtraction, because no alignment of exponents is necessary. In other words, the mantissas can be multiplied as if they were fixed-point integers, and the exponents will simply be added. If, however, this addition of exponents results in an exponent overflow (or underflow), a **floating-point overflow** (or underflow) has to be recorded. The resultant mantissa could have at most one leading zero, which requires a single shift to the left and a corresponding reduction of the exponent by 1. If the exponent underflows after this reduction by 1, the floating-point underflow must be recorded. If, on the other hand, either operand is zero, a floating-point zero has to be generated.

Floating-point division requires us to divide the mantissas and to subtract the exponent of the divisor from the exponent of the dividend. Whenever the dividend is larger than the divisor, the quotient is larger than 1, in which case the mantissa has to be shifted a single position to the right while its exponent is increased by 1. If the exponent overflows (or underflows), a floating-point overflow (or underflow) must be recorded. In those cases where the dividend is zero, a floating-point zero has to be generated. On the other hand, if the divisor is zero, a floating-point overflow must be recorded. Finally, if both the dividend and the divisor are zero, the result is identified as an undefined number.

To speed up this floating-point arithmetic, high-performance computers and workstations have floating-point accelerators, which are special ASICs that incorporate fast algorithms for floating-point arithmetic that is implemented directly in hardware.

2.10 BINARY CODES FOR DECIMAL NUMBERS

Since computers process and store all information in terms of binary digits or bits, in a digital system, we represent a decimal number by a string of bits. For example, we can use 4 bits to represent decimal digits by using a very natural encoding which assigns 0000 to the decimal digit 0, 0001 to 1, 0010 to 2, and so on, concluding with the assignment of 1001 to 9. Thus the three-digit decimal number 123 is represented by the 12-bit string 0001 0010 0011.

In general, any set of objects can be represented by a set of bit strings within which the different bit strings represent the different objects. This set of bit strings is called a **code**, and a particular bit string in the set is called a **code word**. The assignment of code words to objects can be given by an algebraic expression or by a table. You should note, however, when the assignments are given in a tabular form, there may be no logical explanation as to how code words are related to objects. Note also that not all possible bit strings must be used as code words.

As indicated above, at least 4 bits are needed to represent the 10 decimal digits. However, there are $\binom{16}{10} = 16!/10!6!$ different ways to choose 10 specific code words from the 16 possible 4-bit strings and 10! ways to assign each choice to 10 decimal digits. Thus there are $16!10!/10!6! = 16!/6! = 29,059,430,400$ different 4-bit decimal codes. Furthermore, only a few of these are actually used, the most common of which are listed in Table 2.7.

The most frequently used decimal code is **binary-coded decimal** (BCD), which assigns a 4-bit unsigned binary representation to each of the digits 0 through 9, while the code words 1010 through 1111 are not used. The conversion between BCD and decimal representations can be accomplished simply by substituting a 4-bit BCD digit for each decimal digit, and vice versa. In practice, though, we usually pack two BCD digits into one 8-bit byte, which can then represent any one of the values from 0 to 99.

The negative BCD numbers can be expressed in several ways, including sign-magnitude and 10's-complement representations. In each of these representations, the sign uses one extra digit position. In signed-magnitude BCD, the + and − signs could be represented by any 4-bit string, in 10's-complement representation, + is represented by 0000, whereas − is represented by 1001.

TABLE 2.7

Common Decimal Codes

DECIMAL DIGIT	BCD	2421	EXCESS-3	BIQUINARY
0	0000	0000	0011	0100001
1	0001	0001	0100	0100010
2	0010	0010	0101	0100100
3	0011	0011	0110	0101000
4	0100	0100	0111	0110000
5	0101	1011	1000	1000001
6	0110	1100	1001	1000010
7	0111	1101	1010	1000100
8	1000	1110	1011	1001000
9	1001	1111	1100	1010000

The addition of two pairs of the BCD numbers is performed one digit at a time, starting with the least significant digits. The addition of two BCD digits is the same as the addition of two 4-bit, unsigned binary numbers, with one exception: If the sum of these two BCD digits is between 10 and 19, it must be corrected by subtracting 10 and generating the proper carry for the next digit position. In reality, this can be accomplished simply by adding 6 to the overflowed digit, since for 4-bit binary numbers, adding 6 is equivalent to subtracting 10. Moreover, adding 6 automatically produces the proper carry. Note that we can also generate the proper carry into the next digit position either by adding two BCD digits whose sum is equal to or greater than 16.

BCD is what we call a **weighted code**, since the value of each decimal digit is equal to the sum of all the products of the binary values in each bit position and their associated weights. The weights for the BCD bits are 8, 4, 2, and 1, respectively; for this reason, the code is sometimes called the **8421 code**. Alternatively, the weights 2, 4, 2, 1 are used to generate the **2421 code** that is shown in Table 2.7. This letter code is called **self-complementing**, since for any digit 0 through 9, the code word for the 9's complement can be obtained by complementing each bit in the digit's code word.

We have also shown another self-complementing code in Table 2.7, the **excess-3 code**. This code is not a weighted code but is generated from the BCD code by adding 0011 (binary 3) to each code word.

Decimal codes can also have more than 4 bits. For example, the **biquinary code** shown in Table 2.7 uses 7 bits. In this code the first bit in a code word is used to indicate whether the decimal digit falls in the range between 5 and 9, while the second bit indicates the range from 0 to 4. The last 5 bits of each code word are used to select one of the five numbers in the range, with each bit position corresponding to one number in that range.

As you can see from the table, the biquinary code would require 7 bits to represent the same amount of information as the other three codes in the table represent with 4 bits. However, the advantage of this biquinary code lies in its ability to detect single-bit errors, since all code words have the same property: they all have two 1's, one among the two most significant bits and one more among the five least significant bits. Given this property, any accidental change of any bit in any valid code word results in a noncode word, enabling us to detect that the code word is in error. We discuss such codes in detail in Section 2.12.

2.11 CHARACTER CODES

In general, a given string of bits can represent any character, whether numeric or nonnumeric. Since most data processing includes text, the most frequently used characters will be parts of an alphabet, each of which is represented in the computer by a particular bit string.

The most commonly used character code is **ASCII** (the American Standard Code for Information Interchange), in which each character is represented by a 7-bit string. This code accommodates 128 different characters, including uppercase and lowercase letters, the numerals, various punctuation marks, and a number of control characters. All 128 of these code words are shown in Table 2.8, which tells us, for example, that the word "DESIGN" is represented by the following six code words:

$$1000100 \quad 1000101 \quad 1010011 \quad 1001001 \quad 1000111 \quad 1001110$$

TABLE 2.8

American Standard Code for Information Interchange[a]

$b_3b_2b_1b_0$	$b_6b_5b_4$							
	000	001	010	011	100	101	110	111
0000	NUL	DLE	SP	0	@	P	`	p
0001	SOH	DC1	!	1	A	Q	a	q
0010	STX	DC2	"	2	B	R	b	r
0011	ETX	DC3	#	3	C	S	c	s
0100	EOT	DC4	$	4	D	T	d	t
0101	ENQ	NAK	%	5	E	U	e	u
0110	ACK	SYN	&	6	F	V	f	v
0111	BEL	ETB	'	7	G	W	g	w
1000	BS	CAN	(	8	H	X	h	x
1001	HT	EM	)	9	I	Y	i	y
1010	LF	SUB	*	:	J	Z	j	z
1011	VT	ESC	+	;	K	[	k	{
1100	FF	FS	,	<	L	\	l		
1101	CR	GS	–	=	M	]	m	}
1110	SO	RS	.	>	N	^	n	~
1111	SI	US	/	?	O	_	o	DEL

[a]Control code abbreviations:
NUL, null; SOH, start of heading; STX, start of text; ETX, end of text; EOT, end of transmission; ENQ, enquiry; ACK, acknowledge; BEL, bell; BS, backspace; HT, horizontal tab; LF, line feed; VT, vertical tab; FF, form feed; CR, carriage return; SO, shift out; SI, shift in; SP, space; DLE, data link escape; DC1, device control 1; DC2, device control 2; DC3, device control 3; DC4, device control 4; NAK, negative acknowledgment; SYN, synchronize; ETB, end transmission block; CAN, cancel; EM, end of medium; SUB, substitute; ESC, escape; FS, file separator; GS, group separator; RS, record separator; UN, unit separator; DEL, delete or rubout.

Each of these ASCII code words is usually stored in one byte, which includes an extra parity bit that is used for error detection.

2.12 CODES FOR ERROR DETECTION AND CORRECTION

Within a digital system, an **error** can be caused by temporary or permanent physical failures and can be defined as the difference between transmitted and received data. For example, a cosmic ray could cause the temporary failure of a memory circuit by changing the value of a single memory cell. Alternatively, a high package temperature could cause permanent disconnection of the tiny wires inside a microchip. To detect such errors, we need to secure the data with the help of error-detecting codes. To understand these error-detecting codes, however, we first need to introduce the concept of Boolean distance, which in term requires the definition of an n-cube.

Any n-bit string can be visualized as one of the vertices of a binary **n-cube**, which is a cube with a total of 2^n vertices, each of which corresponds to a particular string with n bits. Within this cube, two vertices are connected by an edge if and only if the strings to which they correspond differ in one bit. In Figure 2.11(a) through (d), we show four n-cubes, for $n = 1, 2, 3$, and 4, respectively. The cubes with larger n are more difficult to visualize, although they can be useful in explaining the coding and minimization procedures described in Chapter 4.

Within an n-cube, there can be a number of **m-subcubes**, each containing a set of 2^m vertices. Within these m-subcubes, $n - m$ of the bits at each vertex have the same value, and the remaining m bits take on all 2^m combinations of values 0 and 1. For example, in Figure 2.11(c), the vertices 000, 001, 010, 011 form a 2-subcube within the 3-cube. From the definition of a subcube above, we know that each subcube is characterized by the $n - m$ bits that are the same for each vertex within that subcube. Such a subcube can therefore be specified by a single n-bit string, containing its $n - m$ characteristic binary values and using X in the remaining m positions, to indicate the don't-care bits. In other words, any binary values in place of don't-care bits will produce strings that belong to this m-subcube.

At a conceptual level, the n-cube is useful because it provides a geometrical interpretation of the concept of **distance**, sometimes called **Hamming distance**. The distance between any two vertices is equal to the shortest path between them, which, in turn, is equal to the number of bit positions in which they have different binary values. In other words, any two adjacent vertices will always have a distance of 1. Furthermore, any nonadjacent vertices within any 2-subcube always have a distance

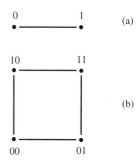

(a)

(b)

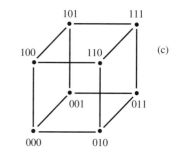

(c)

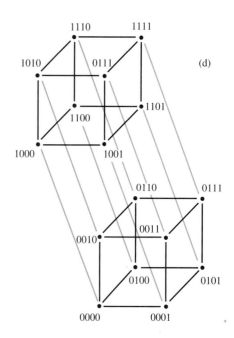

(d)

FIGURE 2.11

n-cubes for $n = 1, 2, 3$, and 4.

of 2. For example, in Figure 2.11(c), vertices 000 and 011 have a distance of 2; similarly, vertices 001 and 010 in the $0XX$-subcube always have a distance of 2. This concept of distance is essential for an understanding of error-detecting codes.

2.12.1 Error-Detecting Codes

Any given n-bit code can be regarded as a subset of all possible n-bit strings. Strings included in that particular subset are called **code words**, while strings not included are called **noncode words**. A code is called an **error-detecting code** if it has the property that certain types of errors will change a code word into a noncode word. Thus assuming that we use only code words for data communication, any errors introduced during transmission will be apparent immediately because they will change code words into noncode words. In other words, if the string received is a code word, the data is correct; if it is a noncode word, the data must contain an error.

To detect a single-bit error—that is, to detect a single bit that has been changed from 0 to 1 or from 1 to 0—it is essential that any two code words in the code have a distance ≥ 2. In other words, we must choose code words in such a way that no two vertices that represent code words would be adjacent in its corresponding n-cube. In Figure 2.12(a), for example, we show a 3-bit code consisting of four code words: 000, 011, 100, and 110. Since a single-bit error could change the code word 100 to code words 000 or 110, this code cannot detect all single-bit errors. However, if we omit 100 from the set of code words and add 101 instead, we can produce a code with the capability to detect single-bit errors. As shown in Figure 2.12(b), within this cube, no single-bit error could change one code word into another, since all the code words are at a distance of 2.

In general, to maintain a distance of 2 in an arbitrary code, we need an equal number of code words and noncode words. Thus to accomplish this goal for an n-bit data, usually called **information bits**, we can use $(n + 1)$-bit code words by adding one more bit, usually called the **parity bit**. The value of this parity bit can be set in such a way that the number of 1's in the code word is even for all code words and odd for all noncode words, or vice versa. When each valid $(n + 1)$-bit code word has an even number of 1's, the code is called an **even-parity code**. On the other hand, a code in which the total number of 1's in a valid $(n + 1)$-bit code word is odd is called an **odd-parity code**. In such cases these codes are called **1-bit parity codes** to emphasize the fact that they each use a single parity bit. As an example, Figure 2.12(b) shows a n-bit even-parity code, consisting of four words: 000, 011, 101, 110. As we can see,

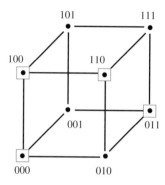

(a) Ordinary code

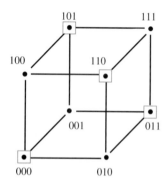

(b) Even-parity code

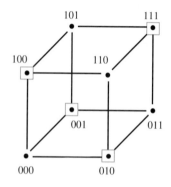

(c) Odd-parity code

FIGURE 2.12
Three different codes.

each code word contains either zero or two ones, while each noncode word contains either one or three ones. Note that in this code, the most-significant two bits are the information bits, while the least-significant bit is the parity bit. Conversely, we could also define a 3-bit odd-parity code as shown in Figure 2.12(c). Note that this code also contains four code words, although in this case, each code word will have either one or three ones.

As you would imagine, these 1-bit parity codes cannot detect 2-bit errors, since changing any two bits from 0 to 1 or from 1 to 0 does not affect the parity. However, they can detect errors that occur when 3 bits in a code word have been changed. In general, a 1-bit parity code can detect changes that have occurred in an odd number of bits but will not detect changes that involve an even number of bits. Thus these 1-bit parity codes can only be used for the detection of single-bit errors. Such parity codes are frequently used in both global and local communications by attaching one parity bit to every 7-bit ASCII code.

Whenever a byte with incorrect parity is received, the received byte, or sometimes the entire message, has to be retransmitted.

2.12.2 Error-Correcting Codes

To actually correct a single-bit error, we need more than one parity bit, since this single bit can indicate only that an entire code word is correct or incorrect. To gain more precise information, we need an extra $\log_2 n$ parity bits for each n information bits so we can determine which information bit is in error. The incorrect bit can then be corrected by changing its value from 0 to 1, or from 1 to 0.

To demonstrate an error-correcting code, we assume that only a single bit of information is to be transmitted and that 0 is to be encoded as 000 and 1 as 111. As shown by the 3-cube in Figure 2.13, this code has a minimum distance of 3. Thus if a single-bit error occurs during the transmission of a code word, it changes that code word into a noncode word, as was the case with the 1-bit parity codes discussed above. In this case, however, the noncode word received would be at a distance of 1 from the code word originally transmitted, and at a distance of 2 from any other code word. Therefore, it is easy to identify the bit in error and to change the received noncode word into the code word that was originally transmitted. As you can see in Figure 2.13, for example, if 000 is transmitted, a single bit error can change it into 100, 010, or 001. However, if we receive a noncode word with one 1 in it, we change it into 000. On the other hand, if we receive a noncode word with two 1's in it, we change it to 111.

Note that the code discussed above can also detect, but not correct, cases where there are two single-bit errors. For example, if 000 is transmitted and 011, 101, or 110 is received, it is obvious that an error has occurred. However, it is not possible to correct this error, since it is not clear whether it was 000 that was originally transmitted and two bits changed, or it was 111 that was transmitted and only one bit changed. For this reason we can use this code either to detect and correct single-bit errors, or to detect up to two errors, but not for both purposes.

There are, however, codes that allow both error detection and error correction, and these are called **error-correcting codes**. In general, a code needs a minimum distance of $2x + 1$ to be useful in correcting up to x single-bit errors. In the simple example presented above, x was equal to 1. Alternatively, we could use a code with a minimum distance of $2x + y + 1$ to correct up to x single-bit errors while detecting up to y additional errors. The task of discovering which code words were originally transmitted is called **decoding**, and the hardware that performs this task is called an **error-correcting decoder**.

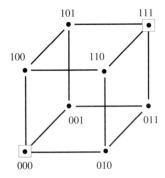

FIGURE 2.13

Example of an error-correcting code.

2.13 HAMMING CODES

In 1950, R. W. Hamming proposed a general method for constructing error-correcting codes by using a minimum distance of three. According to this method, for every integer m there is a $(2^m - 1)$-bit **Hamming code** which contains m parity bits and $2^m - 1 - m$ information bits. Within this Hamming code, the parity bits are intermixed with the information bits as follows: If we number the bit positions from 1 to $2^m - 1$, the bits in position 2^k, where $0 \leq k \leq m - 1$, are the parity bits, and the bits in the remaining positions are information bits. Thus parity bits are always in positions $1, 2, 4, 8, \ldots, 2^{m-1}$. In general, the value of each parity bit is chosen so that the total number of 1's in a specific group of bit positions is even, and these groups are chosen so that no information bit is covered by the same combination of parity bits. It is this arrangement that gives the code its correcting capability. More precisely, for each parity bit in position 2^k, its corresponding group of information bits includes all those bits in the position whose binary representation has a 1 in position 2^k.

To demonstrate parity groups, we begin with the 7-bit Hamming code shown in Figure 2.14, which has information bits in positions 7, 6, 5, and 3 and parity bits in positions 4, 2, and 1. As the shaded squares indicate, each bit in this code is used in the computation of one or more parity values. Since 111 is the binary representation of 7, for example, the information bit in position 7 is used to compute the value of all three parity bits. On the other hand, the information bit in position 6, whose binary representation is 110, is used only for computing the value of the parity bits in positions 4 and 2, while the information bit in position 5 is used in computing the values of the parity bits in positions 4 and 1. Finally, the information bit 3 is used to compute the value of the parity bits in positions 2 and 1.

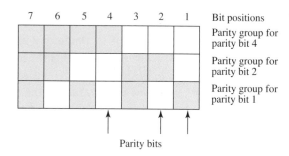

FIGURE 2.14

Computation of parities in a 7-bit Hamming code.

According to these parity groups, the value of the parity bit in position 1 has to be chosen so that the number of 1's in positions 7, 5, 3, and 1 is even, whereas the value of the parity bit in position 2 makes the

Code Words with Four Information Bits in Minimum-Distance-3 and Minimum-Distance-4 Hamming Codes

MINIMUM-DISTANCE-3 CODE		MINIMUM-DISTANCE-4 CODE	
INFORMATION BITS	PARITY BITS	INFORMATION BITS	PARITY BITS
0000	000	0000	0000
0001	011	0001	0111
0010	101	0010	1011
0011	110	0011	1100
0100	110	0100	1101
0101	101	0101	1010
0110	011	0110	0110
0111	000	0111	0001
1000	111	1000	1110
1001	100	1001	1001
1010	010	1010	0101
1011	001	1011	0010
1100	001	1100	0011
1101	010	1101	0100
1110	100	1110	1000
1111	111	1111	1111

number of 1's even in positions 7, 6, 3, and 2, and the value of the parity bit in position 4 makes the number of 1's even in positions 7, 6, 5, and 4. In Table 2.9 we show all the code words for this 7-bit Hamming code.

On the basis of the information in this table, it is easy to see that the minimum distance of a Hamming code must be 3, since this means that for any two code words, we have to make at least three single-bit changes to convert one code word into another. We can prove this intuitively, by demonstrating that a 1- or 2-bit change never produces anything but noncode words, which do not have correct values of parity bits. To prove that a 1-bit change will always generate a noncode word, note that a 1-bit change in a code word affects at least one parity bit, since each bit in the code word is included in at least one parity group. Therefore, a 1-bit change should always make at least one parity value incorrect.

On the other hand, a 2-bit change in a code word does not change the value of a parity bit if both bits are in the same parity group. However, this is not possible, since for any two positions in a code word, there is always one parity group that does not include both positions. In other words, since any two bits must have different positions, their binary numbers must differ in at least one bit, so there is always at least one parity group with only one bit changed, which will produce a noncode word with at least one incorrect parity value. Therefore, we must conclude that Hamming codes have a distance of 3 or more.

On the basis of this explanation, it is not difficult to see how to correct single-bit errors when we are receiving corrupted code words. To correct a single-bit error, we need to compute the parity for each parity group. Next, we add the position numbers of all these parity bits whose groups have odd parity. This sum will indicate the position of the bit that is in error. In Figure 2.15 we demonstrate this procedure for one example, assuming that the proper code word 1010101 was transmitted but that a single-bit error in position 6 occurred during transmission which changed the code word 1010101 into the noncode word 1110101. When we count the number of 1's that are in bit positions 7, 6, 5, and 4 of the code word we received, we find that the number is odd. Similarly, we find that the bits in positions 7, 6, 3, and 2 contain an odd number of 1's. Therefore, we know that it must be the parity bits in positions 4 and 2 that are in error. Since the sum of their position numbers is 6, we know that the error has occurred in the sixth bit position.

This distance-3 Hamming code could easily be modified into a distance-4 code by adding one more parity bit, the value of which is chosen so that the number of 1's in all the bits, including the new one, is even. All the code words for this modified distance-3 code are shown in Table 2.9. As was the case with the 1-bit even-parity code, this additional bit ensures that we can detect an odd number of single-bit errors

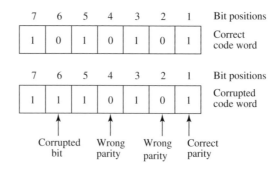

FIGURE 2.15
Correction procedure for distance-3 Hamming code.

should they occur. In particular, any 3-bit error is detectable with this code.

Distance-3 and distance-4 Hamming codes are commonly used for the detection and correction of errors in computer memories. Since these memory components represent a major part of any computer system, Hamming codes provide us with a cost-efficient way to improve system reliability, because the number of parity bits used for memory correction grows only logarithmically with the width of the memory word.

2.14 CHAPTER SUMMARY

In this chapter we have discussed the various data types that are used in digital systems and the way they are represented in binary form. In particular, we described the data types used for arithmetic computation (fixed- and floating-point numbers) and procedures for performing basic arithmetic operations: addition, subtraction, multiplication, and division. These procedures will be used in later chapters as initial specifications in design of arithmetic components.

We also introduced various types of codes, especially the codes we use for error detection (parity codes) and error correction (Hamming codes). These codes are used whenever we need to transmit data from one processor to another over noisy channels or whenever errors are likely to result from unstable environmental conditions. Since such codes require special encoding and decoding hardware, which increases the cost and decreases the performance of a digital system, forcing the designers who use these codes to trade cost and performance for data security.

This chapter was intended to be introductory; the material covered here will permeate the remainder of the book. In the next chapter we introduce basic digital components as well as rules for combining those components into circuits capable of performing binary arithmetic and other digital functions.

2.15 FURTHER READINGS

Knuth, D. E. *The Art of Computer Programming: Semi-numerical Algorithms*. Reading, MA: Addison-Wesley, 1969.

Classic work with an in-depth treatment of fixed- and floating-point numbers as well as the algorithms used for their manipulation.

Peterson, W. W., and E. J. Welden. *Error-Correcting Codes*, 2nd ed. Boston: MIT Press, 1972.

A classic text, with a formal treatment of error-detection and error-correcting codes. Recommended only for readers who are theoretically inclined.

Schmid, H. *Decimal Computation*. New York: Wiley, 1974.

A collection, a catalog, and a review of BCD computation techniques. Describes how each of the most common arithmetic and transcendental operations can be implemented in a variety of ways.

Scott, N. R. *Computer Number Systems and Arithmetic*. Englewood Cliffs, NJ: Prentice Hall, 1985.

A highly readable introductory text on number systems and their application in digital circuits.

Stein, M. L., and R. W. D. Munro. *Introduction to Machine Arithmetic*. Reading, MA: Addison-Wesley, 1971.

Explains the basic algorithms of computer arithmetic, using a mathematical rather than an engineering point of view. Nonetheless, the reader does not need a great deal of mathematical knowledge to understand its material.

Sterbenz, P. H. *Floating-Point Computation*. Englewood Cliffs, NJ: Prentice Hall, 1974.

A formal treatment of floating-point computation and error analysis. What actually happens when floating-point arithmetic is performed during the execution of programs is described.

Wakerly, J. F. *Error-Detecting Codes, Self-Checking Circuits, and Applications*. New York: North-Holland, 1978.

An excellent introduction to various codes used in computer systems and their implementation in many practical applications.

Waser, S., and M. J. Flynn. *Introduction to Arithmetic for Digital System Designers*. New York: Holt, Rinehart and Winston, 1982.

A more detailed treatment of computer arithmetic, intended for those who design arithmetic circuits.

2.16 PROBLEMS

2.1 (Binary representation) Express the following decimal numbers as binary numbers.

    (a) 129

    (b) 511

    (c) 1000

    (d) 2048

2.2 (Binary representation) What is the largest number that we can represent with (a) 9, (b) 10, (c) 15, and (d) 16 bits?

2.3 (Binary representation) List all the digits and their binary representations in base 13.

2.4 (Number conversion) Convert the following binary digits to hexadecimal notation.

    (a) 1010101010

    (b) 10000001

    (c) 11111111111

    (d) 100110011001

2.5 (Number conversion) Give the binary equivalents of the following hexadecimal numbers.

    (a) 123.45

    (b) 1000.50

    (c) BAD.CAB

    (d) DA7.35C

2.6 (Number conversion) Convert the following decimal numbers to radix-6 numbers.

    (a) 131

    (b) 208

    (c) 1001

    (d) 5050

2.7 (Number conversion) Find the decimal equivalents of the following radix-7 numbers.

    (a) 606

    (b) 123

    (c) 6650

    (d) 345.6

2.8 (Number conversion) Convert the following numbers from the given base to the bases that are indicated.

    (a) Decimal 112_{10} to binary, octal, and base 9

    (b) Hexadecimal $1AB2.C_{16}$ to decimal, binary, and base 7

    (c) Binary 101101101_2 to octal, decimal, and base 12

    (d) Base-12 $12AB_{12}$ to binary, base 6, and base 7

2.9 (Number conversion) Formulate a procedure for converting numbers from base 3 to base 9

2.10 (Number conversion) Find the value of x if $23_x = 111100010_2$.

2.11 (Addition rules) Add the following numbers without converting them to decimal representations.

    (a) 01110_2 and 110011_2

    (b) $98A_{12}$ and 234_{12}

    (c) ABC_{16} and $A78_{16}$

2.12 (Binary arithmetic) Evaluate the following expressions by performing binary arithmetic.

    (a) $(101101 + 11101)^2$

    (b) $(100101 + 101101)(100101 - 101101)$

    (c) $(111011 + 10101)/(110111 - 101101)$

2.13 (Number complements) Find the 10's complement of the following decimal numbers.

    (a) 123456

    (b) 987654

    (c) 900900

    (d) 000000

2.14 (Number complements) Find the two's complement of the following binary numbers.

    (a) 1010101

    (b) 111101111

    (c) 0000001

    (d) 100000

    (e) 000000

2.15 (Subtraction rules) Perform subtraction by taking the 10's complement of the subtrahend.

    (a) $3421 - 1567$

    (b) $1682 - 2682$

    (c) $1000 - 1$

    (d) $3003 - 2002$

2.16 (Subtraction rules) Perform binary subtraction by taking the two's complement of the subtrahend.

    (a) $101110 - 10001$

    (b) $111111 - 11110$

    (c) $11110 - 1001$

    (d) $100001 - 10001$

2.17 (BCD arithmetic) Convert the following decimal numbers to binary, and then perform binary multiplication.

    (a) 15×16

    (b) 120×21

    (c) 17×13

    (d) 21×100

2.18 (Multiplication rules) Perform binary multiplication with the following two's-complement numbers.

    (a) 011011×0011

    (b) 111101×0011

    (c) 010101×1001

    (d) 111101×1001

2.19 (Division rules) Divide the following binary numbers.

    (a) $11011/1001$

    (b) $11111/1111$

    (c) $1010101/10111$

    (d) $11001100/10011$

2.20 (Division algorithms) Define the procedure and draw the flowchart for the division of:

    (a) Nonnegative binary numbers

    (b) Two's-complement binary numbers

    (c) Sign-magnitude binary numbers

2.21 (Floating-point algorithms) Define the procedure for (a) adding, (b) subtracting, (c) multiplying, and (d) dividing floating-point numbers.

2.22 (BCD code) Represent the following decimal numbers in BCD.

    (a) 13675

    (b) 23567

    (c) 33441

    (d) 9753

2.23 (Binary codes) Determine the binary code for each of the 10 decimal digits using weighted codes with weights 7, 4, 2, and 1.

2.24 (Binary codes) Represent the decimal number 9876 in

    (a) 8421-code

    (b) 2421-code

    (c) Excess-3 code

    (d) Biquinary code

2.25 (Error-detecting codes) Make a BCD error-detecting code by adding (a) an even-parity bit, and (b) an odd-parity bit in the least-significant position.

2.26 (Character codes) Write the title of this book in ASCII.

2.27 (Character codes) Decode the following ASCII code:

1000010 1001111 1010010 1001001 1001110 1000111

2.28 (Error-detecting codes) Determine how many distinct subcubes of the following sizes would be in any n-cube.

(a) $n - 1$

(b) m

2.29 (Error-detecting codes) How many errors can be detected by a code with a minimum distance of d?

2.30 (Error-detecting codes) Define a distance-3 Hamming code with 11 information bits.

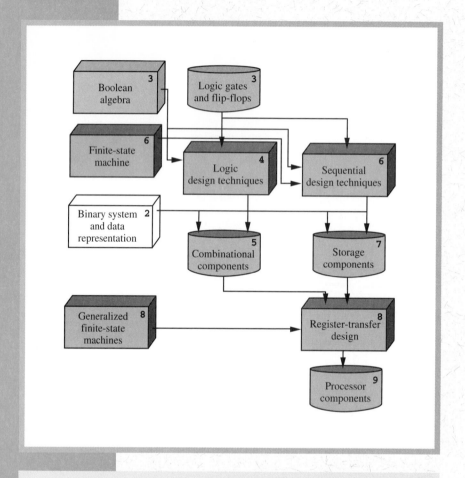

In Chapter 2 we learned the rules for performing binary arithmetic. In this chapter we learn how to design circuits that implement those rules. In general, every digital circuit is implemented with the same basic logic components, called gates and flip-flops. Since every gate is the implementation of one or more Boolean algebra operations, we must understand the properties of Boolean algebra before we can learn to design logic circuits. Once we have discussed Boolean algebra, we will be able to describe and design logic circuits using a given library of logic components. For this purpose we create our own generic library of logic components and describe different technologies that are available for manufacturing digital systems.

CHAPTER

3

Boolean Algebra and Logic Design

The success of computer technology is primarily based on simplicity of designing digital circuits and ease of their manufacture. Digital circuits are composed of basic processing elements, called gates, and basic memory elements, called flip-flops.

The simplicity in digital circuit design can be contributed to the fact that input and output signals of each gate or flip-flop can assume only two values, 0 and 1, and that the changes in signal values are governed by laws of Boolean algegra. The fact that Boolean algebra is finite and richer in properties than ordinary algebra leads to simple optimization techniques for Boolean functions during their implementations with gates and flip-flops. In order to learn techniques for design of digital circuits, usually called logic design, we must understand first the properties of Boolean algebra.

3.1 ALGEBRAIC PROPERTIES

Boolean algebra can be defined with a set of elements, a set of operators, and a number of axioms that are taken as true without the need for proof. In general, a set of elements is defined as any collection of objects that possess a common property. If S is a set and x is an object, then $x \in S$ denotes that x is a member of the set S, and $x \notin S$ denotes that x is not an element of S. A set with a finite number of elements can be specified by listing all its elements inside a pair of braces. For example, $A = \{1, 2, 3, 4\}$ denotes the set A, whose elements are the numbers $1, 2, 3,$ and 4. A **binary operator** defined on the set S is a rule that assigns to each pair of elements in S another unique element that is also included in S.

What we refer to as the **axioms** of any algebra are the basic assumptions from which all the other properties of the system, called theorems, can be deduced. Listed below are the axioms most commonly used in defining an algebraic structure.

CLOSURE. A set S is closed with respect to a binary operator • if and only if for every $x, y \in S, x • y \in S$. For example, the set of natural numbers $N = \{1, 2, 3, 4, \ldots\}$ is closed with respect to addition, since for all $a, b \in N$, we can obtain a unique number c such that $c = a + b$ and $c \in N$. On the other hand, the set of natural numbers is not closed with respect to subtraction, because negative numbers are not in N.

ASSOCIATIVITY. A binary operator • defined on a set S is said to be associative if and only if for all $x, y, z \in S$,

$$(x • y) • z = x • (y • z)$$

IDENTITY ELEMENT. A set S is said to have an identity element with respect to a particular binary operator • whenever there exists an element $e \in S$ such that for every $x \in S$,

$$e • x = x • e = x$$

For example, 0 is an identity element with respect to addition on the set of integers

$$I = \{\ldots, -3, -2, -1, 0, 1, 2, 3, \ldots\}$$

because for any $x \in I$,

$$x + 0 = 0 + x = x$$

COMMUTATIVITY. A binary operator • defined on a set S is said to be commutative if and only if for all $x, y \in S$,

$$x • y = y • x$$

INVERSE ELEMENT.   A set S that has the identity element e with respect to a binary operator $\bullet$ is said to have an inverse if and only if for every $x \in S$, there exists an element $y \in S$ such that

$$x \bullet y = e$$

For example, with respect to addition, the inverse of each $x \in I$ is $(-x)$ since $x + (-x) = 0$.

DISTRIBUTIVITY.   If $\bullet$ and $\square$ are two binary operators on a set S, $\bullet$ is said to be distributive over $\square$ if for all $x, y, z \in S$,

$$x \bullet (y\square z) = (x \bullet y)\square(x \bullet z)$$

3.2 AXIOMATIC DEFINITION OF BOOLEAN ALGEBRA

In 1854, George Boole introduced the formalism that we use for the systematic treatment of logic, which is now called **Boolean algebra**. In 1938, C. E. Shannon applied this particular algebra to demonstrate that the properties of electrical switching circuits can be represented by a two-valued Boolean algebra, which is called **switching algebra**. The formal definition of Boolean algebra that is given below was first formulated in 1904 by E. V. Huntington.

At the most general level, Boolean algebra is an algebraic structure that is defined on a set of elements B with two binary operators, $+$ and $\cdot$, which satisfies the following axioms.

Axiom 1 (Closure Property).   (a) B is closed with respect to the operator $+$; (b) B is also closed with respect to the operator $\cdot$.

Axiom 2 (Identity Element).   (a) B has an identity element with respect to $\cdot$, designated by 1; (b) B also has an identity element with respect to $+$, designated by 0.

Axiom 3 (Commutativity Property).   (a) B is commutative with respect to $+$; (b) B is also commutative with respect to $\cdot$.

Axiom 4 (Distributivity Property).   (a) The operator $\cdot$ is distributive over $+$; (b) similarly, the operator $+$ is distributive over $\cdot$.

Axiom 5 (Complement Element).   For every $x \in B$, there exists an element $x' \in B$ such that (a) $x + x' = 1$ and (b) $x \cdot x' = 0$. This second element, x', is called the complement of x.

Axiom 6 (Cardinality Bound).   There are at least two elements $x, y \in B$ such that $x \neq y$.

As you can see, several differences emerge when we compare Boolean algebra with ordinary algebra. Note, for example, that:

1. In ordinary algebra, $+$ is not distributive over $\cdot$.

2. Boolean algebra does not have inverses with respect to $+$ and $\cdot$; therefore, there are no subtraction or division operations in Boolean algebra.

3. Complements are available in Boolean algebra but not in ordinary algebra.

4. Boolean algebra applies to a finite set of elements, whereas ordinary algebra applies to the infinite set of real numbers.

5. Huntington's definition of Boolean algebra does not include associativity, since it can be derived from the other axioms.

Despite these differences, though, Boolean algebra does resemble ordinary algebra in many respects. Using the familiar symbols $+$ and $\cdot$, for example, facilitates Boolean algebraic manipulations. The novice logic designer, however, must be careful not to use the rules of ordinary algebra when they do not apply.

According to this definition, it should now be clear that to formulate a Boolean algebra, we need to (a) define a set of elements B, (b) define two binary operators on B, and (c) verify that set B, together with the two operators, satisfies the six Huntington axioms. In carrying out these procedures, however, we could formulate many different Boolean algebras, simply because we can define set B and the two operations in a number of different ways. In the rest of the book, we will be working with the two-valued Boolean algebra defined by Shannon, that is, an algebra in which the set B has only two elements. This two-valued Boolean algebra is the accepted basis of mathematical logic in which two elements are "false" and "true" and logic design in which these two elements are 0 and 1.

The **two-valued Boolean algebra** is defined on a set of two elements, $B = \{0, 1\}$, with two binary operators OR $(+)$ and AND $(\cdot)$ as defined in Tables 3.1 and 3.2. As you can see from these tables, the Huntington axioms are valid for the two-valued Boolean algebra defined above.

Axiom 1. Closure is evident in Tables 3.1 and 3.2, since the result of each operation is an element of B.

Axiom 2. The identity elements in this algebra are 0 for the operator $+$ and 1 for the operator $\cdot$. From the Tables 3.1 and 3.2, for example, we see that

(a) $0 + 0 = 0$, and $0 + 1 = 1 + 0 = 1$
(b) $1 \cdot 1 = 1$, and $1 \cdot 0 = 0 \cdot 1 = 0$

which demonstrates that 0 and 1 are both identity elements.

TABLE 3.1

AND
Operator

x	y	$x \cdot y$
0	0	0
0	1	0
1	0	0
1	1	1

TABLE 3.2

OR Operator

x	y	$x + y$
0	0	0
0	1	1
1	0	1
1	1	1

Axiom 3.   The commutativity laws follow from the symmetry of the operator tables.

Axiom 4.   The distributivity of this algebra can be demonstrated by checking both sides of the equation $x \cdot (y + z) = (x \cdot y) + (x \cdot z)$ for every possible case of variable values. If we are to claim distributivity, in other words, we must be able to show that for any value of binary variables x, y, and z, $x \cdot (y + z)$ will have the same value as $(x \cdot y) + (x \cdot z)$. Table 3.3 shows that they do. Similarly, the distributive law of $+$ over $\cdot$ will also hold, as shown in Table 3.4.

T A B L E   3.3

Proof of Distributivity of ·

x	y	z	y + z	x(y + z)	xy	xz	(xy) + (xz)
0	0	0	0	0	0	0	0
0	0	1	1	0	0	0	0
0	1	0	1	0	0	0	0
0	1	1	1	0	0	0	0
1	0	0	0	0	0	0	0
1	0	1	1	1	0	1	1
1	1	0	1	1	1	0	1
1	1	1	1	1	1	1	1

T A B L E   3.4

x	y	z	yz	x + (yz)	x + y	x + z	(x + y)(x + z)
0	0	0	0	0	0	0	0
0	0	1	0	0	0	1	0
0	1	0	0	0	1	0	0
0	1	1	1	1	1	1	1
1	0	0	0	1	1	1	1
1	0	1	0	1	1	1	1
1	1	0	0	1	1	1	1
1	1	1	1	1	1	1	1

   Note that in two-valued Boolean algebra, proofs are often made, as here, by tables that demonstrate validity for every possible case of variable values.

Axiom 5.   0 and 1 are complements of each other, since $0 + 0' = 0 + 1 = 1$ and $1 + 1' = 1 + 0 = 1$; furthermore, $0 \cdot 0' = 0 \cdot 1 = 0$ and $1 \cdot 1' = 1 \cdot 0 = 0$.

Axiom 6.   The cardinality axiom is satisfied, since this two-valued Boolean algebra has two distinct elements, 1 and 0, and $1 \neq 0$.

TABLE 3.5

NOT
Operator

x	x'
0	1
1	0

Generally speaking, this Boolean algebra is established on a set of two elements, 1 and 0, and two binary operators, AND and OR. However, since Axiom 5 establishes the complement operator, NOT (shown in Table 3.5), this two-valued Boolean algebra is frequently defined in terms of three operators: AND, OR, and NOT. This definition is very convenient, since these three operators clearly correspond to the AND, OR, and NOT gates that are used most often in logic design. As mentioned above, this two-valued Boolean algebra is also called **switching algebra** by design engineers. For the sake of brevity, we drop the adjective two-valued in the rest of the book and refer to this algebra simply as Boolean algebra.

3.3 BASIC THEOREMS OF BOOLEAN ALGEBRA

In addition to the axioms that are given in the definition of a Boolean algebra, we can also derive additional laws, called **theorems** of Boolean algebra. These theorems are particular useful when we perform algebraic manipulations of Boolean expressions in the process of optimizing a logic design. Table 3.6 lists six basic theorems of Boolean algebra. In this table the notation has been simplified by omitting the AND operator whenever we can do so without confusion. Like the axioms, these theorems have been listed in pairs, indicating that they can be derived from each other by the duality principle.

TABLE 3.6

Basic Theorems of Boolean Algebra

Theorem 1	(a)	$x + x$	$= x$
(idempotency)	(b)	xx	$= x$
Theorem 2	(a)	$x + 1$	$= 1$
	(b)	$x \cdot 0$	$= 0$
Theorem 3	(a)	$yx + x$	$= x$
(absorption)	(b)	$(y + x)x$	$= x$
Theorem 4		$(x')'$	$= x$
(involution)			
Theorem 5	(a)	$(x + y) + z$	$= x + (y + z)$
(associativity)	(b)	$x(yz)$	$= (xy)z$
Theorem 6	(a)	$(x + y)'$	$= x'y'$
(De Morgan's law)	(b)	$(xy)'$	$= x' + y'$

As mentioned above, axioms are given and need no proof. Theorems, on the other hand, must be proven, either from axioms or from other theorems that have already been proven. In other words, each step in a proof must be justified by an axiom or by another theorem. As an example, we give the proof of Theorems 1(a) and 1(b).

THEOREM 1(a) (Idempotency). $x + x = x$.

PROOF:

$$
\begin{aligned}
x + x &= (x + x) \cdot 1 && \text{by identity [Axiom 2(a)]} \\
&= (x + x)(x + x') && \text{by complement [Axiom 5(a)]} \\
&= x + xx' && \text{by distributivity [Axiom 4(b)]} \\
&= x + 0 && \text{by complement [Axiom 5(b)]} \\
&= x && \text{by identity [Axiom 2(b)]}
\end{aligned}
$$

The dual Theorem 1(b) can be obtained by repeating the proof of Theorem 1(a), interchanging $+$ and $\cdot$, 0 and 1, and (a) and (b) in each line of the proof. To demonstrate duality, the complete proof of Theorem 1(b) is shown below.

THEOREM 1(b) (Idempotency). $x \cdot x = x$.

PROOF:

$$
\begin{aligned}
x \cdot x &= xx + 0 && \text{by identity [Axiom 2(b)]} \\
&= xx + xx' && \text{by complement [Axiom 5(b)]} \\
&= x(x + x') && \text{by distributivity [Axiom 4(a)]} \\
&= x \cdot 1 && \text{by complement [Axiom 5(a)]} \\
&= x && \text{by identity [Axiom 2(a)]}
\end{aligned}
$$

The proofs of the other theorems in Table 3.6 have been left to serve as exercises at the end of the chapter.

Since the two-valued Boolean algebra has only two elements, we can also show the validity of these theorems by using truth tables. To do this, a truth table is constructed for each side of the equation that is stated in the theorem. Then both sides of the equation are checked to see that they yield identical results for all possible combinations of variable values. For example, the Table 3.7 proves De Morgan's first theorem: $(x + y)' = x'y'$. On the basis of this truth table, we can see that the columns headed by $(x + y)'$ and $x'y'$ will have identical results for all combinations of x and y values. Thus we know that the theorem holds.

The Huntington axioms given in Section 3.2 and the basic theorems described above are generally listed in pairs. One of each pair of axioms can be obtained from the other by using an important property of Boolean algebra called the **duality principle**. This principle states that

TABLE 3.7

Proof of De Morgan's First Theorem

x	y	$x + y$	$(x + y)'$	x'	y'	$x'y'$
0	0	0	1	1	1	1
0	1	1	0	1	0	0
1	0	1	0	0	1	0
1	1	1	0	0	0	0

any algebraic equality derived from these axioms will still be valid whenever the OR and AND operators, and identity elements 0 and 1, have been interchanged. In other words, the dual of any algebraic equality can be obtained by changing every OR into AND, every AND into OR, every 1 into 0, and every 0 into 1.

The duality principle is very useful since we can invoke it to prove any statement about Boolean algebra whose dual is known to be true. For example, the complete proof of Theorem 1(b) presented above was not necessary since Theorem 1(b) follows from Theorem 1(a) by the duality principle. Furthermore, we can use the duality principle to prove that every Boolean expression and its dual with complemented variables are complements of each other. More precisely, if $E(x_1, x_2, \ldots, x_n)$ is a Boolean expression of n variables, and $E_d(x_1, x_2, \ldots, x_n)$ is its dual expression, then

$$E'(x_1, x_2, \ldots, x_n) = E_d(x_1', x_2', \ldots, x_n') \tag{3.1}$$

Using this property of Boolean algebra, we can generalize De Morgan's law given in Theorem 6 to more than two variables as follows:

$$(x_1 + x_2 + \cdots + x_n)' = x_1' x_2' \cdots x_n' \tag{3.2}$$

$$(x_1, x_2 \cdots x_n)' = x_1' + x_2' + \cdots + x_n' \tag{3.3}$$

3.4 BOOLEAN FUNCTIONS

In general, **functions** can be defined as algebraic expressions that are formed from variables, operators, parentheses, and an equal sign. More specifically, **Boolean expressions** are formed from binary variables and the Boolean operators AND, OR, and NOT.

When we compute the values of Boolean expressions, we must adhere to a specific order of computation: namely, (1) parentheses, (2) NOT, (3) AND, and (4) OR. In other words, the expression inside the parentheses must be evaluated first, and if there are no parentheses, NOT must be evaluated before AND, and AND before OR. Binary variables in these expressions can take only two values, 0 and 1. For a given value of the variables, then, the value of the function is either 0 or 1. Consider, for example, the Boolean function

$$F_1 = xy + xy'z + x'yz \tag{3.4}$$

This function equals 1 if $x = 1$ and $y = 1$, or if $x = 1$, $y = 0$, and $z = 1$, or if $x = 0$, $y = 1$, and $z = 1$; otherwise, $F_1 = 0$.

The Boolean expression in the definition of F_1 can be characterized as having one **OR term** and three **AND terms**. The first AND term contains two literals while the second and third have three literals each, where a **literal** indicates a variable or its complement. The number of terms and literals is usually used as a measure of the expression's complexity and frequently as a measure of its implementation cost.

The preceding example shows how we define a Boolean function by an algebraic expression. However, any Boolean function can also be defined by a truth table, which lists the value the function has for each combination of its variable values. For example, in Table 3.8 we define two Boolean functions in three variables. As is evident from the table, there are eight distinct ways that the values of 0 or 1 could be assigned to three variables. The columns labeled F_1 and F_1' contain the function value for all possible combination of variable values. From this table, then, we see that F_1 is equal to 1 for four combinations of variable values:

(a) $x = 0, y = 1, z = 1$;
(b) $x = 1, y = 0, z = 1$;
(c) $x = 1, y = 1, z = 0$;
(d) $x = 1, y = 1, z = 1$.

On the other hand, for all other combinations of variable values, F_1 equals 0.

As a general rule, the truth table for any Boolean function of n variables has 2^n rows, which represent every possible combination of variable values, so that the value entered in the function column in each row is the value of the function for that particular combination of variable values. Note that the rows in any table could be numbered from 0 to $2^n - 1$, to correspond to the binary numbers represented by the variable values.

3.4.1 Complement of a Function

The complement of any function F is F', and its value can be obtained by interchanging the 0's for 1's and 1's for 0's in the value of F. To determine the algebraic expression for the complement of a function, we apply the generalized form of De Morgan's theorem given by Equations (3.2) and (3.3) as many times as necessary. For example, the algebraic expression for F_1' is obtained from the expression for F_1 as follows:

$$F_1' = (xy + xy'z + x'yz)' \quad \text{by definition of } F$$
$$= (xy)'(xy'z)'(x'yz)' \quad \text{by De Morgan's theorem}$$
$$= (x' + y')(x' + y + z')(x + y' + z') \quad \text{by De Morgan's theorem}$$

TABLE 3.8

Truth Tables for $F_1 = xy + xy'z + x'yz$ and its Complement $F_1' = (x' + y')(x' + y + z')(x + y' + z')$

ROW NUMBER	x	y	z	F_1	F_1'
0	0	0	0	0	1
1	0	0	1	0	1
2	0	1	0	0	1
3	0	1	1	1	0
4	1	0	0	0	1
5	1	0	1	1	0
6	1	1	0	1	0
7	1	1	1	1	0

In this example we see that in the final expression for F_1', all ANDs and ORs have been interchanged, all unprimed variables have been primed, and all primed variables have become unprimed.

A much simpler way of deriving a complement of a function would be to use a dual with complemented variables as specified by Equation (3.1). Thus the complement of an expression can also be obtained simply by interchanging AND and OR operators and by complementing each literal where that literal has been defined earlier as a primed or unprimed variable. Thus the expression for F_1' derived directly from the expression for F_1 given in Equation (3.4):

$$F_1' = (xy + xy'z + x'yz)'$$
$$= (x' + y')(x' + y + z')(x + y' + z') \tag{3.5}$$

3.4.2 Algebraic Manipulation

In addition to algebraic expressions described above, a Boolean function can be expressed graphically by connecting together AND, OR, and NOT operators, as specified by the algebraic expression that was used to define the function. For example, function F_1, which was defined by Equation (3.1), could be represented with five AND, two OR, and two NOT operators, as shown in Figure 3.1(a). By contrast, F_1', which was defined by Equation (3.5), would need five OR, two AND, and three NOT operators, as shown in Figure 3.1(b). F_1 could also be obtained from F_1' by using an additional NOT operator, as shown in Figure 3.1(b). Note that this second implementation of F requires two more NOT operators.

This example demonstrates that the same function can be specified by two or more different algebraic expressions. Before we can use one expression in place of the other, we must prove, however, that these two algebraic expressions actually define the same function, which could be achieved either by a truth-table comparison or by algebraic manipulation. In the first method, the two algebraic expressions of n binary variables are said to be equal if and only if they have the same values for all 2^n possible combinations of the n variables. In the second method, one or both expressions have to be transformed, using axioms and theorems of Boolean algebra, until both algebraic expressions are the same. Consider, for example, two of the algebraic expressions that define the function F_1:

$$F_1 = xy + xy'z + x'yz$$
$$F_1 = xy + xz + yz \tag{3.6}$$

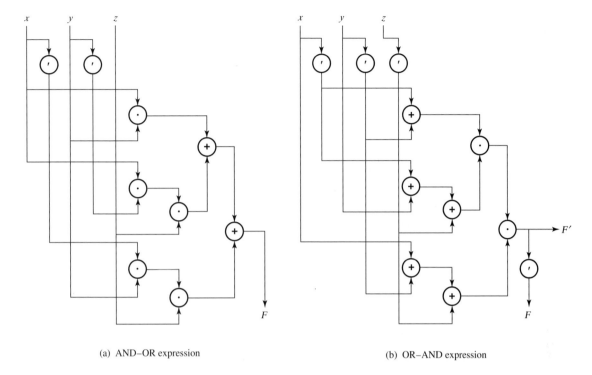

(a) AND–OR expression   (b) OR–AND expression

FIGURE 3.1
Graphic representation of two expressions for F_1.

To show that these two expressions are the same, we can reduce the first
expression to the second one as follows:

$$
\begin{aligned}
xy + xy'z + x'yz &= xy + xyz + xy'z + x'yz && \text{by absorption} \\
&= xy + x(y + y')z + x'yz && \text{by distributivity} \\
&= xy + x1z + x'yz && \text{by complement} \\
&= xy + xz + x'yz && \text{by identity} \\
&= xy + xyz + xz + x'yz && \text{by absorption} \\
&= xy + xz + (x + x')yz && \text{by distributivity} \\
&= xy + xz + 1yz && \text{by complement} \\
&= xy + xz + yz && \text{by identity}
\end{aligned}
$$

Once we have proven equivalence of two expressions, we can use
the simpler one, which requires fewer operators. From the graphic
representation or just counting the operators we can easily find that
$xy + xz + yz$ needs only three AND and two OR operators instead of
the five AND, two OR, and two NOT operators required by the expression $xy + xy'z + x'yz$. Thus since the second expression requires fewer
operators, we could speculate that it would also require less hardware
when it is implemented as a logic circuit.

As you can infer from this example, there is a general rule that the number of AND and OR operators in an expression will be equal to the number of literals less 1. The first expression, for example, has eight literals and needs five AND and two OR operators, for a total of seven; the second expression, which has only six literals, needs three AND and two OR operators, for a total of five. Thus we know that a reduction in the number of literals will be equivalent to a reduction in the number of operators, so that reducing the number of ANDs and ORs can be achieved by reducing the number of literals in an expression.

As this example shows, the number of operators in a Boolean function can generally be minimized by means of algebraic manipulation. Unfortunately, though, we have no established procedure to follow that guarantees the minimal number of operators or literals in the expression. As a result, designers usually use a trial-and-error technique, employing the various axioms, the basic theorems, and any other manipulation rules that they develop through experience. In the next sections we introduce a unique form for specifying Boolean functions and show how to use this form as a starting point for finding simpler functional expressions.

3.5 CANONICAL FORMS

In Section 3.4 we showed how Boolean functions can be defined by truth tables. In this section we show how these truth tables can be converted into algebraic expressions. As you know, for an n-variable function, each row in the truth table represents a particular assignment of binary values to those n variables. We can define a Boolean function, usually called a **minterm**, that is equal to 1 in only one row of its truth table and 0 in all other rows. Since there are 2^n different rows in the truth table, there are also 2^n minterms for any n variables. Each of these minterms, denoted as m_i, can also be expressed as a product, or AND term, of n literals, in which each variable is complemented if the value assigned to it is 0, and uncomplemented if it is 1. More formally, this means that each minterm m_i can be defined as follows.

Let $i = b_{n-1} \cdots b_0$ be a binary number between 0 and $2^n - 1$, which represents an assignment of binary values to the n binary variables x_j such that $x_j = b_j$ for all j where $0 \leq j \leq n - 1$. In this case a minterm of n variables $x_{n-1}, x_{n-2}, \ldots, x_0$, could be represented as

$$m_i(x_{n-1}, \ldots, x_0) = y_{n-1} \cdots y_0$$

where for all k such that $0 \leq k \leq n - 1$,

$$y_k = \begin{cases} x_k & \text{if } b_k = 1 \\ x'_k & \text{if } b_k = 0 \end{cases}$$

In Table 3.9 we show all minterms of the three binary variables, x, y, and z.

In general, the unique algebraic expression for any Boolean function can be obtained from its truth table by using an OR operator to combine all minterms for which the function is equal to 1. These minterms are call **1-minterms**, and the other minterms are called **0-minterms**. For example, the expression for the function F_1 in Table 3.8 could be obtained by ORing all four of its 1-minterms:

$$F_1 = m_3 + m_5 + m_6 + m_7 = x'yz + xy'z + xyz' + xyz \qquad (3.7)$$

Similarly, we can obtain the complement of F_1 by ORing all the 0-minterms:

$$F_1' = m_0 + m_1 + m_2 + m_4 = x'y'z' + x'y'z + x'yz' + xyz' \qquad (3.8)$$

These examples demonstrate an important property of Boolean algebra:

Any Boolean function can be expressed as a sum of its 1-minterms.

The ORing of these minterms is referred to here as a sum because of its resemblance to addition.

At times, it is more convenient to describe the sum-of-minterms form by means of the following short notation:

$$F(\text{list of variables}) = \sum(\text{list of 1-minterm indices})$$

By this notation the summation symbol Σ stands for the ORing of those minterms whose indices are listed in parentheses. The variables listed in parentheses following F are the same variables presented in the same order as they take when the minterm is written as an AND term. Therefore, the short form for F_1, for example, is $F_1(x, y, z) = \sum(3, 5, 6, 7)$, and for F_1' it is $F_1'(x, y, z) = \sum(0, 1, 2, 4)$.

Any Boolean expression can be converted into this sum-of-minterms form by first expanding the given expression into a sum of AND terms. Then each term that is missing one or more variables has to be expanded further, by ANDing the term with an expression such as $x + x'$, where x is one of the missing variables. We demonstrate this expansion procedure in the following example.

___

EXAMPLE 3.1   Sum-of-minterms expansion

PROBLEM   Express the Boolean function $F = x + yz$ as a sum of minterms.

SOLUTION   This function has three variables: x, y, and z. The first term, x, is missing two variables, while the second term,

TABLE 3.9
Minterms for Three Binary Variables

x	y	z	MINTERMS	NOTATION
0	0	0	$x'y'z'$	m_0
0	0	1	$x'y'z$	m_1
0	1	0	$x'yz'$	m_2
0	1	1	$x'yz$	m_3
1	0	0	$xy'z'$	m_4
1	0	1	$xy'z$	m_5
1	1	0	xyz'	m_6
1	1	1	xyz	m_7

TABLE 3.8
Truth Tables for $F_1 = xy + xy'z + x'yz$ and its Complement $F_1' = (x' + y')(x' + y + z')(x + y' + z')$

ROW NUMBER	VARIABLE VALUES			FUNCTION VALUES	
	x	y	z	F_1	F_1'
0	0	0	0	0	1
1	0	0	1	0	1
2	0	1	0	0	1
3	0	1	1	1	0
4	1	0	0	0	1
5	1	0	1	1	0
6	1	1	0	1	0
7	1	1	1	1	0

yz, is missing one variable. Thus we need to expand the first term by ANDing it with $(y + y')(z + z')$, and we expand the second with $(x + x')$. In other words,

$$F = x + yz$$
$$= x(y + y')(z + z') + (x + x')yz$$
$$= xyz + xy'z + xyz' + xy'z' + xyz + x'yz$$

After removing duplicates, in accordance with Theorem 1, and rearranging the minterms in ascending order, we finally obtain

$$F = x'yz + xy'z' + xy'z + xyz' + xyz$$
$$= m_3 + m_4 + m_5 + m_6 + m_7$$
$$= \sum(3, 4, 5, 6, 7)$$

There is also an alternative procedure for obtaining a sum-of-minterms expression, which requires us to convert the given algebraic expression into a truth table and then read the minterms from the truth table. This procedure is demonstrated in the next example.

EXAMPLE 3.2   Conversion to a sum of minterms

PROBLEM   Convert the Boolean function $F = x + yz$ into a sum of minterms by using a truth table.

SOLUTION   The truth table shown in Table 3.10 is derived directly from the algebraic expression, showing that $F = 1$ for all those combinations of variable values for which $x = 1$ or for which $yz = 11$. From the truth table it is easy to identify the five minterms that make the functional value $F = 1$: m_3, m_4, m_5, m_6, and m_7. Thus, as before, the sum-of-minterms expression would be

$$F = m_3 + m_4 + m_5 + m_6 + m_7$$

Similarly to an AND term of n literals being called a minterm, an OR term of n literals is called a **maxterm**. Similarly to the definition of a minterm, a maxterm can be defined as a Boolean function that is equal to 0 in only one row of its truth table and 1 in all other rows. Each maxterm, M_i, can be expressed as a sum, or OR term, of n literals in which each variable would be uncomplemented if the value assigned to it is 0, and complemented if it is 1. In Table 3.11 we have listed the eight

T A B L E   3.10

Truth Table for
$F = x + yz$

x	y	z	F
0	0	0	0
0	0	1	0
0	1	0	0
0	1	1	1
1	0	0	1
1	0	1	1
1	1	0	1
1	1	1	1

T A B L E   3.11

Maxterms for Three Binary Variables

x	y	z	MAXTERMS	NOTATION
0	0	0	$x + y + z$	M_0
0	0	1	$x + y + z'$	M_1
0	1	0	$x + y' + z$	M_2
0	1	1	$x + y' + z'$	M_3
1	0	0	$x' + y + z$	M_4
1	0	1	$x' + y + z'$	M_5
1	1	0	$x' + y' + z$	M_6
1	1	1	$x' + y' + z'$	M_7

maxterms for three variables, together with their symbolic designations. For any number of variables, maxterms could be determined in a similar manner. Note that each maxterm is the complement of its corresponding minterm, and vice versa, so that

$$m_i' = M_i \quad \text{and} \quad M_i' = m_i$$

Note also that if we take the complement of the expression for F_1 given in Equation (3.7), we obtain the function F_1' as follows:

$$
\begin{aligned}
(F_1)' &= (x'yz + xy'z + xyz' + xyz)' \\
&= (x + y' + z')(x' + y + z')(x' + y' + z)(x' + y' + z') \\
&= M_3 M_5 M_6 M_7
\end{aligned}
$$

Similarly, by complementing the expression given in Equation (3.8), we obtain the function F_1 as follows:

$$
\begin{aligned}
F_1 &= (F_1')' \\
&= (x'y'z' + x'y'z + x'yz' + xyz')' \\
&= (x + y + z)(x + y + z')(x + y' + z)(x' + y' + z) \\
&= M_0 M_1 M_2 M_4
\end{aligned}
$$

Taken together, these examples demonstrate that the unique algebraic expression for any Boolean function can be obtained from its truth table by using an AND operator to combine all the maxterms for which the function is equal to 0. These maxterms are called **0-maxterms** as opposed to **1-maxterms**, for which the function is equal to 1. With this in mind, we can express the second unique property of Boolean algebra:

Any Boolean function can be expressed as a product of its 0-maxterms.

The ANDing of maxterms is called a *product* because of its resemblance to multiplication. It is often more convenient, however, to express products of maxterms as follows:

$$F(\text{list of variables}) = \prod(\text{list of 0-maxterm indices})$$

The product symbol, $\prod$, denotes the ANDing of those maxterms whose indices are contained in parentheses. Any Boolean function that is expressed as a sum of minterms or as a product of maxterms is said to be in its **canonical form**. From the definitions of both canonical forms, we can derive a general conversion procedure that could be stated as follows:

> **To convert from one canonical form to another, interchange the symbols Σ and Π, and list the numbers that were excluded from the original form.**

The missing terms will be easy to find, since each Boolean function of n variables will have 2^n minterms and 2^n maxterms numbered from 0 to $2^n - 1$.

As a rule, any Boolean expression of n binary variables could be converted to a product of maxterms. For this purpose the Boolean expression must first be converted into a form that uses OR terms, which is done by using the distributive law, $x + yz = (x + y)(x + z)$. At this point, any OR term with a missing variable, such as x, is expanded by ORing it with xx', for example. This procedure is clarified in the following example.

EXAMPLE 3.3   Product-of-maxterms expansion

PROBLEM   Derive the product-of-maxterms form for the Boolean function $F = x'y' + xz$.

SOLUTION   First, we need to convert the function into the product-of-OR terms by using the distributive law as follows:

$$
\begin{aligned}
F &= x'y' + xz \\
  &= (x'y' + x)(x'y' + z) \\
  &= (x' + x)(y' + x)(x' + z)(y' + z) \\
  &= (x + y')(x' + z)(y' + z)
\end{aligned}
$$

At this point, each OR term in the expression is missing one variable, so we add zz' to the first term and yy' and xx' to the second and third terms, respectively. Thus each term gets expanded into two maxterms:

$$
\begin{aligned}
x + y' &= x + y' + zz' = (x + y' + z)(x + y' + z') \\
x' + z &= x' + z + yy' = (x' + y + z)(x' + y' + z) \\
y' + z &= y' + z + xx' = (x + y' + z)(x' + y' + z)
\end{aligned}
$$

Finally, when we combine all these terms and remove those that appear more than once, we obtain the following expression:

$$
\begin{aligned}
F &= (x + y' + z)(x + y' + z')(x' + y + z)(x' + y' + z) \\
  &= M_2 M_3 M_4 M_6 = \textstyle\prod(2, 3, 4, 6)
\end{aligned}
$$

In Example 3.3 we converted the given algebraic expression to a product-of-OR terms before expanding it to the product of maxterms. Alternatively, we can first generate the truth table and then derive canonical forms from it. The next example demonstrates this approach.

EXAMPLE 3.4   Conversion to a product of maxterms

PROBLEM   Convert the Boolean function

$$F = x'y' + xz$$

into the product-of-maxterms form.

SOLUTION   First, we derive the truth table from the algebraic expression, as shown in Table 3.12. Note that the function value $F = 1$ appears in all of the rows where the variables $xy = 00$ or $xz = 11$. Therefore, the minterms for the function in Table 3.12 are m_0, m_1, m_5, and m_7. Thus, when the function is defined as a sum of minterms, it would be

$$F(x, y, z) = \sum(0, 1, 5, 7)$$

Since there must be a total of eight minterms in a function of three variables, we can now determine that the missing minterms are m_2, m_3, m_4, and m_6. Therefore, when the function is expressed in its product-of-maxterm form, it is

$$F(x, y, z) = \prod(2, 3, 4, 6)$$

Note that the same answer was obtained in Example 3.3 when we used term expansion.

TABLE 3.12

Truth Table for
$F = x'y' + xz$

x	y	z	F
0	0	0	1
0	0	1	1
0	1	0	0
0	1	1	0
1	0	0	0
1	0	1	1
1	1	0	0
1	1	1	1

3.6 STANDARD FORMS

The two canonical forms described in Section 3.5 provide unique expressions for any Boolean functions defined by truth tables. However, these forms are very seldom the ones with the fewest number of operators, since, by definition, each minterm or maxterm requires $n - 1$ AND or OR operators.

As an alternative, though, we can also define Boolean functions in **standard form**, whereas each term may require fewer than $n - 1$ operations. There are two types of standard forms, the sum of products and the product of sums. As before, the **sum of products** could be defined as a Boolean expression that contains AND terms, called **product terms** or **implicants**, comprising one or more literals each. The **sum** denotes the ORing of these terms. An example of a function that is expressed as a sum of products is

$$F_1 = xy + x'yz + xy'z$$

Note that this expression has three product terms, comprising two or three literals each.

By contrast, a **product-of-sums** expression is an AND expression that contains OR terms, called **sum terms** or **implicates**, whereas the **product** denotes the ANDing of these terms. Each of the sum terms can have any number of literals, and the product can have any number of sum terms. An example of a function been expressed as a product of sums is

$$F_1' = (x' + y') \cdot (x + y' + z') \cdot (x' + y + z')$$

Note that the expression has three sum terms of two or three literals each.

These sum-of-products and product-of-sums standard forms are not unique, in the sense that there can be several different sums of products and products of sums for a given function. However, even though these standard forms are not unique, they are useful nonetheless because they require fewer operators than canonical forms do. These standard forms would be derived from the canonical forms by combining the terms that differ in one literal, using the axioms of Boolean algebra.

For example, the expression $xyz + xyz'$ could be reduced to xy as follows:

$$\begin{aligned} xyz + xyz' &= xy(z + z') && \text{by distributivity [Axiom 4(a)]} \\ &= xy \cdot 1 && \text{by complement [Axiom 5(a)]} \\ &= xy && \text{by identity [Axiom 2(a)]} \end{aligned}$$

Similarly, the expression $xyz + xyz' + xy'z + xy'z'$ could be reduced to x by applying the procedure above twice:

$$\begin{aligned} xyz + xyz' + xy'z + xy'z' &= xy(z + z') + xy'(z + z') \\ &= xy + xy' \\ &= x(y + y') \\ &= x \end{aligned}$$

We can also obtain a standard form with fewer operators by applying this procedure several times on different groups of terms, as the following example demonstrates.

EXAMPLE 3.5   Standard form

PROBLEM   Derive a standard form with a reduced number of operators for the function $F_1 = xyz + xyz' + xy'z + x'yz$.

SOLUTION   As you can see, the term xyz can be combined with the second, third, and fourth terms in this expression. Thus we replicate it twice before combining it with other terms:

$$F_1 = xyz + xyz' + xy'z + x'yz$$
$$= xyz + xyz' + xyz + xy'z + xyz + x'yz$$
$$= xy(z + z') + x(y + y')z + (x + x')yz$$
$$= xy + xz + yz$$

In general, we can combine terms and eliminate literals in a standard form until no more reduction is possible. In this case, each product term in a sum-of-products form is called a prime implicant and a sum product in a product-of-sums form, a prime implicate.

Each prime implicant represents one or more 1-minterms. Note that each 1-minterm may be included in several prime implicants. If a 1-minterm is included in only one prime implicant we call that implicant an **essential prime implicant** since it cannot be omitted from any standard form without changing the given function. Similarly, we can define essential prime implicates for the product-of-sums standard form. We discuss systematic procedures for obtaining a reduced standard form consisting of prime implicants in Chapter 4.

Even though these standard forms may require fewer operators than the canonical forms, these expressions still might not contain an absolutely minimal number of operators. On the contrary, by factoring literals, we can express a given Boolean function in a nonstandard form that sometimes requires even fewer operators. For example, the number of operators in the expression $xy + xy'z + xy'w$ can be reduced further if we first factor the variable x and then factor y':

$$xy + xy'z + xy'w = x(y + y'z + y'w)$$
$$= x(y + y'(z + w))$$

As you can see, this form is neither a sum of products nor a product of sums, although it can be converted to a standard form by using the distributive laws to remove the parentheses.

EXAMPLE 3.6   Nonstandard forms

PROBLEM   Reduce the number of operators in the standard form of the function $F_1 = xy + xz + yz$.

SOLUTION   There are three nonstandard forms of the function F_1 that require fewer operators: Each of these require two ANDs and two ORs, in comparison with three ANDs and two ORs in the standard form.

$$F_1 = xy + xz + yz$$
$$= xy + (x + y)z$$
$$= x(y + z) + yz$$
$$= xz + y(x + z)$$

As we have shown in this section, we can use several strategies to reduce the number of operators in the Boolean expression, all of which can be combined into the design strategy shown in Figure 3.2. Following this strategy, we first convert each algebraic expression into a truth table. Second, we generate a canonical form. Then we reduce the number of operators by creating subcubes and converting a canonical form into a standard form. Finally, we could reduce this number further by factoring all the common subexpressions and creating a nonstandard form.

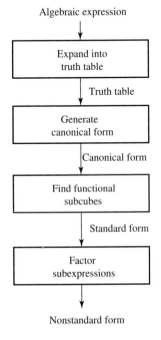

FIGURE 3.2

Strategy for operator minimization in Boolean expressions.

3.7 OTHER LOGIC OPERATIONS

So far, we have discussed only two Boolean functions of two variables, AND and OR. As we demonstrated in Section 3.6, however, there will be 2^{2^n} Boolean functions for any n binary variables, which means that there will be a total of 16 Boolean functions for two variables. Since the AND and OR functions are only two of the 16 possible Boolean functions, in this section we define the other 14 functions of two variables.

In Table 3.13 we have given all 16 functions of two binary variables, x and y. Each row in this table represents one possible function of these two variables, and the names of these functions are given in the first column of the table. The truth tables for all 16 functions are presented in the third column of the table. Since each of these functions can also be expressed algebraically, we have given the corresponding Boolean expressions in the fourth column of the table. Note that each function has been designated by F_i, where i is the decimal equivalent of the binary number that can be obtained by interpreting the function values in the third column as binary numbers.

As you know, each of these functions can be given in a standard form by using operators AND, OR, and NOT. Since there is no reason why we cannot assign a special operator symbol to each function, each function can also be represented by the operator symbols that are listed in the second column of the table. As a rule, though, with the exception of the XOR symbol, these symbols are not commonly used by designers. Finally, the last column contains English-language descriptions that explain each of the 16 functions.

T A B L E   3.13

Boolean Expressions for the 16 Functions of Two Variables

NAME	OPERATOR SYMBOL	FUNCTION VALUES FOR $x, y =$				ALGEBRAIC EXPRESSION	COMMENT
		00	01	10	11		
Zero		0	0	0	0	$F_0 = 0$	Binary constant 0
AND	$x \cdot y$	0	0	0	1	$F_1 = xy$	x and y
Inhibition	x/y	0	0	1	0	$F_2 = xy'$	x but not y
Transfer		0	0	1	1	$F_3 = x$	x
Inhibition	y/x	0	1	0	0	$F_4 = x'y$	y but not x
Transfer		0	1	0	1	$F_5 = y$	y
XOR	$x \oplus y$	0	1	1	0	$F_6 = xy' + x'y$	x or y but not both
OR	$x + y$	0	1	1	1	$F_7 = x + y$	x or y
NOR	$x \downarrow y$	1	0	0	0	$F_8 = (x + y)'$	Not-OR
Equivalence	$x \odot y$	1	0	0	1	$F_9 = xy + x'y'$	x equals y
Complement	y'	1	0	1	0	$F_{10} = y'$	Not y
Implication	$x \subset y$	1	0	1	1	$F_{11} = x + y'$	If y, then x
Complement	x'	1	1	0	0	$F_{12} = x'$	Not x
Implication	$x \supset y$	1	1	0	1	$F_{13} = x' + y$	If x, then y
NAND	$x \uparrow y$	1	1	1	0	$F_{14} = (xy)'$	Not-AND
One		1	1	1	1	$F_{15} = 1$	Binary constant 1

As you can see from the comments, the 16 functions we listed can be subdivided into three categories according to the number of variables that actually influence the function value:

1. There are two functions that generate constants: *Zero* and *One*. For every combination of variable values, the *Zero* function will return 0, whereas the *One* function will return 1.

2. There are four functions of one variable, which indicate *Complement* and *Transfer* operations. Specifically, the *Complement* function will produce the complement of one of the binary variables. The *Transfer* function, by contrast, will reproduce one of the binary variables at the output, so that the variable will pass through the logic—or transfer to the output—unchanged.

3. There are 10 functions that define eight specific binary operations: *AND, Inhibition, XOR, OR, NOR, Equivalence, Implication*, and *NAND*.

Of these eight binary operators, *Inhibition* and *Implication* are never used in computer design, just because they are very difficult to implement as individual components but can easily be implemented by using *AND* or *OR* operators in conjunction with a *NOT* operator at one of the inputs. As a rule, though, designers prefer the *NOR* and *NAND* operators to the *OR* and *AND* operators, simply because *NOR* and *NAND* can be implemented with fewer transistors.

Basically, the *NOR* function is the complement of the *OR* function; in fact, its name is an abbreviation of not-OR. Similarly, *NAND* is the complement of *AND*, and its name is an abbreviation of not-AND. *XOR*, which is the abbreviation of exclusive-OR, is similar to *OR* except that it will exclude a result of 1 whenever x and y are both equal to 1. The *Equivalence* operator will produce an output of 1 whenever both binary variables have the same value—that is, when they are both equal to 0 or both equal to 1. Given these properties, it should be apparent that the *XOR* and *Equivalence* functions are actually complements of each other, as can be verified by comparing the truth tables for F_6 and F_9 given in Table 3.13. Because of this complementarity, the equivalence function is often called exclusive-*NOR*, or *XNOR*.

Of the 16 functions defined in Table 3.13, you can see that only 12 are unique, since four of these functions are repeated twice. *Zero* and *One* are particularly easily implemented, by connection to the power-supply lines, and do not require any circuitry. Two of these functions, *Inhibition* and *Implication*, are neither commutative nor associative, which makes them inconvenient for use in logic design. The other eight, however, can easily be implemented as standard logic gates and therefore are frequently used in logic design.

3.8 DIGITAL LOGIC GATES

In previous sections we learned how to specify Boolean functions and how to derive expressions for computing function values. To implement these Boolean expressions, we construct **logic networks** or **logic circuits** with variables in the expression as inputs to this logic network, which contains one or more logic gates. Each **logic gate** performs one or more Boolean operations that we have defined in previous sections. The collection of logic gates that we use in constructing logic networks is called the gate library, and the gates in the library are called **standard gates**. Although every Boolean operator can be implemented as a logic gate and included in the **gate library**, modern gate libraries rarely include more than a dozen gates, to lower the cost of library maintenance and simplify the development of CAD tools for logic design. Before selecting which operators are to be included in the gate library, we generally consider the following criteria:

1. Frequency of use in typical logic design, defined by its ability to implement a variety of Boolean functions in conjunction with other gates.

2. Operator extensibility to more than two variables, which requires its commutativity and associativity.

3. Construction simplicity, defined by the number of transistors needed for its construction and the time needed for the signal change to propagate through the gate.

On the basis of these criteria, we generally select only eight operators to be implemented as standard gates, namely, the *Complement, Transfer, AND, OR, NAND, NOR, XOR,* and *XNOR* operators. Among logic designers, the *Complement* operator is frequently called the *Inverter* or *NOT* operator, and the *Transfer* operator is usually called the *Driver* since it is used for driving large loads and long connection lines.

In Table 3.14, we show the graphic symbols and Boolean expressions of each of these eight gates. Note that each gate has one or two binary inputs, designated by x and/or y, and one binary output, designated by F. As you can see, Table 3.14 also shows the cost of each gate in terms of the number of transistors it would require when constructed with CMOS technology and the normalized delay of signal propagation through that particular gate.

Since the function of the inverter is to complement the logic value of its input, we place a small circle at the output of its graphic symbol to indicate this logic complementation. We also use a triangle symbol to designate a driver circuit, which implements the transfer function by replicating the input value at its output. In general, a driver is equivalent to two inverters that are connected in cascade, so that the output of the first inverter serves as the input of the second.

As mentioned above, AND and OR gates are used to implement the binary operators AND and OR, whereas the NAND and NOR gates are used to implement those functions that are the complements of AND and OR. As you can see, there is a small circle at each of these outputs which indicates this complementation. Among logic designers, these NAND and NOR gates are used extensively and are far more popular than the AND and OR gates, simply because their implementation requires only four transistors, in comparison with AND and OR gates, which require six transistors. Furthermore, because they require fewer transistors, the NAND and NOR gates are faster than the corresponding AND and OR gates.

TABLE 3.14

Basic Logic Library

NAME	GRAPHIC SYMBOL	FUNCTIONAL EXPRESSION	COST (NUMBER OF TRANSISTORS)	GATE DELAY (NS)
Inverter	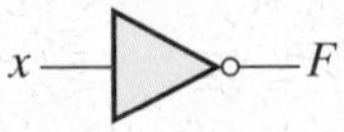 x —▷o— F	$F = x'$	2	1
Driver	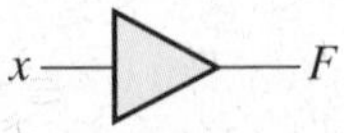 x —▷— F	$F = x$	4	2
AND	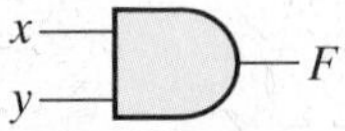 x, y —D— F	$F = xy$	6	2.4
OR	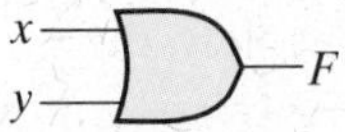 x, y —D— F	$F = x + y$	6	2.4
NAND	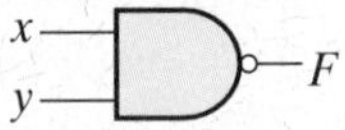 x, y —Do— F	$F = (xy)'$	4	1.4
NOR	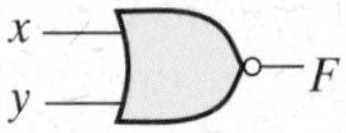 x, y —Do— F	$F = (x + y)'$	4	1.4
XOR	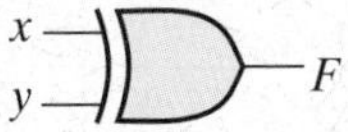 x, y —⫘D— F	$F = x \oplus y$	14	4.2
XNOR	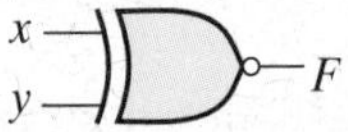 x, y —⫘Do— F	$F = x \odot y$	12	3.2

As indicated in Table 3.14, the graphic symbol of the XOR gate is almost the same as that of the OR gate, except that it has an additional curved line at the input. Note that the XNOR gate is the complement of the XOR gate, as indicated by the small circle on its output line.

When we are implementing Boolean functions with this basic gate library, we are usually trying to find the Boolean expression that will best satisfy a given set of design requirements. Generally, these requirements involve restrictions on cost, which can be given in terms of the number of transistors and/or signal delay through the logic network, which is usually specified in nanoseconds. Very frequently, our main goal is to find the fastest design, or, to put this another way, to find the design with the smallest input/output delay. On the other hand, our main goal will just as often be to find the least expensive design. By their very nature, these two goals tend to be in conflict, since a faster design will usually evaluate common subexpressions in parallel, which means that it will require more gates than a lower-cost design in which the subexpressions are factored out and executed serially.

In the following example, we demonstrate several of these different design trade-offs in the design of a full adder.

◼ **EXAMPLE 3.7** Full-adder design

PROBLEM Design a full adder based on the specifications given in Table 2.3, using the basic logic library that was given in Table 3.14. The primary goal is to minimize the propagation delay from c_i to c_{i+1}, while the secondary goal is to use the smallest possible number of transistors.

SOLUTION First, we derive an expression that contains a minimum number of operators. The expression for s_i can be reduced to two XOR gates:

$$
\begin{aligned}
s_i &= x_i'y_i'c_i + x_i'y_ic_i' + x_iy_i'c_i' + x_iy_ic_i \\
&= (x_i'y_i + x_iy_i')c_i' + (x_i'y_i' + x_iy_i)c_i \\
&= (x_i \oplus y_i)c_i' + (x_i \odot y_i)c_i \\
&= (x_i \oplus y_i)c_i' + (x_i \oplus y_i)'c_i \\
&= (x_i \oplus y_i) \oplus c_i
\end{aligned}
$$

As we have seen in Example 3.5, the expression for carry function c_{i+1} could be reduced to $x_iy_i + c_i(x_i + y_i)$. However, if we convert it to another form, we will be able to use the subexpression $x \oplus y$, which is already part of the expression for s_i.

$$
\begin{aligned}
c_{i+1} &= x_iy_ic_i' + x_iy_ic_i + x_i'y_ic_i + x_iy_i'c_i \\
&= x_iy_i(c_i' + c_i) + c_i(x_i'y_i + x_iy_i') \\
&= x_iy_i + c_i(x_i \oplus y_i)
\end{aligned}
$$

At this point we can share the common subexpressions in the expressions for s_i and c_{i+1}, which allows us to implement the full adder with five gates, as shown in Figure 3.3(a). Note that this implementation requires 46 transistors and has a delay of 4.8 ns from c_i to c_{i+1}. This implementation uses AND, OR, and XOR gates, which are slower than the corresponding NAND, NOR, and XNOR gates. If, however, we modify the expressions for s_i and c_{i+1}, we can take advantage of the faster, less expensive NAND and NOR gates. To do this, we first transform the expression for c_{i+1} as follows, using

TABLE 2.3

Addition of Binary Digits

$x_i + y_i + c_i$			c_{i+1}	s_i
0	0	0	0	0
0	0	1	0	1
0	1	0	0	1
0	1	1	1	0
1	0	0	0	1
1	0	1	1	0
1	1	0	1	0
1	1	1	1	1

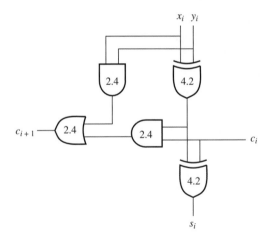

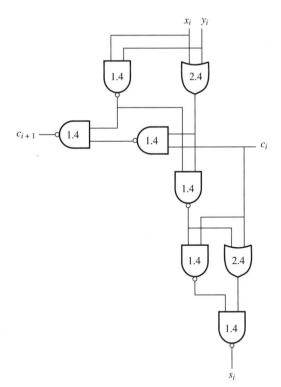

INPUT/OUTPUT PATH	DELAY (ns)
c_i to c_{i+1}	4.8
c_i to s_i	4.2
x_i, y_i to c_{i+1}	9.0
x_i, y_i to s_i	8.4

(a) Design with minimum
number of operators

(b) Input/output delays
for the design in part (a)

INPUT/OUTPUT PATH	DELAY (ns)
c_i to c_{i+1}	2.8
c_i to s_i	3.8
x_i, y_i to c_{i+1}	5.2
x_i, y_i to s_i	7.2

(c) Design with NANDs and ORs

(d) Input/output delays
for the design in part (c)

FIGURE 3.3
Full-adder design.

De Morgan's theorems:

$$c_{i+1} = x_i y_i + c_i(x_i + y_i)$$
$$= ((x_i y_i)'(c_i(x_i + y_i))')'$$

Similarly, we transform the expression for s_i as follows:

$$s_i = (x_i \oplus y_i)c_i' + (x_i \odot y_i)c_i$$
$$= (x_i \odot y_i)'c_i' + (x_i \odot y_i)c_i$$
$$= (x_i \odot y_i) \odot c_i$$

In addition, we can also implement $x_i \odot y_i$ with two NANDs and one OR gate:

$$x_i \odot y_i = x_i y_i + x_i' y_i'$$
$$= ((x_i y_i)'(x_i' y_i')')'$$
$$= ((x_i y_i)'(x_i + y_i))'$$

Using these expressions, we can implement the faster full adder shown in Figure 3.3(c). Note that this adder takes only 2.8 ns from c_i to c_{i+1}, in comparison to 4.8 ns for the previous design. This implementation would also be less expensive, since it uses only 36 transistors instead of the 46 required previously.

On the basis of Example 3.7, we can generalize and say that the attempt to minimize the number of operators will not necessarily yield the fastest or even the least expensive design, but if we try to find the expression that uses the fastest or least expensive gates in the library, we may achieve this goal.

3.9 EXTENSION TO MULTIPLE INPUTS AND MULTIPLE OPERATORS

There are, however, other ways to lower the cost and delay of an implementation, one of which involves expanding the library by constructing gates that have more than two inputs. As a rule, any gate can be extended to have multiple inputs as long as the binary operation it implements is commutative and associative, as it guarantees that the variables can be connected to gate inputs in any order. Since the AND and OR operations possess these two properties by the definition of Boolean algebra, they are the easiest to extend.

The NAND and NOR functions, however, are commutative but not associative. Nonetheless, it is possible to think of multiple-input NAND and NOR functions as the complements of the AND and OR functions, respectively. Thus the multiple-input NAND and NOR functions are defined as follows:

$$\text{NAND}(x, y, z, \ldots) = (xyz \cdots)' \neq x \uparrow y \uparrow z \uparrow \cdots$$
$$\text{NOR}(x, y, z, \ldots) = (x + y + z + \cdots)' \neq x \downarrow y \downarrow z \downarrow \cdots$$

Since the XOR and XNOR gates are both commutative and associative, they can be extended to more than two inputs. In other words, any one of the gates in Table 3.14, except for the inverter and driver, could be extended to have more than two inputs.

On the other hand, we do not usually build multiple-input XOR and XNOR gates because most of the logic functions in digital design, with the exception of parity functions, can be designed by using XOR or XNOR gates with only two-inputs. Furthermore, even these 2-input XOR and XNOR gates are usually constructed from NANDs, NORs, and NOTs, to simplify the gate library.

Thus most extended libraries would include NAND, NOR, AND, and OR gates that have 3 or 4 inputs each. It is possible to build gates with a larger number of inputs, but they are the most difficult to construct, and since they are also the least frequently used, the cost of library and CAD tool maintenance tends to outweigh this limited usefulness. It is for these reasons that we have included only 3- and 4-input gates in our extended library. The graphic symbols for these 3- and 4-input AND, OR, NAND, and NOR gates have been shown in Table 3.15, with their corresponding expressions, cost, and delay.

There is another way to improve the performance and cost in the implementation of Boolean functions, and that involves extending the library to include gates that can each perform more than one Boolean operation. Since in many cases, for example, the Boolean functions are implemented using the standard sum-of-product or product-of-sum forms, it is beneficial to have standard gates that could implement those forms efficiently. As shown in Table 3.16, these multiple-operator gates are called AND-OR-INVERT (AOI) and OR-AND-INVERT gates. By using these gates, we can construct standard-form implementations that have a lower cost and smaller delays than they do when they have been implemented with single-operator gates. For example, a 2-wide, 3-input AOI, which implements the sum of two products having three literals each, requires 12 transistors and introduces a delay of 2.2 ns, whereas 20 transistors and 4.2 ns are required for the same sum of products when implemented with two 3-input AND gates and one 2-input NOR gate.

TABLE 3.15
Multiple-input Standard Logic Gates

NAME	GRAPHIC SYMBOL	FUNCTIONAL EXPRESSION	COST (NUMBER OF TRANSISTORS)	GATE DELAY (NS)
3-input AND		$F = xyz$	8	2.8
4-input AND		$F = xyzw$	10	3.2
3-input OR		$F = x + y + z$	8	2.8
4-input OR		$F = x + y + z + w$	10	3.2
3-input NAND		$F = (xyz)'$	6	1.8
4-input NAND		$F = (xyzw)'$	8	2.2
3-input NOR		$F = (x + y + z)'$	6	1.8
4-input NOR		$F = (x + y + z + w)'$	8	2.2

Gates that have multiple inputs and can perform multiple operations are frequently called **complex gates**. In the next two examples, we demonstrate their usefulness.

EXAMPLE 3.8   Implementation with multiple-input gates

PROBLEM   Implement the full adder from Example 3.7 using the multiple-input gates shown in Table 3.15 whenever they are appropriate.

SOLUTION   To use multiple-input gates, we need to start from a standard form, specifically from the one with the fewest possible operators, which will allow us to minimize cost. Furthermore, we attempt to use the fastest gates in the library, to obtain the shortest possible delay. Usually, the fastest gates

T A B L E 3.16

Multiple-operator Standard Logic Gates

NAME	GRAPHIC SYMBOL	FUNCTIONAL EXPRESSION	COST (NUMBER OF TRANSISTORS)	GATE DELAY (NS)
2-wide, 2-input AOI		$F = (wx + yz)'$	8	2.0
3-wide, 2-input AOI		$F = (uv + wx + yz)'$	12	2.4
2-wide, 3-input AOI		$F = (uvw + xyz)'$	12	2.2
2-wide, 2-input OAI		$F = ((w + x)(y + z))'$	8	2.0
3-wide, 2-input OAI		$F = ((u + v)(w + x)(y + z))'$	12	2.2
2-wide, 3-input OAI		$F = ((u + v + w)(x + y + z))'$	12	2.4

in the library are NAND and NOR gates, so to utilize them, we apply De Morgan's theorems until we have converted the selected standard form into an expression that uses NANDs or NORs.

In case of the full adder, we modify the expressions for c_{i+1} and s_i as follows:

$$c_{i+1} = x_i y_i + c_i x_i + c_i y_i$$
$$= ((x_i y_i)'(c_i x_i)'(c_i y_i)')'$$

and

$$s_i = x_i' y_i' c_i + x_i' y_i c_i' + x_i y_i' c_i' + x_i y_i c_i$$
$$= ((x_i' y_i' c_i)'(x_i' y_i c_i')'(x_i y_i' c_i')'(x_i y_i c_i)')'$$

In Figure 3.4(a) we have shown an implementation derived from these modified expressions. As you can see, the delay from any input to the output s_i is only 5.0 ns, and to c_{i+1} is only 3.2 ns. Unfortunately, though, the design requires 56 transistors for its implementation, which could probably be reduced by using multiple-operator gates.

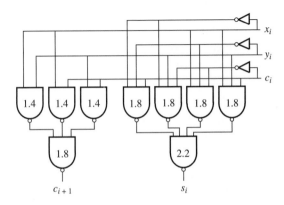

(a) Design with multiple-input gates

INPUT/OUTPUT PATH	DELAY (ns)
c_i to c_{i+1}	3.2
c_i to s_i	5.0
x_i, y_i to c_{i+1}	4.2
x_i, y_i to s_i	5.0

(b) Input/output delays for the design in part (a)

FIGURE 3.4
Full-adder design with multiple-input gates.

EXAMPLE 3.9   Implementation with multiple-operator gates

PROBLEM   Implement the full adder using the multiple-operator gates shown in Table 3.16 whenever they are appropriate.

SOLUTION   When using multiple-operator gates, we would begin by transforming the functional expressions into AOI and OAI subexpressions. Since the expression for the sum s_i has four AND terms containing three literals each, the best choice for its implementation would be a 3-input, 4-wide AOI gate. However, since we do not have this kind of gate in our library, we can best implement it as shown below by using two 3-input, 2-wide AOI gates, in conjunction with a NAND gate:

$$s_i = x_i'y_i'c_i + x_i'y_ic_i' + x_iy_i'c_i' + x_iy_ic_i$$
$$= ((x_i'y_i'c_i + x_i'y_ic_i')'(x_iy_i'c_i' + x_iy_ic_i)')'$$

To use a single 2-input, 3-wide AOI gate for the implementation of the carry function, we must generate the expression for its complement:

$$c_{i+1} = x_iy_i + c_ix_i + c_iy_i$$
$$= ((x_iy_i)'(c_ix_i)'(c_iy_i)')'$$
$$= ((x_i' + y_i')(c_i' + x_i')(c_i' + y_i'))'$$
$$= (x_i'y_i' + c_i'x_i' + c_i'y_i')'$$

The result is shown in Figure 3.5(b). Note that the delay from c_i to c_{i+1} is 3.4 ns, which is only 0.2 ns longer than in the implementation that used multiple-input gates. On the other hand, the delay from c_i to s_i is only 4.6 ns, which is 0.4 ns shorter than in the implementation that used multiple-input gates. Furthermore, the use of multioperation gates has reduced the cost from 56 to 46 transistors.

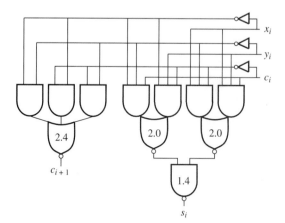

INPUT/OUTPUT PATH	DELAY (ns)
c_i to c_{i+1}	3.4
c_i to s_i	4.4
x_i, y_i to c_{i+1}	3.4
x_i, y_i to s_i	4.4

(a) Design with multiple-operator gates

(b) Input/output delays for the design in part (a)

FIGURE 3.5

Full-adder design with multiple-operator gates.

In Examples 3.7, 3.8, and 3.9, we have demonstrated algebraic manipulation of Boolean expressions for implementation with various types of gates. As you have seen, it is not obvious at the outset which types of gates will yield the best design. Usually, we have to try several alternatives until we find the best solution. In Chapter 4, we discuss the systematic procedures for implementing Boolean functions and optimizing those implementations for different libraries.

3.10 GATE IMPLEMENTATIONS

In Sections 3.8 and 3.9 we introduced different types of gates that perform one or more Boolean operations. These gates are electronic circuits composed of resistors, diodes, and transistors that can be connected in a different way to perform different Boolean operations. Early gates were constructed primarily from resistors and diodes since transistors were expensive. With advances in semiconductor technology, however, the fabrication of transistors became simple and inexpensive, so that contemporary gates are constructed exclusively with transistors.

The style in which transistors are connected characterizes each logic family or library and gives it its unique name. Before we discuss the basic logic families, we define several metrics that can be used for the comparison of different families.

3.10.1 Logic Levels

The gate implementations are electronic circuits whose behavior can be explained very well in terms of voltage levels measured in volts (V) but not necessarily in terms of Boolean values 0 and 1. However, to accommodate these Boolean values, gate circuits are designed in such a way that only two voltage levels, high (H) and low (L), are observable in steady state at gate inputs and outputs. Therefore, the Boolean function performed by such a gate circuit depends on the interpretation of the voltage levels H and L, or in other words, the mapping of 0 and 1 to voltage levels H and L. This mapping can be accomplished in two different ways, resulting in two different logic systems: positive and negative.

In the **positive logic system**, 0 is assigned to L and 1 is assigned to H, while in the **negative logic system** the opposite is true: L represents 1 and H represents 0. Thus each gate circuit performs different Boolean functions in the positive logic system than in the negative logic system. For example, the gate circuit whose output is L only when both inputs are H [Figure 3.6(a)] performs the NAND operation in positive logic [Figure 3.6(b)] and the NOR operation in negative logic [Figure 3.6(c)].

Similarly, a gate circuit whose output is L whenever one of the inputs is H [Figure 3.7(a)] can be used to perform the NOR operation

INPUTS	OUTPUTS
L L	H
L H	H
H L	H
H H	L

(a) Gate behavior

INPUTS	OUTPUTS
0 0	1
0 1	1
1 0	1
1 1	0

(b) Positive logic NAND

INPUTS	OUTPUTS
1 1	0
1 0	0
0 1	0
0 0	1

(c) Negative logic NOR

FIGURE 3.6
Interpretation of the gate circuit whose output is L only when both inputs are H.

INPUTS	OUTPUTS
L L	H
L H	L
H L	L
H H	L

(a) Gate behavior

INPUTS	OUTPUTS
0 0	1
0 1	0
1 0	0
1 1	0

(b) Positive logic NOR

INPUTS	OUTPUTS
1 1	0
1 0	1
0 1	1
0 0	1

(c) Negative logic NAND

FIGURE 3.7
Interpretation of the gate circuit whose output is L whenever one of the inputs is H.

in positive logic [Figure 3.7(b)] or the NAND operation in negative logic [Figure 3.7(c)].

To distinguish positive and negative logic systems we use a small triangle as a polarity indicator for negative logic on any input and output signal line. The presence of this polarity indicator signifies that negative logic is assumed for voltage values on that particular signal. Using polarity indicators, we can mix positive and negative logic values as shown in Table 3.17.

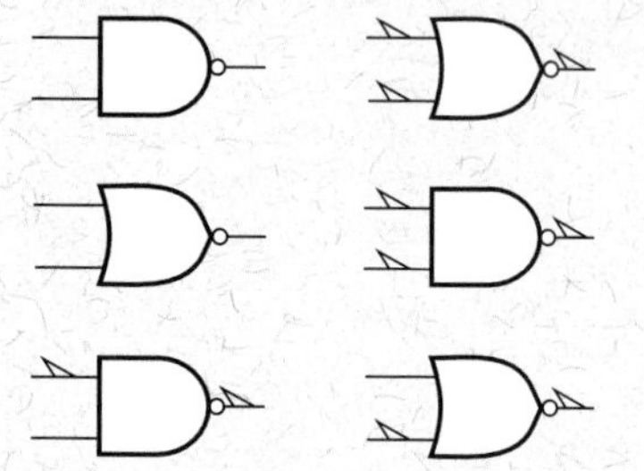

The mixing of logic levels was practiced quite frequently in the past when designers mixed gates from different logic families on the same board. Since in the last decade or so, all new ICs have been made with the CMOS logic family, which uses positive logic, negative logic has fallen out of favor with designers, so that modern CAD tools predominately use positive logic. For this reason we also use only positive logic throughout this book.

TABLE 3.17

Examples of Positive and Negative Logic Symbols

POSITIVE LOGIC	NEGATIVE LOGIC

3.10.2 Noise Margins

The gate circuits are constructed to sustain variations in input and output voltage levels. These variations are usually the result of several different factors. For example, batteries get older and lose their full potential, causing the supply voltage to drop. Similarly, high operating temperatures may cause a drift in transistor voltage and current characteristics. On the other hand, spurious pulses may be introduced on signal lines by normal surges of current in neighboring supply lines. All of these undesirable voltage variations that are superimposed on the normal operating voltage levels are called **noise**.

All gates are designed to tolerate a certain amount of noise on their input and output ports. The maximum noise voltage level that is tolerated by a gate is called a **noise margin**. The noise margin can be derived from input/output voltage characteristics that are measured under different operating conditions and supplied in the gate documentation. Such an input/output characteristic for transistor-transistor logic family is shown in Figure 3.8, in which the output voltage V_O is plotted as a function of the input voltage V_I.

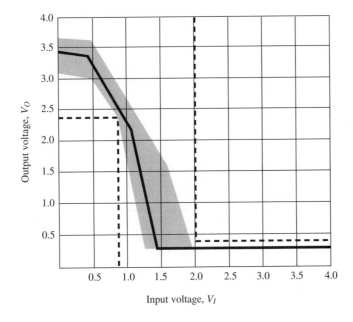

FIGURE   3.8
Typical input/output characteristics for gates in the transistor-transistor logic family.

Since the input/output characteristics drifts under different operating conditions, we have also shown the drifting range by the shaded area in Figure 3.8. From the figure we can see that the given gate operates in three different modes: high output, transition and low output. In the first mode, when V_I is between 0 and 0.8 V, the output voltage V_O is greater than 2.4 V and less than the supply voltage V_{CC}, which is usually 5.0 V. In the transition mode, when V_I is between 0.8 and 2.0 V, the gate switches from H to L. Finally, in the third mode, when V_I is greater than 2.0 V, the output voltage V_O is higher than 0 and less than 0.4 V.

To determine noise margins, we must compare the output and output voltage ranges of gates in the same family as shown in Figure 3.9,

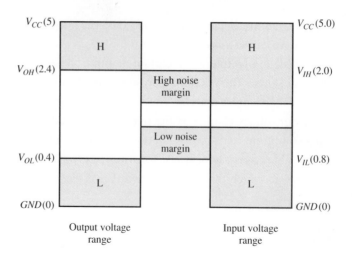

FIGURE 3.9
High and low noise margins.

in which we see the output voltage range of a driving gate on the left side and the input voltage range of the driven gates on the right side.

Any voltage between V_{OH} and V_{CC} is considered H and any voltage between 0 and V_{OL} is considered L. Similarly, any voltage between V_{IH} and V_{CC} is considered H and any voltage between 0 and V_{IL} is considered to be L.

The voltage difference $V_{OH} - V_{IH}$ is called the high-level noise margin, since any noise voltage smaller than $V_{OH} - V_{IH}$ will be tolerated and will not change the output value of the driven gate. For the same reason, the voltage difference $V_{IL} - V_{OL}$ is called the low-level noise margin. In the example of transistor–transistor logic, $V_{OH} = 2.4$, $V_{IH} = 2.0$, $V_{IL} = 0.8$, and $V_{OL} = 0.4$, and both high and low noise margins are equal to 0.4 V. In other words, any noise smaller than 0.4 V will not disturb the gate operation. Such high noise margins, which are not available in analog circuits, make digital designs superior to analog.

3.10.3 Fan-out

As we mentioned in previous subsections, each gate can drive several other gates. The number of gates that each gate can drive, while providing voltage levels in the guaranteed range, is called the **standard load** or **fan-out**.

The fan-out really depends on the amount of electric current a gate can source or sink while driving other gates. As we can see from Figure 3.10, when the gate output is H, the gate behaves as a current source since the current I_{OH} flows out of the driver gate and into the set of driven gates. The current I_{OH} is equal to the sum of all input currents, indicated by I_{IH}, flowing into the driven gates. On the other hand, when the gate output is L, the gate behaves as a current sink, since the current I_{OL} flows into the gate and out of the driven gates. The current I_{OL} is again equal to the sum of all the input currents I_{IL} flowing out of all driven gates.

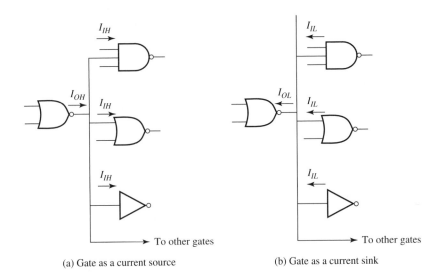

(a) Gate as a current source   (b) Gate as a current sink

FIGURE 3.10
Current flow in a typical logic circuit.

Since all the gates in a logic family are constructed in such a way that each gate requires the same I_{IH} and the same I_{IL}, we can compute fan-out in the following way:

$$\text{Fan} - \text{out} = \max(I_{OH}/I_{IH}, \ I_{OL}/I_{IL})$$

For example, the input and output current for the transistor–transistor logic family are the following:

$$I_{OH} = 400 \ \mu\text{A}$$
$$I_{OL} = 16 \ \mu\text{A}$$
$$I_{IH} = 40 \ \mu\text{A}$$
$$I_{IL} = 1.6 \ \mu\text{A}$$

Therefore, the fan-out is equal to $\max(400/40, \ 16/1.6) = 10$. This means that each gate can drive 10 other gates in the same family without getting out of its guaranteed range of operations. In case more than 10 gates are connected to the output of a single gate, the output voltage levels will degrade and the gate will slow down.

The modern metal-oxide-semiconductor (MOS) logic families have a fan-out of about 50, since each gate must source or sink a current only during the transition from H to L or L to H.

3.10.4 Power Dissipation

Each gate is connected to a power supply V_{CC} and draws a certain amount of current during its operation. Since each gate can be in a high state, transition or low state, we can distinguish three different currents drawn from the power supply: I_{CCH}, I_{CCT}, and I_{CCL}. In older logic families such as TTL, the transition current I_{CCT} is negligible in comparison to I_{CCH} and I_{CCL}. Assuming that the gate spends an approximately equal amount of time in the high and the low states, and almost no time in the transition state, the average current is equal to $(I_{CCH} + I_{CCL})/2$. The average **power dissipation** can be computed as a product of average current and power supply voltage. In other words,

$$P_{\text{avg}} = V_{CC} \times (I_{CCH} + I_{CCL})/2$$

The power dissipation is measured in milliwatts (mW) and for the TTL logic family this value is approximately 10 mW.

In modern technologies such as the CMOS family, the steady-state currents I_{CCH} and I_{CCL} are negligible in comparison with I_{CCT} and the average power dissipation is

$$P_{\text{avg}} = V_{CC} \times I_{CCT}$$

where I_{CCT} alone is an average of the current during the transition period. Since this current is relatively small, the typical power dissipation of CMOS gates is small. Obviously, the power dissipation increases with the frequency with which the gate output is changing.

The power dissipation is an important metric for two reasons. First, the amount of current and power available in a battery is nearly constant. Thus the power dissipation of a circuit or a product defines the battery life. In other words, the larger the power dissipation, the shorter the battery life.

Second, the power dissipation is proportional to the heat generated by the microchip or product. Excessive heat dissipation may increase operating temperature and cause gate circuitry to drift out of its normal operating range, which will cause the gates to generate improper output values. For both of these reasons, we must keep the power dissipation of any gate implementation as low as possible.

3.10.5 Propagation Delay

The propagation delay given for each gate in Tables 3.12 to 3.14 is defined as an average time needed for input change to propagate to the output. This propagation delay is usually measured in nanoseconds, which are equal to 10^{-9} second. The propagation delay can be obtained from gate input and output waveforms as shown in Figure 3.11. From the figure we can observe the following:

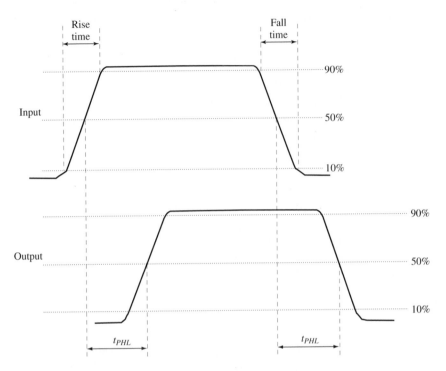

FIGURE 3.11
Propagation delay.

1.   Input and consequently output signals do not switch their values instantly.

2. H to L and L to H changes can be delayed for different amounts of time.

Since signal values do not change instantly, we can define **rise time** as a delay for a signal to switch from 10% to 90% of its nominal value. Similarly, we can define the **fall time** as a time for a signal to switch from 90% to 10% of its nominal value. Since H-to-L and L-to-H transitions are not delayed equally, we can define H-to-L propagation delay t_{PHL} and L-to-H propagation delay t_{PLH}. The t_{PHL} is the time necessary for the output signal to reach 50% of its nominal value on the H-to-L transition after the input signal reached 50% of its nominal value. The t_{PLH} is defined similarly. The **propagation delay** t_P can be defined as the average value of t_{PHL} and t_{PLH}. Thus

$$t_P = (t_{PHL} + t_{PLH})/2$$

As an example, the typical 2-input NAND gate in the TTL family has a nominal $t_{PHL} = 7$ ns and $t_{PLH} = 11$ ns for a nominal $t_P = (7 + 11)/2 = 9$ ns. The modern CMOS logic family has $t_P = 1$ ns. Since IC manufacturers cannot guarantee the same nominal value on every gate they fabricate, they also give the maximal delay values which guarantee that no gate will ever exceed this maximal value.

For example, the maximal propagation delays for 2-input NAND gates in the TTL family are $t_{PHL} = 22$ ns and $t_{PLH} = 15$ ns, with an average delay $t_P = 18.5$ ns. In the past these maximal delay values were used in the design, since different gates were supplied by different manufacturers and there was no guarantee that all slow gates would not appear on the same critical path from input to output. Presently, all gates are manufactured on one microchip at the same time, so that manufacturing variations apply equally to all of them. In this case, every delay from input to output changes proportionately and the whole IC gets slower or faster depending on manufacturing variations. The slower ICs are sold at a lower price and faster ones at a higher price. For this reason, designers today use nominal delay rather than maximal delays during the design of an IC.

3.10.6 Bipolar Logic Families

In Section 3.9 we presented different types of gates that perform one or more Boolean operations. These gates could be constructed using two different transistor technologies: bipolar and metal-oxide-semiconductor.

A **bipolar transistor** can be modeled as a voltage-controlled switch with three terminals: emitter, collector and base. As shown in Figure 3.12, the switch between the emitter and collector is open when the voltage on its base is low and closed when the voltage is high. Each gate in bipolar technology is constructed from resistors, diodes, and transistors. Resistors are fabricated as transistors without a base whose switches are always closed, and diodes are fabricated as transistors with a missing collector that allow current to go in one direction but not in another.

All gates in a particular logic family are constructed in the same style, exhibiting certain distinguished characteristics that give the name to all the gates in the family. An early family in use in the 1960s was **resistor–transistor logic** (RTL), in which one resistor and one transistor were used for every gate input. This logic family emerged at the time when transistors were expensive to fabricate and the goal of designers was to minimize the number of transistors used in the gate design. RTL logic was in use before integrated circuits were invented, and logic gates were assembled at that time from separately manufactured components. After the invention of integrated circuits, fabrication of transistors be-

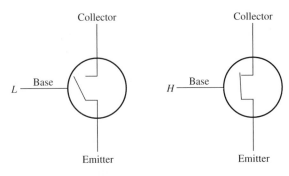

Collector

Base

L

Emitter

(a) Low voltage on base

Collector

Base

H

Emitter

(b) High voltage on base

FIGURE 3.12

Bipolar transistor model.

came less expensive, so that input resistors in gate circuits were replaced by diodes and given the name **diode–transistor logic** (DTL). Standard gates in the DTL family had shorter rise and fall times but required more components.

With the invention of multiemitter transistors, input diodes were replaced with multiemitter transistors, giving rise to the popular **transistor–transistor logic** (TTL) family, which dominated digital designs in the 1970s and 1980s.

As shown in Figure 3.13, a typical TTL gate consists of three parts: input gate logic, phase splitter, and the totem-pole output stage. The input logic performs the required Boolean function, while the phase splitter provides two signals of opposite polarity to drive the two output transistors, which are not open or closed at the same time, except during the transition. These two transistors, usually called **pull-up** and **pull-down transistors**, alternate their states in a lock-step manner. When the pull-up transistor is closed and the pull-down is open, the gate output is H and the gate is sourcing the current I_H. On the other hand, when the pull-up transistor is open and the pull-down is closed, the gate output is L and the gate is sinking the current I_L.

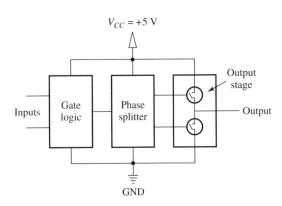

$V_{CC} = +5$ V

Inputs

Gate logic

Phase splitter

Output stage

Output

GND

FIGURE 3.13

TTL gate implementation.

In addition to totem-pole output, the TTL logic family also offered gates with two other output styles: open collector and tri-state outputs. The **open collector** (OC) style is obtained by omitting the pull-up transistor and its associated resistance. This style was offered to obtain more complex functions, such as AND-OR-INVERT, without offering AOI gates. Using OC gates, we can tie their outputs and connect them to a power supply through a separate pull-up resistor, as shown in Figure 3.14(a). In such a case the tied output is H only if each OC gate is H and L whenever one of the OC gates is L. In this way we obtained an AND function by tieing together OC gates without using additional gates. Since no physical gate is used, such an AND function is called a **wired-AND gate**, whose symbol is shown in Figure 3.14(b). As you can see from the figure, the output Boolean function obtained this way is equal to an AOI gate since

$$F = (wx)'(yz)' = (wx + yz)'$$

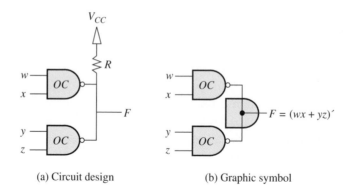

(a) Circuit design   (b) Graphic symbol

FIGURE 3.14

Wired-AND of two open collector gates in TTL logic family.

The **tri-state** or **3-state** output is used for driving buses. In this case, the phase splitter in Figure 3.13 is upgraded to provide three possible states of the output drivers: high (H), low (L), and high-impedance state (Z).

In the high and low states, the totem-pole output works as before, while in the high-impedance state both transistors are open and the gate output is disconnected from the bus for all practical purposes. The tri-state output is required for driving large buses with many bus drivers since wired-ANDs can only be used for small buses in which only a few gates are used to drive the bus. The wire-AND is limited to small buses because of the leakage current through the pull-down transistor when it is open. If too many gates are wired together, the sum of all the leakage currents may be large enough to lower H on the bus to an unacceptable range.

Since TTL logic was the dominant logic family in the 1970s and 1980s, many different variations of the basic family were offered for low-power and high-speed applications. In low-power variations, power consumption was reduced at the expense of speed, and in high-performance variants, the delay was reduced in a trade-off for increased power dissipation. Such a TTL variant was the Schottky TTL, which used specially built transistors named after one of the transistor's inventors.

For really high-speed applications such as supercomputers and communications, designers used a bipolar family called emitter-coupled logic (ECL). The ECL family offered the highest speed of all the families by reducing the time for transistors to switch from H to L, and vice versa. Main logic parameters for the various logic families are compared in Table 3.18.

TABLE 3.18

Characteristics of 2-input NAND for Various Logic Families

LOGIC FAMILY	NUMBER OF RESISTORS	NUMBER OF DIODES	NUMBER OF TRANSISTORS	NOISE MARGIN	FAN OUT	POWER DISSIPATION	DELAY (NS)
RTL	3	—	2	0.4	5	20	25
DTL	4	3	2	1.0	8	12	30
TTL	4	1	5	0.4	10	10	9
Schottky TTL	5	2	7	0.4	10	19	3
ECL	8	2	6	0.15	25	25	2
CMOS	—	—	4	0.5	30–50	0.1–0.3	1

3.10.7 MOS Logic Families

The second logic family, which started as a competitor to bipolar technology in 1980 because of its reduced power consumption but has emerged as a dominant technology in IC design, is **metal-oxide-semiconductor (MOS) logic**. A MOS transistor is built from a layer of metal above a layer of semiconductor with a layer of silicon dioxide serving as an insulation between them. As shown in Figure 3.15, a transistor can also be modeled as a voltage-controlled switch with three terminals: source, gate, and drain.

In MOS technology it is possible to fabricate two complementary transistors: a P-transistor and an N-transistor. As shown in Figure 3.15(a), the P-transistor is closed when the gate voltage is high and open when the gate voltage is low. On the other hand, as shown in Figure 3.15(b), the N-transistor is closed when the gate voltage is low and open

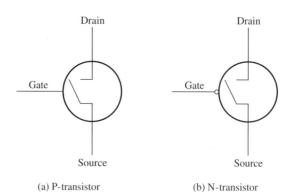

FIGURE 3.15
MOS transistor models.

(a) P-transistor

(b) N-transistor

when it is high. This complementary nature of MOS transistors can be exploited in the design of output stages in gate circuits by using the N-transistor as a pull-up and the P-transistor as a pull-down. Since these two transistors are complementary, they can be driven by the same signal without requiring the phase splitter that is necessary with the TTL logic family. Furthermore, since MOS transistors do not source or sink any gate current except during the transition, we can combine the gate logic and the output stage and reduce the number of transistors. The logic family based on these observations called **complementary MOS (CMOS) logic**, is used exclusively for IC design in 1990. Its popularity can be contributed to its low power dissipation, high fan-out value, and simplicity in fabrication.

The schematics of the basic logic gates for the CMOS family are shown in Figure 3.16. The inverter circuit shown in Figure 3.16(a) consists of only two transistors. As you can see from the truth table in Figure 3.16(b), when the input signal x is L, the pull-up transistor T_1 is closed and the pull-down transistor is open. Since the pull-up transistor is closed, the output F is at 5.0 V, which represents the high-voltage level, H. On the other hand, when x is H, the pull-up T_1 is open, the pull-down T_2 is closed, and the output is at 0 V (GND), which represents the low-voltage level, L.

More complex gates operate in the same fashion, although their pull-ups and pull-downs consist of more than one transistor. As shown in Figure 3.10(c), a NAND gate has a pull-up section that consists of two transistors T_1 and T_2 connected in parallel, and a pull-down section that consists of two transistors T_3 and T_4 connected in series. As shown in the truth table in Figure 3.16(d), when at least one of the input signals x or y is L, at least one of the transistors T_1 or T_2 will be closed, at least one of the transistors T_3 and T_4 will be open, and the output F will be H. On the other hand, when both signals x and y are H, transistors T_1 or T_2 are both open, T_3 and T_4 are both closed, and the output F is L.

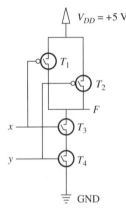

	$V_{DD} = +5$ V

(a) Inverter

x	T_1	T_2	F
L	on	off	H
H	off	on	L

(b) Inverter truth table

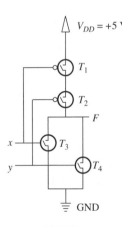

(c) NAND gate

x	y	T_1	T_2	T_3	T_4	F
L	L	on	on	off	off	H
L	H	on	off	off	on	H
H	L	off	on	on	off	H
H	H	off	off	on	on	L

(d) NAND truth table

(e) NOR gate

x	y	T_1	T_2	T_3	T_4	F
L	L	on	on	off	off	H
L	H	on	off	off	on	L
H	L	off	on	on	off	L
H	H	off	off	on	on	L

(f) NOR truth table

FIGURE 3.16
Schematics of basic gates in CMOS technology.

The NOR gate is constructed in the symmetrically opposite way. As we can see from Figure 3.16(e), the pull-up sections consist of two transistors T_1 and T_2 connected in series, while the pull-down section has parallel connections of transistors T_3 and T_4. In this case the gate operates as shown in the truth table in Figure 3.16(f). When both input signals x and y are L, both pull-up transistors T_1 or T_2 are closed, both pull-down transistors T_3 and T_4 are open, and the output F is H. In the case when either of the input signals x or y is H, at least one of the pull-up transistors is open, one of the pull-down transistors is closed, and the output F is L.

As we can see from the discussion above, CMOS gate implementation is very simple, which gives CMOS logic enormous advantages over bipolar logic. Since CMOS requires the fewest number of transistors per gate, it is the logic family with the highest density, which is measured in numbers of gates per area of silicon. Furthermore, since silicon dioxide is a very good insulator, the gate terminal is well insulated from the source and drain, and therefore CMOS transistors source current only during transition from H to L and sink it during the transition from L to H. Since there is no current in a steady state, the CMOS logic has no static power dissipation, although it has a small dynamic power dissipation, which is measured in microwatts per megahertz (μW/MHz). For a frequency of 100 MHz this dynamic power dissipation is between 0.1 and 0.3 μW. Furthermore, since only a small amount of current is needed during the transition, a CMOS gate has a very high fan-out value of approximately 30 to 50. The only weakness exhibited by CMOS logic in the early 1980s was a propagation delay that was longer than the delay exhibited in bipolar logic. However, with advances in fabrication techniques, today we can fabricate CMOS transistors that are approximately 1 micron in width, with delays below 1 ns. The CMOS logic, with such small transistors, also outperforms bipolar logic in speed, as you can see from Table 3.18. For these reasons, CMOS became the dominant logic family of 1990 and with reductions in transistor sizes to the submicron range, it is probably without competition in the foreseeable future.

3.11 VLSI TECHNOLOGY

At the most basic level, digital designs are implemented with integrated circuits, or ICs, which are built on a small silicon crystal, or **chip**. The surface of each chip contains a number of transistors, which are produced through a fabrication process that alters the chip's surface chemically. The transistors are interconnected to form the various types of gates, and the gates can then be used to form larger components, such as memories and processors. Each silicon chip is mounted in a ceramic or plastic container such as the one shown in Figure 3.17 and connected to external pins on the package to form an integrated circuit. The number of pins on each chip can range from 14 in the smaller IC packages to several hundred in the larger packages. Regardless of its number of pins, though,

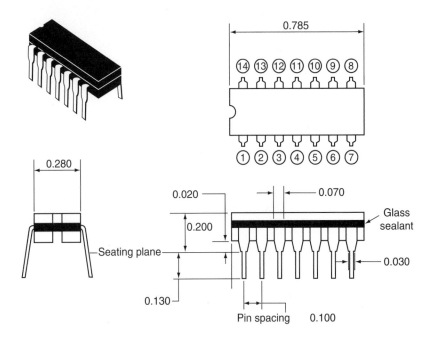

FIGURE 3.17

14-pin ceramic package (all linear dimensions are in inches).

each IC package is very small, so small that an entire microprocessor could be enclosed within a 40-pin IC package that has dimensions of $2.0 \times 0.6 \times 0.2$ inches. When it is produced, each IC is given a numeric designation that is printed on its surface for purposes of identification. In addition, IC vendors publish data books that contain all the important information about the electrical and mechanical properties of these ICs, including functional descriptions, flowcharts of operations, and timing diagrams for input and output signals.

Frequently, digital ICs are categorized according to the number of transistors or logic gates contained in a single package, and these categories are customarily referenced as either small-, medium-, large-, or very-large-scale integration devices. **Small-scale-integration** (SSI) devices contain up to 10 independent gates in a single package. Since the inputs and outputs of these gates are connected directly to the pins on the package, the number of gates is limited by the number of pins available in the IC. In Figure 3.18 we show six typical SSI devices in series 7400 of the TTL logic family.

Medium-scale integration (MSI) devices have a complexity of approximately 10 to 100 gates in a single package. These devices usually contain several bit slices of standard digital storage or arithmetic components such as registers, counters, register files, adders, multipliers, and parity generators. Figure 3.19, for example, shows a TTL 9-bit add/even-parity generator housed in a 14-pin package. We introduce these components in Chapters 5 and 7.

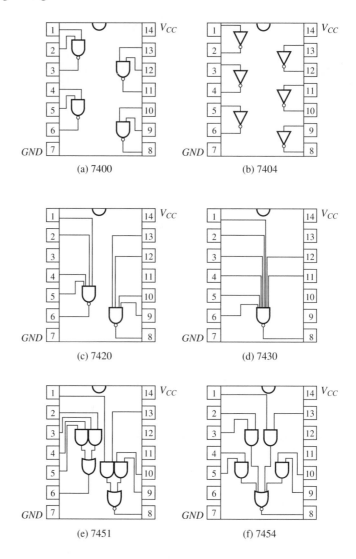

FIGURE 3.18
Basic TTL packages in series 7400.

Large-scale integration (LSI) devices contain between 100 and several thousand gates in a single package. This category of devices includes digital components such as controllers, data paths, memory chips, and programmable logic components. We describe some of these components in Chapters 7 and 8.

Finally, **very-large-scale integration** (VLSI) devices contain hundreds of thousands of gates within a single package. Examples of such devices are large memories and microprocessors, microcomputer chips, and system subfunctions, such as graphics and floating-point accelerators. The small size and low cost of VLSI chips have revolutionized design technology, as they provide designers with an unprecedented opportunity to create low-cost, high-performance, application-specific ICs

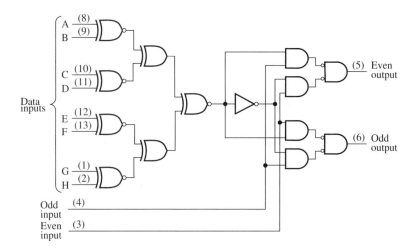

FIGURE 3.19
9-bit odd/even-parity generator (SN74180 in TTL family).

(ASICs) that can perform a single application task very efficiently and are well tuned to certain applications. At present, VLSI components are the only components in use, since SSI, MSI, and LSI components were predominant in the 1970s and 1980s but are available today only as replacement parts for older equipment.

The advent of VLSI technology has brought about one important change in the evaluation of design cost. For example, the hardware cost of a product designed with SSI, MSI, or LSI components used to be measured by the total number of ICs on a PC board. In the newer technology, however, the hardware cost of a VLSI chip is measured by its silicon area. Since this area is proportional to the number of transistors or gates in a logic schematic or to the number of storage bits in a memory design, it makes sense that designers should try to implement these designs with the minimal number of gates and the smallest necessary memory, as this allows them to minimize the cost.

The VLSI chips that are used in most designs come in three flavors: custom, semicustom, or programmable design. In the **custom approach**, VLSI chips, or some of their parts, are designed by hand, so that each transistor and each wire is individually defined by a set of polygons which are then used to generate the photographic masks needed in the fabrication process. Since designing by hand is very tedious, a standard cell design methodology has been developed to shorten the design time by allowing the use of standard cells or predesigned components as the building blocks from which large logic circuits can be constructed.

As a rule, each standard cell contains a single gate of one of the types shown in Tables 3.14, 3.15, and 3.16. All of these cells are of the same height but vary in width and they all have their inputs and outputs on the top or the bottom of the cell. Thus the standard cells can be placed in rows and connected with wires that are placed in the channels between the rows. Horizontal and vertical wires are generally fabricated on two different layers that are located above the standard cells, as shown in Figure 3.20.

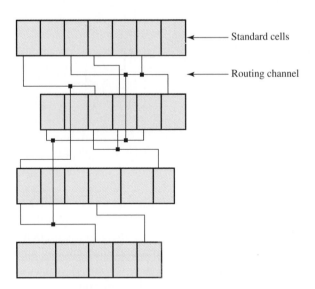

Standard cells

Routing channel

FIGURE 3.20
Standard-cell approach.

The standard cells can be collected into standard-cell libraries, which are used by designers throughout the design process. This design process for standard cells consists of several tasks: namely, capture, simulation, placement, and routing. In the first task, the design must be captured with schematic editors, which allow designers to work on a computer screen positioning and connecting the graphic symbols of the gates being used. Then, to verify the logic functions that have been captured and the delay from input to output, the designer simulates the captured schematic with a logic simulator, which generates the logic values for each signal or connection with respect to time. After simulation has confirmed the validity of the schematic, the standard cells can be placed on a silicon surface. For this purpose the designer uses a CAD placement tool, which defines the proper row for each cell and its position in the row. The goal of placement is to minimize routing areas by using a minimal number of routing tracks in each channel. Finally, after placement has been completed, the designer uses a routing tool to connect all the cells together. The goal of routing is to connect all the nets with wires of a minimum length.

In Figure 3.21, we show an implementation of the full-adder functions sum and carry, with standard cells. Note that the placement of the cells in this figure requires four horizontal tracks for routing in the top channel, and five tracks in the bottom channel.

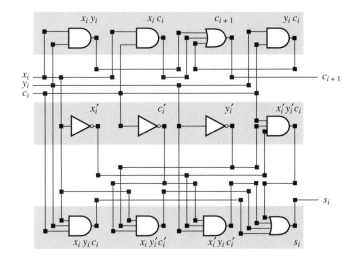

FIGURE 3.21
Full-adder implementation with standard cells.

In contrast to the custom approach, the **semicustom approach** to logic design employs an IC that is partially prefabricated and is known as a **gate array** because it incorporates a large number of identical gates that are laid out in a regular two-dimensional array. For the present-day technology, the number of gates on a given chip can range from 100,000 to 1,000,000. These gates are usually of the 3- or 4-input NAND or NOR type. Since all these gates are prefabricated, all we need to add are their interconnections. Moreover, since the manufacture of these interconnections requires only metal deposition, the cost of manufacturing gate arrays is substantially lower than it is for the custom approach. On the other hand, the density of gate arrays is much lower than that of custom chips, since a gate array of the same size as a custom chip will contain one-fourth to one-tenth the number of gates as the corresponding custom chip.

The design process for a gate array is similar to that used for custom design, except that we must perform an additional step of optimization, called technology mapping, after the schematic capture and simulation. The purpose of technology mapping is to convert all the components in the captured schematic into a single gate type that is available in the gate array selected. For example, if a gate array contains 3-input NAND gates, all of the Boolean functions in the schematic must be implemented with 3-input NAND gates. When this technology mapping has been accomplished, the placement and routing can be performed with the same CAD tools that we used for standard-cell design.

As an example of this type of semicustom design, consider how we would implement the full-adder functions sum and carry with a gate array of 3-input NAND gates. First, these sum and carry expressions have to be converted into 3-input NAND implementations using

De Morgan's theorems:

$$c_{i+1} = xy + yc_i + xc_i$$
$$= ((x_iy_i)'(y_ic_i)'(x_ic_i)')'$$

and

$$s_i = x_i'y_i'c_i + x_i'y_ic_i' + x_iy_i'c_i' + x_iy_ic_i$$
$$= (x_i'y_i'c_i + x_i'y_ic_i' + x_iy_i'c_i') + xyc_i$$
$$= ((x_i'y_i'c_i + x_i'y_ic_i' + x_iy_i'c_i')'(x_iy_ic_i)')'$$
$$= ((((x_i'y_i'c_i)'(x_i'y_ic_i')'(x_iy_i'c_i')')')'(x_iy_ic_i)')'$$

In Figure 3.22 you can see a full-adder implementation that uses a NAND-type gate array. Note that the carry has been implemented with four gates, which is the minimal number of gates required for this function. On the other hand, the sum function requires seven gates, since the 4-input NAND will require three gates when it is to be implemented with 3-input NAND gates.

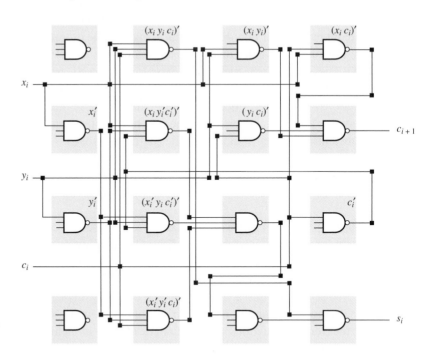

FIGURE 3.22

Full-adder implementation with gate array technology.

The third approach to design, known as the **field-programmable approach**, avoids the fabrication cost and time as a trade-off for lower gate densities of field-programmable devices, which are arrays of logic components whose connectivity can be established simply by loading the appropriate configuration data into the device's internal memory. Since these field-programmable devices can be reprogrammed any number of times, they are well suited for use in new designs in which the design specification is evolving, or in those designs where the hardware must be customized for users. In addition, field-programmable devices are ideal for prototyping, and they also offer a cost-effective solution for small-volume production. Unfortunately, the density and speed of these devices tend to be lower than that of devices available through the custom and semicustom approaches.

As shown in Figure 3.23(a), a field-programmable gate array (FPGA) contains an array of programmable logic blocks (PLBs)

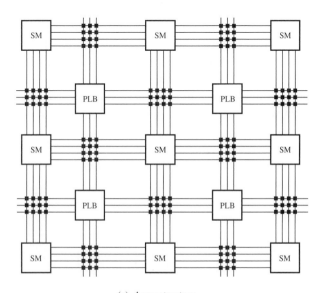

(a) Array structure

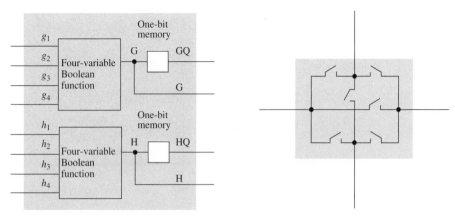

(b) Programmable logic blocks (PLB)

(c) Interconnect point

FIGURE 3.23

Field-programmable gate array.

surrounded by programmable interconnect and several I/O blocks placed on the perimeter of the chip, which are used to drive other components that are located off the chip. Each PLB consists of two four-variable logic blocks and two one-bit memory elements, as indicated in Figure 3.23(b). Note that each logic block can be programmed to implement any Boolean function of four variables, and the functional value it generates could either be outputted to another PLB immediately, or alternatively, can be stored for later use in a one-bit memory element.

Within an FPGA, the programmable interconnect contains of a set of horizontal and vertical wires that can be interconnected through a **switching matrix** (SM). In each $n \times n$ SM, there will be $m \leq n \times n$ interconnect points which can be used to connect the horizontal and vertical wires in several different ways. As shown in Figure 3.23(c), each interconnect point contains six switches, which can be programmed to be open and closed. Depending on which switches we close, we can select one of the 64 different connections between the top, bottom, left, and right wires. Interconnect points are also used to connect PLBs to horizontal and vertical wires as shown in Figure 3.23(a).

As shown in Figure 3.24, the FPGA technology enables us to implement the full adder with one PLB, within which the carry and sum

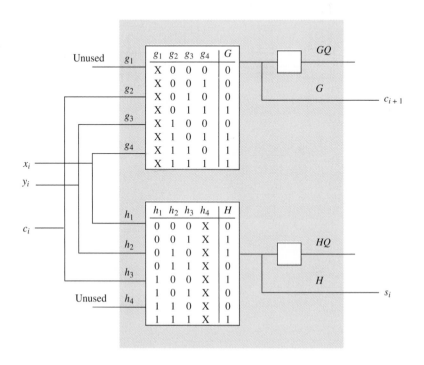

F I G U R E 3.24

Full-adder implementation with one PLB.

functions are each implemented with one logic block. Note that since sum and carry are both three-variable functions, one input to each block is unused.

3.12 CHAPTER SUMMARY

We began this chapter with an axiomatic definition of Boolean algebra, which constitutes the formal basis for all logic design. We have also presented the main theorems of Boolean algebra, because these theorems are critical for the correct manipulation of Boolean expressions.

In addition, we have introduced Boolean functions and shown how to define them in terms of truth tables and how to derive their Boolean expressions. As we have indicated, these Boolean expressions can be given in three ways, using canonical, standard, or nonstandard forms. Although the canonical form has the advantage of being unique, it will not necessarily use the minimal number of operators for a given Boolean function. In comparison with this canonical form, the standard form tends to require fewer operators, and the nonstandard form tends to use the smallest number of the three. Each of the two forms can be obtained from the canonical form through algebraic manipulation. It is important to remember, though, that the standard and nonstandard forms are not unique, as this means that for each Boolean function, there could be several different standard and nonstandard expressions. One of the primary design tasks is to find the one expression among all the possible nonstandard forms that has the smallest number of operators. In this chapter we have worked through several examples of how this expression can be found through algebraic manipulation but have not presented any systematic technique that could guarantee minimality or near minimality.

We have also introduced the simple logic gates that are used to implement Boolean operators as well as the more complex gates that can implement several Boolean operators at once. These simple and complex gates constitute the standard logic library used by designers in logic design. We have also introduced VLSI technology and the various ways of manufacturing microchips while using custom, semicustom, and programmable technologies. As expected, each technology uses its own library and requires its own optimization techniques for implementing Boolean functions.

In conclusion we can say that the main problem of logic design is trying to find the implementation of a Boolean function that will best satisfy cost and delay requirements, which are generally stated as highest performance (minimal delay) at minimal cost. In Chapter 4, we investigate some of the systematic techniques for solving this problem. Since these techniques differ for the given technology and the library we will also focus our attention on design trade-offs and logic design exploration.

3.13 FURTHER READINGS

Boole, G. *An Investigation of the Laws of Thought.* New York: Dover, 1954.

Reprint of the original work on Boolean algebra.

Friedman, A. D. and P. R. Menon. *Theory and Design of Switching Circuits.* Rockville, MD: Computer Science Press, 1975.

One of the early textbooks on logic design and switching circuits. Provides a thorough treatment of the material and research results from the 1960s and early 1970s.

Hayes, J. P. *Introduction to Digital Logic Design.* Reading, MA: Addison-Wesley, 1993.

A comprehensive text on introductory logic design that relates well to VLSI technology without requiring previous knowledge of circuit theory and design.

Huntington, E. V. "Sets of independent postulates for the algebra of logic." *Transactions of the American Mathematical Society*, Vol. 5 (1904), pp. 288–209.

The article that introduced the axiomatic formulation of Boolean algebra that is presented in this book.

Shannon, C. E. "A symbolic analysis of relay and switching circuits." *Transactions of the AIEE*, Vol. 57 (1938), pp. 713–723.

The first paper showing how Boolean algebra can be applied to the design of logic circuits that are implemented by electronic relays.

Weste, N., and K. Eshragian. *Principles of CMOS VLSI Design*, 2nd ed. Reading, MA: Addison-Wesley, 1993.

Combines VLSI technology and logic design, with an emphasis on custom design methodology. Recommended for engineering students with some knowledge of circuit theory and practice.

3.14 PROBLEMS

3.1 (Theorems of Boolean algebra) Give proofs of the following theorems.
  (a) Theorem 2(a) and (b)
  (b) Theorem 3(a) and (b)
  (c) Theorem 4(a) and (b)
  (d) Theorem 5(a) and (b)
  (e) Theorem 6(a) and (b)

3.2 (Theorems and proofs) Using truth tables, prove the validity of the following identities.
  (a) $(xyz)' = x' + y' + z'$
  (b) $xy' + x'y = (xy + x'y')'$
  (c) $xy + x'z + yz = xy + x'z$
  (d) $(x + y + z)' = x'y'z'$

3.3 (Theorems and proofs) Prove algebraically these extensions of De Morgan's theorem.
  (a) $(xyz)' = x' + y' + z'$
  (b) $(x + y + z)' = x'y'z'$

3.4 (Boolean functions) Derive truth tables for the following Boolean functions.
  (a) $F(x, y, z, w) = xz + yw + xz'$
  (b) $F(x, y, z, w) = x'y'z + x'z'w' + xzw' + xy'w$
  (c) $F(x, y, z) = (x + z)'$
  (d) $F(x, y, z) = (x + z)'(x + y')$

3.5 (Boolean functions) Derive the complements of the functions in Problem 3.3, using De Morgan's law.

3.6 (Boolean algebra) Prove by algebraic manipulation that the following expressions are equivalent.

(a) $x'y' + xy = (xy' + x'y)'$
(b) $x'z + xy = x'y'z + yz + xy$
(c) $xy'z' + x' + xyz'' = x' + z'$
(d) $x + xy + y = x + y$

3.7 (Canonical forms) Derive the sum-of-minterms and the product-of-maxterms canonical forms for the following Boolean functions.

(a) $F = x \oplus y \oplus z$
(b) $F = zw' + xy'w' + xy'z$

3.8 (Canonical forms) Derive the complements of the Boolean functions presented in Problem 3.6.

3.9 (Standard forms) For the Boolean functions specified in Problem 3.6, derive the sum-of-products and product-of-sums standard forms, using the minimal number of operators.

3.10 (Algebraic manipulation) Minimize the number of operators in the following Boolean expressions.

(a) $x'y' + xy + xy'$
(b) $(x + y)(x + y')$
(c) $x'y' + x'y + xz$
(d) $y'z' + x'y' + x'z + yz'$

3.11 (Algebraic manipulation) Explain the difference between reducing the number of operators and reducing the number of literals.

3.12 (Boolean functions) Prove or disprove the commutativity of the following operations.

(a) Inhibition
(b) Equivalence
(c) Implication
(d) Exclusive-or

3.13 (Boolean functions) Prove or disprove the associativity of the operators given in Problem 3.12.

3.14 (Boolean implementations) Implement the XOR function by means of:

(a) NAND gates only
(b) NOR gates only
(c) AND, OR, and NOT gates

3.15 (Boolean implementations) Implement $x \oplus y \oplus z$ using the components in the basic logic library presented in Table 3.14. Find the implementation that has:

(a) The smallest cost
(b) The shortest delay
(c) The smallest cost–delay product

3.16 (Logic libraries) Using the basic logic library presented in Table 3.14, implement the full subtractor that is specified by the following table:

x_i	y_i	b_i	b_{i+1}	d_i
0	0	0	0	0
0	0	1	1	1
0	1	0	1	1
0	1	1	1	0
1	0	0	0	1
1	0	1	0	0
1	1	0	0	0
1	1	1	1	1

Find the implementation that has:

(a) The smallest cost
(b) The shortest delay

3.17 (Logic libraries) Redo Problem 3.15 using only the gates that are given in Tables 3.15 and 3.16.

3.18 (Logic libraries) Redo Problem 3.15 using any of the standard logic gates that are given in Tables 3.14, 3.15 and 3.16.

3.19 (Gate arrays) Using nothing but three-input NAND gates, derive a logic schematic of a:

(a) Full adder
(b) Full subtractor

3.20 (Gate arrays) Using a 3-input NAND implementation of the (a) full adder, and (b) full subtractor, determine the position of each gate in a 4×4 gate array so that none of the vertical or horizontal routing channels has more than four routing tracks.

3.21 (Field-programmable gate arrays) Program a PLB cell so that whenever the control input is equal to 1, it acts as a full adder, whereas a control input that is equal to 0 will turn it into a full subtractor. Assume that the carry and borrow signals share the same input.

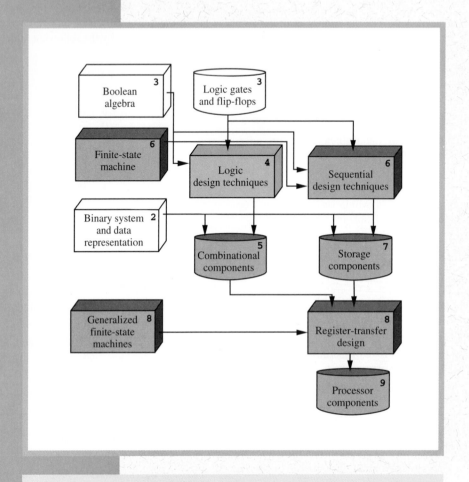

So far we have learned the basic principles of Boolean algebra and discussed how we implement Boolean functions with various logic gates. Since these gates all have different costs, sizes, and delays, so do implementations of Boolean functions constructed from these gates. Since the cost, size, and delay of such implementations depend strongly on the form of the Boolean expression and type of gates used, we need to know how to derive the proper expression and select proper types of gates that yield minimal cost, size, or delay of an implementation. In this chapter, then, we learn some of the design techniques that help us to optimize logic designs with respect to cost and delay. In addition, we discuss how these techniques can be applied to different technologies.

Simplification of Boolean Functions

In Chapter 3 we showed through several examples how to implement Boolean functions with logic gates. We also showed that the cost and delay of a given implementation depend on the form of the Boolean expression and the logic library used in its construction. For example, we showed that a Boolean function can be specified in the form of a truth table, on the basis of which we can then define the canonical, standard, and nonstandard forms of Boolean expression for that function. As mentioned in Chapter 3, these three types of forms have different properties. Although the canonical form is unique, it generally contains too many operators to serve as a basis for an efficient

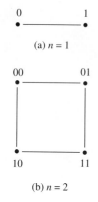

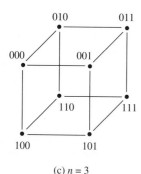

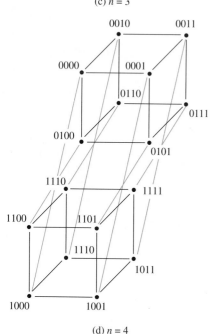

Boolean cubes for $n = 1, 2, 3$, and 4.

implementation. On the other hand, a standard form, which generally contains fewer operators, is not unique. Similarly, a nonstandard form, which has even fewer operators than the standard form, is not unique either. Since these forms are not unique, then, we need a procedure that allows us to find the nonstandard form that has the minimum number of operators, since Boolean expressions with fewer operators will require fewer gates and fewer inputs per gate, thus enabling us to generate less costly implementations.

At the same time, though, while minimizing the number of operators helps us to produce less costly implementations, such implementations often have longer delays, since the input signal may have to propagate through more gates as a consequence of maximally factored expressions. To minimize this delay, then, we need to concentrate on reducing the number of operators on each critical path from input to output. Furthermore, we must try to ensure that the types of operators on these critical paths can be implemented with the fastest gates in the gate library.

In Chapter 3 we showed how we can minimize the number of operators in an expression through certain types of algebraic manipulation. In this chapter we describe the systematic techniques that enable us, first, to minimize the number of operators in standard and nonstandard forms, and then to map these operators on the gates in a given library.

4.1 MAP REPRESENTATION

The map method is a simple, straightforward procedure for minimizing the number of operators in standard-form expressions. To generate such a standard form we begin with a convenient form of a truth table called a map, which was proposed by Veitch and later modified by Karnaugh. The map is designed to help us identify the smallest possible number of subcubes that define a given Boolean function. Each subcube represents a product in a standard sum-of-products form.

In Chapter 2 we introduced the Boolean n-cubes, which provide the basis for these maps. Figure 4.1, for example, shows the Boolean cubes for $n = 1, 2, 3$, and 4. As mentioned earlier, each vertex in each **n-cube** represents a minterm of an n-variable Boolean function. Thus each Boolean function could be represented visually in the form of an n-cube by marking those vertices in which the value of that function is 1, and leaving unmarked vertices to indicate the function values of 0. Each cube representation is equivalent to the truth table representation of the same function, since there is a one-to-one correspondence between each row in the truth table and each vertex in the Boolean n-cube. In

Figure 4.2, for example, we show the truth table and the corresponding cube representations of the popular carry and sum functions, used
extensively as examples in Chapter 3.

To find the standard form of a function that contains the minimal number of operators, we use the concept of a Boolean subcube. In
general, an **m-subcube** of an n-cube can be defined as that set of 2^m
vertices in which $n - m$ of the variables will have the same value at every vertex, while the remaining m variables will take on the 2^m possible
combinations of the values 0 and 1. Thus each subcube can be characterized by the $n - m$ variable values that are the same for every vertex
in the subcube. For example, if a Boolean function has a value of 1 in
each vertex of the m-subcube, the 2^m 1-minterms in that subcube could
be expressed by a single term of $n - m$ literals, which represents the
variable values that are the same for each vertex of the subcube. To
demonstrate this fact, let $x_1, x_2, \ldots, x_{n-m}$ be the variables whose values
are the same in each vertex of the n-cube, and let $l_1, l_2, \ldots, l_{n-m}$ be the
literals such that $l_i = x_i$ whenever the value of $x_i = 1$, and $l_i = x_i'$ whenever the value of $x_i = 0$. Then the function value of the m-subcube is
equal to

$$
\begin{aligned}
& l_1 l_2 \cdots l_{n-m}(x'_{n-m+1} x'_{n-m+2} \cdots x'_n + x'_{n-m+1} x'_{n-m+2} \cdots x_n \\
& + \cdots + x_{n-m+1} x_{n-m+2} \cdots x_n) \\
= \ & l_1 l_2 \cdots l_{n-m}
\end{aligned}
$$

Note that the expression in parentheses represents the sum of all possible minterms of m variables, which will always be equivalent to 1.

On the basis of this demonstration, we know that any Boolean
function can be described in a standard sum-of-products form, within
which each term will be a subcube of 1-minterms and each 1-minterm will
be in at least one subcube. To minimize the number of OR operators
in such a form, we have to choose as few subcubes as possible while
still covering all its 1-minterms, and to minimize the number of AND
operators, we have to choose the largest possible subcubes, which are
known as prime implicants

In general, a **prime implicant** (PI) is defined as a subcube that is not
contained within any other subcube, and an **essential prime implicant**
(EPI) is the subcube that includes a 1-minterm that is not included in any
other subcube. These prime implicants can be determined and selected
visually from a cube representation, or we could derive them from the
two-dimensional form of this cube, which is called a **Karnaugh map**, or
map for short. The map is an array of squares arranged in rows and
columns. The variables are divided into row and column variables, each
row representing a particular assignment of 0's and 1's to row variables
and each column representing a similar assignment to column variables.

c_i	x_i	y_i	c_{i+1}	s_i
0	0	0	0	0
0	0	1	0	1
0	1	0	0	1
0	1	1	1	0
1	0	0	0	1
1	0	1	1	0
1	1	0	1	0
1	1	1	1	1

(a) Truth table

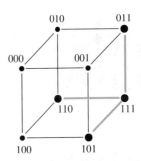

(b) Carry function c_{i+1}

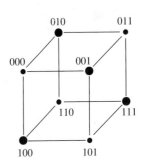

(c) Sum function s_i

FIGURE 4.2

Representation of carry
and sum functions with
Boolean cubes.

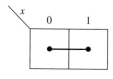

(a) $n = 1$

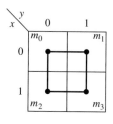

(b) $n = 2$

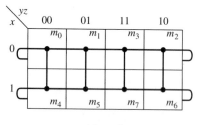

(c) $n = 3$

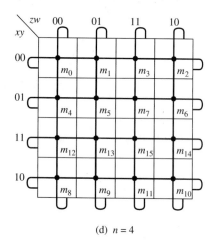

(d) $n = 4$

FIGURE 4.3

Boolean cubes and corresponding Karnaugh maps for $n = 1$, 2, 3, and 4.

In other words, each square corresponds to one vertex of the cube—that is, one minterm of the Boolean function. If the minterm is a 1-minterm, a 1 will be placed inside its square, while the square will be left empty to indicate a 0-minterm.

In Figure 4.3 we can see that there is a one-to-one correspondence between Boolean cubes and Karnaugh maps. In other words, these maps are simply two-dimensional representations of Boolean cubes. They are more useful than truth tables simply because they can show adjacency and can therefore aid in identifying subcubes.

Figure 4.3(a), for example, is a single-variable map consisting of two squares that indicate $x = 0$ and $x = 1$. This map could be used to represent all four single-variable functions: 0, x, x', and 1. However, since the expressions for these functions are easy to remember, this map is rarely used. A more useful map is the two-variable version shown in Figure 4.4(a). This map consists of four squares, which represent the four minterms of a two-variable Boolean function, namely, $x'y'$, $x'y$, xy', and xy. The largest subcube in a two-variable map is a 1-cube, which represents a single variable or its complement. For example, Figure 4.4(b) shows three such subcubes of size 1. A two-variable map could be used to represent each of the two-variable functions. As an example, the Boolean functions AND, OR, and XOR are shown in the truth table in Figure 4.5(a) and again in the maps in Figure 4.5(b), (c), and (d).

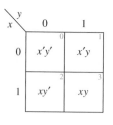

(a) Map organization

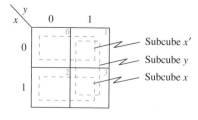

(b) Example subcubes of size 1

FIGURE 4.4

Two-variable map.

In Figure 4.6(a) we show a **three-variable map**, which consists of eight squares, which correspond to the eight minterms of a three-variable Boolean function. From the map you can see that the largest subcubes are of size 2 and that these subcubes can be expressed by a single literal. In Figure 4.6(b) we show three of the six possible subcubes of size 2, and in Figure 4.6(c) we show several subcubes of size 1.

	yz			
x	00	01	11	10
0	$x'y'z'$	$x'y'z$	$x'yz$	$x'yz'$
1	$xy'z'$	$xy'z$	xyz	xyz'

(a) Map organization

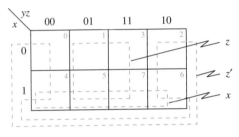

(b) Examples of 2-subcubes

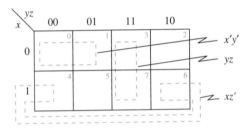

(c) Examples of 1-subcubes

FIGURE 4.6
Three-variable map.

x	y	AND	OR	XOR
0	0	0	0	0
0	1	0	1	1
1	0	0	1	1
1	1	1	1	0

(a) Truth table

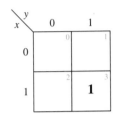

(b) AND: xy

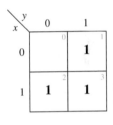

(c) OR: $x + y$

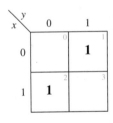

(d) XOR: $x'y + xy'$

FIGURE 4.5
Map representation of three two-variable Boolean functions.

As an example of a map representation, in Figure 4.7 we have presented the truth table and maps of the carry and sum functions defined in Chapter 2 and used as examples in Chapter 3. Note that the carry function could be expressed as the sum of three subcubes of size 1: x_iy_i, c_ix_i, and c_iy_i. As you can see from the map, all three subcubes are essential prime implicants, since each subcube contains one minterm that is not included in any of the other subcubes. On the other hand, the sum function cannot be simplified, because it has no subcubes of two or more minterms in its map representation. In other words, the sum function does not have a standard form that differs from its canonical form.

In Figure 4.8(a) we show a **four-variable map**, which consists of 16 squares, which correspond to the 16 minterms of a four-variable function. Each square in this map is adjacent to four other squares that differ in the

c_i	x_i	y_i	c_{i+1}	s_i
0	0	0	0	0
0	0	1	0	1
0	1	0	0	1
0	1	1	1	0
1	0	0	0	1
1	0	1	1	0
1	1	0	1	0
1	1	1	1	1

(a) Truth table

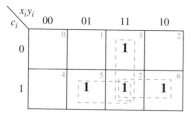

(b) Carry function: $c_{i+1} = x_i y_i + c_i x_i + c_i y_i$

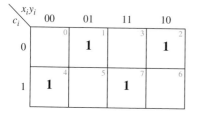

(c) Sum function:
$$s_i = x_i' y_i' c_i + x_i' y_i c_i' + x_i y_i' c_i' + x_i y_i c_i$$

FIGURE 4.7

Map representation of carry and sum functions.

value of one variable, including the squares on the map boundaries. In case of squares on the boundary, we remember that the map represents a 4-cube and that a square in the top row and the square in the same column in the bottom row are adjacent to each other, as are a square in the leftmost column and the square in the same row in the rightmost column. With this in mind, in Figure 4.8(b) and (c) we show some samples of 2- and 3-subcubes in a four-variable map.

As an example of a four-variable function, consider a two-bit comparator, which compares two-bit binary numbers $x = x_1 x_0$ and $y = y_1 y_0$, whose values can be 0, 1, 2, or 3. In this comparator the greater-than function G is equal to 1 whenever $x > y$, whereas the less-than function L is equal to 1 whenever $x < y$. The equality function E, indicating that $x = y$, can be obtained from G and L, since $E = (G + L)'$. In Figure 4.9(a) we present the truth table for G, E, and L, while in Figure 4.9(b) and (c), you can see the map representations of functions G and L. Note that functions G and L are symmetrical with respect to the main diagonal, and that each could be described by the sum of one 2-subcube and two 1-subcubes. Note also that each of these subcubes is an essential prime implicant.

Unfortunately, the maps that we use to represent five- and six-variable functions are not as convenient as two-, three-, and four-variable maps, simply because, at this level of complexity, adjacency is more difficult to visualize. For example, in the four-variable map, each square was adjacent to four other squares: on the top, the bottom, the left, and the right. To show such adjacency in a **five-variable map**, however, we need to use two four-variable maps that are positioned next to each other, as shown in Figure 4.10(a). In this representation we assume that the second map is overlaid on top of the first map so as to create a three-dimensional object. With this in mind, each square can be seen to be adjacent to four other squares in its own map, as well as to the squares that are in the same row and column of the other map.

In Figure 4.10(b) we show several examples of 3- and 4-subcubes within this five-variable map. The subcubes that span both maps can be recognized easily since they consist of two halves that occupy the same place in both maps. In other words, an m-subcube could be represented by two identical $(m - 1)$-subcubes, one in each map, or by a single m-subcube that appears in only one of the maps.

Similar conclusions can be drawn for **six-variable maps** such as the one shown in Figure 4.11(a). In this map you can see that an m-subcube could consist of (1) four $(m-2)$-subcubes that occupy the same position in all four maps, (2) two $(m - 1)$-subcubes that appear in the same position in two adjacent maps, or (3) a single m-subcube that appears in only one of the maps. Several examples of these 4-subcubes are shown in Figure 4.11(b).

xy \ zw	00	01	11	10
00	$x'y'z'w'$ (0)	$x'y'z'w$ (1)	$x'y'zw$ (3)	$x'y'zw'$ (2)
01	$x'yz'w'$ (4)	$x'yz'w$ (5)	$x'yzw$ (7)	$x'yzw'$ (6)
11	$xyz'w'$ (12)	$xyz'w$ (13)	$xyzw$ (15)	$xyzw'$ (14)
10	$xy'z'w'$ (8)	$xy'z'w$ (9)	$xy'zw$ (11)	$xy'zw'$ (10)

(a) Map organization

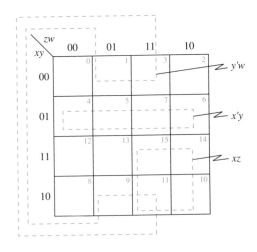

(b) Examples of 2-subcubes

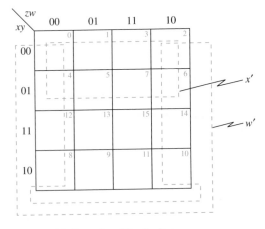

(c) Examples of 3-subcubes

FIGURE 4.8
Four-variable map.

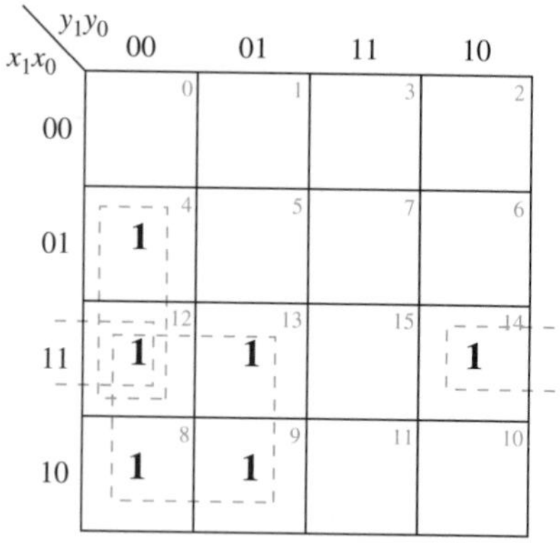

(b) Greater-than function:
$$G = x_1 y_1' + x_0 y_1' y_0' + x_1 x_0 y_0'$$

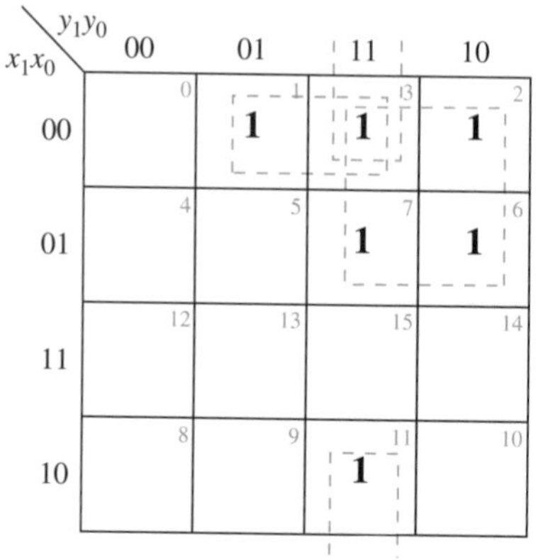

x_1	x_0	y_1	y_0	G	E	L
0	0	0	0	0	1	0
0	0	0	1	0	0	1
0	0	1	0	0	0	1
0	0	1	1	0	0	1
0	1	0	0	1	0	0
0	1	0	1	0	1	0
0	1	1	0	0	0	1
0	1	1	1	0	0	1
1	0	0	0	1	0	0
1	0	0	1	1	0	0
1	0	1	0	0	1	0
1	0	1	1	0	0	1
1	1	0	0	1	0	0
1	1	0	1	1	0	0
1	1	1	0	1	0	0
1	1	1	1	0	1	0

(a) Truth table

(c) Less-than function:
$$L = x_1' y_1 + x_1' x_0' y_0 + x_0' y_1 y_0$$

FIGURE 4.9

Representation of greater-than and less-than functions in maps.

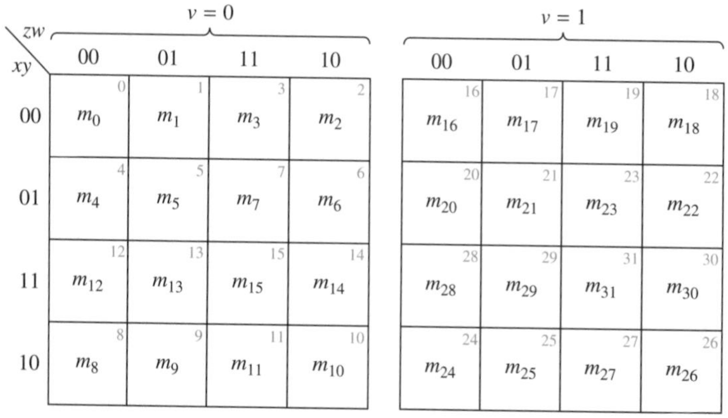

(a) Map organization

FIGURE 4.10

Five-variable map.

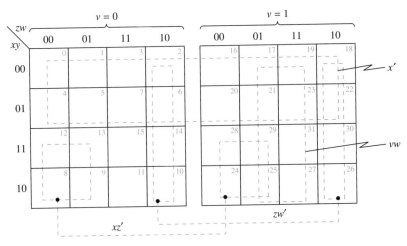

(b) Examples of 3-subcubes and 4-subcubes

FIGURE 4.10
Continued.

	$v = 0$				$v = 1$			
zw xy	00	01	11	10	00	01	11	10
00	m_0	m_1	m_3	m_2	m_{16}	m_{17}	m_{19}	m_{18}
01	m_4	m_5	m_7	m_6	m_{20}	m_{21}	m_{23}	m_{22}
11	m_{12}	m_{13}	m_{15}	m_{14}	m_{28}	m_{29}	m_{31}	m_{30}
10	m_8	m_9	m_{11}	m_{10}	m_{24}	m_{25}	m_{27}	m_{26}

$u = 0$

	00	01	11	10	00	01	11	10
00	m_{32}	m_{33}	m_{35}	m_{34}	m_{48}	m_{49}	m_{51}	m_{50}
01	m_{36}	m_{37}	m_{39}	m_{38}	m_{52}	m_{53}	m_{55}	m_{54}
11	m_{44}	m_{45}	m_{47}	m_{46}	m_{60}	m_{61}	m_{63}	m_{62}
10	m_{40}	m_{41}	m_{43}	m_{42}	m_{56}	m_{57}	m_{59}	m_{58}

$u = 1$

(a) Map organization

FIGURE 4.11
Six-variable map.

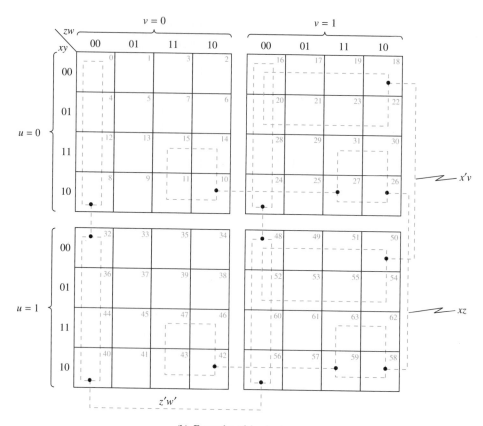

(b) Examples of 4-subcubes

FIGURE 4.11
Continued.

4.2 MAP METHOD OF SIMPLIFICATION

As mentioned above, the primary purpose of these map representations is to help us simplify standard forms by reducing the number of operators they contain. As shown in Figure 4.12, the procedure for operator reduction, which is usually called the map method, consists of four basic steps.

MAP GENERATION. In the first step, any other representation of a given Boolean function is converted into a map representation. A truth table, for example, is converted into a map by placing a 1 into the squares that correspond to 1-minterms. Similarly, a canonical form is converted into a map by inserting a 1 for each minterm in the form. A standard form can either be expanded into a canonical form first, or it can be directly converted by inserting $(n - m)$ 1's into each $(n - m)$-subcube in the map for each m-literal term in the standard form.

PRIME IMPLICANT GENERATION. In the second step, a list of prime implicants is developed by inspecting each 1-minterm, finding the largest possible subcube of 1-minterms that includes the minterm in question, and then adding that subcube to the list of prime implicants. If two or more different subcubes are discovered, they are all added to the list. On the other hand, if we rediscover a subcube that is already on the list, it will not be added the second time.

ESSENTIAL IMPLICANT SELECTION. In the third step, we look for any 1-minterm that is included in only one prime implicant, because this implicant is an essential prime implicant and will automatically be added to the cover list, which is explained below.

CREATE MINIMAL COVER. The goal of this step is to generate a cover list consisting of the smallest possible number of prime implicants, which are selected in such a way that each 1-minterm is contained in at least one prime implicant. To create this list, one may take several approaches, the simplest of which is the greedy approach, explained below. In this method we find the prime implicant that contains the greatest number of not-covered 1-minterms and move it from the prime implicant list to the cover list. If we happen to have two prime implicants that both include the same number of not-covered minterms, one is chosen randomly. This procedure is then repeated until all the minterms have been covered. The following example provides a demonstration of this approach.

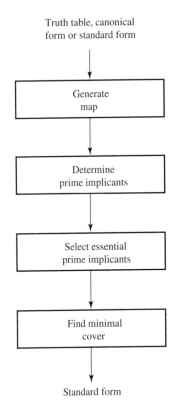

FIGURE 4.12

Map method for Boolean simplification.

■ ***EXAMPLE 4.1*** Map method

PROBLEM Using the map method, simplify the Boolean function $F = w'y'z' + wz + xyz + w'y$.

SOLUTION Following the procedure given in Figure 4.12, we first generate a map from this algebraic expression by inserting 1's for all the subcubes that are given in the expression. In this case these subcubes are $w'y'z'$, wz, xyz, and $w'y$, as shown in Figure 4.13(a). Note that the term xyz is redundant, as its minterms $x'yzw$ and $xyzw$ are included in the subcubes wz and $w'y$, respectively.

Having developed the four-variable map, we determine all the prime implicants and generate a PI list, as shown in Figure 4.13(b) and (c). To generate the PI list, we inspect each 1-minterm and add to the list all the prime implicants that contain that minterm. As mentioned above, if we discover an implicant that is already on the list, we do not duplicate it.

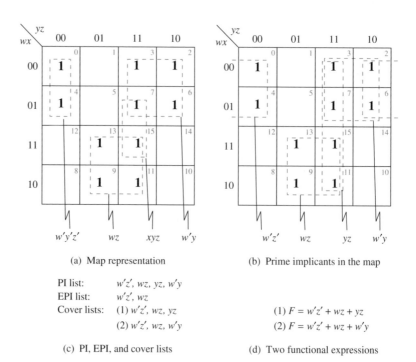

(a) Map representation

(b) Prime implicants in the map

PI list: $w'z'$, wz, yz, $w'y$

EPI list: $w'z'$, wz

Cover lists: (1) $w'z'$, wz, yz (1) $F = w'z' + wz + yz$

               (2) $w'z'$, wz, $w'y$ (2) $F = w'z' + wz + w'y$

(c) PI, EPI, and cover lists

(d) Two functional expressions

FIGURE 4.13
Boolean simplification.

In our case we start with minterm m_0, which turns out to be contained within the prime implicant $w'z'$. Minterm m_2 is contained in two prime implicants, $w'y$ and $w'z'$. At this point, though, we add only $w'y$ to the list, since $w'z'$ is already on it. Similarly, minterm m_3 is contained in both yz and $w'y$, but only yz is added to the list. Minterms m_4, m_6, and m_7 do not add any new prime implicants to the list. Minterm m_9, however, adds wz to the list. Since none of the other minterms add any new prime implicants to the list, we know that the complete PI list consists of four prime implicants, as shown in Figure 4.13(c).

At this point we are ready to perform the third step by selecting the essential prime implicants. As you can see, minterms m_0 and m_4 are covered only by the prime implicant $w'z'$, whereas minterms m_9 and m_{13} are covered only by the prime implicant wz. Thus the essential prime implicant list, or EPI list, consists of the two prime implicants $w'z'$ and wz, as shown in Figure 4.13(c).

Finally, we need to find the minimal number of prime implicants that will cover the remaining minterms m_3 and m_7. From the map in Figure 4.13(b), we can see that both minterms are covered by either yz or $w'y$. Since both of these prime implicants are the same size, either could be chosen

for the final cover. For this reason, Figure 4.13(c) shows
two different cover lists and Figure 4.13(d) shows two simplified expressions, each of which requires the same number
of operators. Note that each of these simplified expressions
require three AND operators and two OR operators, in contrast to the six AND and three OR operators required by the
original expression. In other words, our simplification procedure has resulted in a 50% reduction in AND operators
and a 33% reduction in OR operators.

Although the procedure described above has been effective in this
case, we cannot always rely on this strategy to yield the minimal number
of prime implicants. In some cases, for example, the size of the final
cover is affected by the order in which the prime implicants have been
selected, as you will see in the following example.

EXAMPLE 4.2 Selection of prime implicants

PROBLEM Simplify the Boolean function $F = w'x'yz' + w'xy + wxz + wx'y' + w'x'y'z'$.

SOLUTION In Figure 4.14(a) we present the map generated
from the expression above. As you can see, this map shows
that there are eight prime but no essential implicants for this

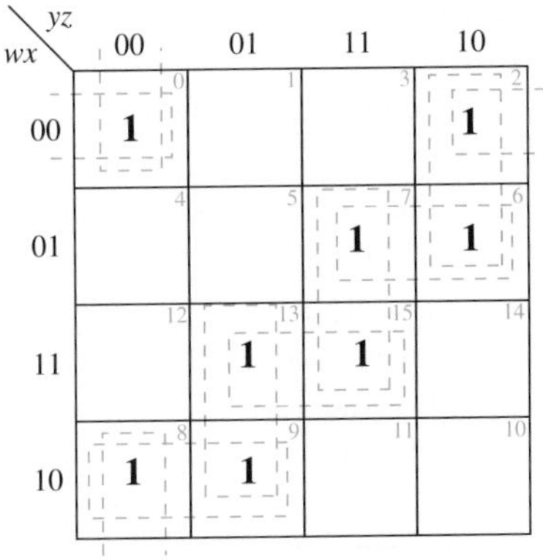

(a) Map representation

PI list: $w'x'z'$, $w'xy$, wxz, $wx'y'$, $x'y'z'$, $wy'z$, xyz, $w'yz'$
EPI list: empty
Cover lists: (1) $w'x'z'$, $w'xy$, wxz, $wx'y'$
              (2) $x'y'z'$, $wy'z$, xyz, $w'yz'$

(b) PI, EPI, and cover lists

FIGURE 4.14

Boolean simplification example.

function. In addition, Figure 4.14(b) shows that we can find two completely different covers for this function, both of which require the same number of operators.

Note that selecting the prime implicants for each cover is a tricky task because we are forced to select prime implicants randomly since all the prime implicants are the same size. If, however, we select prime implicant $w'x'z'$ first and implicant xyz next, we need three more prime implicants to complete the cover. In other words, we need one more implicant than we used in either of the two covers shown in Figure 4.14(b), each of which required only four prime implicants. Note also that these two minimal covers are disjoint, since they have no prime implicants in common.

In Example 4.2 we have demonstrated that the order in which we select prime implicants can be extremely important and that the heuristic procedure described in Figure 4.12 will not always be sufficient to find the minimal covers. In Section 4.4 we introduce an alternative procedure that can be relied on to find all the minimal covers for a given Boolean function.

4.3 DON'T-CARE CONDITIONS

In previous sections we have considered only those Boolean functions that are **completely specified**—that is, we have assumed that a function has a value of 0 or 1 for every combination of variable values. Under this assumption, we could define each Boolean function in terms of a set of 0-minterms and a set of 1-minterms. In practice, however, we specify only the set of 1-minterms and assume that all the minterms not in that set are 0-minterms. In many applications, however, a Boolean function is not specified for certain combinations of variable values, because those combinations never occur. For example, the BCD code for decimal digits uses only 10 of the 16 possible combinations to specify the decimal digits 0 through 9. In other words, six of these combinations, representing the numbers 10, 11, 12, 13, 14, and 15, are never used. For this reason, any Boolean function that uses the BCD code as input would have to be considered unspecified for the combinations that represent the numbers 10, 11, 12, 13, 14, and 15. Such a Boolean function, which has unspecified outputs for some input combinations, is called an **incompletely specified function**, and the minterms for which the function is not specified are called **don't-care minterms** (d-minterms) or **don't-care conditions**.

Don't-care minterms can be used to further simplify the Boolean expression of such an incompletely specified function. Since these don't-care conditions never occur, we can assign to these minterms a functional value of either 0 or 1 in a way that makes prime implicant subcubes larger and therefore functional expressions smaller. Within the map itself we distinguish these don't-care conditions from 0's and 1's by placing a X in the appropriate squares, which indicates intuitively that we do not care whether a functional value of 0 or 1 is assigned to that particular minterm.

When using maps with don't-care conditions during prime implicant generation, we inspect each 1-minterm, find the largest possible subcube of 1-minterms and, in this case, d-minterms, that includes the minterm in question and then add this subcube to the prime implicant list, if it is not already included. In other words, we implicitly assign a functional value of 1 to all those d-minterms that are included in at least one prime implicant and assign a value of 0 to all the others. We demonstrate this procedure in the following example.

■ **EXAMPLE** *4.3*   Simplification with don't care conditions

PROBLEM   Derive Boolean expressions for the nine's complement of a BCD digit.

SOLUTION   We know from Section 2.5 that the complement of a decimal number is equal to its nine's complement incremented by 1. Furthermore, we know that the nine's complement of a decimal number can be obtained by subtracting each of its digits from 9. Therefore, the nine's complements of digits 0, 1, 2, 3, 4, 5, 6, 7, 8, and 9 are 9, 8, 7, 6, 5, 4, 3, 2, 1, and 0, as shown in Figure 4.15(a). If we assume BCD encoding, each of these digits is represented by a 4-bit binary number $x_3x_2x_1x_0$, and its nine's complement by the other 4-bit binary number $y_3y_2y_1y_0$, as indicated in the same figure. As you can see, the combinations 1010, 1011, 1100, 1101, 1110, and 1111 are never used in encoding of decimal digits of their nine's complements. These combinations represent the don't-care conditions of the four Boolean functions that define the encoding of the nine's complement. From the table of decimal digits and their nine's complement shown in Figure 4.15(a), we can derive the map representations shown in Figure 4.15(b). Note that the six don't-care combinations have been indicated by the symbol $\times$ in each of these maps.

To reduce the number of terms in the Boolean expression and the number of literals in each term, we must assign the appropriate values to the don't cares in each map. When simplifying the expression for y_3, for example, we assume that all the don't cares have a value of 0, which makes $y_3 = x_3'x_2'x_1'$.

DIGITS		NINE'S COMPLEMENTS	
DECIMAL	BCD	DECIMAL	BCD
	$x_3x_2x_1x_0$		$y_3y_2y_1y_0$
0	0 0 0 0	9	1 0 0 1
1	0 0 0 1	8	1 0 0 0
2	0 0 1 0	7	0 1 1 1
3	0 0 1 1	6	0 1 1 0
4	0 1 0 0	5	0 1 0 1
5	0 1 0 1	4	0 1 0 0
6	0 1 1 0	3	0 0 1 1
7	0 1 1 1	2	0 0 1 0
8	1 0 0 0	1	0 0 0 1
9	1 0 0 1	0	0 0 0 0

(a) Nine's-complement table

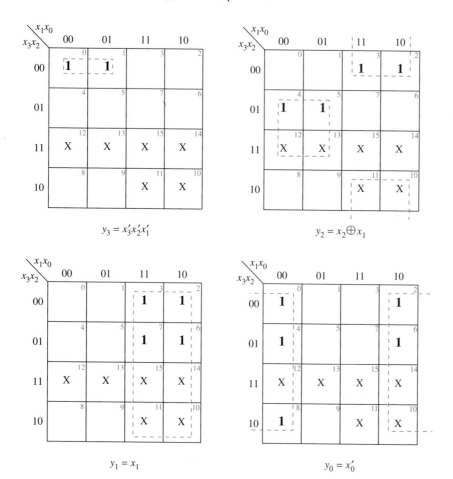

(b) Map representation

FIGURE 4.15
Simplification of nine's-complement functions.

Alternatively, the expression for y_2 is simplified by assuming that only two of the don't-care minterms m_{14} and m_{15} have a value of 0, while all the others have a value of 1. Similarly, when simplifying the expression for y_1, we assume that don't-care minterms m_{10}, m_{11}, m_{14}, and m_{15} have a value of 1, and in the expression for y_0, we assume that the minterms m_9, m_{11}, and m_{14} are equal to 1.

If we did not use these don't-care minterms, we would obtain one extra literal per term in the expressions for y_2, y_1, and y_0, in addition to one extra term in the expression for y_0. Needless to say, these d-minterms can be used in a similar fashion to further simplify product-of-sum forms, or any other nonstandard forms, for that matter.

The preceding example has shown that in a given map, the d-minterms can be used to our benefit, since we can choose to assign a functional value of 0 or 1 to each of these d-minterms, depending on their positions within the map. Once this choice has been made, the incompletely specified function will be transformed into a completely specified one, whose expression will no longer indicate what choice was made in assigning 0 or 1 to the d-minterms.

4.4 TABULATION METHOD

As you can see from the description in Section 4.3, the map method is essentially a trial-and-error procedure because it requires a person to recognize subcube patterns in the map. As the number of variables increases above six, it becomes increasingly difficult for people to recognize subcubes and select a minimal set of prime implicants.

By contrast, the **tabulation method** does not have these disadvantages, simply because if does not rely on pattern recognition. To be sure, this tabulation method is quite tedious for human designers, who are prone to make mistakes in this monotonous and lengthy process. Nonetheless, it is quite suitable for machine computation, since it searches almost exhaustively for the prime implicants and eventually finds all possible covers. Many modern CAD tools use a derivation of this method, which was first proposed by Quine and later improved by McCluskey, and therefore is frequently referred to as the Quine–McCluskey method.

This tabulation method of Boolean simplification starts with the sum-of-products canonical form and consists of two steps. In the first step, we find all the prime implicants of a given Boolean function. In the second step, we identify the essential implicants and then use them to find all the minimal covers.

4.4.1 Prime Implicant Generation

To determine all the prime implicants, the tabulation method requires us first to compare each minterm in the canonical form with all its other minterms and find all the subcubes of size 1, or a 1-subcube. In other words, we try to find all pairs of two minterms that differ in the value of only one variable. This comparison process is usually accelerated by first grouping those minterms that have the same number of variables whose values are equal to 1, called a 1's-count, and then sorting these groups in ascending order by their 1's-count. By grouping and sorting in this manner, we can find any two minterms that differ in exactly one variable simply by comparing the minterms in one group with only the minterms in the next group. Through this comparison, we generate a number of 1-subcubes, which can then be grouped and ordered according to their own 1's count. Next, we compare minterms in the two groups of 1-subcubes, whose 1's-counts differ by one, and generate 2-subcubes. This process can be repeated as many times as necessary until no new subcubes can be generated, or until all the minterms have been grouped into one n-subcube, which would mean that the function is equal to 1. In the following example, we use the Boolean function presented in Example 4.1 to demonstrate this procedure.

■ **EXAMPLE 4.4** Prime implicants generation

PROBLEM Generate all the prime implicants for the function F that was originally defined by the map in Figure 4.13(a), and has been duplicated in Figure 4.16(a).

SOLUTION According to this map, the canonical form of this function contains ten 1-minterms that can be grouped into five groups: G_0, G_1, G_2, G_3, and G_4. Each group G_i, where $0 \leq i \leq 4$, contains those minterms whose 1's count is equal to i. For example, the first group, G_0, contains only the minterm m_0, because this minterm represents the combination $wxyz = 0000$, and its 1's count is therefore equal to 0. Similarly, group G_1 contains the minterms m_2 and m_4, since these minterms represent the combinations $wxyz = 0010$ and $wxyz = 0100$, whose 1's count is equal to 1. We can define all other groups in the same manner. Each group contains minterms that can be thought of as 0-subcubes, as shown in the list of 0-subcubes in Figure 4.16(b).

As you can see from this list, each element consists of four items: the name of the group, G_i, the minterm indices that are included in that particular subcube, the variable values for the subcube, and a flag indicating whether or not that

$wx \backslash yz$	00	01	11	10
00	0: **1**	1:	3: **1**	2: **1**
01	4: **1**	5:	7: **1**	6: **1**
11	12:	13: **1**	15: **1**	14:
10	8:	9: **1**	11: **1**	10:

(a) Map representation

GROUP ID	SUBCUBE MINTERMS	SUBCUBE VALUE *w*	*x*	*y*	*z*	SUBCUBE COVERED
G_0	(0)	0	0	0	0	yes
G_1	(2)	0	0	1	0	yes
	(4)	0	1	0	0	yes
G_2	(3)	0	0	1	1	yes
	(6)	0	1	1	0	yes
	(9)	1	0	0	1	yes
G_3	(7)	0	1	1	1	yes
	(11)	1	0	1	1	yes
	(13)	1	1	0	1	yes
G_4	(15)	1	1	1	1	yes

(b) List of 0-subcubes

GROUP ID	SUBCUBE MINTERMS	SUBCUBE VALUE *w*	*x*	*y*	*z*	SUBCUBE COVERED
G_0	(0, 2)	0	0	–	0	yes
	(0, 4)	0	–	0	0	yes
G_1	(2, 3)	0	0	1	–	yes
	(2, 6)	0	–	1	0	yes
	(4, 6)	0	1	–	0	yes
G_2	(3, 7)	0	–	1	1	yes
	(3, 11)	–	0	1	1	yes
	(6, 7)	0	1	1	–	yes
	(9, 11)	1	0	–	1	yes
	(9, 13)	1	–	0	1	yes
G_3	(7, 15)	–	1	1	1	yes
	(11, 15)	1	–	1	1	yes
	(13, 15)	1	1	–	1	yes

(c) List of 1-subcubes

GROUP ID	SUBCUBE MINTERMS	SUBCUBE VALUE *w*	*x*	*y*	*z*	SUBCUBE COVERED
G_0	(0, 2, 4, 6)	0	–	–	0	no
G_1	(2, 3, 6, 7)	0	–	1	–	no
G_2	(3, 7, 11, 15)	–	–	1	1	no
	(9, 11, 13, 15)	1	–	–	1	no

(d) List of 2-subcubes

FIGURE 4.16
Prime implicants generation.

subcube is covered by a larger subcube. The flag will be set to "yes" or "no" after we have generated the list of next-larger subcubes. Note that since the canonical form contained 10 minterms, this list of 0-subcubes will consist of 10 elements, each of which occupies one row.

To generate a list of 1-subcubes, we need to compare each of the minterms in group G_i with each of the minterms in group G_{i+1}, and generate a 1-subcube for group G_i in the list of 1-subcubes if these minterms differ in one variable. For example, according to Figure 4.16(b), minterm m_0 can be combined with minterm m_2 to generate a 1-subcube that contains m_0 and m_2 and has the variable values $wxyz = $ 00–0. This 1-subcube can be represented by $w'x'z'$. Similarly, minterm m_0 can also be combined with minterm m_4, generating a 1-subcube whose variable values are $wyxz =$ 0–00, which can be represented by the expression $w'y'z'$. At this point, then, we have completed the generation of 1-subcubes for group G_0, since there are no more minterm pairs in which the first minterm is in group G_0 and the second one in group G_1. Using the same technique, we can then generate the rest of the 1-subcubes for groups G_1, G_2, and G_3. Note that since every minterm on the list of 0-subcubes has been used in at least one 1-subcube, we have inserted a "yes" in every row of the fourth column of Figure 4.16(b).

Having obtained a complete list of 1-subcubes, we can now generate a list of 2-subcubes, as shown in Figure 4.16(d). As you can see, each of the 2-subcubes in this list contains four minterms and can be described by a two-literal term. Again, these 2-subcubes are generated by comparing the 1-subcubes in two succeeding groups, of the 1-subcube list and combining them into 2-subcubes if they differ in the value of exactly one variable; that is, we generate a 2-subcube whenever we find that there is one variable in both 1-subcubes that has a value of 0 in one and of 1 in the other. Note that "–" is not an indication of the value of a variable but is rather a placeholder for a variable that has already been eliminated from the expression. As you can see from Figure 4.16(d), a comparison of all the 1-subcube pairs in Figure 4.16(c) eventually yields a total of four 2-subcubes. Note also that since each 1-subcube was used in generating a 2-subcube, we have inserted a "yes" in every row of the fourth column of Figure 4.16(c).

At this point we now try to combine the 2-subcubes on our list into 3-subcubes, but in this case no 3-subcubes can be found. Therefore, all the 2-subcubes that appear in the list in Figure 4.16(d) are the prime implicants. In other words, the four prime implicants of the function that is specified in Figure 4.16(a) are $w'z'$, $w'y$, yz, and wz. Note that no 1-subcube or 0-subcube is a prime implicant, since each of them is covered by at least one 2-subcube.

4.4.2 Minimal Cover Generation

To determine the minimal cover for a function, we have to determine the EPIs that are to be included in every cover, since EPIs are the implicants which contain those minterms that are covered only once, although an EPI may contain other minterms as well. The best way to find EPIs is to construct a selection table in which each row represents one PI and each column represents a minterm. Within this table we enter an $\times$ at the intersection of a row and a column if and only if the minterm represented by that column is included in the PI represented by that row. After filling out the table we know that the columns that have only one $\times$ in them represent those minterms that are covered only once. Such an $\times$ is then circled, and the corresponding PI is included in the list of essential prime implicants. This procedure is demonstrated below as we continue Example 4.4.

■ **EXAMPLE** *4.5*   EPI selection

PROBLEM   Find all the minimal covers for the function whose PIs were determined in Example 4.4.

SOLUTION   In Example 4.4 we identified four PIs: $w'z'$, $w'y$, yz, and wz. Therefore, we construct our EPI selection table as shown in Figure 4.17(a), indicating in each row the name, expression, and minterm indices of one of the PIs, and assigning one column to every 1-minterm. We then enter an $\times$ to indicate where a given minterm is covered by a given PI. For example, starting with the first row we enter an $\times$ into columns 0, 2, 4, and 6 since we know that the prime implicant P_1 contains the minterms m_0, m_2, m_4, and m_6.

After entering all the required $\times$'s for all the rows, we then indicate those columns that have only one $\times$ by circling that $\times$. As you can see from our table, columns 0, 4, 9, and 13 have only one $\times$ each. Therefore, P_1 and P_4 are EPIs, since they are the only PIs that cover the minterms m_0, m_4, m_9, and m_{13}. Fortunately, P_1 and P_4 also cover the minterms m_2, m_6, m_{11}, and m_{15}, which means that the only

PRIME IMPLICANT NAME	PRIME IMPLICANT EXPRESSION	IMPLICANT MINTERMS	FUNCTION MINTERMS										
			0	2	3	4	6	7	9	11	13	15
P_1	$w'z'$	$(0, 2, 4, 6)$	⊗	×		⊗	×					
P_2	$w'y$	$(2, 3, 6, 7)$		×	×		×	×				
P_3	yz	$(3, 7, 11, 15)$			×			×		×		×
P_4	wz	$(9, 11, 13, 15)$							⊗	×	⊗	×

EPI covered minterms: 0   2   4   6   9   11   13   15
Not covered minterms: 3   7

(a) EPI selection table

PI list: $w'z', w'y, yz, wz$
EPI list: $w'z', wz$
Cover lists: (1) $w'z', wz, w'y$
              (2) $w'z', wz, yz$

(b) PI, EPI, and cover lists

(1) $F = w'z' + wz + w'y$
(2) $F = w'z' + wz + yz$

(c) Minimal-cover expressions

FIGURE 4.17

Selection of prime implicants for Example 4.5.

minterms not covered by either P_1 or P_4 are the minterms m_3 and m_7. Since both of these minterms could be covered by either P_2 or P_3, we have now obtained two minimal covers: As shown in Figure 4.17(b), one cover would contain P_1, P_2, and P_4, while the other would consist of P_1, P_3, and P_4. In Figure 4.17(c) we have shown two minimal sum-of-products expressions corresponding to these two covers.

In Example 4.5 we identified two EPIs that could cover eight of the 10 minterms, which meant that finding a minimal cover was a relatively simple task. In many cases, however, the task of selecting the rest of the PIs to complete the minimal cover may not be as easy as selecting the EPIs. Quite frequently, though, we have a large number of PIs from which to choose, which complicates our selection significantly. One way to find all of these possible covers is to generate first a product of sums, in which each sum represents a set of PIs that covers a particular minterm that has not been covered by any of the EPIs. Next, we multiply out the product-of-sums form to obtain a sum-of-products form in which each product, together with all the EPIs, represents one of the possible covers. Among all the covers, those covers that have the smallest possible number of PIs are the minimal covers. We demonstrate this procedure in the following example.

EXAMPLE 4.6   Minimal cover generation

PROBLEM   Find all the possible minimal covers for the Boolean function given by the map in Figure 4.18(a).

SOLUTION   The generation of the PIs is shown in Figure 4.18(b) and (c), the EPI selection table in Figure 4.18(d), and the list of all the PIs in Figure 4.18(e). In the selection table we find that there are two EPIs, P_1 and P_2, that cover the minterms m_2, m_6, m_8, and m_9.

There are, however, three minterms that are left uncovered by P_1 and P_2: m_7, m_{13}, and m_{15}. Within this group, minterm m_7 could be covered by either P_3 or P_5, m_{13} could be covered by either P_4 or P_6, and m_{15} could be covered by either P_5 or P_6, which can be expressed in terms of the following product of sums of these PIs:

$$(P_3 + P_5)(P_4 + P_6)(P_5 + P_6)$$

Multiplying the second and third sums produces the following expression:

$$(P_3 + P_5)(P_4 P_5 + P_5 P_6 + P_4 P_6 + P_6)$$

Since P_6 covers the same minterms as do P_5 and P_6 and has fewer PIs, we can remove the product $P_5 P_6$ from the expression. For the same reason we can also remove the product $P_4 P_6$, which reduces the cover expression to

$$(P_3 + P_5)(P_4 P_5 + P_6)$$

Multiplying out this expression yields the following lower expression:

$$P_3 P_4 P_5 + P_4 P_5 + P_3 P_6 + P_5 P_6$$

Since P_3, P_4, and P_5 do not constitute the smallest set of PIs, we can remove that set from consideration. According to the remaining expression, then, we are able to cover the minterms m_7, m_{13}, and m_{15} by using P_4 and P_5, or P_3 and P_6, or P_5 and P_6. Finally, by combining these three options with the EPIs defined above, we obtain the three different minimal covers that are shown in Figure 4.18(e).

wx \ yz	00	01	11	10
00				1
01			1	1
11		1	1	
10	1	1		

(a) Map representation

GROUP ID	SUBCUBE MINTERMS	SUBCUBE VALUE w	x	y	z	SUBCUBE COVERED BY 1-SUBCUBE
G_1	(2)	0	0	1	0	yes
	(8)	1	0	0	0	yes
G_2	(6)	0	1	1	0	yes
	(9)	1	0	0	1	yes
G_3	(7)	0	1	1	1	yes
	(13)	1	1	0	1	yes
G_4	(15)	1	1	1	1	yes

(b) List of 0-subcubes

GROUP ID	SUBCUBE MINTERMS	SUBCUBE VALUE w	x	y	z	SUBCUBE COVERED BY 2-SUBCUBE
G_1	(2, 6)	0	–	1	0	no
	(8, 9)	–	0	0	1	no
G_2	(6, 7)	0	1	1	–	no
	(9, 13)	1	0	–	1	no
G_3	(7, 15)	–	1	1	1	no
	(13, 15)	1	–	1	1	no

(c) List of 1-subcubes

PRIME IMPLICANT NAME	PRIME IMPLICANT EXPRESSION	IMPLICANT MINTERMS	FUNCTION MINTERMS 2	6	7	8	9	13	15
P_1	$w'yz'$	(2, 6)	⊗	×					
P_2	$x'y'z$	(8, 9)				⊗	×		
P_3	$w'xy$	(6, 7)		×	×				
P_4	$wx'z$	(9, 13)					×	×	
P_5	xyz	(7, 15)			×				×
P_6	wyz	(13, 15)						×	×
EPI covered minterms:			2	6		8	9		
Not covered minterms:					7			13	15

(d) EPI selection table

PI list: $w'yz'$, $x'y'z$, $w'xy$, $wx'z$, xyz, wyz;

EPI list: $w'yz'$, $x'y'z$;

Cover lists: (1) $w'yz'$, $x'y'z$, $wx'z$, xyz;
(2) $w'yz'$, $x'y'z$, $w'xy$, wyz;
(3) $w'yz'$, $x'y'z$, xyz, wyz

(e) PI, EPI, and cover lists

FIGURE 4.18

PI generation and cover selection for Example 4.6.

As you can see from these examples, this tabulation method works well for Boolean functions that have relatively few prime implicants. Unfortunately, though, when the number of variables grows beyond 10 and the number of implicants grows beyond 100, this tabulation method becomes less efficient, even for CAD tools that are running on high-performance workstations. For this reason, most of the fast CAD tools use a variety of heuristics tailored to a special set of goals, applications, libraries, and technologies.

4.5 TECHNOLOGY MAPPING FOR GATE ARRAYS

In Section 4.4, we discussed certain techniques that are used to derive the standard and factored forms of Boolean functions having n variables. Any one of these forms uses the standard Boolean operators AND, OR, and NOT and can easily be implemented with AND, OR, and NOT gates of up to n inputs.

To reduce the cost and turnaround time, many designs are currently being manufactured with gate-array technology. As described in Section 3.11, a gate array is a two-dimensional arrays of cells within which each cell contains a single gate that has a fixed number of inputs. These gates within the cells are usually m-input NAND (NOR) gates, or, most frequently, 3-input NAND (NOR) gates. To use these gate arrays, then, we need to convert an expression or schematic consisting of AND, OR, and NOT gates into one that consists entirely of m-input NAND (NOR) gates.

This conversion process, called **technology mapping**, includes several distinct tasks that we describe in this section. First, we demonstrate a technique for translating a schematic consisting of various AND, OR, and NOT gates into a schematic comprising nothing but NAND (NOR) gates. This translation task itself involves two distinct parts, conversion and optimization. During conversion, we replace each AND and OR gate with an equivalent NAND (NOR) gates, while during optimization we eliminate any double inverters that were introduced during conversion. After explaining conversion and optimization, we go on to show how an AND (OR) gate with n inputs can be decomposed into an AND (OR) gate with m inputs. Finally, we demonstrate how this decomposition technique can be used to minimize the delay in a NAND (NOR) schematic.

The conversion rules are based on the involution theorem and De Morgan's Law and can be summarized as follows:

$$\text{Rule 1:} \qquad xy = ((xy)')'$$
$$\text{Rule 2:} \quad x + y = ((x + y)')')' = (x'y')'$$
$$\text{Rule 3:} \qquad xy = ((xy)')' = (x' + y')'$$
$$\text{Rule 4:} \quad x + y = ((x + y)')')'$$

Rules 1 and 2 are generally used for the conversion to NAND schematics, while Rules 3 and 4 are generally used for the conversion to NOR schematics. All four of these rules have been shown graphically in Figure 4.19(a). We also use a single optimization rule, which states that any double inverters can be eliminated, since $(x')' = x$ according to the involution theorem. This rule is shown graphically in Figure 4.19(b). Note that in practice, the inverters are implemented with NAND (NOR) gates that have all their inputs tied together. In this discussion we use the inverter symbol instead of the NAND (NOR) symbol so that inverters can easily be distinguished from NAND (NOR) gates.

In simple terms, the procedure for translating AND-OR schematics into NAND (NOR) schematics can be stated as follows:

Replace AND and OR gates with NAND (NOR) gates by using Rules 1 and 2 (3 and 4), and eliminate double inverters whenever possible.

As shown in Table 4.1, this translation procedure can be easily applied to standard sum-of-products and product-of-sums forms. In this table, for example, you can see that a sum-of-products form can be converted to a NAND implementation simply by replacing each gate with a NAND gate. Alternatively, a sum-of-products form can be translated to

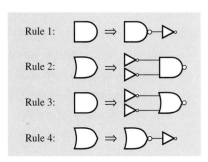

(a) Conversion rules

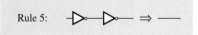

(b) Optimization rule

FIGURE 4.19

Conversion and optimization rules.

TABLE 4.1

Translation of Sum of Products and Product of Sums to NAND and NOR Schematics

FORM TYPE	STANDARD FORM IMPLEMENTATION	NAND IMPLEMENTATION	NOR IMPLEMENTATION
Sum of products			
Product of sums			

a NOR schematic by replacing each gate with a NOR gate and inserting an inverter on each input and output port. You can also see that the reverse is true whenever we are coverting a product-of-sums form to a NAND or NOR implementation. Because of the additional inverters, however, we would rarely use a product-of-sums form to obtain a NAND implementation or a sum-of-products form to obtain a NOR implementation.

EXAMPLE 4.7   Conversion to NAND (NOR) gates

PROBLEM   Derive the NAND and NOR implementations of the carry function originally defined in Table 2.3 and reproduced in map form in Figure 4.20(a).

SOLUTION   In Figure 4.20(b) we show the standard sum-of-products and product-of-sums forms, and on the left-hand

c_i \\ $x_i y_i$	0	01	11	10
0			1	
1		1	1	1

(a) Map definition of the carry function

$$c_{i+1} = x_i y_i + x_i c_i + y_i c_i$$
$$c_{i+1} = (x_i + y_i)(x_i + c_i)(y_i + c_i)$$

(b) Standard forms

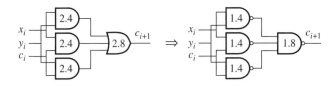

(c) NAND implementation

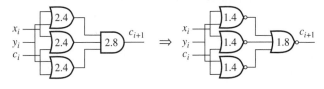

(d) NOR implementation

FIGURE 4.20

NAND and NOR implementations of the carry function.

side in Figure 4.20(c) and (d) we show the straightforward implementations of these forms with AND and OR gates. When converting the sum-of-products implementation into the NAND implementation shown in Figure 4.20(c), we simply replace each AND gate with a NAND gate that is followed by an inverter (Rule 1), and then replace each OR gate with a NAND gate with inverters at its inputs (Rule 2). After eliminating any double inverters, we would then obtain the NAND implementation that has been shown on the right-hand side in Figure 4.20(c).

In a similar fashion, we could use Rules 3 and 4 to translate the product-of-sums implementation into a NOR implementation. After the double-inverter elimination, we obtain the NOR implementation shown on the right in Figure 4.20(d).

In these figures and from the data presented in Table 3.14 you can see the improved performance of these NAND and NOR implementations, which have a delay of only 3.2 ns from any input to the output, in contrast to the AND–OR and OR–AND implementations, which required 5.2 ns. Furthermore, we know that these NAND and NOR implementations have a lower cost as well, since they require 16 transistors, in contrast to the 24 transistors required by the AND–OR and OR–AND implementations.

In Example 4.7 we have seen how to convert AND and OR gates into NAND (NOR) gates. However, if we are to use the NAND (NOR) gates that are available in a gate array, we need to be aware that the gates in such an array will have only m inputs, whereas AND and OR terms may have up to n inputs, where n may be much larger than m. To be able to use m-input NAND (NOR) gates, we must learn to decompose these larger AND and OR terms into m-input AND and OR gates.

In this procedure, sometimes called **term decomposition**, each n-input AND (OR) gate is decomposed into a tree of m-input AND (OR) gates. This tree has $\lceil \log_m n \rceil$ levels and $\lceil (n-1)/(m-1) \rceil$ m-input gates, assuming that the symbol $\lceil x \rceil$ indicates the smallest integer that is greater than x, and the symbol $\lfloor x \rfloor$ indicates the largest integer that is smaller than x. On the first level of this tree, there are $\lfloor n/m \rfloor$ gates; the outputs of these gates, together with the remaining $(n - m(\lfloor n/m \rfloor))$ inputs from the first level, serve as the inputs to gates on the second level. This procedure can then be repeated for each of the $\lceil \log_m n \rceil$ levels. In the following example we demonstrate this decomposition procedure.

EXAMPLE 4.8   Gate decomposition

PROBLEM   Decompose the 10-variable AND term $x_9x_8x_7x_6x_5$ $x_4x_3x_2x_1x_0$ into a tree of three-input AND gates.

SOLUTION   For a 10-variable term, we have $\lceil \log_3 10 \rceil = 3$ levels of gates in the tree and require $\lceil (10-1)/(3-1) \rceil = 5$ gates. Since this AND tree has 10 inputs, it requires $\lfloor 10/3 \rfloor = 3$ gates on the first level. On the second level, it has $3 + (10 - 3(\lfloor 10/3 \rfloor)) = 4$ inputs and therefore requires $\lfloor 4/3 \rfloor = 1$ gate, and on the third level, it has $1 + (4 - 3(\lfloor 4/3 \rfloor)) = 2$ inputs and 1 gate. These computations, which determine the proper number of gates in each level, are summarized in Figure 4.21(a).

LEVEL NUMBER	NUMBER OF INPUTS	NUMBER OF GATES
1	10	$\lfloor 10/3 \rfloor = 3$
2	$3 + (10 - 3(\lfloor 10/3 \rfloor)) = 4$	$\lfloor 4/3 \rfloor = 1$
3	$1 + (4 - 3(\lfloor 4/3 \rfloor)) = 2$	1

(a) Input and gate computation on each level

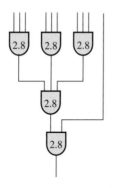

(b) One possible decomposition

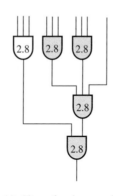

(c) Alternative decomposition

FIGURE   4.21
Decomposition of 10-input AND gate into 3-input AND gates.

Once we have determined the number of gates on each level, we still need to determine how the inputs should be connected to the gates on the first level, and how gate outputs on one level are to be connected to the gate inputs on the next level. This can be accomplished in several ways, each of which can result in a different combination of delays between some inputs and the output. In Figures 4.21(b) and (c) we present two possible decompositions that would enable us to implement the 10-input AND gate with five 3-input AND gates. Note that these two possible decompositions differ only in the propagation delay of some of its input/output paths. In Figure 4.21(b), for example, the propagation delay to the output from all the inputs except the rightmost one is 8.4 ns, and the propagation delay from the rightmost input to the output is only 2.8 ns. By contrast, in Figure 4.21(c), the propagation delay from the three leftmost inputs and the rightmost input to the output is 5.6 ns, while the propagation delay from the other inputs to the output is 8.4 ns.

As a rule, the decomposition of AND and OR gates must precede the conversion task whenever the number of literals in a given product or sum term exceeds m. In other words, the conversion to NAND (NOR) gates and the double-inverter elimination can be performed only after the decomposition, as the following example demonstrates.

EXAMPLE 4.9   Technology mapping for gate arrays

PROBLEM   Implement the full-adder sum function using 3-input NAND gates.

SOLUTION   The sum function, defined initially in Table 2.3, is represented by the map shown in Figure 4.22(a). As you know by now, its sum-of-products form, which we derived in Figure 4.7(c), can be written as follows:

$$s_i = x_i'y_i'c_i + x_i'y_ic_i' + x_iy_i'c_i' + x_iy_ic_i$$

From this standard form, then, we can obtain the AND–OR implementation shown in Figure 4.22(b).

Since the OR gate in this schematic has four inputs, we need to decompose it into two OR gates with no more than three inputs each, as shown in Figure 4.22(c). After this decomposition, we can now use the first two inversion rules to convert each gate into a three-input NAND gate, which would yield the schematic that is shown in Figure 4.22(d). Finally, we can eliminate any double inverters to obtain the optimized NAND schematic shown in Figure 4.22(e).

As shown in Example 4.8, the decomposition of a large gate can produce a NAND (NOR) tree network in which different paths through the network may incur different delays. This fact can be used to our advantage when we are optimizing a given logic network for performance.

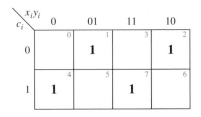

(a) Map representation

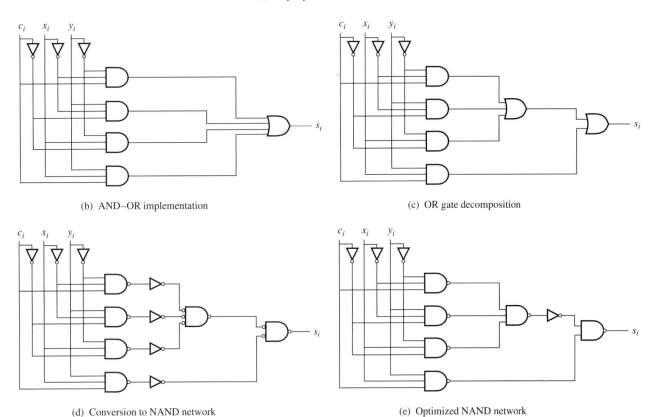

(b) AND–OR implementation

(c) OR gate decomposition

(d) Conversion to NAND network

(e) Optimized NAND network

FIGURE 4.22
Sum function implementation with 3-input NAND gates.

This task of performance optimization, called **retiming**, is generally conducted after the decomposition, conversion, and inverter elimination tasks, when the various delays through the schematic can be calculated accurately. During retiming, we assign the paths that have the shortest delays through the tree networks to the signals with the longest delay through the entire logic network. After retiming, we often have to repeat the conversion and elimination procedures one more time. We demonstrate this retiming process in the following example.

EXAMPLE 4.10 Design retiming

PROBLEM Implement the carry-look-ahead function c_4 using 3-input NAND gates.

SOLUTION The carry function out of the ith bit can be defined by the following equation, where $g_i = x_i y_i$ and $p_i = x_i + y_i$:

$$c_{i+1} = g_i + p_i c_i$$

Therefore, we can derive the following equations to represent the first four carries:

$$c_1 = g_0 + p_0 c_0$$
$$c_2 = g_1 + p_1 c_1$$
$$c_3 = g_2 + p_2 c_2$$
$$c_4 = g_3 + p_3 c_3$$

Through forward substitution, we can express c_4 more directly, in terms of c_0, g_i, and p_i, where $0 \leq i \leq 3$:

$$c_4 = g_3 + p_3 g_2 + p_3 p_2 g_1 + p_3 p_2 p_1 g_0 + p_3 p_2 p_1 p_0 c_0$$

This function is called the 4-bit carry-look-ahead function, since the output carry c_4 does not depend on the intermediate carries c_1, c_2, and c_3. In Figure 4.23(a) we show a straightforward AND–OR implementation that is based on this expression. In Figure 4.23(b) we present one possibility for decomposing this implementation into 3-input AND and OR gates. Next, a conversion to NAND gates and the elimination of double inverters yields the NAND schematic shown in Figure 4.23(c). As you can see from Figure 4.23(c), the maximum input/output delay for this carry-look-ahead network is 8.2 ns.

It is possible, however, that an alternative decomposition of the OR gate would result in a shorter delay. This alternative decomposition assigns the shorter paths through the OR gate to the terms $p_3 p_2 p_1 g_0$ and $p_3 p_2 p_1 c_0$, thereby producing the new performance-optimized decomposition of the carry-look-ahead function shown in Figure 4.23(d). Then, after converting to NAND gates and eliminating double inverters, we obtain the NAND network shown in Figure 4.23(e). Note that the maximum delay through this NAND network is only 6.4 ns, which represents an impressive 30% reduction in the critical-path delay.

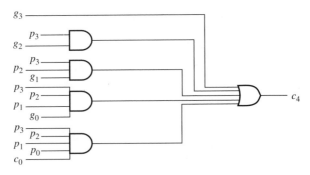

(a) AND–OR implementation

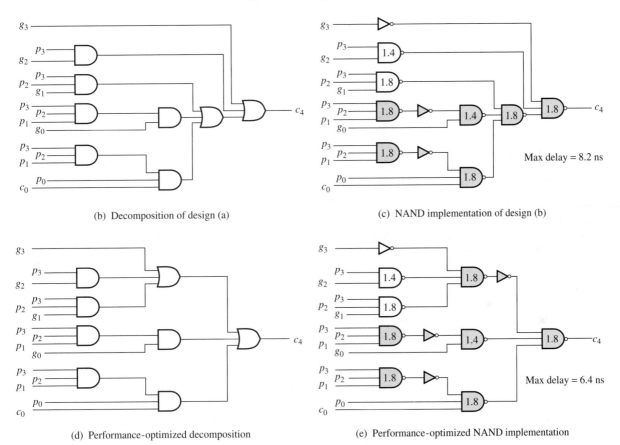

(b) Decomposition of design (a)

(c) NAND implementation of design (b)

(d) Performance-optimized decomposition

(e) Performance-optimized NAND implementation

FIGURE 4.23

Two NAND implementations of the 4-bit carry-look-ahead function.

In Figure 4.24 we present a flowchart of the translation procedure used for gate arrays, in which multilevel AND–OR networks are to be converted into networks of m-input NAND gates. As we demonstrated

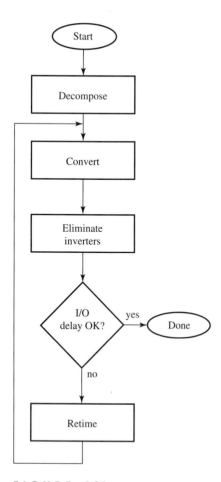

F I G U R E 4.24

Technology mapping procedure for gate arrays.

in Example 4.10, this procedure consists of four tasks: decomposition, conversion, elimination, and retiming. In the decomposition task we break large AND and OR gates into trees of m-input AND and OR gates. In the conversion task we replace each of these AND–OR gates with an equivalent combination of NAND (NOR) and NOT gates. Then the elimination task removes unnecessary double inverters. After elimination we calculate the input/output delays for all input/output paths, and paths that have the longest delay are flagged for closer examination. If possible, these delays on the critical paths are reduced by retiming, which can be iterated as many times as necessary, until we reach the point where no further reduction of critical-path delay is possible.

4.6 TECHNOLOGY MAPPING FOR CUSTOM LIBRARIES

In previous sections we discussed the conversion task of transferring a schematic consisting of AND, OR, and NOT gates into a NAND or NOR schematic in which every NAND or NOR gate has only m-inputs. As our examples have shown, the conversion task can be quite simple in this context, since once the original expression or schematic has been decomposed into m-input AND and OR gates, conversion is basically a matter of replacing each m-input AND or OR gate with the unique combination of a NAND or NOR gate. When we are working with custom libraries, however, this conversion procedure becomes more complex, just because these libraries contain complex gates such as AOI and OAI gates, which means that each gate in the original schematic could be replaced by more than one gate in the library. Furthermore, this also means that each gate in the library could replace several gates in the original schematic. For this reason, technology mapping for custom libraries requires us to group the gates in the original schematic in such a way that each group will represent one of the library gates, while at the same time, the mapped schematic will have the minimal delay or implementation cost.

The task of grouping the gates in the original schematic can be thought of as a task of covering the original schematic with library gates. By minimizing delay, then, we mean selecting that cover for which the maximum delay from any input to the output is minimal. Similarly, by minimizing cost, we mean selecting the cover for which the cost is minimal.

Although it is sometimes possible to minimize delay and cost at the same time, delay and cost minimization generally turn out to be two contradictory goals. To minimize delay, for example, input signals should pass through as few gates as possible. For this reason, delay-optimized circuits tend to use a standard sum-of-products (product-of-sums) form, which requires only two levels of gates, although these forms may require more gates and also gates with a larger number of inputs than the nonstandard forms. To minimize cost, however, the opposite is true, as the implementation schematic should have as few gates as possible, and each gate should have as few inputs as possible. For this reason, cost-optimized circuits tend to use maximally factored nonstandard forms, with more than two levels of gates, which require fewer gates and gates with fewer inputs than the standard forms. From this discussion we see that cost minimization can be seen to increase the delay by introducing extra levels of gates, whereas delay minimization tends to increase the cost by increasing the number of gates and the number of inputs required for each gate.

In many cases, however, these two goals can be synchronized while we perform technology mapping. Since the goal of delay minimization is to reduce the delay on the longest input/output path, called the **critical path**, there is no reason why all the noncritical paths could not be optimized for cost, as long as the delay of the noncritical paths does not exceed the delay of the critical path. Therefore, when we perform technology mapping, we always begin by minimizing the delay of the critical path and then proceed to minimize the cost of the noncritical paths. To determine the critical path, we generally map the given schematic into a NAND or NOR schematic, since NAND and NOR gates are usually the fastest gates in any library. In the following example, we demonstrate this task of technology mapping for a custom library.

EXAMPLE *4.11*   Technology   mapping   for   custom libraries

PROBLEM   Convert the expression $w'z' + z(w + y)$ into a logic schematic using any of the gates from the library defined in Tables 3.14, 3.15, and 3.16.

SOLUTION   As shown in Figure 4.25(a), the expression $w'z' + z(w + y)$ can easily be implemented with the AND, OR, and NOT gates found in this library. By adding the individual gate delays that have been indicated inside the symbol for each gate, we can see that the longest delay is from input y or w to output F and is equal to 7.2 ns. Furthermore, since we know that each 2-input AND or OR gate requires six transistors, and each inverter requires two transistors, we can also see that the total cost of this implementation is equal to 28 transistors.

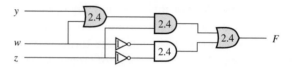

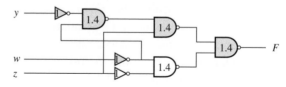

(a) AND–OR implementation (delay = 7.2 ns, cost = 28)

(b) NAND implementation (delay = 5.2 ns, cost = 22)

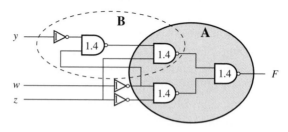

(c) Two possible conversions

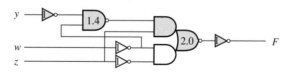

(d) Alternative A (delay = 5.4 ns, cost = 20)

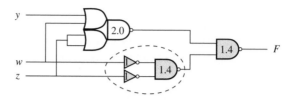

(e) Alternative B (delay = 3.8 ns, cost = 20)

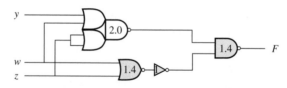

FIGURE 4.25
Example of technology mapping tasks.

(f) Cost-optimized alternative B (delay = 3.8 ns, cost = 18)

On the other hand, if we convert this schematic to NAND gates by following the procedure described in Section 4.5, we can obtain the schematic shown in Figure 4.25(b), for which the delay on the critical path is only 5.2 ns and the total cost is only 22 transistors. As you can see in Figure 4.25(c), this schematic allows two possible conversions on the critical path from y or w to F, shown here as alternatives A and B. If we implement alternative A, we replace three gates with a 2-wide, 2-input AOI gate and an inverter, as shown in Figure 4.25(d). Unfortunately, this substitution increases the delay on the critical path by 0.2 ns, even while it reduces the total cost to 20 transistors. By contrast, if we implement alternative B, replacing three gates with a 2-wide, 2-input OAI gate, as shown in Figure 4.25(e), we can reduce the delay on the critical path to 3.4 ns and reduce the cost to 20 transistors. At the same time, though, we will be introducing a new critical path from inputs w and z to output F, which will have a delay of 3.8 ns.

Since we have generated a new critical path, we need to turn our attention to reducing its delay. For this critical path, however, no delay reduction can be achieved, although a slight cost reduction can be obtained by replacing the group of two inverters and the 2-input NAND gate indicated in Figure 4.25(e) by a 2-input NOR gate and one inverter. The final result, shown in Figure 4.25(f), has a critical-path delay of 3.8 ns and a total cost of 18 transistors.

As a rule, the conversion procedure demonstrated in Example 4.10, which is summarized in the flowchart in Figure 4.26, could be applied to any schematic and any library. To begin with, we convert the given schematic into a NAND or NOR implementation, because this will enable us to estimate its input/output delays more accurately. Then we sort all its paths according to the amount of their delays. Having determined which is the longest path, we try to cover one gate on its critical path with one of the gates in the library. For every possibility that we try, we record its performance and cost gain with the goal of finding the single gate cover that achieves the highest gain. This procedure is repeated until all the gates on the critical path have been covered by at least one of the library gates. At that point we select the most profitable alternative and recompute the delays on the rest of the paths and use the same procedures to cover the longest of the noncovered paths. Finally, when all the paths in the schematic have been covered, the conversion

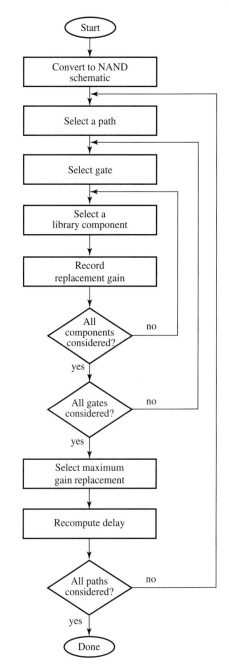

FIGURE   4.26
Conversion   procedure   for   custom libraries.

procedure terminates and we can proceed with inverter elimination and retiming, as described in Figure 4.24.

4.7 HAZARD-FREE DESIGN

When designing combinatorial circuits, we must ensure that the circuit operates properly under all possible conditions. One condition that may make a circuit malfunction is called a **hazard**. Hazards generate short unwanted glitches that appear at the output because of different propagation delays on different but converging paths through the circuit. More precisely, a **glitch** is a short-duration change in the output value when no output change is expected.

We demonstrate the concept of a hazard on the example in Figure 4.27, in which we show the map representation and the corresponding logic schematic for the Boolean function $F = xy' + yz$.

From the schematic in Figure 4.27(b), we see that there are two different paths labeled a and b, from input y to the output F with two different propagation delays. The delay on path a, which goes from y to F through the inverter, an AND gate, and the OR gate, is 5.8 ns, while the delay on path b, which only goes through an AND gate, and the OR gate is 4.8 ns. In the case when $x = z = 1$ and $y = 1$, the output F will be 1 through path b. Similarly, when $x = z = 1$ and $y = 0$, the output F will be 1 through path a. Therefore, in an ideal design, in which each gate has 0 delay, the output F should stay 1 when y changes from 1 to 0, since a becomes equal to 1 at the time that b becomes 0. However, in reality, a needs 3.4 ns to become equal to 1, while b becomes equal to 0 in 2.4 ns, forcing F to 0 for 1 ns. This situation is shown in Figure 4.27(c), in which y changes to 0 at t_0, followed by b changing to 0 at $t_0 + 2.4$ ns, and a changing to 1 at $t_0 + 3.4$.

Since F is equal to the value or a of the value of b, F changes to 0 at $t_1 = t_0 + 4.8$ ns and back to 1 at $t_2 = t_0 + 5.8$ ns. This 1-ns glitch is caused by a **static 1-hazard**, in the implementation of the Boolean function F. More precisely, we say that a logic schematic has a static 1-hazard if there are two 1-minterms that differ in only one variable but are not covered by a common product term in a sum-of-products implementation. Similarly, we can define a **static 0-hazard** as a condition in which there are two 0-minterms not covered by a common sum term in a product-of-sums implementation. For example, if we implement function F in Figure 4.27 using the product-of-sums from $(x + y)(y' + z)$, we can observe a 1-ns positive glitch when y changes from 0 to 1 and $x = z = 0$.

The definition of hazard suggests the technique for designing hazard-free circuits. From the hazard definition, we know that a 1-

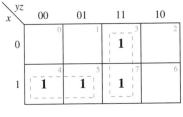

$$F = xy' + yz$$

(a) Map representation

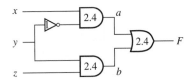

(b) Logic schematic

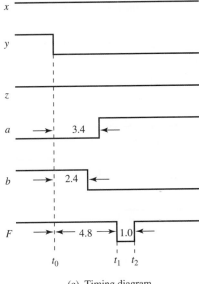

(c) Timing diagram

F I G U R E *4.27*
Design with static 1-hazard.

hazard exists because two different product terms are used to cover two adjacent 1-minterms. Therefore, to eliminate a hazard we must include an additional prime implicant covering both adjacent 1-minterms in the sum-of-products form. This additional prime implicant is redundant since the sum-of-products form with and without it defines the same Boolean function.

In Figure 4.28 we have demonstrated the elimination of the hazard for the example presented in Figure 4.27. As we have seen from

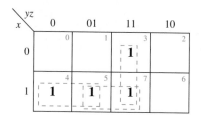

$$F = xy' + yz + xz$$

(a) Map representation

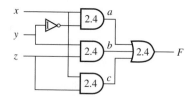

(b) Logic schematic

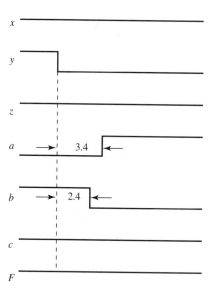

(c) Timing diagram

FIGURE 4.28
Hazard-free design.

Figure 4.27, the minimal sum-of-products form contains two essential prime implicants: xy' and yz. In Figure 4.28(a) we indicated two adjacent 1-minterms, m_5 and m_7, that are covered by two different prime implicants. These two minterms introduce the glitch when variable y

changes from 1 to 0 as shown in Figure 4.27(c). To avoid this glitch we must add the prime implicant xz to the sum of products. This prime implicant will introduce an additional gate whose output is labeled c in the logic schematic in Figure 4.28(b). As shown in the timing diagram in Figure 4.28(c), this redundant gate prevents the occurrence of a glitch since the value of $c = xz$ is equal to 1 during the change in the value of y as long as $x = z = 1$. A similar technique for designing hazard-free circuits can be applied to product-of-sum form, in which we add redundant prime implicants to avoid static 0-hazards.

In general, static hazards are caused by two complementary signals (such as y and y'), which become equal for short periods of time due to different delays on different paths through the schematic. If, in addition, two signals that always have the same value become different for a short period of time, we say that the design has a **dynamic hazard**. This situation occurs when the same variable value propagates through the design on two different paths with different delays. A dynamic hazard causes a glitch on the output after transition from 0 to 1 or 1 to 0.

As an example, let us consider the design in Figure 4.29, which was obtained by adding an AND and an OR gate to the design with static 1-hazard from Figure 4.27(b). As shown in the timing diagram in Figure 4.29(b), signal c generates a glitch at $t_0 + 4.8$ ns after y changes from 1 to 0 at t_0. On the other hand, signal d changes from 0 to 1 at $t_1 = t_0 + 3.4$ ns. Since c is equal to 1 at that time, the output F will change to 1 at $t_2 = t_1 + 2.4$ ns. However, the glitch on signal c will appear at the output at $t_2 + 1.4$ ns and disappear 1 ns later at $t_2 + 2.4$ ns.

This dynamic hazard can be eliminated from the design in several different ways. One way is to eliminate the static hazard by introducing a redundant prime implicant, as explained earlier. The other way is to delay the change on d until t_2 by inserting another gate with a delay of 2.4 ns or more on d between the OR gate and the output AND gate. This additional delay will postpone the change of d from 0 to 1 until t_2 and the change of F from 0 to 1 until $t_2 + 2.4$ ns when the glitch has already disappeared.

So far we have demonstrated static and dynamic hazards that cause a circuit to malfunction during single-variable changes. The detection and elimination of hazard situations for multiple-variable changes is more difficult and beyond the scope of this book.

In conclusion, the hazards in combinatorial logic are not so critical since outputs reach the proper steady value after some time. On the other hand, hazards in sequential circuits are critical since glitches can be mistaken for valid signal pulses and steer a sequential component into the wrong state without the possibility to recover from this malfunction.

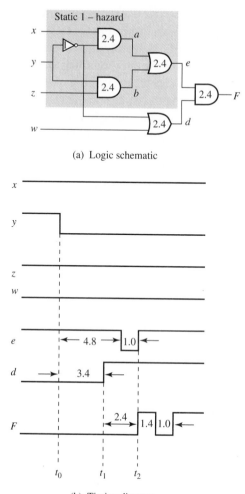

(a) Logic schematic

(b) Timing diagram

FIGURE 4.29
Dynamic hazard.

4.8 CHAPTER SUMMARY

In this chapter we introduced two methods for simplifying expressions of Boolean functions. The first method is based on the map representation of a Boolean function, which is very convenient for visual identification of prime implicants. Although the map method is very useful in this identification, it does not provide a systematic procedure for selecting the proper implicants to be included in the minimal cover. The tabulation method, on the other hand, provides a systematic procedure for finding all the prime implicants, selecting the essential prime implicants, and finding all the minimal covers that will be used for implementation of a Boolean function. Although the tabulation method guarantees finding all minimal covers, it is not computationally practical for Boolean functions with a large number of variables since it requires a long time to find all the minimal covers. For this reason, most of the CAD tools for logic synthesis use a variety of heuristics to shorten the running time of synthesis algorithms.

Including map and tabulation methods, most methods for the simplification of Boolean functions minimize the number of operators in the expression that is used for function implementation. Since those implementations are constructed with gates from different libraries, we need to follow the simplification task with a procedure for technology mapping which maps the operators in a Boolean expression to gates from the given library. In this chapter we introduced two methods for technology mapping. The first method is designed for gate arrays in which the entire library consists of a single NAND or NOR gate with a fixed number of inputs. In this method we first decompose the large gates to smaller gates with the same number of inputs as the NAND or NOR gate in the library and then convert each gate into library gates by using the given conversion rules. After the gate conversion we perform inverter elimination to reduce cost and retiming to reduce the propagation delay on the critical paths.

The second method presented is designed for custom libraries which include complex gates that can perform several different Boolean operations concurrently. In this method we first implement a Boolean function with NAND and NOR gates to estimate propagation delay accurately and find critical paths in the implementations. After the delay estimation, we first attempt to reduce the delay on critical paths and then attempt to reduce the cost of noncritical paths. In this way we can satisfy both of the two contradictory goals of cost and performance optimization.

4.9 FURTHER READINGS

Devadas, S., A. Ghosh, and K. Keutzer. *Logic Synthesis.* New York: McGraw-Hill, 1994.

>A very detailed mathematical exposition of algorithms used in CAD tools for logic synthesis. Recommended for students who are interested in logic synthesis algorithms and CAD tools.

Karnaugh, M. "A map method for synthesis of combinatorial logic circuits." *Transactions of the AIEE, Communications and Electronics*, Vol. 72, Part I (November 1953), pp. 593–599.

>The paper that introduced the map method.

McCluskey, E. *Logic Design Principles.* Englewood Cliffs, NJ: Prentice Hall, 1986.

>An introductory book on logic design by one of the pioneers in the field. Includes a good overview of design principles, hazard-free design, and testing methods, as well as McCluskey's original formulation of the tabulation method.

Quine, W. "The problem of simplifying truth functions." *American Mathematical Monthly*, Vol. 59 (October 1952), pp. 521–531.

>The paper that introduced the tabulation method.

4.10 PROBLEMS

4.1 (Cube representation) For the following Boolean functions, specify the cube representations and identify all the subcubes.
 (a) $F = y_1'y_0' + x_0y_1' + x_1y_1' + x_1x_0 + x_1y_0'$
 (b) $F = w'z' + wz + w'y$
 (c) $F = w'x' + xy + wy'$
 (d) $F = x'y'z' + wy'z + xyz' + w'yz'$

4.2 (Map representation) Generate the map representations for the following Boolean functions.
 (a) $F = w'x' + xy + wy' + wx$
 (b) $F = x_1'x_0' + x_1'y_0 + y_1y_0 + x_1'y_1 + x_0'y_1$
 (c) $F = w'z' + wz + w'y + yz$
 (d) $F = w'x'z' + w'xy + wxz + wx'y + w'yz'$

4.3 (Standard forms) Using the map method, find the standard sum-of-products form for the following Boolean functions.
 (a) $F = y_1'(y_0' + x_0) + x_1(y_1' + x_0 + y_0')$
 (b) $F = x_1'x_0'y_1'y_0' + x_1'x_0y_1'y_0 + x_1x_0y_1y_0 + x_1x_0'y_1y_0'$
 (c) $F = w'z' + yz + wz$
 (d) $F = w'y'z' + xy'z + wyz + x'yz'$

4.4 (Map method) Using the map method, determine the prime implicants of the following Boolean functions.
 (a) $F = x_1'x_0' + y_1y_0 + x_1'x_0y_1'y_0 + x_1'x_0y_1y_0' + x_1x_0'y_1y_0'$
 (b) $F = w'x' + w'xy + wx'y' + wx$
 (c) $F = w'y'z' + xy'z + wyz + x'yz'$
 (d) $F = w'y + w'x'z + xyz' + wx'y' + wy'z'$

4.5 (Map method) Find all of the essential prime implicants for the following Boolean functions.
 (a) $F = y_1'(y_0' + x_0 + x_1) + x_1(x_0 + y_0')$
 (b) $F = x_1'x_0'y_1'y_0' + x_1'x_0y_1'y_0 + x_1x_0y_1y_0 + x_1x_0'y_1y_0'$
 (c) $F = w'x'z' + w'x'y + wxz + wx'y'$
 (d) $F = y'z + wyz + w'(y' + z')$

4.6 (Map method) Find all the minimal covers for the following Boolean functions.
 (a) $F = w'x' + w'xy + wx + wx'y' + xy$
 (b) $F = yz + w'z' + wy'z$
 (c) $F = x'y'z' + wy'z + xyz + w'yz'$
 (d) $F = wy'z' + wx'y' + w'y + w'x'y'z + wxyz'$

4.7 (Tabulation method) Using the tabulation method, find all the prime implicants for the following Boolean expressions.
 (a) $F = \sum(0, 4, 5, 8, 9, 10, 12, 13, 14, 15)$
 (b) $F = \sum(0, 1, 2, 4, 5, 6, 9, 11, 13, 15)$
 (c) $F = \sum(1, 2, 3, 6, 7, 8, 9, 12, 14)$
 (d) $F = \sum(0, 2, 4, 5, 10, 11, 13, 15)$

4.8 (Tabulation method) Using the tabulation method, find all the essential prime implicants and minimal covers for the following Boolean expressions.
 (a) $F = \sum(0, 1, 2, 3, 5, 6, 7, 10, 11, 15)$
 (b) $F = \sum(0, 1, 2, 3, 6, 7, 8, 9, 12, 13, 14, 15)$
 (c) $F = \sum(0, 2, 4, 5, 10, 11, 13, 15)$
 (d) $F = \sum(1, 2, 3, 6, 7, 8, 9, 12, 14)$

4.9 (Tabulation method) Using the tabulation method, find all the minimal covers for the following Boolean functions.
 (a) $F = wx + x'y' + w'y$
 (b) $F = w'y'z' + xy'z + wyz + wx'y + w'x'z'$
 (c) $F = wx'y'z' + wxz' + x'y'z + w'y$
 (d) $F = x_1'x_0'y_0 + x_1y_1 + x_1x_0'y_1y_0$

4.10 (Gate-array mapping) Convert the function $wx'y' + yw'z' + yxz + yxw$ into:
 (a) 2-input NAND gates
 (b) 3-input NAND gates
 (c) 4-input NAND. gates

4.11 (Gate-array mapping) Convert the following functions to 3-input NOR gates.
 (a) $F = wx'y' + xyz + w'yz' + wxy$
 (b) $F = wx'y' + y(w'z' + x(z + w))$
 (c) $F = wx'y' + w'yz + xz(w + y)$
 (d) $F = w'(yz' + xy) + w(x'y' + xz)$

4.12 (Gate-array mapping) Assume that the following expressions are to be implemented with 2-input NOR gates and perform the gate decomposition that will minimize their delay.
 (a) $F = w'xyz' + w'y'z' + wy'z + yz + w'x'yz'$
 (b) $F = w'y + wz + w'z'$
 (c) $F = w'x' + wx + w'xy + wy'z' + wx'y'z$
 (d) $F = wy' + xy + w'x + wxyz$

4.13 (Technology mapping) Using the library defined by Tables 3.14, 3.15 and 3.16, perform technology mapping and minimize the delay for the following Boolean functions.
 (a) $F = y_1'(y_0' + x_0 + x_1) + x_1(x_0 + y_0')$
 (b) $F = w'(x'z' + xy) + w(xz + x'y')$
 (c) $F = w'x'z + w'xy + wxz + wx'y'$
 (d) $F = wx'y' + y(w'z' + x(z + w))$

4.14 (Technology mapping) Redo Problem 4.13 using only the library defined by Table 3.14.

4.15 (Technology mapping) Redo Problem 4.13 using only the library defined by Table 3.16.

4.16 (Technology mapping) Beginning with the full subtractor defined by the table in Problem 3.15, design a minimal-delay implementation that uses:

    (a) The custom library defined by Table 3.14.

    (b) The custom library defined by Tables 3.14 and 3.15.

    (c) The custom library defined by Tables 3.14, 3.15, and 3.16.

4.17 (Technology mapping) Derive a minimum-delay implementation for the carry-look-ahead function $c_4 = g_3 + p_3 g_2 + p_3 p_2 g_1 + p_3 p_2 p_1 g_0 + p_3 p_2 p_1 p_0 c_0$ that uses:

    (a) The custom library defined by Table 3.14.

    (b) The custom library defined by Tables 3.14 and 3.15.

    (c) The custom library defined by Tables 3.14, 3.15, and 3.16.

4.18 (Hazard-free design) Detect and correct all of the static hazards for the proposed solution in Example 4.1.

4.19 (Hazard-free design) Design a hazard-free implementation for the Boolean function given in Example 4.2.

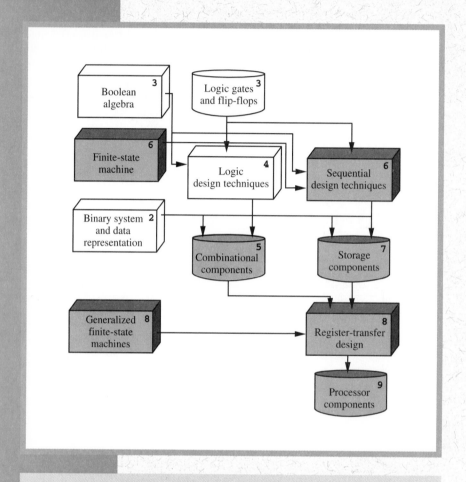

Most digital systems, including computers, are designed to transform data. These transformations can be of various types, including arithmetic operations, logic operations, encoding and decoding of data, and data reorganization. In general, these transformations are performed by register-level combinatorial components, which consist of nothing but gates, and can be used in the construction of processors and other ASICs. In this chapter we use the digital design techniques we discussed in previous chapters to design a library of generic register-level combinatorial components. Throughout the rest of this book we use these components in the specification and implementation of various microchip architectures.

CHAPTER

5

Combinatorial Components

In this chapter we design the basic combinatorial components that are used at the register level of digital design. These combinatorial components, together with a variety of storage components, make up the microarchitecture of all standard processors as well as custom application-specific ICs. Combinatorial components can be used for data transformation, for interconnection, and for control. More specifically, data transformation components perform arithmetic operations (addition, subtraction, multiplication and division), logic operations (AND, OR, XOR, and complement), comparison operations (greater than, equal to and less than), and bit manipulation operations (shift, rotation, extraction, and insertion). The interconnect components, comprising selectors and buses, are used to connect the arithmetic and storage components. Conversion components such as decoders and encoders are used for conversion between different codes. Finally, universal components such as read-only memories (ROMs) and programmable-logic arrays (PLAs) are used primarily in the design of control units.

In the following sections we describe all of these components and show how they can be constructed from standard gates. To simplify the explanations, we use only generic AND, OR, XOR, and NOT gates and do not attempt to optimize each design for a particular technology or library.

5.1 RIPPLE-CARRY ADDERS

In this section we describe the arithmetic components that we used to perform binary addition. As we explained in Chapter 2, we add two binary numbers, such as $x = x_{n-1} \cdots x_0$ and $y = y_{n-1} \cdots y_0$, by adding together each pair of bits x_i and y_i, as well as the carry bit c_i, which is carried over from the previous bit position. By adding these bits for each position i between 0 and $n-1$, we can produce the sum bit s_i and an output carry bit c_{i+1}. This procedure for single-bit addition was described in the truth table in Table 2.3 and is repeated in Figure 5.1(a).

To obtain the logic schematic for this binary adder, we need to convert the truth table in Figure 5.1(a) into the map representation in Figure 5.1(b). From this representation we can then derive Boolean expressions that have a minimal number of literals, which we will need for the design of this single-bit adder. Since this adder performs the addition of two operand bits x_i and y_i, and the carry bit c_i, it is generally known as a **full adder** (FA). As you will recall, we used this FA extensively in Chapter 3 as our example of how to implement a given Boolean function with different libraries (Examples 3.7 and 3.8) and technologies (Figures 3.21, 3.22, and 3.24). In Figure 5.1(c) we show the logic schematic for this FA, consisting of five generic gates.

As a rule, any binary adder can be implemented as a serial connection of FAs, arranged such that the output carry of each FA serves as the input carry for the next-higher significant FA. For example, an 8-bit adder consists of eight FAs that have been connected according to the schematic in Figure 5.1(d). In general, any n-bit adder, whose graphic symbol has been shown in Figure 5.1(e), could be constructed in this manner. As you can see, the longest delay in such an adder would

x_i	y_i	c_i	c_{i+1}	s_i
0	0	0	0	0
0	0	1	0	1
0	1	0	0	1
0	1	1	1	0
1	0	0	0	1
1	0	1	1	0
1	1	0	1	0
1	1	1	1	1

(a) Truth table for full adder

$$s_i = x_i \oplus y_i \oplus c_i$$

$$c_{i+1} = x_i y_i + c_i(x_i \oplus y_i)$$

(b) Map representation

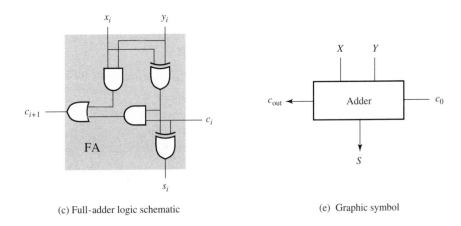

(c) Full-adder logic schematic

(e) Graphic symbol

(d) Eight-bit adder unit

FIGURE 5.1
Ripple-carry adder.

be from the input carry c_0, or the least significant bits x_0 and y_0, to the output carry c_{out}. In other words, any change in c_0, x_0, or y_0 has to propagate or ripple through all the FAs, which is why we refer to this kind of adder as a **ripple-carry adder**.

5.2 CARRY-LOOK-AHEAD ADDERS

It is possible, however, to reduce the delay of the carry chain in this kind of ripple-carry adder by using what we call the carry-look-ahead technique. This technique takes advantage of the fact that the major part of the expressions for each carry in the chain can be precomputed. To explain this concept, we look first at precomputing carries for a 4-bit adder slice, which adds $x_{i+3}x_{i+2}x_{i+1}x_i$, $y_{i+3}y_{i+2}y_{i+1}y_i$, and the input carry c_i. In this adder slice, if we define carry-generate function $g_i = x_iy_i$ and carry-propagate function $p_i = x_i \oplus y_i$, the four carries $c_{i+1}, \ldots, c_{i+4}$ can be expressed as follows:

$$c_{i+1} = g_i + p_ic_i \tag{5.1}$$

$$c_{i+2} = g_{i+1} + p_{i+1}c_{i+1} \tag{5.2}$$

$$c_{i+3} = g_{i+2} + p_{i+2}c_{i+2} \tag{5.3}$$

$$c_{i+4} = g_{i+3} + p_{i+3}c_{i+3} \tag{5.4}$$

Furthermore, after forward substitution, we can express each of these four carries in terms of c_i, as in the following expressions:

$$c_{i+1} = g_i + p_ic_i \tag{5.5}$$

$$c_{i+2} = g_{i+1} + p_{i+1}g_i + p_{i+1}p_ic_i \tag{5.6}$$

$$c_{i+3} = g_{i+2} + p_{i+2}g_{i+1} + p_{i+2}p_{i+1}g_i + p_{i+2}p_{i+1}p_ic_i \tag{5.7}$$

$$c_{i+4} = g_{i+3} + p_{i+3}g_{i+2} + p_{i+3}p_{i+2}g_{i+1}$$
$$+ p_{i+3}p_{i+2}p_{i+1}g_i + p_{i+3}p_{i+2}p_{i+1}p_ic_i \tag{5.8}$$

Equations (5.5)–(5.8) show that carries $c_{i+1}, c_{i+2}, c_{i+3}$, and c_{i+4} can be computed directly from input bits and input carry c_i without the ripple effect. In other words, none of Equations (5.5)–(5.8) depends on $c_{i+1}, c_{i+2}, c_{i+3}$, or c_{i+4}. However, this technique cannot easily be extended to n-bit slices, where n is larger than four, because of fan-in and fan-out limitations. As we can observe from Equations (5.5)–(5.8), the number of product terms and the number of literals in each product term increases by one with each successive equations, which, in turn, requires gates with $n + 1$ inputs for an n-bit slice. If the available library contains gates with much smaller fan-in, these large gates must be implemented with multiple levels of gates as we have shown in Example 4.10. Such an implementation with multiple gates introduces longer delays, which contradicts the goal of speeding up carry propagation.

Similarly to increase in the number and size of terms in Equations (5.5)–(5.8), we can observe an increase in variable appearance in those terms. More precisely, each variable p_{i+k}, $0 \le k \le n - 1$, appears $(k + 1)(n - k)$ times in the carry equations. For example, p_i appears four times, and p_{i+1}, p_{i+2}, and p_{i+3} appear 6, 6, and 4 times, respectively. With a higher number of variable appearances, we must increase the fan-out of their drivers, which in turn increases the size and delay of the entire implementation. For these practical reasons n is usually limited to 4.

Equation (5.8) can then be also rewritten as

$$c_{i+4} = g_{(i,i+3)} + p_{(i,i+3)}c_i \qquad (5.9)$$

in which

$$g_{(i,i+3)} = g_{i+3} + p_{i+3}g_{i+2} + p_{i+3}p_{i+2}g_{i+1}$$
$$+ p_{i+3}p_{i+2}p_{i+1}g_i \qquad (5.10)$$

$$p_{(i,i+3)} = p_{i+3}p_{i+2}p_{i+1}p_i \qquad (5.11)$$

In Equations (5.5)–(5.11), we have defined the combinatorial component, which is called a **carry-look-ahead** (CLA) **generator**. In Equations (5.10) and (5.11), specifically, we have defined the carry-generate and carry-propagate functions for a 4-bit slice that can be used by the higher-order CLAs for generating carries beyond a 4-bit slice.

This CLA generator can be used to replace the 4-bit carry chain that computes $c_{i+1}, c_{i+2}, c_{i+3}$ and c_{i+4}, thereby making the adder faster. Consider, for example, how a carry-look-ahead adder compares to a ripple-carry adder. As you can see in Figure 5.2(a), the 4-bit carry chain in the ripple-carry adder consists of four FA carry chains, which appear inside the colored strip in this figure. Within this 4-bit carry chain, each one of the four FA carry chains consists of one AND and one OR gate, used to compute $c_{i+1} = g_i + p_i c_i$.

If, however, we were to replace this carry chain with the CLA generator shown in Figure 5.2(b), we would obtain the CLA adder that is shown in Figure 5.2(c). In this version of the adder the CLA generator would be able to produce four carries with less delay than the ripple-carry chain. The input/output delays for the ripple-carry adder from Figure 5.2(a) and the CLA adder from Figure 5.2(c) have been summarized in Table 5.1. As you can see from the table, the CLA generator takes only 4.8 ns to generate c_{i+4}, which is significantly less than the 19.2 ns required by the ripple-carry chain. Similarly, the delay from x_i or y_i to c_{i+4} is 13.0 ns for the CLA adder, as opposed to 23.4 ns for the ripple-carry adder. From this comparison, then, it is clear that a 4-bit CLA generator will produce a faster 4-bit adder, and that by connecting several of these 4-bit adders, we could significantly improve the speed of larger adders as well. Such a 16-bit adder consisting of four 4-bit carry-look-ahead adders is shown in Figure 5.3(a). The adder is constructed

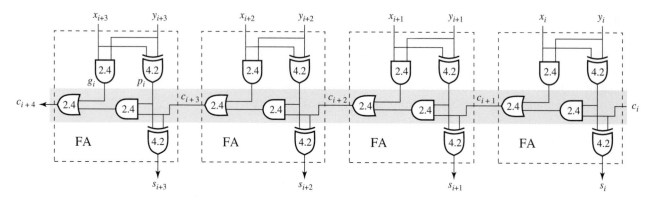

(a) Four-bit slice of a ripple-carry adder

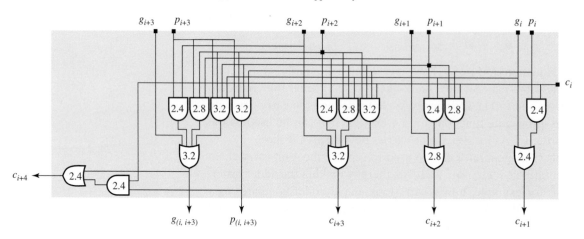

(b) Logic schematic of CLA

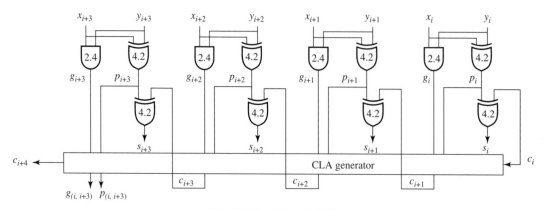

(c) Four-bit adder slice with CLA generator

FIGURE 5.2
CLA generator.

in such a way that carries inside each 4-bit adder are computed with a CLA generator, while 4-bit carries c_4, c_8, c_{12}, and c_{16} ripple through the 4-bit slices in such a way that the output carry from one generator will serve as the input carry to the next more significant generator.

TABLE 5.1

Ripple and CLA Delays for 4-Bit Adder Slice[a]

CARRY CHAIN	RIPPLE DELAY	CLA DELAY
$c_i(x_i, y_i)$ to c_{i+1}	4.8 (9.0)	4.8 (9.0)
$c_i(x_i, y_i)$ to c_{i+2}	9.6 (13.8)	5.6 (9.8)
$c_i(x_i, y_i)$ to c_{i+3}	14.4 (18.6)	6.4 (10.6)
$c_i(x_i, y_i)$ to c_{i+4}	19.2 (23.4)	4.8 (13.0)
$c_i(x_i, y_i)$ to $g_{(i, i+3)}$	Not applicable	6.4 (10.6)
$c_i(x_i, y_i)$ to $p_{(i, i+3)}$	Not applicable	3.2 (7.4)

[a]Values in parentheses are delays from x_i or y_i.

This kind of adder, in which CLA generators are used to speed up carries inside 4-bit slices, while carries between the generators ripple through the adder is called a single-level CLA adder. We can also speed up the generation of 4-bit carries c_4, c_8, c_{12}, and c_{16} by using an additional CLA generator.

Using Equation (5.9), we can express carries c_4, c_8, c_{12}, and c_{16} as follows:

$$c_4 = g_{(0,3)} + p_{(0,3)}c_0 \qquad (5.12)$$

$$c_8 = g_{(4,7)} + p_{(4,7)}c_4 \qquad (5.13)$$

$$c_{12} = g_{(8,11)} + p_{(8,11)}c_8 \qquad (5.14)$$

$$c_{16} = g_{(12,15)} + p_{(12,15)}c_{12} \qquad (5.15)$$

Since Equations (5.12)–(5.15) have the same form as Equations (5.1)–(5.4), we can use a CLA generator to generate carries c_4, c_8, c_{12}, and c_{16} as shown in Figure 5.3(b). Note that in this two-level design, the carries do not ripple through the CLA generators; instead, the second level generates these carries for the first-level CLA generators. In this design, then, the output carries c_4, c_8, c_{12}, and c_{16} from the first level of generators are not used. Instead, the $g_{(i,i+3)}$ and $p_{(i,i+3)}$ outputs from the first-level generators are used to generate those carries within the second-level CLA generator.

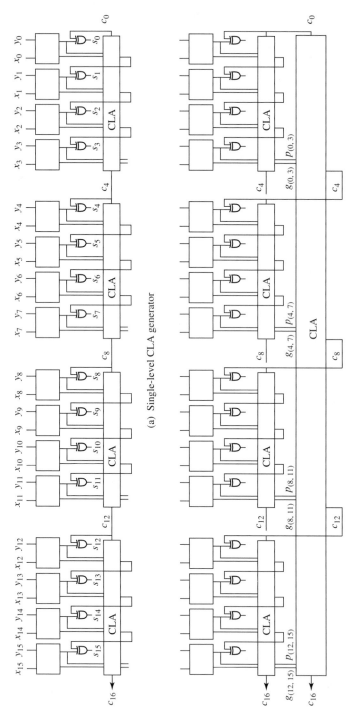

(a) Single-level CLA generator

(b) Two-level CLA generator

FIGURE 5.3

16-bit CLA adder.

Similar to Equation (5.9), we can define carry c_{16} in terms of the input carry c_0 with the following equation:

$$c_{16} = g_{(0,15)} + p_{(0,15)}c_0 \qquad (5.16)$$

The 16-bit carry-generate and carry-propagate functions, $g_{(0,15)}$ and $p_{(0,15)}$, have the same form as those given by Equations (5.10) and (5.11) and they can be used for the generation of higher-order carries c_{16}, c_{32}, c_{48}, and c_{64} in a 64-bit adder with three levels of CLA generators.

In general, in an n-bit adder, we can use $\lceil \log_4 n \rceil$ levels of CLA generators. In Table 5.2 we have compared the delays of the 16-bit adders with one and two levels of CLA generators from Figure 5.3(a) and (b) with the 16-bit ripple-carry adder.

TABLE 5.2

Carry Chain Delays for 16-Bit Adder[a]

CARRY CHAIN	RIPPLE DELAY	ONE-LEVEL CLA	TWO-LEVEL CLA
$c_0(x_0, y_0)$ to c_4	19.2 (23.4)	4.8 (13.0)	4.8 (13.0)
$c_0(x_0, y_0)$ to c_8	38.4 (42.6)	9.6 (17.8)	5.6 (16.2)
$c_0(x_0, y_0)$ to c_{12}	57.6 (61.8)	14.4 (22.6)	6.4 (17.0)
$c_0(x_0, y_0)$ to c_{16}	76.8 (81.0)	19.2 (27.4)	4.8 (19.4)

[a]Values in parentheses are delays from x_0 or y_0.

From the table we see that the 16-bit adder with two levels of CLA generators is approximately 30 percent faster than an adder that uses only a single level of CLA generators, in addition to being approximately four times as fast as a ripple-carry adder. The reason for this difference in delay is in the construction of the carry chains in the ripple-carry and carry-look-ahead adders. To compare these delays, we will assume that every gate has the same delay. Under this assumption, an n-bit ripple-carry adder has $2n$ gate delays, as can be seen from Figure 5.2(a). On the other hand, the n-bit adder with $\lceil \log_4 n \rceil$ levels of CLA generator requires $(2\lceil \log_4 n \rceil)$ gate delays to generate top-level carries and another $2(\lceil \log_4 n \rceil - 1)$ gate levels to generate carries for each bit as demonstrated in Figure 5.3(b). Thus a total gate delay in a CLA adder grows logarithmically with the number of bits, while it grows linearly in a ripple-carry adder.

For the sake of simplicity, we use the ripple-carry technique throughout the rest of the book, although you should keep in mind that, in practice, the CLA technique is used most often in high-performance designs.

5.3 ADDERS/SUBTRACTORS

As a rule, binary subtraction is performed by adding the minuend to the two's complement of the subtrahend. The two's complement is obtained by complementing every bit in the subtrahend and then adding 1. This addition of 1 is accomplished by setting the input carry c_0 to 1 while we are adding the minuend to the subtrahend's complement. In other words, subtraction is generally performed through addition, and for this reason it is usually most convenient to construct a functional unit that can perform both addition and subtraction.

Usually, this **adder/subtractor** will have two inputs, $A = a_{n-1} \cdots a_0$ and $B = b_{n-1} \cdots b_0$, and one output, $F = f_{n-1} \cdots f_0$, as well as one select signal, S. Whenever $S = 0$, the adder/subtractor will perform addition, and whenever $S = 1$, it will perform subtraction. The functional table for this adder/subtractor is provided in Figure 5.4(a),

S	FUNCTION	COMMENT
0	$A + B$	Addition
1	$A + B' + 1$	Subtraction

(a) Truth table

(b) Graphic symbol

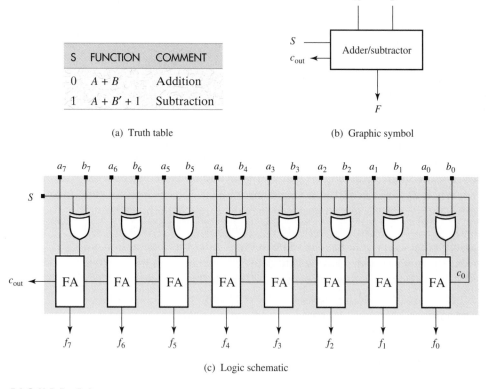

(c) Logic schematic

FIGURE 5.4

Two's-complement adder/subtractor.

and its graphic symbol is shown in Figure 5.4(b). Finally, as an example, an 8-bit adder/subtractor is shown in Figure 5.4(c). Note that this figure represents a ripple-carry design, although a CLA implementation like the one demonstrated in Section 5.2, could also be used. Within this implementation, the complement of the input B is obtained by performing an XOR operation between S and B.

5.4 LOGIC UNIT

In the most general terms, a **logic unit** enables us to perform one of several Boolean functions on any two operands, $X = x_{n-1} \cdots x_0$ and $Y = y_{n-1} \cdots y_0$. In other words, whenever the function f_j is selected, the logic unit will generate the result $S = f_j(X, Y) = f_j(x_{n-1}, y_{n-1}) \cdots f_j(x_0, y_0)$. Since a logic unit that can perform all 16 Boolean functions of two variables is not too complex, we will use such a unit to demonstrate the general procedures we use to design any given logic unit.

In Figure 5.5(a) we have shown all 16 of the Boolean functions that use two variables. Since there are 16 of them, we have to use the four select variables S_3, S_2, S_1, and S_0 to be able to select any one of these functions. The encoding of these selection variables for a given function is such that the select variable S_i, for which $0 \le i \le 3$, is equal to 1 if and only if the minterm $m_i = 1$ for that function. For example, the OR function $f_{14} = m_3 + m_2 + m_1$, so the values of select variables $S_3 S_2 S_1 S_0 = 1110$. Note that when the value of the select variables $S_3 S_2 S_1 S_0$ is interpreted as a binary number, it will be equal to the index of the function they select. In other words, in the case of the function f_{14}, the value of $S_3 S_2 S_1 S_0$ is equal to 1110, which is also the binary representation for the integer 14.

Since each selection variable will control one minterm, we can write an expression for a bit slice of a logic unit (LU) as follows:

$$s_i = S_0 m_0 + S_1 m_1 + S_2 m_2 + S_3 m_3$$

$$= S_0 x_i' y_i' + S_1 x_i' y_i + S_2 x_i y_i' + S_3 x_i y_i$$

The logic diagram of such a bit slice of a logic unit is shown in Figure 5.5(b), and the graphic symbol of an n-bit logic unit is shown in Figure 5.5(c). In general, any n-bit logic unit will consist of n bit slices that execute concurrently, as in the case with the 8-bit logic unit shown in Figure 5.5(d).

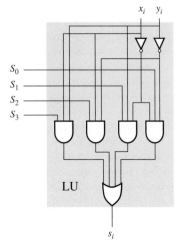

(b) Logic-unit implementation

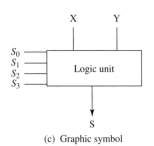

(c) Graphic symbol

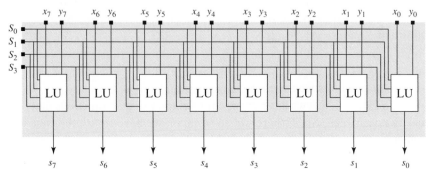

x_i	y_i	f_0	f_1	f_2	f_3	f_4	f_5	f_6	f_7	f_8	f_9	f_{10}	f_{11}	f_{12}	f_{13}	f_{14}	f_{15}	
m_0	0	0	0	1	0	1	0	1	0	1	0	1	0	1	0	1	0	1	S_0
m_1	0	1	0	0	1	1	0	0	1	1	0	0	1	1	0	0	1	1	S_1
m_2	1	0	0	0	0	0	1	1	1	1	0	0	0	0	1	1	1	1	S_2
m_3	1	1	0	0	0	0	0	0	0	0	1	1	1	1	1	1	1	1	S_3

(a) Boolean functions of two variables

(d) 8-bit logic unit

FIGURE 5.5
Logic unit.

5.5 ARITHMETIC-LOGIC UNIT

An **arithmetic-logic unit** (ALU) performs the basic arithmetic and logic operations in a microprocessor. Its arithmetic operations include, for example, addition, subtraction, increment, and decrement, and its logic operations include AND, OR, identity, and complement operations. Since all the arithmetic operations are based on addition, we can design an ALU simply by modifying the inputs of a ripple-carry or CLA adder. The modifying logic used for arithmetic operations is sometimes called an **arithmetic extender** (AE), and the modifying logic used for logic operations is called a **logic extender** (LE). Either one or both of these extenders is connected to the input of the adder, as indicated by the dashed lines in Figure 5.6. We now show how to design these extenders one at a time.

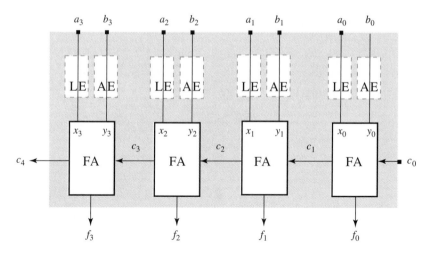

FIGURE 5.6
4-bit adder with arithmetic (AE) and logic (LE) extenders.

Since our ALU is to perform four arithmetic and four logic operations, we need to introduce a mode control variable M, which will select either arithmetic or logic operations in such a way that whenever $M = 1$, the ALU will perform arithmetic operations, and whenever $M = 0$, it will perform logic operations. We also need to use two select variables, S_1 and S_0, which will enable us to select any one of the four arithmetic or four logic operations. The values assigned to S_1 and S_0 for each arithmetic operation are summarized in the functional table in Figure 5.7(a).

As you can see, this table also shows the value of the ALU output F, as well as the values for the adder inputs X, Y, and c_0 which are required to achieve that value of F. Note that according to this table, the X input of the adder always requires the value of A, while the Y input can require all 1's, B, B', or all 0's. These values for the Y input will be generated by the AE, the truth table for which has been shown in Figure 5.7(b). This table was obtained from the functional table in Figure 5.7(a) simply by expanding column Y into columns b_i and y_i. In Figure 5.7(c) we show the map representation of the AE, from which we can see that its Boolean expression would be

$$y_i = MS_1'b_i + MS_0'b_i'$$

Finally, the logic schematic of this AE is shown in Figure 5.7(d).

Having shown the procedure for designing an AE, we can now turn to the design of a LE, which starts with the **functional table** describing its operations, as shown in Figure 5.8(a). From this table you can see that

M	S_1	S_0	FUNCTION NAME	F	X	Y	c_0
1	0	0	Decrement	$A - 1$	A	all 1's	0
1	0	1	Add	$A + B$	A	B	0
1	1	0	Subtract	$A + B' + 1$	A	B'	1
1	1	1	Increment	$A + 1$	A	all 0's	1

(a) Functional table

M	S_1	S_0	b_i	y_i
1	0	0	0	1
1	0	0	1	1
1	0	1	0	0
1	0	1	1	1
1	1	0	0	1
1	1	0	1	0
1	1	1	0	0
1	1	1	1	0

(b) Truth table

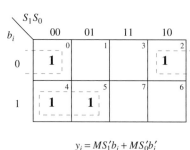

$$y_i = MS_1'b_i + MS_0'b_i'$$

(c) Map representation

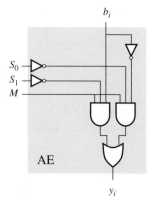

AE

(d) Logic schematic

F I G U R E   5.7
Arithmetic extender.

the Y and c_0 inputs always require a value of 0 for any one of the logic operations, whereas the X input requires a different Boolean expression for each of these operations. On the basis of this functional table, we are able to develop a truth table for the LE, which is shown in Figure 5.8(b), and its map representation, which is presented in Figure 5.8(c). From this map representation we are able to derive the following Boolean expression to describe the LE:

$$x_i = M'S_1'S_0'a_i' + M'S_1S_0b_i + S_0a_ib_i + S_1a_i + Ma_i$$

Having obtained this expression, we then proceed to construct the logic schematic for the LE, shown in Figure 5.8(d).

At this point we have obtained logic schematics for both the AE and the LE, and our next task is to connect them with an adder, thus forming a complete arithmetic-logic unit like the 4-bit ALU shown in Figure 5.9(a). Note that in the ALU, the logic operations are performed in the logic extender, and the FAs are used to pass the LE's results without change. In other words, the FAs are used as connections that have a fixed delay.

M	S_1	S_0	FUNCTION NAME	F	X	Y	c_0
0	0	0	Complement	A'	A'	0	0
0	0	1	AND	A AND B	A AND B	0	0
0	1	0	Identity	A	A	0	0
0	1	1	OR	A OR B	A OR B	0	0

(a) Functional table

M	S_1	S_0	x_i
0	0	0	a_i'
0	0	1	$a_i b_i$
0	1	0	a_i
0	1	1	$a_i + b_i$
1	X	X	a_i

(b) Truth table

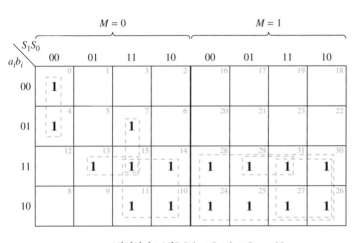

$$x_i = M'S_1'S_0'a_i' + M'S_1S_0b_i + S_0a_ib_i + S_1a_i + Ma_i$$

(c) Map representation

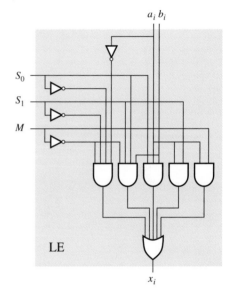

(d) Logic schematic

FIGURE 5.8
Logic extender.

Note also that the carry-out of the most significant bit represents an overflow in the case of unsigned arithmetic and that the EX-OR of the carry-outs of the two most significant bits represents the overflow in the case of 2's-complement arithmetic. If necessary, the 4-bit ALU shown in Figure 5.9(a) can be extended into an n-bit ALU, by using an n-bit adder in conjunction with n AEs and n LEs. The graphic symbol for such an ALU has been shown in Figure 5.9(b). In the industry, most ALUs used in real products are constructed in this fashion, except that they can differ in the type and number of their arithmetic and logic operations and in the implementation of their carry chains.

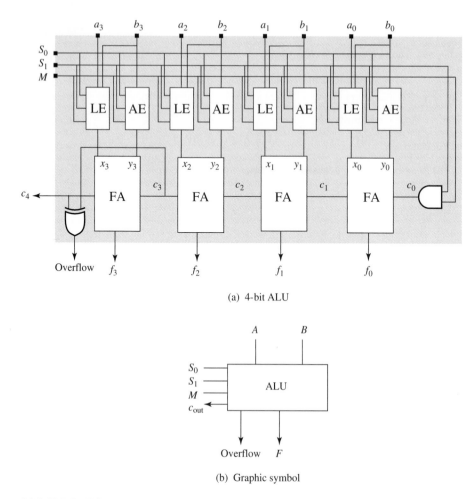

(a) 4-bit ALU

(b) Graphic symbol

FIGURE 5.9
Final ALU design.

5.6 DECODERS

Decoders (sometimes also called **demultiplexers**) are frequently incorporated into larger units for use whenever we need to activate or enable only one of n subcomponents. In such a case, each subcomponent can be assigned an index between 0 and $n - 1$ which is represented by a binary address A. To activate a particular subcomponent at any given time, this address A is decoded into n enable lines, out of which only one line is equal to 1. In general, an m-to-n decoder has $m = \log_2 n$ input lines, $A_{m-1}, \ldots, A_0$, and n output lines,

$C_{n-1}, \ldots, C_0$, as well as a control input, E. This control input enables the outputs in the following way: whenever $E = 0$ all the outputs are 0, and whenever $E = 1$, only the output C_i will be 1, where i is the integer whose value is equal to the binary value on inputs $A_{m-1}, \ldots, A_0$.

As an example, Figure 5.10 shows a 1-to-2 decoder, the graphic symbol and truth table of which appear in Figure 5.10(a) and (b). As you can see, the decoder has one address line, A_0, and one enable line, E, along with two output lines, C_0 and C_1. As long as line E equals 1, $C_0 = 1$ whenever $A_0 = 0$ and $C_1 = 1$ whenever $A_0 = 1$. The Boolean expressions for outputs C_1 and C_0 are shown in Figure 5.10(c), while its gate implementation is presented in Figure 5.10(d).

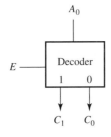

(a) Graphic symbol

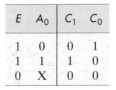

E	A_0	C_1	C_0
1	0	0	1
1	1	1	0
0	X	0	0

(b) Truth table

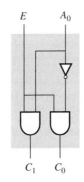

(d) Logic diagram

$$C_0 = EA_0'$$
$$C_1 = EA_0$$

(c) Boolean expression

FIGURE 5.10
1-to-2 decoder.

If necessary, this 1-to-2 decoder can be extended into a 2-to-4 decoder, as shown in Figure 5.11. Note that the decoder now has two address lines, A_1 and A_0, the enable line, E, and four output lines, $C_3, C_2, C_1,$ and C_0. As explained above, this 2-to-4 decoder is used to decode the binary number represented by A_1 and A_0, and then to assign a 1 to the output line whose index is equal to that binary number.

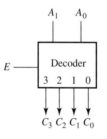

A_1 A_0

E —— Decoder

3 2 1 0

C_3 C_2 C_1 C_0

(a) Graphic symbol

E	A_1	A_0	C_3	C_2	C_1	C_0
1	0	0	0	0	0	1
1	0	1	0	0	1	0
1	1	0	0	1	0	0
1	1	1	1	0	0	0
0	X	X	0	0	0	0

(b) Truth table

$C_0 = EA_1'A_0'$

$C_1 = EA_1'A_0$

$C_2 = EA_1A_0'$

$C_3 = EA_1A_0$

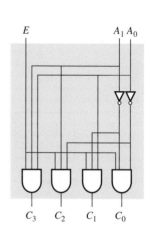

C_3 C_2 C_1 C_0

FIGURE 5.11
2-to-4 decoder.

(c) Boolean expression

(d) Logic diagram

It is also possible to build larger m-to-n decoders from 1-to-2 and 2-to-4 decoders. For example, if we use 1-to-2 decoders in the construction, the m-to-n decoder will have $\log_2 n$ levels of 1-to-2 decoders, each of which will decode one address bit. In other words, the most significant address bit will be decoded by one decoder, the next most significant bit by two decoders, and so on, until the least significant bit is being decoded by $n/2$ decoders. Each output of each decoder on a particular level will enable one of the decoders on the next level, so that the number of decoders on each successive level will double with its distance from the top decoder. In Figure 5.12, for example, we show a 3-to-8 decoder constructed from 1-to-2 decoders. Its truth table is shown in Figure 5.12(a) and its implementation in Figure 5.12(b). The same principles apply when we use 2-to-4 decoders, except for the fact that a 2-to-4 decoder can decode 2 bits at a time, so an m-to-n decoder constructed from 2-to-4 decoders needs only half as many levels and half as many decoders as one constructed from 1-to-2 decoders, as Figure 5.12(c) clearly demonstrates this point.

E	A_2	A_1	A_0	C_7	C_6	C_5	C_4	C_3	C_2	C_1	C_0
1	0	0	0	0	0	0	0	0	0	0	1
1	0	0	1	0	0	0	0	0	0	1	0
1	0	1	0	0	0	0	0	0	1	0	0
1	0	1	1	0	0	0	0	1	0	0	0
1	1	0	0	0	0	0	1	0	0	0	0
1	1	0	1	0	0	1	0	0	0	0	0
1	1	1	0	0	1	0	0	0	0	0	0
1	1	1	1	1	0	0	0	0	0	0	0
0	X	X	X	0	0	0	0	0	0	0	0

(a) Truth table

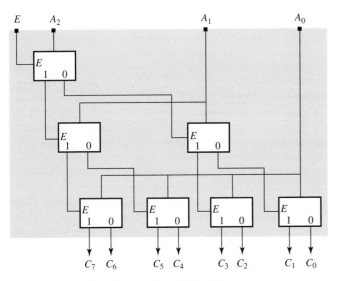

(b) Implementation with 1-to-2 decoders

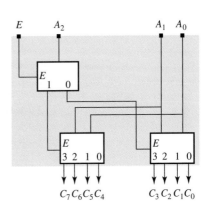

(c) Implementation with 2-to-4 decoders

FIGURE 5.12
3-to-8 decoder.

5.7 SELECTORS

In many designs we encounter components that need to use data from different sources at different times. For such designs we need a **selector** or **multiplexer** (MUX), which is a combinatorial component that can select one of several data sources to be used as operands for an ALU, to be stored in a memory or to be sent over a bus. In general, a selector will have n inputs, one output, and $\log_2 n$ select signals that will select data from any one of the n inputs to be passed to the output. Although we could construct any n-to-1 selector, in practice most logic libraries would include only 2-to-1 and 4-to-1 selectors, simply because selectors with a larger number of inputs can easily be constructed from 2-to-1 and 4-to-1 selectors.

In Figure 5.13 we show a 2-to-1 selector, presenting the graphic symbol in Figure 5.13(a) and the truth table in Figure 5.13(b). As you can see, this 2-to-1 selector has two inputs, D_1 and D_0, and one output, Y, in addition to one select signal, S, which selects one of the inputs as follows: Whenever $S = 0$, the output $Y = D_0$, whereas whenever $S = 1$, the output $Y = D_1$. The Boolean expression for the output Y is provided in Figure 5.13(c), and the complete logic diagram of this 2-to-1 selector is presented in Figure 5.13(d).

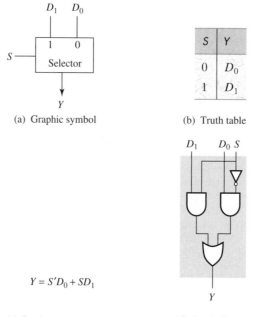

S	Y
0	D_0
1	D_1

(a) Graphic symbol   (b) Truth table

$Y = S'D_0 + SD_1$

FIGURE 5.13
2-to-1 selector.   (c) Boolean expression   (d) Logic diagram

By contrast, Figure 5.14 shows a 4-to-1 selector, which selects any one of four data lines as directed by the two selection signals S_1 and S_0. In this figure you can see the graphical symbol, the truth table, the output Boolean expression, and the logic diagram for this 4-to-1 selector.

Wherever they are required, larger selectors can be constructed from a number of 2-to-1 selectors. For an n-to-1 selector, for example, where n is a power of 2, we use $\log_2 n$ selection signals and $\log_2 n$ levels of 2-to-1 selectors. Each selection signal will serve to control one of the levels of selectors. On the first level, each selector will select between

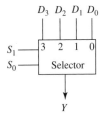

D_3 D_2 D_1 D_0

S_1 ——

S_0 ——

| 3 | 2 | 1 | 0 |

Selector

Y

(a) Graphic symbol

S_1	S_0	Y
0	0	D_0
0	1	D_1
1	0	D_2
1	1	D_3

(b) Truth table

$$Y = S_1'S_0'D_0 + S_1'S_0D_1$$
$$+ S_1S_0'D_2 + S_1S_0D_3$$

(c) Boolean expression

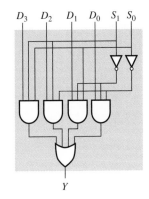

(d) Logic diagram

FIGURE   5.14

4-to-1 selector.

two data sources, while on the second level, each selector will select between the two selector outputs from the first level. In other words, on every level beyond the first, each selector is used to select one of the two outputs produced by selectors at the preceding level. As an example of these larger selectors, Figure 5.15 shows an 8-to-1 selector, with its truth table in Figure 5.15(a) and an implementation that uses 2-to-1 selectors in Figure 5.15(b).

It would be possible to implement the same 8-to-1 selector by using logic gates as shown in Figure 5.16. In this case, as you can see, we use a 3-to-8 decoder to decode the control signals. Although this gate implementation seems quite simple, it has the disadvantage that it is not easily scalable. In other words, the number and size of the gates in the decoder, as well as the size of the output OR gate, would have to increase with the number of inputs, so that the larger gates have to be implemented as trees of gates, which significantly increases the cost and delay of the selector. For this reason we generally use this gate implementation only for small values of n, while the selectors for larger values of n are constructed by the method described earlier, using several levels of 2-to-1 or 4-to-1 selectors.

S_2	S_1	S_0	Y
0	0	0	D_0
0	0	1	D_1
0	1	0	D_2
0	1	1	D_3
1	0	0	D_4
1	0	1	D_5
1	1	0	D_6
1	1	1	D_7

(a) Truth table

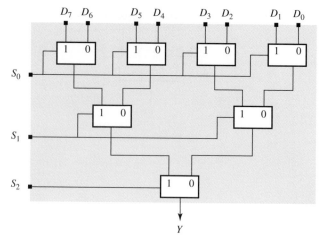

(b) Implementation with 2-to-1 selectors

FIGURE 5.15

8-to-1 selector.

S_2	S_1	S_0	Y
0	0	0	D_0
0	0	1	D_1
0	1	0	D_2
0	1	1	D_3
1	0	0	D_4
1	0	1	D_5
1	1	0	D_6
1	1	1	D_7

(a) Truth table

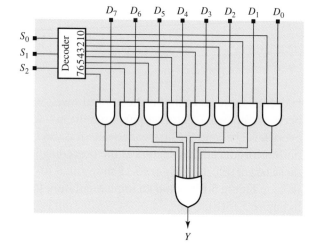

(b) Implementation with a decoder

FIGURE 5.16

Alternative 8-to-1 selector.

5.8 BUSES

Although the selectors described in previous sections are in common use, selectors that have a large number of inputs can be difficult to manufacture, since they require many wires to be brought together to a central place where the selector is located. Fortunately, there is one elegant solution to this problem, called a **bus**, which can be easily routed around the other objects on a microchip or a PCB. To construct a bus, we use a component called a tristate driver, whose output provides three different values, 0, 1, and Z. The value Z represents a high-impedance state, which for all practical purposes can be thought of as a disconnection from the bus.

As you can see in Figure 5.17(a) and (b), a **tristate driver** has a data line, D, an enable line, E, and an output line, Y. Whenever E equals 1, the output Y will follow the input data line D. Conversely, whenever

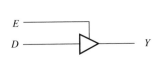

(a) Tristate driver symbol

E	Y
0	Z
1	D

(b) Truth table for tristate driver

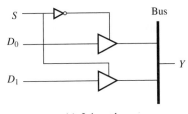

(c) 2-input bus

S	Y
0	D_0
1	D_1

(d) Truth table for 2-input bus

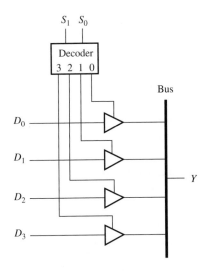

(e) 4-input bus

S_1	S_0	Y
0	0	D_0
0	1	D_1
1	0	D_2
1	1	D_3

(f) Truth table for 4-input bus

FIGURE 5.17
Bus implementation.

E becomes 0, the output value will be equal to Z. Each bus contains a set of tristate drivers in which one driver is used for each source that is connected to the bus. Since only one source can be allowed to drive the bus at a given time, the enable lines of different drivers can be encoded into a source address for efficient storage and transmission of these addresses.

In its function, a bus is equivalent to a selector, since it can have n data inputs but allows only one data on the bus at a time. For example, the 2-input bus shown in Figure 5.17(c) has two data lines, D_1 and D_0, and one address line, S, so that when $S = 0$, Y will equal D_0, and when $S = 1$, Y will equal D_1. Note that the truth table for this 2-input bus, shown in Figure 5.17(d), is equivalent to the truth table of a 2-to-1 selector. Using the same principles, we can also construct buses that have more inputs, such as the 4-input bus shown in Figure 5.17(e), which corresponds to the truth table in Figure 5.17(f). As you can see, this bus incorporates a 2-to-4 decoder, which will convert the two address lines S_1 and S_0 into the four enable lines we need for the four tri-state drivers that drive the bus Y.

In general, buses are very easy to manufacture and very easy to modify if we need to add new sources or delete old ones. For this reason, buses are very common in local networks where there are many sources to be connected together in the same room or the same building.

5.9 PRIORITY ENCODERS

A priority encoder is almost the complement of a decoder, in the sense that a priority encoder connected to the outputs of a decoder would produce an identity function—that is, the input to the decoder would be equal to the output of the priority encoder. On the other hand, a decoder connected to the outputs of an encoder would not produce an identity function, because a priority encoder is designed to encode the position of the most significant input with a value of 1 and to disregard the values of all the inputs that are in less significant positions. For this reason, the encoder's input values could not be reproduced at the outputs of the decoder that is connected to it.

In general terms, a **priority encoder** has n inputs, $D_{n-1}, \ldots, D_0$, where $n = 2^m$ for some m. It also has $\log_2 n = m$ outputs, $A_{m-1}, \ldots, A_0$, as well as an additional output called Any, which will be 1 whenever any of the inputs has a value that is different from 0. The outputs $A_{m-1}, \ldots, A_0$ represent the index of the most significant input bit D_i that has a value equal to 1.

The simplest of all possible encoders is the 2-to-1 priority encoder shown in Figure 5.18. Its graphic symbol is shown in Figure 5.18(a) and its truth table in Figure 5.18(b). As you can see, the 2-to-1 priority encoder has two inputs, D_1 and D_0, and one output, A_0, in addition to the *Any* output described above. In this encoder, whenever $D_1 = 0$ and $D_0 = 1$, then $A_0 = 0$, and conversely, whenever $D_1 = 1$ and D_0 is a don't care, then $A_0 = 1$. The Boolean expressions for the output can easily be derived from the truth table and are shown in Figure 5.18(c). Finally, in Figure 5.18(d) is shown the logic schematic for this 2-to-1 priority encoder.

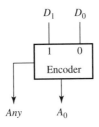

D_1 D_0

1	0
Encoder	

Any A_0

(a) Graphic symbol

D_1	D_0	A_0	ANY
0	0	0	0
0	1	0	1
1	X	1	1

(b) Truth table

$$A_0 = D_1$$
$$Any = D_0 + D_1$$

(c) Boolean expression

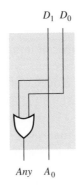

D_1 D_0

Any A_0

(d) Logic diagram

FIGURE   5.18
2-to-1 priority encoder.

More useful than this 2-to-1 priority encoder, however, is the 4-to-2 priority encoder shown in Figure 5.19, which has four inputs, D_3, D_2, D_1, and D_0, and two address outputs, A_1 and A_0, in addition to the *Any* output. Its graphic symbol is shown in Figure 5.19(a) and its truth table in Figure 5.19(b). As before, we can now use the map method to derive the output Boolean expressions, which are shown in Figure 5.19(c), and these expressions can be translated in turn into the logic schematic that is presented in Figure 5.19(d).

The importance of 2-to-1 and 4-to-1 encoders is that by combining them with selectors we can construct priority encoders with a larger

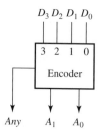

$D_3\, D_2\, D_1\, D_0$

| 3 | 2 | 1 | 0 |

Encoder

Any A_1 A_0

(a) Graphic symbol

D_3	D_2	D_1	D_0	A_1	A_0	ANY
0	0	0	0	0	0	0
0	0	0	1	0	0	1
0	0	1	X	0	1	1
0	1	X	X	1	0	1
1	X	X	X	1	1	1

(b) Truth table

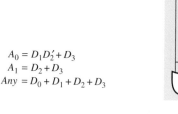

$$A_0 = D_1 D_2' + D_3$$
$$A_1 = D_2 + D_3$$
$$Any = D_0 + D_1 + D_2 + D_3$$

(c) Boolean expression

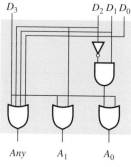

D_3 $D_2\, D_1\, D_0$

Any A_1 A_0

(d) Logic diagram

FIGURE 5.19
4-to-2 priority encoder.

number of inputs. When we use 2-to-1 encoders to design these larger components, we group inputs into pairs so that each group of two is encoded by one of the 2-to-1 priority encoders. Proceeding in this manner, we use on the first level a total of $n/2$ 2-to-1 encoders, which will generate $n/2$ candidates for the least significant address bit, A_0. One of these candidates will be selected by a $(n/2)$-to-1 selector. To produce the next most significant address, A_1, we have to encode $n/2$ *Any* outputs from the $n/2$ first-level encoders, once again grouping them into pairs. For this second level of encoding, we use $n/4$ priority encoders and a $(n/4)$-to-1 selector which selects the bit A_1. In addition, these $n/4$ encoders generate $n/4$ *Any* outputs, which can then be encoded to produce the next most significant address bit, A_2. This procedure is repeated until only one *Any* output remains.

At each level of the encoder we use 2-to-1 selectors, in order to select the proper address bit. Each 2-to-1 selector selects one of the outputs from a group of two encoders, using the encoding of their *Any* outputs as the control line for this selection. As an example we show in Figure 5.20(b) an implementation of an 8-to-3 priority encoder which uses 2-to-1 encoders and 2-to-1 selectors. The truth table for this encoder appears in Figure 5.20(a). Alternatively, the same 8-to-3 encoder could be implemented by using two 4-to-2 encoders, one 2-to-1 encoder, and two 2-to-1 selectors, as shown in Figure 5.20(c).

D_7	D_6	D_5	D_4	D_3	D_2	D_1	D_0	A_2	A_1	A_0	ANY
0	0	0	0	0	0	0	0	0	0	0	0
0	0	0	0	0	0	0	1	0	0	0	1
0	0	0	0	0	0	1	X	0	0	1	1
0	0	0	0	0	1	X	X	0	1	0	1
0	0	0	0	1	X	X	X	0	1	1	1
0	0	0	1	X	X	X	X	1	0	0	1
0	0	1	X	X	X	X	X	1	0	1	1
0	1	X	X	X	X	X	X	1	1	0	1
1	X	X	X	X	X	X	X	1	1	1	1

(a) Truth table

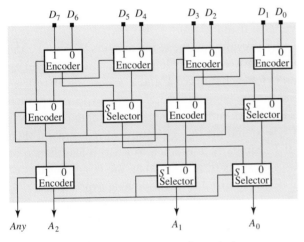

(b) Implementation with 2-to-1 encoders and selectors

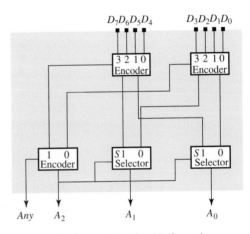

(c) Implementation using 4-to-2 encoders

FIGURE 5.20

8-to-3 priority encoder.

5.10 MAGNITUDE COMPARATORS

Many programming languages include relational operators that enable us to evaluate certain conditions and determine when certain actions are to be taken. Within these languages, these conditions are generally expressed in terms of relations between two entities X and Y, which can represent constants, variables, or arithmetic expressions. These relational expressions use three basic operators, "greater than" ($X > Y$), "equal to" ($X = Y$), and "less than" ($X < Y$). In addition, each of these operations has a complement: The operator "greater than or equal to" ($X \geq Y$) is the complement of "less than," "less than or equal to" $(X \leq Y)$ is the complement of "greater than," and "not equal to" $(X \neq Y)$, of course, is the complement of "equal to." The result of any one of these relational operations is a Boolean variable, which can have a value of 0 or 1.

As a rule, these relational operations are performed by units called **comparators**. It is possible to construct a comparator for each relational operator, but in this section we demonstrate how to design a universal comparator that can be used to evaluate any one of the relational operators. In general terms, such a universal comparator compares the two positive integers $X = x_{n-1} \cdots x_0$ and $Y = y_{n-1} \cdots y_0$ and then generates the two Boolean results G and L as an output, indicating the following: When the output $G = 1$, then $X > Y$, and when $G = 0$, then $X \leq Y$; at the same time, when $L = 1$, then $X < Y$, and when $L = 0$, then $X \geq Y$. Thus we know that $X \neq Y$ whenever $G = 1$ or $L = 1$, and conversely, that $X = Y$ whenever $G = 0$ and $L = 0$.

To determine these results for the n-bit integers X and Y, the comparator starts its comparison with the least significant bits x_0 and y_0, computing the G_i and L_i for each suffix of X and Y, where the ith suffixes of X and Y are defined as the integers $x_i x_{i-1} \cdots x_0$ and $y_i y_{i-1} \cdots y_0$ such that $i \leq n - 1$. Thus for the ith suffix of X and Y, G is equal to 1 if x_i is greater than y_i or if $x_i = y_i$ and the $(i - 1)$th suffix of X is greater than the $(i - 1)$th suffix of Y. Similarly, L is equal to 1 if x_i is less than y_i or if $x_i = y_i$ and the $(i - 1)$th suffix of X is less than the $(i - 1)$th suffix of Y. These values can be summarized by the following expressions:

$$G_i = (x_i > y_i) \text{ or } ((x_i = y_i) \text{ and } (G_{i-1} > L_{i-1}))$$
$$L_i = (x_i < y_i) \text{ or } ((x_i = y_i) \text{ and } (G_{i-1} < L_{i-1}))$$

As you can see, we have reduced the entire comparison to a comparison of the 2-bit numbers $x_i G_{i-1}$ and $y_i L_{i-1}$. At this point, then, we can design a basic 2-bit comparator that can compare the two 2-bit numbers $a_1 a_0$ and $b_1 b_0$, and then use it to construct larger n-bit comparators.

In Figure 5.21(a) we show a truth table for a 2-bit comparator whose inputs are the two 2-bit integers $a_1 a_0$ and $b_1 b_0$, and the outputs are G and L. The map representation of this comparator, with the Boolean expressions for G and L, is shown in Figure 5.21(b) and its logic schematic in Figure 5.21(c).

As mentioned above, the 2-bit comparator can be used in serial and parallel implementations of n-bit comparators that can compare any of two unsigned integers X and Y. In a serial implementation, for example, we use one 2-bit comparator for every pair of bits, represented by x_i and y_i. For each 2-bit comparator, the input values x_i and y_i are connected to its a_1 and b_1 inputs, while the values G_{i-1} and L_{i-1} obtained from the $(i - 1)$th suffix comparison are connected to the inputs a_0 and

a_1	b_1	a_0	b_0	G	L
0	0	0	0	0	0
0	0	0	1	0	1
0	0	1	0	1	0
0	0	1	1	0	0
0	1	0	0	0	1
0	1	0	1	0	1
0	1	1	0	0	1
0	1	1	1	0	1
1	0	0	0	1	0
1	0	0	1	1	0
1	0	1	0	1	0
1	0	1	1	1	0
1	1	0	0	0	0
1	1	0	1	0	1
1	1	1	0	1	0
1	1	1	1	0	0

(a) Truth table

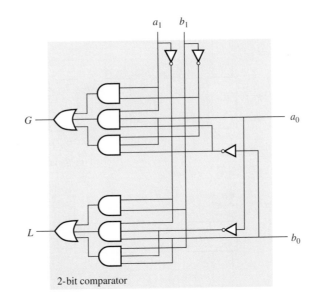

(c) Logic schematic

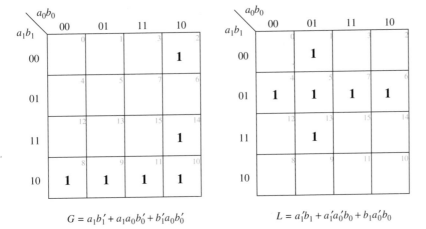

$$G = a_1 b_1' + a_1 a_0 b_0' + b_1' a_0 b_0'$$

$$L = a_1' b_1 + a_1' a_0' b_0 + b_1 a_0' b_0$$

(b) Map representation

FIGURE 5.21
2-bit magnitude comparator.

b_0. In this manner, each 2-bit comparator produces the outputs G and L, which represent the functions G_i and L_i. In Figure 5.22(a) we show a serial implementation of an 8-bit magnitude comparator. As you can see, this 8-bit comparator requires only seven 2-bit comparators since we have used only one 2-bit comparator to compare $x_1 x_0$ and $y_1 y_0$.

As a general rule, the comparison of any two n-bit integers always requires $(n-1)$ 2-bit comparators regardless of whether we use a serial or

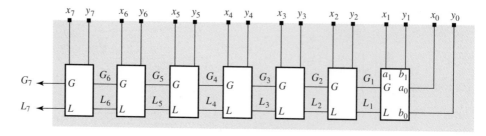

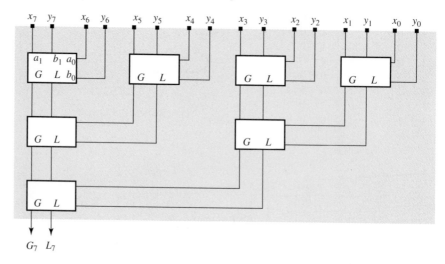

(a) Serial implementation

(b) Parallel implementation

FIGURE 5.22
8-bit magnitude comparator.

a parallel implementation. The serial implementation described above, though, does have a major disadvantage, since the delay of the n-bit comparator will be equal to $(n - 1)$ times the delay of a single 2-bit comparator. In a parallel implementation, by contrast, this delay can be reduced to $\lceil \log_2 n \rceil$, simply because the parallel implementation divides the n-bit comparison into two-bit comparisons on the first level. Then the results of these two-bit comparisons are compared on the next level, yielding 4-bit comparisons, which are then compared on the next level, yielding 8-bit comparisons, and so on. Proceeding in this manner, we need $\lceil \log_2 n \rceil$ levels to obtain an n-bit comparison. As an example of this kind of parallel comparison, Figure 5.22(b) shows an implementation for the 8-bit magnitude comparator. Note that this parallel implementation still requires $(n-1)$ 2-bit comparators, but its delay is only $\lceil \log_2 n \rceil$ times the delay of a single 2-bit comparator.

5.11 SHIFTERS AND ROTATORS

In digital design we frequently use shifting and rotation operations for packing and unpacking digits and characters, for field extraction and insertion, and for floating-point arithmetic operations. Each processor, for example, has at least several instructions for 1-bit left and right shift and left and right rotation. The shift operation can be performed in logic or arithmetic mode. During a logic shift operation, a word is shifted m bit positions to the left or right. As a result of this operation, m bits are shifted out of the word, as m new bits have to be shifted in. During an arithmetic shift operation the word being shifted is assumed to be a number, so that the m-bit shift to the right represents division by 2^m and m-bit shift to the left represents multiplication by 2^m. If the shifted number is a 2's-complement number, m copies of the sign have to be shifted in during arithmetic right shift and m 0's shifted in during arithmetic left shift. In addition, the MSB must be made a duplicate of the sign bit after the arithmetic left shift. During a rotation operation, on the other hand, no bits are lost, since the bits that are shifted out on one side are simultaneously shifted back in on the other side of the word.

The **shifters** and **rotators** we use for these operations are implemented with selectors. For example, the universal shifter/rotator shown in Figure 5.23, which can perform logic shift or rotate one bit position to the left or to the right, has one data input, $D = d_n \cdots d_0$, one output, $Y = y_n \cdots y_0$, and three selection lines, S_2, S_1, and S_0, which determine the operation to be performed. According to the functional table in Figure 5.23(a), when $S_2 = 0$, the input data will be passed unchanged to the output, whereas when $S_2 = 1$, a shift or rotation operation will be performed. Whether these operations move to the left or right depends on the value of S_1: that is, $S_1 = 0$ indicates that the data movement will be to the left, whereas $S_1 = 1$ indicates that the movement will be to the right. Finally, S_0 is used to differentiate between shift and rotation operations, so that when $S_0 = 0$, the shifter/rotator will shift, and when $S_0 = 1$, it will rotate.

Implementation of an 8-bit shifter/rotator is shown in Figure 5.23(b). This unit can shift or rotate one bit position to the left or right, or can pass the data through unchanged. As you can see, this shifter/rotator has been implemented with a 4-to-1 selector for each bit position, arranged such that each selector can choose the input bit that is positioned to the left, the bit that is positioned to the right, or the bit that is at its own position. In addition, this shifter has two extra 2-to-1 selectors, which can choose the leftmost or rightmost bit during a shift or a rotation operation.

S_2	S_1	S_0	Y	COMMENT
0	0	X	D	No shift
0	1	X		Not used
1	0	0	shl(D)	Shift left
1	0	1	rtl(D)	Rotate left
1	1	0	shr(D)	Shift right
1	1	1	rtr(D)	Rotate right

(a) Functional table

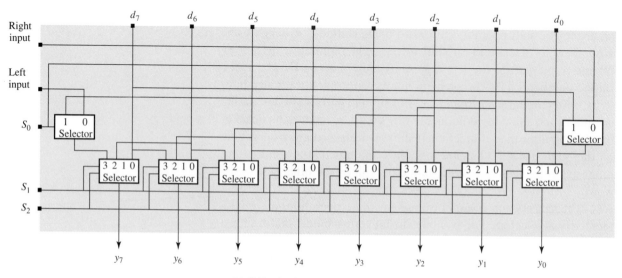

(b) Shifter implemented with 4-to-1 selectors

FIGURE 5.23
8-bit shifter.

As mentioned above, this shifter is capable of shifting or rotating one bit position to the left or right, which means that whenever we require a shift of more than one position, we have to pass the data through this shifter several times. In other words, this type of shifter makes the task of shifting or rotating data by an arbitrary number of positions very slow. To avoid this unnecessary delay, high-performance designs use a **barrel shifter**, which is designed to shift any number of positions at one time. In such an n-bit shifter/rotator, where $n = 2^m$, we use $m = \log_2 n$ levels of 2-to-1 selectors arranged such that the ith level of selectors ($0 \leq i \leq m - 1$) shifts by 2^i positions when its select line $S_i = 1$, or passes the data unchanged when the select line $S_i = 0$. In other words, if we want to shift data by B positions, where B is a binary number $b_{m-1} \cdots b_0$, we set the value of the shifter selection line S_i to b_i for all i such that $0 \leq i \leq m - 1$.

In Figure 5.24 we demonstrate one possible design for a barrel shifter in which, for the sake of simplicity, we have limited the shifter to one function, right rotation. As you can see, this 8-bit barrel rotator has been implemented with three levels of 2-to-1 selectors, which are

S_2	S_1	S_0	y_7	y_6	y_5	y_4	y_3	y_2	y_1	y_0
0	0	0	d_7	d_6	d_5	d_4	d_3	d_2	d_1	d_0
0	0	1	d_0	d_7	d_6	d_5	d_4	d_3	d_2	d_1
0	1	0	d_1	d_0	d_7	d_6	d_5	d_4	d_3	d_2
0	1	1	d_2	d_1	d_0	d_7	d_6	d_5	d_4	d_3
1	0	0	d_3	d_2	d_1	d_0	d_7	d_6	d_5	d_4
1	0	1	d_4	d_3	d_2	d_1	d_0	d_7	d_6	d_5
1	1	0	d_5	d_4	d_3	d_2	d_1	d_0	d_7	d_6
1	1	1	d_6	d_5	d_4	d_3	d_2	d_1	d_0	d_7

(a) Truth table

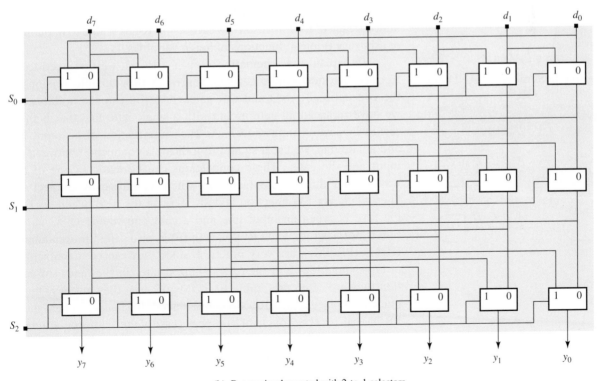

(b) Rotator implemented with 2-to-1 selectors

FIGURE 5.24
8-bit barrel right rotator.

controlled by the selection lines S_0, S_1, and S_2 in the following manner: When $S_0 = 1$, the first level rotates by one bit position; when $S_1 = 1$, the second level rotates by two bit positions; and when $S_2 = 1$, the third level rotates by four bit positions.

In general, the cost of such an 8-bit barrel rotator will be $n \log_2 n$ times the cost of a single 2-to-1 selector, and its delay from any input to any output will be approximately $\log_2 n$ times the delay of a single 2-to-1 selector. To construct a more complex shifter/rotator capable of performing a wider range of operations, we use essentially the same approach but need to use a larger number of 2-to-1 selectors.

5.12 READ-ONLY MEMORIES

A **read-only memory** (ROM) can be thought of as a universal logic element that is able to implement concurrently several different Boolean functions that are defined on the same set of variables. In general terms, each ROM contains n words of m bits each and is usually referred to as an $n \times m$ ROM. It also includes $\log_2 n$ address lines that are used to address each of its n words. Thus each $n \times m$ ROM is able to implement m arbitrary Boolean functions of $\log_2 n$ variables.

To explain the schematic for such a ROM, we first need to introduce two new symbols, which represent programable versions of the conceptional AND and OR gates. As you can see in Table 5.3, we have replaced all gate inputs with a single gate line that is intersected by several input lines. At each intersection of an input line and a gate line, we use a square to indicate a connection between the input and the gate. These connections can be made in one of two ways, either during manufacturing, when we physically connect two lines whenever a connection is desired, or in the field, when we burn the fuse between an input line and a gate line whenever a connection is not desired. Such ROMs with fuses, also called **programmable ROMs** (PROMs), are very practical, since they can be manufactured in large quantities and then personalized later in the field. In addition they are often preferable to ROMs because they are easy to upgrade or replace if the PROM's content needs to change. In fact, such a PROM can best be thought of as a special case of the field-programmable logic arrays (FPGAs) described in Section 3.10; given their functional similarities, these PROMs can be seen as the predecessors of FPGAs, which require a more complex internal organization. In Figure 3.23, for example, you saw that each PLB was implemented with a 16×2 PROM.

TABLE 5.3

Programmable Symbols of AND and OR

COMPUTATIONAL SYMBOL	PROGRAMMABLE SYMBOL

As mentioned above, a typical $n \times m$ ROM or PROM has $k = \log_2 n$ address lines designated $A_{k-1}, \ldots, A_0$, as well as m output lines designated $F_{m-1}, \ldots, F_0$. It consists of a k-to-n address decoder and a programmable OR array. As an example, Figure 5.25 shows a 16×4 ROM in which a 4-to-16 decoder is used to select any one of the 16 words in the ROM. Within the programmable OR array, the value of each bit in each word is determined by the presence or absence of a connection between the horizontal and vertical lines: since a black square on an intersection indicates a connection, which, in turn, indicates that a value of 1 has been written into that particular bit position.

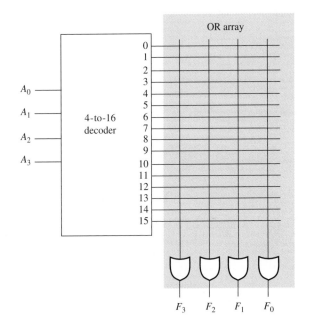

F I G U R E   5.25
16×4 ROM.

In Figure 5.26(a) we use this 16×4 ROM for implementation of the adder/subtractor bit slice presented initially in Figure 5.4. As you can see, this bit slice has one select line, S, which selects whether it performs an addition or subtraction on the two bits a_i and b_i, together with the carry bit c_i which has carried over from the previous bit slice. This bit slice also has two outputs: f_i, which represents a bit of the sum or difference, and the carry output c_{i+1}, which carries to the next bit slice. The truth table for the function of this bit slice has been shown in Figure 5.26(b), and in Figure 5.26(c) we show its ROM implementation. Note that in this implementation, each 1 in the output column of the truth table has been converted into the appropriate connection in the ROM's OR array. In the case of a ROM implementation, then, the input lines S, a_i, b_i, and c_i are mapped into the address lines

A_3 (S)	A_2 (a_i)	A_1 (b_i)	A_0 (c_i)	F_3	F_2	F_1 (c_{i+1})	F_0 (f_i)
0	0	0	0	X	X	0	0
0	0	0	1	X	X	0	1
0	0	1	0	X	X	0	1
0	0	1	1	X	X	1	0
0	1	0	0	X	X	0	1
0	1	0	1	X	X	1	0
0	1	1	0	X	X	1	0
0	1	1	1	X	X	1	1
1	0	0	0	X	X	0	1
1	0	0	1	X	X	1	0
1	0	1	0	X	X	0	0
1	0	1	1	X	X	0	1
1	1	0	0	X	X	1	0
1	1	0	1	X	X	1	1
1	1	1	0	X	X	0	1
1	1	1	1	X	X	1	0

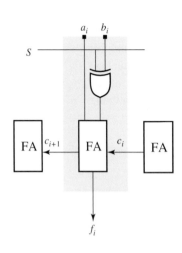

(a) Adder/subtractor bit slice

(b) Truth table

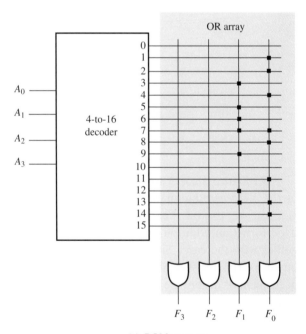

(c) ROM program

FIGURE 5.26

16×4 ROM programmed as an adder/subtractor bit slice.

A_3, A_2, A_1, and A_0, whereas the output lines c_{i+1} and f_i are mapped into F_1 and F_0.

In this implementation it is also important to note that the ROM's words with addresses 0 and 10 are not needed at all. Unfortunately, a ROM implementation will waste words like these whenever the values of all the outputs for a particular word are 0. Because of these wasted words, ROM implementations of functions that have only a few values of 1 are very expensive. On the other hand, ROMs are excellent for storing fixed data, because they have such high bit density in comparison to writable memories. For the same reason, they are very commonly used in the control units of standard processors and application-specific coprocessors to generate values of control signals. Furthermore, ROMs are nonvolatile; in other words, they do not lose the memory content after the power is turned off. For this reason they are used to store programs and data for bootstrapping computers when the power is turned on.

5.13 PROGRAMMABLE LOGIC ARRAYS

In Section 5.12, we noted that ROMs are not very efficient when we use them to implement sparse functions, which have only a small number of 1's, because in such cases, many of the words in the ROM will have a value of 0, which is a waste of silicon area. It was to minimize this waste that **programmable logic arrays** (PLAs) were developed. Basically, PLAs differ from ROMs in their implementation of the address decoder: instead of using a full decoder, as ROMs do, a PLA would use a programmable decoder, called an AND array, which can be programmed to decode only those words that have a nonzero content. Furthermore, in addition to this programmable decoder, a PLA could have a programmable output array to be used whenever we need to complement the output values. This output array can improve the efficiency of the PLA by allowing a greater degree of flexibility in implementing each function. For example, if a given function has only a few 0's, the AND and OR arrays can be programmed to implement the complement of that function, which will require fewer words, and then to complement this function's complement again in the output array.

As a rule, each PLA is characterized by its number of words, designated by n, and its number of outputs, which is defined by m. Moreover, since the number of address lines will not be equal to $\log_2 n$, we also need to specify the PLA's number of input or address lines, which is designated by k. Thus we know that a $k \times n \times m$ PLA will have $A_{k-1}, \ldots, A_0$ address lines in addition to n words, where each word represents one minterm of the address inputs, and m outputs, designated by $F_{m-1}, \ldots, F_0$. We also know that such a PLA can implement m arbitrary Boolean functions of k variables each as long as the number of different terms in those m functions together does not exceed the value of n.

In Figure 5.27 we show the structure of a $4 \times 8 \times 4$ PLA. As you can see, it has the four inputs A_3, A_2, A_1, and A_0, the four outputs F_3, F_2, F_1, and F_0, and 8 AND terms or words. From this definition we know that each AND term can contain up to four literals, that each output function can have up to eight AND terms, and that each output can be produced in either its true or its complemented form.

In Figure 5.28 we use this $4 \times 8 \times 4$ PLA to implement the full-adder functions c_{i+1} and s_i, which were defined in Figure 5.1. Note that we could not use this PLA to implement the adder/subtractor bit slice

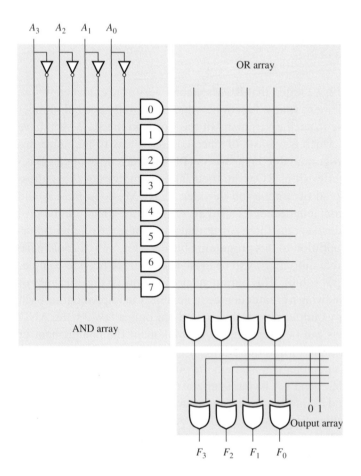

FIGURE 5.27
PLA structure.

A_3	A_2 x_i	A_1 y_i	A_0 c_i	F_3	F_2	F_1 c_{i+1}	F_0 s_i
X	0	0	0	X	X	0	0
X	0	0	1	X	X	0	1
X	0	1	0	X	X	0	1
X	0	1	1	X	X	1	0
X	1	0	0	X	X	0	1
X	1	0	1	X	X	1	0
X	1	1	0	X	X	1	0
X	1	1	1	X	X	1	1

(a) Truth table

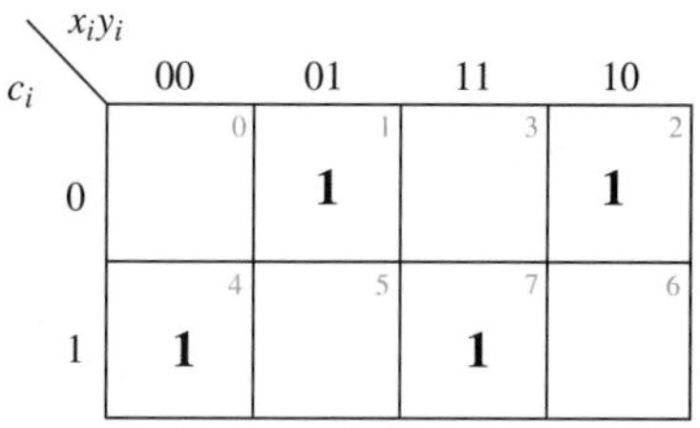

$$s_i = x_i'y_i'c_i + x_i'y_ic_i' + x_iy_i'c_i' + x_iy_ic_i$$

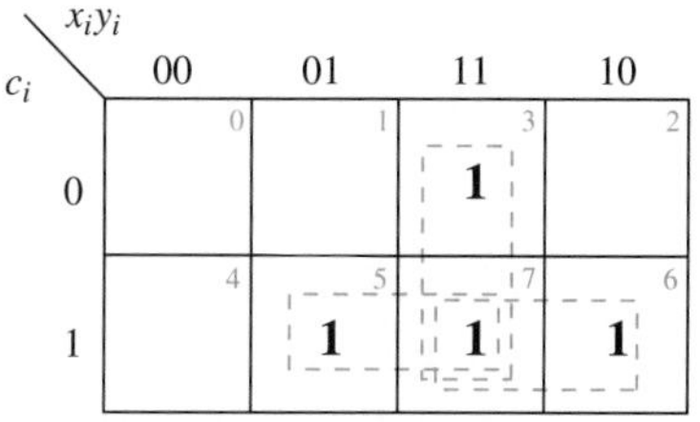

$$c_{i+1} = x_iy_i + x_ic_i + y_ic_i$$

(b) Map representation

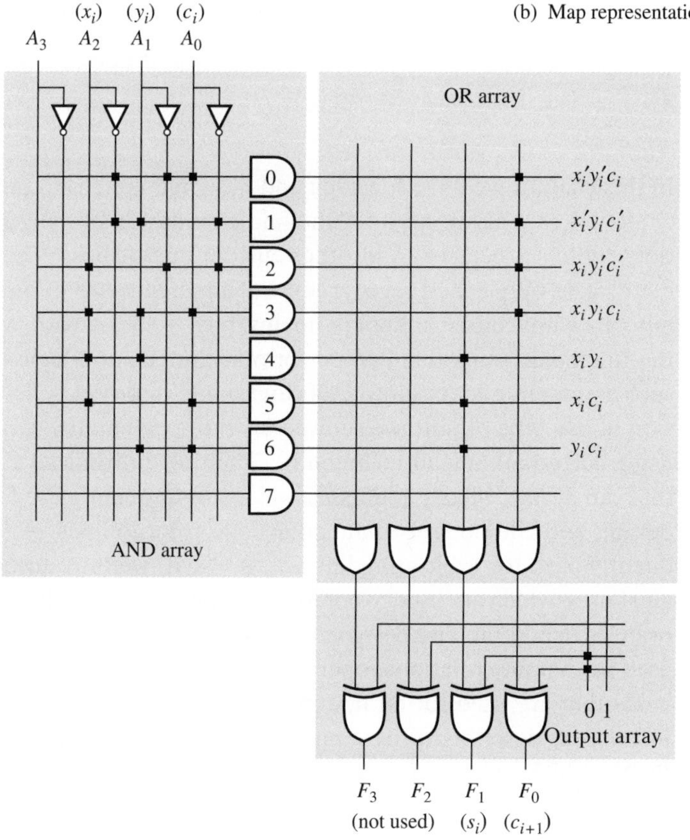

(c) PLA implementation

F I G U R E 5.28
PLA implementation of the full adder.

that was given in Figure 5.26, because such a slice would require eight terms for the functions f_i, and five more terms for the function c_{i+1}, for a total of 13 different terms, which would exceed its limit of eight terms that are available in our PLA.

To implement this full adder, we assign x_i, y_i, and c_i to the address lines A_2, A_1, and A_0, and the outputs c_{i+1} and s_i to the PLA outputs F_1 and F_0. The truth table and map representations for this implementation have been shown in Figure 5.28(a) and (b), and a logic schematic of the PLA, indicating all its connections, is presented in Figure 5.28(c).

PLAs tend to be no less flexible than ROMs and have the additional advantage of being more efficient in their implementation of random logic. Consequently, they are used more often for the implementation of control logics, whereas ROMs are used most frequently for tables of coefficients, startup programs, test vectors, and other random data.

5.14 CHAPTER SUMMARY

In this chapter we have specified and designed the basic combinatorial components that are used for the implementation of data transformations within processors and other custom microchips. These components, generally called register-level components, are designed to manipulate whole binary numbers, not just bits. To begin with, we designed the functional units that can perform arithmetic and logic operations, such as adders, adders/subtractors logic units, and ALUs. In our discussion of this type of unit, we showed how to speed up the carry chain by using carry-look-ahead techniques. Then we introduced components that can decode binary addresses, which are frequently used in memory design, and components that can encode priority lines, which are frequently used for arbitrating bus access. Next, we introduced selectors and buses, which are used to connect the components within a microchip or PCB. In addition, we designed combinatorial components that can be used to compute relational operators, such as comparators, and components that are used for bit manipulation, such as shifters and rotators. Finally, we described programmable components, such as ROMs and PLAs, which are frequently used to implement tables, control logics, and other random logic functions. In most cases we designed these components by starting with their functional tables, converting them into truth tables, and then implementing them with generic gates, all the while drawing on the logic synthesis techniques that we learned in previous chapters.

5.15 FURTHER READINGS

Ercegnovac, M. and T. Lang. *Digital Systems and Hardware/Firmware Algorithms*. New York: Wiley, 1985.

> An excellent and thorough introduction to the construction of combinatorial components and iterative arrays.

Hayes, J. P. *Computer Architecture and Organization*. New York: McGraw-Hill, 1988.

> An introductory architecture book that describes many of the combinatorial register-level components and their uses in processor design.

Neil, H. E., and K. Eshraghiam. *Principles of CMOS VLSI Design*. Reading, MA: Addison-Wesley, 1993.

> Explains to readers who have a knowledge of circuit design and layout techniques the design of combinatorial components on the circuit level and illustrates how to perform transistor layout for many of the components.

5.16 PROBLEMS

5.1 (Adders) Design a 2-bit adder slice that will combine the functions of two FAs. Using the library presented in Table 3.14, compare the delay of your design with that of the design shown in Figure 5.1.

5.2 (Subtractors) Define and design a full subtractor, which would be similar to a full adder, and use it to design a ripple-borrow subtractor.

5.3 (Subtractors) Define and design a borrow-look-ahead function and show how it could be used in a magnitude subtractor.

5.4 (Carry-look-ahead generators) Using the libraries given by the tables noted below, redesign the CLA generator that was shown in Figure 5.2(c).
  (a) Table 3.14,
  (b) Table 3.14 and 3.15,
  (c) Table 3.14, 3.15, and 3.16.

For each design, compare the delays in the generation of the following carries: c_4, c_8, c_{12}, and c_{16}.

5.5 (Carry-look-ahead generators) Design a 64-bit CLA adder, using:
  (a) One level of CLA
  (b) Two levels of CLA
  (c) Three levels of CLA

Compare the delays of these adders.

5.6 (Carry-look-ahead generators) Design the fastest possible CLA adder for:
  (a) 16 bits
  (b) 32 bits
  (c) 64 bits

5.7 (Logic units) Design a logic unit that will perform the following combinations of operations.
  (a) NAND, NOR, transfer, and complement
  (b) XOR and XNOR
  (c) AND, OR, and NOT

5.8 (ALUs) Design an ALU that can perform add, subtract, NAND, and NOR operations.

5.9 (ALUs) Design a logic extender that can perform AND, NAND, OR, NOR, XOR, XNOR, identity, and complement operations.

5.10 (Decoders) Design a 4-to-16 decoder, using:
  (a) 1-to-2 decoders
  (b) 2-to-4 decoders
  (c) AND, OR, and NOT logic gates

5.11 (Encoders) Design a (a) 2-to-1, (b) 4-to-2, (c) 8-to-3, and (d) 16-to-4 code encoder, which is a true complement of a decoder.

5.12 (Selectors) Give an algorithm for construction of n-to-1 selectors from 2-to-1 selectors for any given integer n.

5.13 (Comparators) Design the serial and parallel versions of a comparator that can compare the following types of number representation.
  (a) Sign-magnitude
  (b) Two's complement
  (c) Floating point

5.14 (Comparators) Design comparators that would evaluate the following single relations.

(a) $X > Y$

(b) $X = Y$

(c) $X < Y$

(d) $X \geq Y$

(e) $X \leq Y$

5.15 (Comparators) Redesign the 2-bit comparator that compares $X = x_1 x_0$ with $Y = y_1 y_0$, under the condition that x_0 and y_0 will never be 1 at the same time. How many transistors would you save if you used this 2-bit comparator in the serial implementation of the 8-bit comparator in Figure 5.22(a)?

5.16 (Comparators) Redesign the 2-bit comparator that compares $X = x_1 x_0$ with $Y = y_1 y_0$, under the condition that x_1 and y_1, or x_0 and y_0, or both will never be 1 at the same time. How many transistors would you save if you used this 2-bit comparator in the parallel implementation of the 8-bit comparator in Figure 5.22(b)?

5.17 (Shifters) Design an 8-bit barrel:

(a) Left rotator

(b) Left shifter

(c) Left and right shifter

(d) Left and right shifter/rotator

5.18 (Shifters) Define the operations of an arithmetic left shift (multiplication by 2) and a right shift (division by 2) for sign-magnitude and two's-complement numbers. Design a 1-bit arithmetic shifter for:

(a) Sign-magnitude numbers

(b) Two's-complement numbers

(c) Both types of numbers

5.19 (Shifters) Redesign the universal shifter presented in Figure 5.23 by adding the capacity for two's-complement arithmetic shifting to its set of operations.

5.20 (ROMs) For arbitrary Boolean functions, compare the cost and delay of their implementations with:

(a) A PROM

(b) A PLA

(c) A FPGA

(d) Random logic

5.21 (ROMs) Using a 16×4 PROM, implement a 2-bit comparator that can generate "greater than," "less than," and "equal to" functions.

5.22 (PLAs) Using the type of PLAs indicated in parentheses, implement the following functions.

(a) An adder/subtractor slice (with $4 \times 16 \times 4$ PLA)

(b) A magnitude comparator (with $4 \times 8 \times 4$ PLA)

(c) A CLA generator (with $9 \times 8 \times 6$ PLA)

5.23 (PLAs) Using a $4 \times 8 \times 4$ PLA, add the mode bit M to the full adder presented in Figure 5.28(a), so that whenever $M = 0$, the output $s_i = x_i$, and whenever $M = 1$, the PLA will perform the full-adder function.

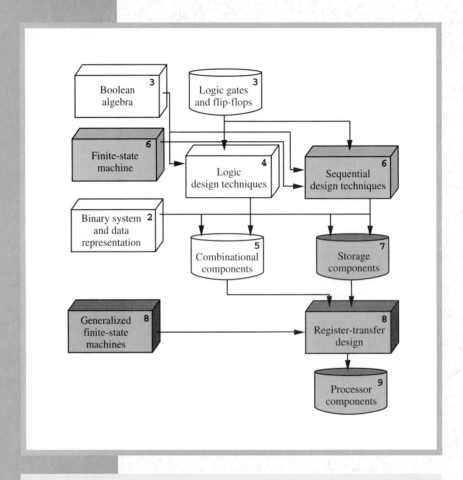

So far, we have learned how to specify and design combinatorial components for data encoding, selection, manipulation, and transformation. In this chapter we learn how to specify and design sequential circuits that contain memory and thus can remember the changes of input signals that occurred in the past. We learn how to model the sequential components using a finite-state-machine model and how to use it in the analysis and synthesis of sequential logic.

6

Sequential Logic

In the previous five chapters we described the design procedure for combinatorial components. The main characteristic of all combinatorial components is the fact that their output values are computed entirely from their present input values. For any change in input values, the output values appear at the output pins with the delay Δ needed to compute those output values. Sequential components differ because they contain memory elements, which combinatorial components do not. As a result, the output values of sequential components are computed using both the present and past input values.

This dependence on the past input values requires the presence of memory elements in sequential circuits. The values stored in memory elements define the state of a sequential component. Thus any change in the input values at time t_i will change the state of the sequential component at time $t_i + \Delta_1$ and the output values at time $t_i + \Delta_2$.

As an example of a sequential circuit, let us consider the ring counter in a telephone answering machine, which counts the number of incoming rings and turns on the message recorder after four rings. Since the ring counter counts up to four, the counter memory must be able to store four digits: 0, 1, 2, and 3. When it is the number 0 that is stored in the memory, we say that the answering machine is in state 0, in which it expects the first ring. In states 1, 2, and 3, the answering machine will have received one, two, or three rings, respectively. When the counter is in state 3 and the fourth ring arrives, the recorder is activated. At this time, further rings will be disabled and the counter will return to state 0. In this example we see that the output of the ring counter depends not just on one ring but on the sequence of rings that occurred before the fourth ring arrives.

This is generally true for all sequential circuits. Their outputs depend on the sequence of input values that have occurred over a period of time. In fact, the term *sequential* comes from this dependence on an input-value sequence instead of just a current input value. As we have seen, this sequence of input values, or some derivative of it, is stored in the memory. Since this memory is always finite, the sequence size must always be finite, which means that the sequential logic can contain only a finite number of states, although the number of states could be quite large.

In general, sequential circuits can be asynchronous or synchronous. **Asynchronous sequential circuits** change their state and output values whenever a change in input values occurs, whereas all **synchronous sequential circuits** change their states and output values at fixed points of time, which are specified by the rising or falling edge of a free-running **clock** signal. In Figure 6.1 we show the timing diagram and nomenclature for a typical clock signal. In this diagram you can see that the **clock period** is the time between successive transitions in the same direction, that is, between two rising or two falling edges. The reciprocal of the clock period is referred to as the **clock frequency**. Usually, the clock period is measured in nanoseconds (ns) and frequency is measured in megahertz (MHz). The **clock width** is the time during which the value of the clock signal is equal to 1. The ratio of clock width and clock period is referred to as the **duty cycle**. A clock signal is said to be **active high** if the state changes occur at the clock's rising edge or during the clock width. Otherwise, the clock signal is said to be **active low**.

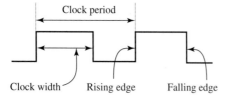

Clock period

Clock width   Rising edge   Falling edge

FIGURE 6.1

Clock signal.

In this chapter we use this nomenclature to discuss synchronous sequential logic. First, we introduce the basic storage elements that can store one bit of information, known as latches and flip-flops. We then give the analysis procedure for sequential logic and establish the finite-state-machine model used for the modeling of sequential logic. We also discuss the synthesis procedure for converting finite-state-machine descriptions into sequential logic schematics. In the course of this presentation, analysis and synthesis procedures are demonstrated on several practical examples.

6.1 SR LATCH

The simplest memory element in digital design is the SR latch, which consists of two cross-coupled NOR gates. As you can see in Figure 6.2(a), the **SR latch** has two input signals, the set signal S and the reset

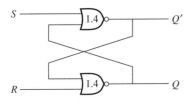

(a) Logic schematic

S	R	Q	Q(next)	Q'(next)
0	0	0	0	1
0	0	1	1	0
0	1	X	0	1
1	0	X	1	0
1	1	X	0	0

(c) Truth table

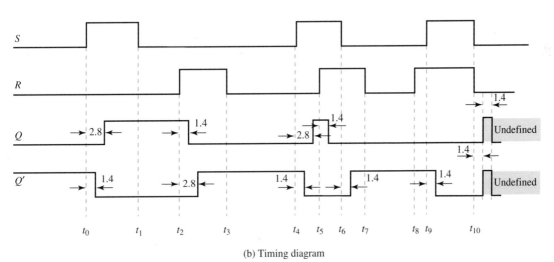

(b) Timing diagram

FIGURE 6.2
SR latch (NOR implementation).

signal R; it also has two output signals, Q and Q'; finally, it has two states, a **set state** when $Q = 1$ ($Q' = 0$) and a **reset state** when $Q = 0$ ($Q' = 1$). As long as both input signals S and R are equal to 0, the SR latch persists in the same state. For example, if $Q = 1$, the output of the top NOR will be equal to 0, which, in turn, will keep the output of the bottom NOR at 1. Similarly, if $Q = 0$, the output of the top NOR will be equal to 1, which will make the output of the bottom NOR equal to 0.

If, however, the S input (R input) becomes equal to 1, the SR latch goes to the set (reset) state. This is demonstrated in the timing diagram in Figure 6.2(c). For example, when S equals 1 at t_0, the output Q' equals 0 at $t_0 + 1.4$ ns, which, in turn, forces Q to go to 1 at $t_0 + 2.8$ ns. Note that when S goes back to 0 at t_1, the SR latch stays in the set state. Similarly, the SR latch can be reset by asserting the reset signal R while keeping S at the value 0. For example, when R becomes 1 at t_2, the Q output becomes 0 at $t_2 + 1.4$ ns, forcing Q' to become 1 at $t_2 + 2.8$ ns. Note also that after R is disasserted at t_3, the latch will stay in the reset state.

If input signals S and R are both equal to 1, both output signals, Q and Q', must be equal to 0. If one of the input signals is disasserted earlier than the other, the latch will end up in the state forced by the signal that was disasserted later. This situation is demonstrated in Figure 6.2(b) at the point when S equals 1 at t_4. As you can see, the latch will follow the normal pattern and enter the set state at $t_4 + 2.8$ ns. Furthermore, when R is asserted at t_5, the Q output equals 0 at $t_5 + 1.4$ ns. Note that as long as both S and R equal 1, both outputs Q and Q' equal 0. However, when S is disasserted at t_6, the latch will enter the reset state at $t_6 + 1.4$ ns and stay in the reset state until S or R is reasserted again.

One problem inherent in the SR latch is the fact that if both S and R are disasserted at the same time, we cannot predict the latch output. In case both gates have exactly the same delay, both gates will become 1 at the same time and then 0 at the same time, and so on, thus oscillating forever, as shown in Figure 6.2(b). For example, when both input signals get disasserted at t_{10}, both NOR gates will become 1 at $t_{10} + 1.4$ ns. Since one of the inputs to each NOR gate is now equal to 1, both NOR gates will become equal to 0 at $t_{10} + 2.8$ ns. This oscillation, usually called a **critical race**, will continue with outputs of both gates equal to 1 at $t_{10} + 1.4 \times (2n + 1)$ and 0 at $t_{10} + 1.4 \times (2n)$ ns for any nonnegative integer n. When both NOR gates do not have exactly the same delay, one NOR gate may be slightly faster than the other. In such a case, the faster NOR gate will prevail and set its output to 1, forcing the other latch output to 0 at $t_{10} + 2.8$ ns. Therefore, when both input signals get disasserted at the same time, the next latch's state is undefined, since we do not know which condition will occur.

In order to avoid this indeterministic behavior, we must ensure that S and R signals are never disasserted at the same time. Unfortunately, this rule is difficult to enforce because of unknown delays in the logic circuits generating the values of S and R. As a result, we must follow a much stricter rule when designing with SR latches; we must ensure that S and R signals should never be asserted at the same time.

From this analysis of SR-latch operation, we can construct the truth table of the latch behavior, shown in Figure 6.2(c). As this table shows, for each moment t_i, $Q(next)$ and $Q'(next)$ indicate the value of output Q at time $t_i + \Delta$, where Δ is equal to or greater than 2.8 ns. The table gives the output values for every combination of input values and the state of the SR latch.

The SR latch can also be implemented with NAND gates. In this case, however, S and R inputs are normally equal to 1. Setting S or R to 0 will set or reset the latch, which is just the opposite of the NOR implementation, where asserting S or R caused the latch to be set or reset. The NAND implementation is shown in Figure 6.3(a), (b), and (c) for completeness.

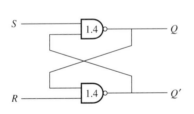

(a) Logic schematic

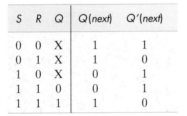

S	R	Q	$Q(next)$	$Q'(next)$
0	0	X	1	1
0	1	X	1	0
1	0	X	0	1
1	1	0	0	1
1	1	1	1	0

(c) Truth table

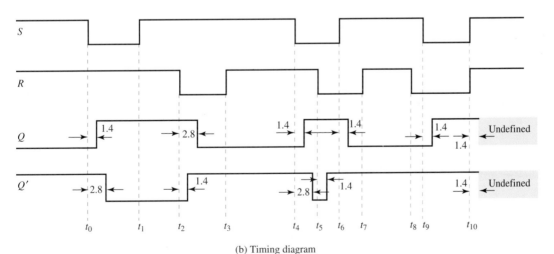

(b) Timing diagram

FIGURE 6.3
SR latch (NAND implementation).

6.2 GATED SR LATCH

The **gated SR latch** is similar to the SR latch, with one exception. As shown in Figure 6.4, this latch has a third control input, C, which enables or disables the operation of the SR latch. In practice, this means that when C equals 1, the gated SR latch operates as an SR latch. When $C = 0$, however, setting or resetting of the latch is disabled and the circuit persists in the preceding state. Consider, for example, the timing diagram in Figure 6.4(d), which demonstrates this behavior, showing that although the latch is in the reset state at t_0, it does not get set when S becomes 1. Note, however, that the setting of the latch is allowed at t_1, when C is asserted; the Q' output becomes 0 at $t_1 + 2.0$ ns and Q equals 1 at $t_1 + 4.0$ ns. Once C is disasserted again at t_2, the changes in

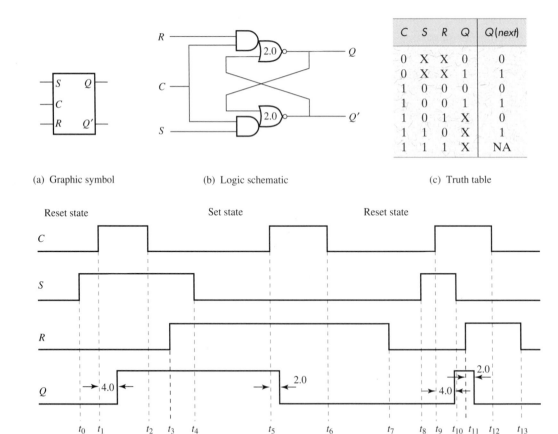

C	S	R	Q	Q(next)
0	X	X	0	0
0	X	X	1	1
1	0	0	0	0
1	0	0	1	1
1	0	1	X	0
1	1	0	X	1
1	1	1	X	NA

(a) Graphic symbol   (b) Logic schematic   (c) Truth table

(d) Timing diagram

FIGURE 6.4
Gated SR latch.

the values of the input signals S and R at t_3 and t_4 cannot affect the state of the latch. When C is asserted again at t_5, however, the value of the input signals is allowed to propagate through the latch. Therefore, the latch is reset at $t_5 + 2.0$ ns.

In general, we can see that the latch follows the changes in the input signals as long as C is equal to 1. For example, when C becomes 1 at t_9, S is equal to 1, so the latch enters set state ($Q = 1$) at $t_9 + 4.0$ ns. When S is disasserted at t_{10} and R is asserted at t_{11}, the latch enters the reset state ($Q = 0$) at $t_{11} + 2.0$ ns.

One precaution is relevant when working with the gated SR latch: The designer must make sure that the input signals do not change during the time window around the falling edge of the control input C. This window starts at setup time t_{setup} before the falling edge of C and ends with hold time t_{hold} after the falling edge of C. In Figure 6.4(d), for example, the following conditions must hold for the third control pulse:

$$t_{12} - t_{11} \geq t_{setup}$$
$$t_{13} - t_{12} \geq t_{hold}$$

Similar inequalities can be written for other falling edges of the control signal in Figure 6.4(d). In the majority of digital designs, the control input is connected to the system clock signal. For this reason, the gated SR latch is also frequently called a **clocked SR latch**.

6.3 GATED D LATCH

As indicated in Section 6.2, designers who are working with SR latches must ensure that inputs S and R never equal 1 at the same time. This nuisance can be removed by using D latches, which have only one input D. The **gated D latch** is constructed from a gated SR latch by connecting the D input to the S input and D' to the R input of the SR latch, as shown in Figure 6.5(b). By connecting D and D' to S and R inputs, we ensure that both S and R will never equal 1 at the same time. A D latch also has a C input, which enables the D latch as it did with the gated SR latch described above. When C equals 1, the output Q will assume the same value as the input D after a short delay time. Conversely, when C equals 0, the output Q maintains the last value of D established before the falling edge of the clock.

The functionality of a gated D latch is demonstrated in the timing diagram in Figure 6.5(d). Note that when C becomes equal to 1 at t_1, Q will become equal to D at $t_1 + 4.0$ ns. Similarly, when C becomes equal to 1 at t_4, Q will become equal to D at $t_4 + 2.0$ ns. Note also that

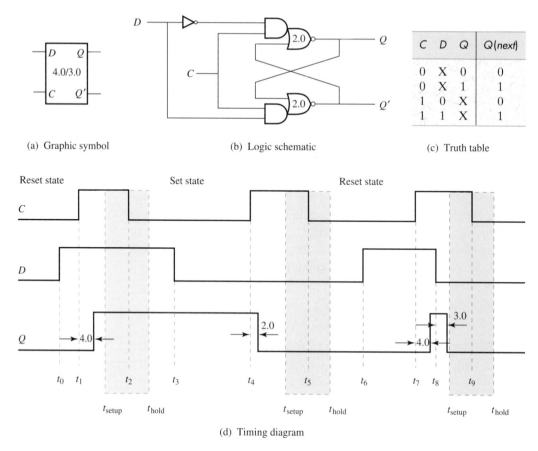

(a) Graphic symbol (b) Logic schematic (c) Truth table

C	D	Q	Q(next)
0	X	0	0
0	X	1	1
1	0	X	0
1	1	X	1

(d) Timing diagram

FIGURE 6.5
Gated D latch.

if D changes during the clock width, Q will follow the changes in input D as long as the changes occur before t_{setup} and after t_{hold}. t_{setup} and t_{hold} are times before and after the falling edge of the C signal during which the D input must be stable. The time interval between t_{setup} and t_{hold} is shown shaded in Figure 6.5(d). In the figure, for example, Q will become equal to 1 at $t_7 + 4.0$ ns, since D was equal to 1 when C became 1. On the other hand, when D changes to 0 at t_8, Q will follow at $t_8 + 3.0$ ns, as long as $t_9 - t_8 \geq t_{setup}$. In general, the gated D latch is easy to work with because the input signal D and the slightly delayed output signal Q always have the same value during the time period in which C is asserted.

As we explained in the preceding paragraph, output Q is delayed by 4.0 ns in the L-to-H transition and 3.0 ns in the H-to-L transition, which is indicated by 4.0/3.0 in the graphic symbol when used in larger schematics.

6.4 FLIP-FLOPS

As explained earlier, gated latches are simple memory elements that are enabled during the entire time interval, during which the control signal C equals 1. These latches are often called **level-sensitive latches** because they are enabled whenever the control signal is at level 1. At any point during that time, the latches will be transparent, in the sense that any input changes will propagate to the output with some small delay. These latches behave as memory elements only after the falling edge of the control signal, when they retain the state set by the last input value that occurred before the falling edge of the control signal.

On the basis of this description you can see that designers must be very cautious when using these latches since long time intervals when latch is transparent can sometimes allow unwanted information to enter the latch. As an example, let's consider a 3-bit shift register consisting of three D latches, as shown in Figure 6.6(a). In this example the input signal X is connected to the D input of the first latch, its output Q_1 is connected to the D input of the second latch, and its output Q_2 is connected to the D input of the third latch. The control input C is connected to the system clock Clk that synchronizes the operation of all the latches. Ideally, this shift register should work in the following way: During each clock width, the X value will enter the first latch, the value in the first latch will be moved into the second latch, and the second value will be moved to the third latch.

As you can see in the detailed timing diagram in Figure 6.6(b), however, the information shift that actually occurs will not be exactly as desired. Let us assume, for example, that all latches are in the reset state ($Q_1 = Q_2 = Q_3 = 0$) and that the input signal X has a value of 1 during the first clock pulse and 0 afterward. In other words, the shift register should start with a content of 000 and contain 100, 010, and 001 after the first, second, and third clock pulses. In reality, however, if our shift register starts with a content of 000, it will be followed by 111, 000, and 000 after the first, second, and third clock pulses. In other words, the shift register has behaved as a single D latch which stores the value of the input signal X in each clock cycle.

Let's observe this behavior in even greater detail, assuming that the clock width $t_w = 15$ ns and that the input signal X becomes equal to 1 at t_0. When the clock signal enables the latching at t_1, the first latch will change to the set state ($Q_1 = 1$) at $t_1 + 4.0$ ns. Since the clock signal retains its value for another 11 ns, however, the second latch will switch to the set state at $t_1 + 8.0$ ns, as will the third latch at $t_1 + 12.0$ ns. After the first falling edge at t_2, then, the content of our shift register will be equal

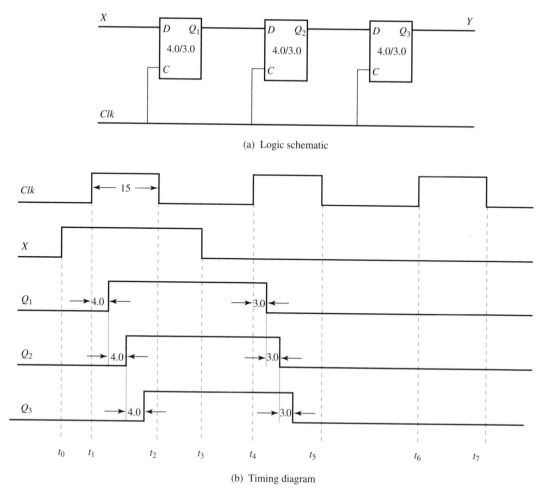

(a) Logic schematic

(b) Timing diagram

FIGURE 6.6
Erroneous shifting with D latches.

to 111. Similar behavior will be exhibited when the second and all succeeding clock pulses have enabled further latching in the shift register.

One possible idea to rectify this erroneous behavior is to shorten the clock width to one propagation delay. The difficulty in this approach, though, is that the delays in setting and resetting latches are not the same, which means that a clock width that works to set the latch may not work for resetting the latch, and vice versa. Furthermore, if the clock width is limited to a time less than the latch delay, the latch may not have time to catch the input value. In any case, the latch manufacturer cannot really guarantee exact delay values simply because of variations in the fabrication process. In this sense, we must keep in mind that the setting and resetting delays that we use are just expected delay values, whereas real delay values are normally distributed around these expected delays.

Given these constraints, there are two possible solutions to our problem: master-slave and edge-triggered flip-flops. **Master-slave flip-flops** are implemented using two latches, referred to as a master latch and a slave latch. As shown in Figure 6.7(a), the input to the master latch is the input to the flip-flop, while input to the slave latch is the output of the master latch. The output of the slave latch is the output of the entire flip-flop. Within the flip-flop, both the master and slave latches are driven by the same clock signal, Clk, the crucial difference being that the master latch will be enabled when the clock signal is equal to 0, and the slave latch will be enabled when the clock signal is equal to 1.

The advantage in using these flip-flops should be clear: Since master and slave latches are never enabled at the same time, the entire master–slave flip-flop is never transparent. When the clock signal Clk is 0, for example, only the master latch is enabled and its content is

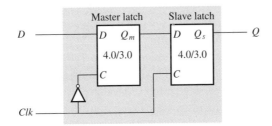

(a) Logic schematic

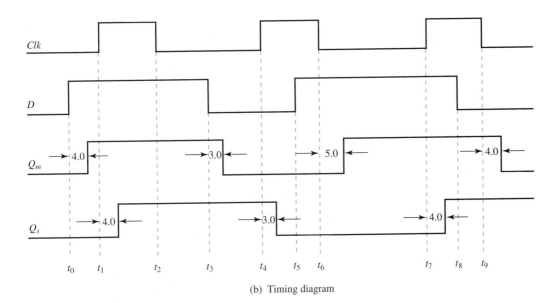

(b) Timing diagram

FIGURE 6.7
Master-slave flip-flop.

transferred to the slave latch only after the clock signal becomes 1. Note that when the clock signal becomes 1, the master latch is disabled and its content does not change.

This is shown in more detail in the timing diagram of Figure 6.7(b), which shows three pulses of the clock signal *Clk*. When D input becomes 1 at t_0, the master latch follows the input change by setting $Q_m = 1$ at $t_0 + 4.0$ ns, since its control input C is equal to 1. This change does not propagate through the slave latch until the *Clk* equals 1 at t_1 and sets $Q_s = 1$ at $t_1 + 4.0$ ns. When D becomes 0 again at t_3, the master latch follows at $t_3 + 3.0$ ns but the change does not propagate through the slave latch until $t_4 + 3.0$ ns. When D changes again to 1 at t_5, the change is not accepted by the master latch until the *Clk* equals 0 at t_6. Thus Q_m becomes 1 at $t_6 + 5.0$ ns. Note that an extra 1-ns delay was added because the inverter driving the C input of the master latch. Furthermore, when the slave latch is enabled at t_7, Q_s equals 1 at $t_7 + 4.0$ ns. A similar change of the input D to 0 at t_8 is not registered by the master latch until $t_9 + 4.0$ ns and not propagated through the slave latch until the clock signal becomes 1 again.

As demonstrated in Figure 6.7, the value of the input D is captured into the master latch before the rising edge of the clock signal and transferred to the slave latch immediately after the same rising edge. For all practical purposes we can say that the value of D was captured on the rising edge of the clock signal.

If we reconstruct the 3-bit shift register discussed above using master–slave flip-flops, we obtain the logic schematic shown in Figure 6.8(a), which corresponds to the timing diagram shown in Figure 6.8(b). Note that this new timing diagram contains the same *Clk* and input signals as in Figure 6.6(b) but has been altered so that for each flip-flop, we show two waveforms: the outputs of the master and slave latches, Q_{im} and Q_{is}, where $1 \leq i \leq 3$.

As the diagram shows, after the input signal X changes to 1 at t_0, only the master latch of the first flip-flop will be set ($Q_{1m} = 1$), at $t_0 + 4.0$ ns. Then, when the clock signal changes to 1 at t_1, the slave latch is set at $t_1 + 4.0$ ns. A little bit later, after the clock signal returns to 0 at t_2, the master latch of the second flip-flop is set ($Q_{2m} = 1$), at $t_2 + 5.0$ ns. Note that when the input signal X returns to 0 at t_3, the master latch of the first flip-flop is reset ($Q_{1m} = 0$). After the next rising edge of the clock, Q_{1s} is returned to 0 at $t_3 + 3.0$ and Q_{2s} is set to 1 at $t_4 + 4.0$. Similarly, at the third rising edge of the clock, Q_{2s} is reset and Q_{3s} is set.

As you can see, shift registers constructed from master–slave flip-flops shift their content by one position to the right on each rising edge of the clock signal. Each clock cycle therefore corresponds to one state

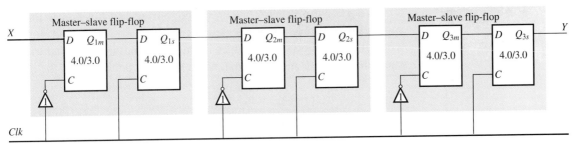

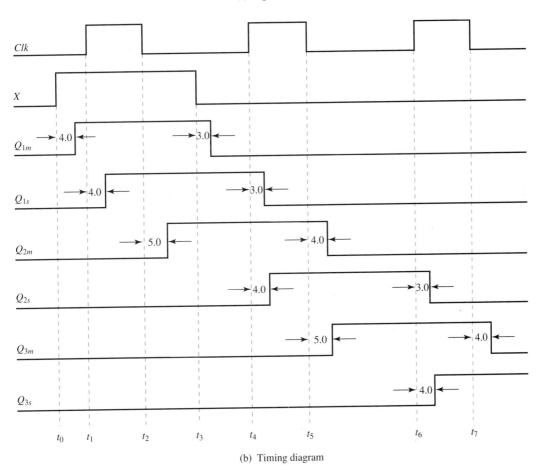

(a) Logic schematic

(b) Timing diagram

FIGURE 6.8
Shifting with master–slave flip-flops.

of the shift register, which [for the sequence of the input signal values shown in Figure 6.8(b)] goes from state 000 through states 100, 010, and 001, and finally, returns to 000.

As shown in Figure 6.9(a), an **edge-triggered flip-flop** is implemented with three interconnected SR latches: set, reset, and output. The set latch follows the changes in the *Clk* signal if *D* is equal to 1 at the rising edge of the *Clk* signal, while the reset latch follows the clock

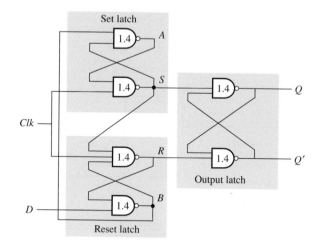

(a) Logic schematic

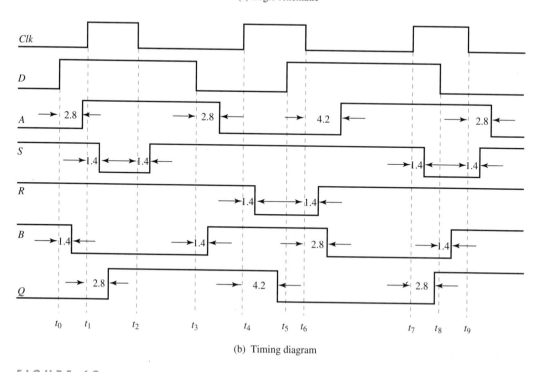

(b) Timing diagram

FIGURE 6.9
Edge-triggered flip-flop.

signal if D is equal to 0 at the rising edge of the clock signal. In other words, signals A and B register changes in D as long as Clk is equal to 0. The detailed operation of the edge-triggered flip-flop is explained in the timing diagram shown in Figure 6.9(b).

While Clk equals 0, S and R signals are both 1, holding the output latch in its present state. When D changes at t_0, B goes to 0 at $t_0 + 1.4$ ns and A goes to 1 at $t_0 + 2.8$ ns. The output Q is not affected until Clk equals 1 at t_1, forcing S to become 0 at $t_1 + 1.4$ ns and Q to become 1 at $t_1 + 2.8$ ns. When Clk returns to 0 at t_2, S returns to 1 at $t_2 + 1.4$ ns, leaving Q at 1. When D goes to 0 at t_3, B becomes 1 at $t_3 + 1.4$ ns and A becomes 0 at $t_3 + 2.8$ ns.

After the rising edge of the Clk signal at t_4, R changes to 0 at $t_4 + 1.4$ ns and Q to 0 at $t_4 + 4.2$ ns. The change in the value of D at t_5 is not registered until the falling edge of the Clk signal at t_6 when R returns to 1 at $t_6 + 1.4$ ns and B becomes 0 at $t_6 + 2.8$ ns and A becomes 1 at $t_6 + 4.2$ ns. At $t_7 + 2.8$ ns, Q is set to 1 after the rising edge of Clk at t_7 and the lowering of S at $t_7 + 1.4$ ns.

Note again that subsequent change in D at t_8 does not propagate to the output Q but is captured when B becomes 1 at $t_8 + 1.4$ ns and A becomes 0 at $t_9 + 2.8$ ns. The value of Q will become 0 at the next rising edge of the Clk signal if D does not change after t_8. If D changes after t_8 and before the next rising edge, values of A and B signals will capture this change and propagate it to the output Q at the next rising edge of the Clk signal.

Since both master–slave and edge-triggered flip-flops change states only during positive clock transitions as we have demonstrated in Figures 6.7 and 6.9, we can define one state of the sequential circuit containing flip-flops to be a time interval between the two rising edges of the clock signal. The value of the sequential circuit in each of its states is defined by the content of all its flip-flops.

6.5   FLIP-FLOP TYPES

In Section 6.4 we showed how to construct a master-slave and edge-triggered flip-flop. Although there are many different ways to construct flip-flops, they all exhibit the following two characteristics: first, a flip-flop will change state only on the positive or negative edge of the clock signal, and second, its data inputs must not change after time t_{setup} before and until time t_{hold} after the triggering edge of the clock signal.

All flip-flops can be divided into four basic types: SR, JK, D, and T. They differ in the number of inputs and in the response evoked by different values of input signals. The four types of flip-flops are defined in Table 6.1. Each of these flip-flops can be uniquely described by its graphical symbol, its characteristic table, its characteristic equations or excitation table. Graphical symbols specify the number and types of inputs and outputs. All flip-flops have output signals Q and Q'. All of them also have the clock signal input. The small triangle at the clock input indicates that the flip-flop is triggered by the rising edge of the clock signal. Conversely, a circle in front of the triangle would indicate that the flip-flop is triggered by the falling edge of the clock signal.

TABLE 6.1

Flip-Flop Types

FLIP-FLOP NAME	FLIP-FLOP SYMBOL	CHARACTERISTIC TABLE	CHARACTERISTIC EQUATION	EXCITATION TABLE

SR

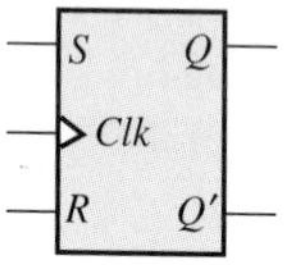

S	R	Q(next)
0	0	Q
0	1	0
1	0	1
1	1	NA

$Q(next) = S + R'Q$

$SR = 0$

Q	Q(next)	S	R
0	0	0	X
0	1	1	0
1	0	0	1
1	1	X	0

JK

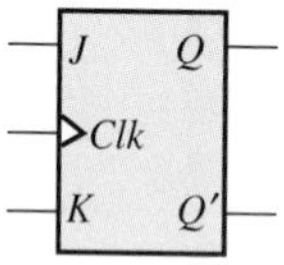

J	K	Q(next)
0	0	Q
0	1	0
1	0	1
1	1	Q'

$Q(next) = JQ' + K'Q$

Q	Q(next)	J	K
0	0	0	X
0	1	1	X
1	0	X	1
1	1	X	0

D

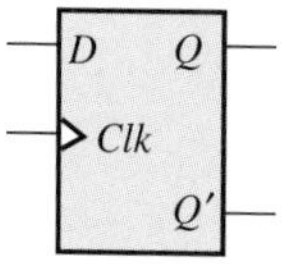

D	Q(next)
0	0
1	1

$Q(next) = D$

Q	Q(next)	D
0	0	0
0	1	1
1	0	0
1	1	1

T

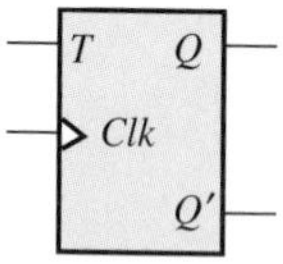

T	Q(next)
0	Q
1	Q'

$Q(next) = TQ' + T'Q$

Q	Q(next)	T
0	0	0
0	1	1
1	0	1
1	1	0

For the sake of simplicity we use throughout this book only flip-flops triggered by the rising edge. Each flip-flop has one or two data inputs that characterize the flip-flop and give it its name, as described earlier. The **SR flip-flop** has two inputs, S (set) and R (reset), that set or reset the flip-flop when asserted. In other words, when $S = 1$ and $R = 0$, the flip-flop output Q is set to 1 and when $S = 0$ and $R = 1$ it is reset to 0. Similar to the SR flip-flop, the **JK flip-flop** has two inputs, J and K, which set or reset the flip-flop when asserted. In addition, when both inputs J and K are asserted at the same time, the JK flip-flop changes its state. As mentioned before, the **D flip-flop** has one input D (data), which sets the flip-flop when $D = 1$ and resets it when $D = 0$. The **T flip-flop** has one input T (toggle), which forces the flip-flop to change states when T equals 1.

In the second column of Table 6.1 we see the **characteristic table**, which is a shorter version of the truth table, that gives for every set of input values and the state of the flip-flop before rising edge the corresponding state of the flip-flop after the rising edge of the clock signal. In the table, Q and $Q(next)$ designate the state of the flip-flop before and after the rising edge of the clock, respectively. The characteristic table is used during the analysis of sequential circuits when the value of flip-flop inputs are known and we want to find the value of the flip-flop output Q after the rising edge of the clock signal. As with any other truth table, we can use the map method to derive a **characteristic equation** for each flip-flop, which are shown in the third column of Table 6.1.

In the fourth column of the table, we show an **excitation table** which is used during the synthesis of sequential circuits. The excitation table is derived from the characteristic table by transposing input and output columns. It gives the value of flip-flop inputs that are necessary to change the flip-flop's present state to the desired next state after the rising edge of the clock signal.

In addition to graphical symbols, tables, or equations, flip-flops can also be described uniquely by means of state diagrams or state graphs, in which case each state would be represented by a circle, and a transition between states would be represented by an arrow. In Table 6.2, for example, the four types of flip-flops are described by this method. Note that each arrow is labeled with the values of its input signals, which will cause a transition from one state to the other. Note also that the same state can be both the source and the destination of a transition. Since transitions occur at the clock edge, each state can be thought of as a time interval between two rising edges of the clock signal.

In the table you can see that the state diagrams of all four flip-flops have the same number of states and transitions: Each flip-flop is in the set state when $Q = 1$ and in the reset state when $Q = 0$. Furthermore,

TABLE 6.2

State Diagrams for Various Flip-Flops

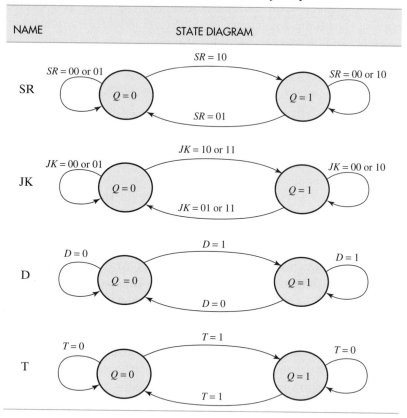

NAME	STATE DIAGRAM
SR	$SR = 00$ or 01 — $Q = 0$ — $SR = 10$ → $Q = 1$ — $SR = 00$ or 10; $SR = 01$ (return)
JK	$JK = 00$ or 01 — $Q = 0$ — $JK = 10$ or 11 → $Q = 1$ — $JK = 00$ or 10; $JK = 01$ or 11 (return)
D	$D = 0$ — $Q = 0$ — $D = 1$ → $Q = 1$ — $D = 1$; $D = 0$ (return)
T	$T = 0$ — $Q = 0$ — $T = 1$ → $Q = 1$ — $T = 0$; $T = 1$ (return)

each flip-flop can move from one state to the other, or it can reenter the same state. The only difference between the four types lies in the values of input signals that cause these transitions. A state diagram is a very convenient way to visualize the operation of a flip-flop or even of large sequential components. In Section 6.7 we generalize these state diagrams, to define the finite-state-machine model used in the design of sequential logic.

Each flip-flop is usually available with and without **asynchronous inputs** that are used to preset and clear the flip-flops independently of other flip-flop inputs. These inputs are used to set flip-flops into the initial state for their standard operation. For example, after power is turned on, the state of each flip-flop is not predictable and thus we must use asynchronous inputs to set the flip-flops properly before the start of their synchronous operation. Preset and clear inputs are called asynchronous because they do not depend on the clock signal and therefore have precedence over all other synchronous operations. In other words, when asynchronous inputs are active, the values on other flip-flop inputs are ignored. This can also be concluded from the logic schematics of a D latch and a D flip-flop with asynchronous inputs that are given in Figure 6.10.

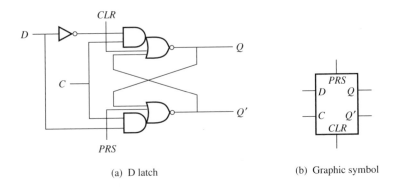

(a) D latch   (b) Graphic symbol

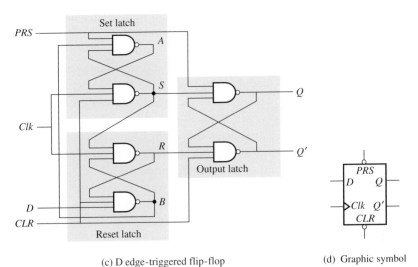

(c) D edge-triggered flip-flop   (d) Graphic symbol

FIGURE 6.10

Storage elements with asynchronous inputs.

As shown in Figure 6.10(a), the gated D latch with asynchronous inputs is the same gated D latch from Figure 6.5, with two additional inputs: PRS and CLR. When preset input (PRS) is equal to 1, the output Q' is equal to 0 and Q to 1. Conversely, when clear input (CLR) is equal to 1, the output Q is equal to 0. As long as one of the PRS or CLR inputs are 1, the flip-flop will persist in the states imposed by the asynchronous inputs. The graphic symbol for a D latch with asynchronous input is shown in Figure 6.10(b).

In contrast to the D latch, the edge-triggered flip-flop in Figure 6.10(c) is preset by the signal PRS when it is equal to 0 and cleared by the signal CLR when it is equal to 0. That fact that a low value of asynchronous signals affects the flip-flops is indicated by the small

TABLE 6.3

Graphic Symbols for
Flip-Flops with
Asynchronous Inputs

FLIP-FLOP NAME	FLIP-FLOP SYMBOL
SR	
JK	
D	
T	

circles in the graphic symbol shown in Figure 6.10(d). Note that the preset and clear signals force all the latches in the Figure 6.10(c) into proper states that correspond to $Q = 1$ and $Q = 0$, respectively. Since active-low preset and clear signals are more frequently found in practice, we will assume throughout this book that all asynchronous inputs are active-low. We show the graphic symbols for all types of flip-flops with active-low asynchronous inputs in Table 6.3.

6.6 ANALYSIS OF SEQUENTIAL LOGIC

Sequential logic is usually specified by means of a logic schematic, which incorporates the flip-flops given in Table 6.1 and the gates given in Tables 3.14, 3.15, and 3.16. Unfortunately, while such a logic schematic may clearly represent the structure of the sequential logic, it does not readily disclose its function, which can be a problem for the designer. During a product redesign, for example, designers usually want to modify the function of the product in order to add new features, or conversely, they may want to use new components and need to verify that the component replacements have not modified the function of the product. In either case, the designers will need to derive the functionality of the sequential logic schematic.

This process, called **analysis**, requires the designer to generate one or more functional descriptions, using state diagrams, state and output tables, and input and output Boolean equations. Once the functional description is derived, designers may also want to develop timing diagrams, which allow them to check their predictions against simulated results. In the following section we demonstrate the complete analysis procedure with several examples.

EXAMPLE 6.1   Modulo-4 counter

PROBLEM   Derive the state table and state diagram for the sequential circuit represented by the schematic in Figure 6.11(a).

SOLUTION   The first step in our analysis is to derive Boolean expressions for the inputs of each flip-flop in the schematic, in terms of external input Cnt and the flip-flop outputs Q_1 and Q_0. Since there are two D flip-flops in our example, we derive two expressions for D_1 and D_0:

$$D_0 = Cnt \oplus Q_0 = Cnt'Q_0 + CntQ_0' \tag{6.1}$$

$$D_1 = Cnt'Q_1 + CntQ_1'Q_0 + CntQ_1Q_0' \tag{6.2}$$

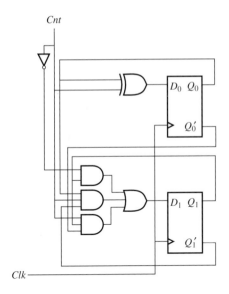

(a) Logic schematic

$$D_0 = Cnt \oplus Q_0 = Cnt' Q_0 + Cnt Q_0'$$
$$D_1 = Cnt' Q_1 + Cnt Q_1'Q_0 + Cnt Q_1Q_0'$$

(b) Excitation equation

$$Q_0(next) = D_0 = Cnt' Q_0 + Cnt Q_0'$$
$$Q_1(next) = D_1 = Cnt' Q_1 + Cnt Q_1'Q_0 + Cnt Q_1Q_0'$$

(c) Next-state equations

PRESENT STATE	NEXT STATE	
Q_1Q_0	$Q_1(next)\,Q_0(next)$	
	$Cnt = 0$	$Cnt = 1$
0 0	0 0	0 1
0 1	0 1	1 0
1 0	1 0	1 1
1 1	1 1	0 0

(d) Next-state table

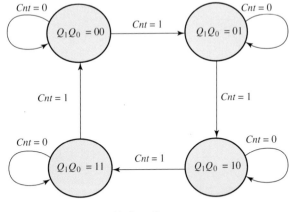

(e) State diagram

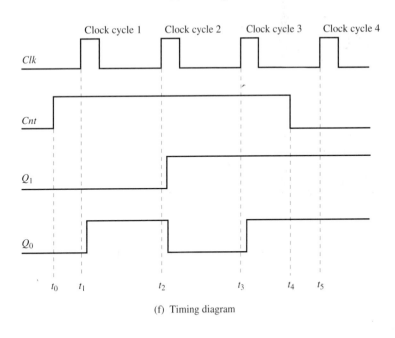

(f) Timing diagram

FIGURE 6.11
Analysis of a sequential circuit.

These Boolean expressions are called **excitation equations** since they represent the inputs to the flip-flops, which, in turn, will determine the state of the sequential circuit in the next clock cycle. After the excitation equations are derived, we can derive the **next-state equations** by converting these excitation equations into flip-flop characteristic equations. In the case of D flip-flops, $Q(next) = D$. Therefore, the next-state equations equal the excitation equations:

$$Q_1(next) = Cnt'Q_0 + CntQ_0' \tag{6.3}$$

$$Q_0(next) = Cnt'Q_1 + CntQ_1'Q_0 + CntQ_1Q_0' \tag{6.4}$$

We now convert these next-state equations into tabular form called the **next-state table**, in which each row corresponds to a state of the sequential circuit and each column represents one set of input values. In general, each state of a sequential circuit is defined by the binary values stored in its flip-flops. In this case, then, since we have only two flip-flops, the number of possible states is four—that is, Q_1Q_0 can be equal to 00, 01, 10, or 11. These values are shown as present states in Figure 6.11(d).

In the next-state part of the table, each entry defines the value of the sequential circuit in the next clock cycle after the rising edge of the *Clk*. Since this value depends on the present state and the value of the input signals, the next-state table will contain one column for each assignment of binary values to the input signals. In our example, since there is only one input signal, *Cnt*, the next-state table shown in Figure 6.11(d) has only two columns, corresponding to $Cnt = 0$ and $Cnt = 1$. Note that each entry in the next-state table indicates the value of the flip-flops in the next state if their value in the present state is in the row header and the input values in the column header. Each of these next-state values has been computed from next-state equations (6.3) and (6.4).

Instead of a next-state table, however, we could use a state diagram to represent the behavior of the sequential circuit. A state diagram is basically a pictorial representation of the next-state table. It has exactly one node, identified by a circle, for each present state in the next-state table. It also has exactly one directed arc going out of each state for each entry in the table. Each arc is labeled with the values of the input signals that cause the transition from the present state (the source of the arc) to the next state (the destination of the arc).

In general, the number of states in a next-state table or a state diagram will equal 2^m, where m is the number of flip-flops; similarly, the number of arcs will equal $2^m \times 2^k$, where k is the number of binary input signals. In the state diagram in Figure 6.11(e), there must be four states and eight transitions. Following these transition arcs, we can see that as long as $Cnt = 1$, the sequential circuit visits the states in the following sequence: $0, 1, 2, 3, 0, 1, 2, \ldots$. On the other hand, when $Cnt = 0$, the circuit stays in its present state until Cnt changes to 1, at which point the counting continues. Since this sequence is characteristic of modulo-4 counting, we can conclude that the sequential circuit represented in Figure 6.11(a) is a modulo-4 counter with one control signal, Cnt, which enables counting when $Cnt = 1$ and disables it when $Cnt = 0$.

In Figure 6.11(f) we show a timing diagram, representing four clock cycles, which enables us to observe the behavior of the counter in greater detail. In this timing diagram we have assumed that Cnt is asserted in clock cycle 0 at time t_0 and is disasserted in clock cycle 3 at time t_4. We have also assumed that the counter is in state $Q_1 Q_0 = 00$ in the clock cycle 0. Note that on the clock's rising edge, at t_1, the counter will go to state $Q_1 Q_0 = 01$ with a slight propagation delay; in cycle 2, after t_2, to $Q_1 Q_0 = 10$; and in cycle 3, after t_3, to $Q_1 Q_0 = 11$. Since Cnt becomes 0 at t_4, we know that the counter will stay in state $Q_1 Q_0 = 11$ in the next clock cycle. To verify the behavior of a sequential circuit completely, we must construct timing diagrams for all possible sequences of input values.

In Example 6.1 we demonstrated the analysis of a sequential circuit that has no outputs by developing a next-state table and a state diagram which describe only the states and the transitions from one state to the next. In the next example we complicate our analysis by adding output signals, which means that we have to upgrade the next-state table and the state diagram to identify the value of output signals in each state. Such a sequential circuit, in which the output values depend solely on its present state, is usually referred to as a **state-based** or **Moore-type sequential circuit**.

EXAMPLE 6.2   State-based modulo-4 counter

PROBLEM   Derive the next state, the output tables, and the state diagram for the sequential circuit given by the schematic shown in Figure 6.12(a).

Cnt

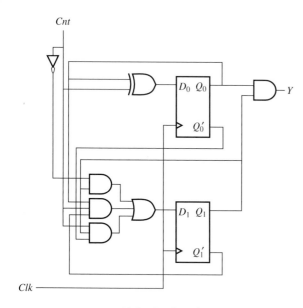

Clk

(a) Logic schematic

$$D_0 = Cnt \oplus Q_0 = Cnt'\, Q_0 + Cnt\, Q_0'$$
$$D_1 = Cnt'\, Q_1 + Cnt\, Q_1'Q_0 + Cnt\, Q_1 Q_0'$$

(b) Excitation equation

$$Q_0(next) = D_0 = Cnt'\, Q_0 + Cnt\, Q_0'$$
$$Q_1(next) = D_1 = Cnt'\, Q_1 + Cnt\, Q_1'Q_0 + Cnt\, Q_1 Q_0'$$
$$Y = Q_1 Q_0$$

(c) Next-state and output equations

PRESENT STATE	NEXT STATE		OUTPUTS
$Q_1 Q_0$	$Q_1(next)\, Q_0(next)$		Y
	$Cnt = 0$	$Cnt = 1$	
0 0	0 0	0 1	0
0 1	0 1	1 0	0
1 0	1 0	1 1	0
1 1	1 1	0 0	1

(d) Next-state and output table

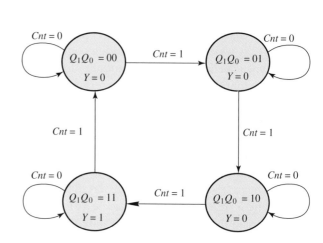

(e) State diagram

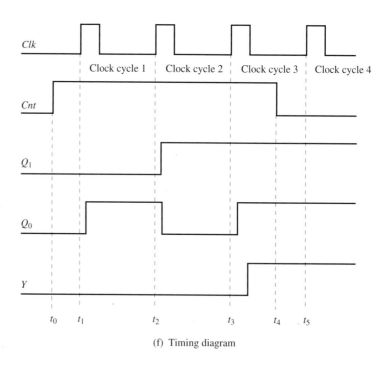

(f) Timing diagram

FIGURE 6.12

Analysis of a state-based modulo-4 counter.

SOLUTION In the figure the input combinatorial logic is the same as in Example 6.1, so the excitation and next-state equations will be the same as in Example 6.1. For the sake of completeness, we have shown these equations in Figure 6.12(b) and (c). In addition, however, we have computed the output equation,

$$Y = Q_1 Q_0 \qquad\qquad (6.5)$$

As this equation shows, the output Y will equal 1 when the counter is in state $Q_1 Q_0 = 11$, and it will stay 1 as long as the counter stays in that state. Since the output Y depends only on the present state of the sequential circuit, we can add one extra column to the state table to convert it to a next-state/output table. We use Equation (6.5) to determine the values to be placed in the output column, as shown in Figure 6.12(d). In general, we add one column for each output signal to convert a next-state table to a next-state/output table.

In Figure 6.12(e) we show how the value of the output signal can be added to each state in the state diagram, and in Figure 6.12(f) how the output Y can be also added to the timing diagram. In Figure 6.12(f), note that the counter will reach the state $Q_1 Q_0 = 11$ only in the third clock cycle, so the output Y will equal 1 after Q_0 changes to 1. Since counting is disabled in the third clock cycle, the counter will stay in the state $Q_1 Q_0 = 11$ and Y will stay asserted in all succeeding clock cycles until counting is enabled again.

In Example 6.2 we have analyzed the sequential logic of a state-based circuit, in which the output signal values were dependent on the state of the sequential circuits but not on the input signal values. In the case of an **input-based** or **Mealy-type sequential circuit**, however, the output values are dependent on the input values as well as the state of the circuit. In analyzing such a circuit, the state and output tables must be modified in order to describe this input-based sequential circuit, which means that every entry in the next-state table will represent the next-state and the output value, separated by a slash (/).

In a state diagram of this type of sequential circuit, the output is not associated with the state but with the transition arc. In this case, each arc is labeled with both the input values that move the circuits from the present state to the next state, and the output values, which correspond to the input-signal values in the present state. This modification is demonstrated by the following example.

___

■ EXAMPLE 6.3 Input-based modulo-4 counter

PROBLEM Derive the state/output table and the state diagram for the sequential circuit given by the schematic shown in Figure 6.13(a).

SOLUTION As you can see from Figure 6.13, this circuit differs from the circuit in Example 6.2 only in the expression of its output, which now depends on the value of the input signal Cnt. From the schematic we can see that the value Y equals 1 when the counter is in state $Q_1Q_0 = 11$ and counting. Thus

$$Y = CntQ_1Q_0 \qquad (6.6)$$

Given this output equation, the state table from Example 6.1 must be modified so that each entry represents the next-state and output values; that is, the next-state value must be computed from the next-state equations, and the output values must be computed from the output equations, shown in Figure 6.13(c). This modified state/output table is shown in Figure 6.13(d).

The state diagram of this input-based circuit will have four states, as before. However, unlike the diagram of the state-based circuit, it now labels each arc with the input and output values in the form X/Y. The label X/Y can be interpreted as follows: If the input signal value at the next positive edge of the clock signal is equal to X, the circuit will transition to the state pointed to by the arc in the next clock cycle. Furthermore, its output during the present clock cycle will be equal to Y as long as the input signal value is equal to X. In Figure 6.13(e), for example, the arc between states $Q_1Q_0 = 01$ and $Q_1Q_0 = 10$ has been labeled $Cnt = 1/Y = 0$, which means that if $Cnt = 1$ during the cycle in which $Q_1Q_0 = 01$, the counter's output will be $Y = 0$ in the present clock cycle and in the next clock cycle the counter will be in state $Q_1Q_0 = 10$. This situation is demonstrated in clock cycle 1 in the timing diagram presented in Figure 6.13(f).

Thus the counter will reach state $Q_1Q_0 = 10$ in clock cycle 2, in which the output signal $Y = 0$. In clock cycle 3,

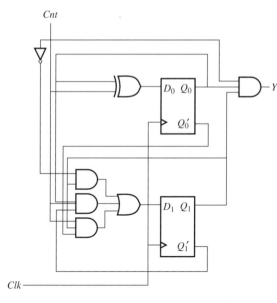

(a) Logic schematic

$$D_0 = Cnt \oplus Q_0 = Cnt'\, Q_0 + Cnt\, Q_0'$$
$$D_1 = Cnt'\, Q_1 + Cnt\, Q_1Q_0 + Cnt\, Q_1Q_0'$$

(b) Excitation equation

$$Q_0(next) = D_0 = Cnt'\, Q_0 + Cnt\, Q_0'$$
$$Q_1(next) = D_1 = Cnt'\, Q_1 + Cnt\, Q_1'Q_0 + Cnt\, Q_1Q_0'$$
$$Y = Cnt\, Q_1Q_0$$

(c) Next-state and output equations

PRESENT STATE	NEXT STATE/OUTPUTS	
Q_1Q_0	$Q_1(next)\ Q_0(next)/Y$	
	$Cnt = 0$	$Cnt = 1$
0 0	0 0/0	0 1/0
0 1	0 1/0	1 0/0
1 0	1 0/0	1 1/0
1 1	1 1/0	0 0/1

(d)   Next-state and output table

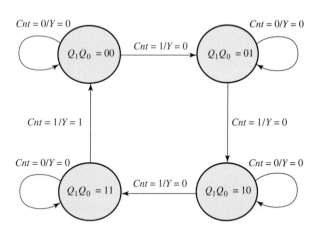

(e) State diagram

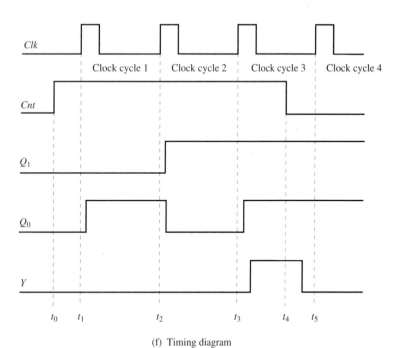

(f) Timing diagram

FIGURE 6.13
Analysis of input-based modulo-4 counter.

the counter will be in state $Q_1Q_0 = 11$ and the output signal Y will equal 1. At t_4, however, the output Y will become equal to 0 because the input signal Cnt now equals 0 even though the counter is still in state $Q_1Q_0 = 11$. In contrast, note that the output Y in Example 6.2 maintained a value of 1 in clock cycle 3, because its value was dependent only on the counter state, which had not changed.

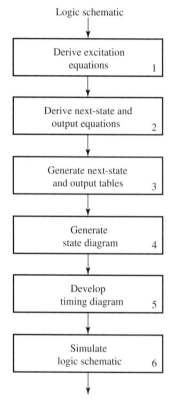

FIGURE 6.14
Analysis procedure for sequential circuits.

On the basis of the tasks applied in Examples 6.1 to 6.3, you should now have a general sense of the various tasks involved in an analysis of sequential circuits. As indicated in Figure 6.14, we start with a logic schematic from which we can derive excitation equations for each flip-flop input. Then, to obtain next-state equations, we insert the excitation equations into characteristic equations. The output equations can also be derived from the schematic, and once we have our output and next-state equations, we can generate next-state and output tables as well as state diagrams. When we reach this stage, we use either the tables or the state diagram to develop a timing diagram, which can then be verified through simulation. We can obtain timing waveforms through simulation on two different levels. On the structural level, we can describe the logic schematic in a simulation language and run the simulation for each set of state and input values using a library of gate and flip-flop models. On the behavioral level, we can describe state diagrams or next-state/output tables in a simulation language and run that through a simulator. In this case we can verify the sequential circuit's functionality but not its real delays, since the state diagram and tables do not contain any information about circuit implementation.

6.7 FINITE-STATE-MACHINE MODEL

At this point we have analyzed several sequential circuits and described them by means of next-state and output Boolean equations, state and output tables, and state diagrams, each of which completely specifies any sequential circuit. All of these descriptions are based on the model of the finite-state machine which we describe in this section.

The finite-state machine (FSM) can be defined abstractly as the quintuple

$$< S, I, O, f, h >$$

where S, I, and O represent a set of states, set of inputs, and a set of outputs, respectively, and f and h represent the next-state and output functions. The next-state function f is defined abstractly as a mapping $S \times I \rightarrow S$. In other words, f assigns to every pair of state and input symbols another state symbol. The FSM model assumes that time is divided into uniform intervals and that transitions from one state to another occur only at the beginning of each time interval. Therefore, the next-state function f defines what the state of the FSM will be in the next time interval given the state and input values in the present interval.

The output function h determines the output values in the present state. There are two different types of finite-state machine, which correspond to two different definitions of the output function h. One type is a **state-based** or **Moore FSM**, for which h is defined as a mapping $S \rightarrow O$. In other words, an output symbol is assigned to each state of the FSM. The other type is an **input-based** or **Mealy FSM**, for which h is defined as the mapping $S \times I \rightarrow O$. In this case, an output symbol in each state is defined by a pair of state and input symbols.

According to our definition, each set S, I, and O may have any number of symbols. However, in reality we deal only with binary variables, operators, and memory elements. Therefore, S, I, and O must be implemented as a cross-product of binary signals or memory elements, whereas functions f and h are defined by Boolean expressions that will be implemented with logic gates.

Thus the FSM can model any sequential circuit with k input signals $A_1, \ldots, A_k$, m flip-flops $Q_1, \ldots, Q_m$, and n output signals $Y_1, \ldots, Y_n$, as shown in Figure 6.15. For such a sequential circuit, S, I, and O are cross products of flip-flops or signals as follows:

$$S = Q_1 \times Q_2 \times \cdots \times Q_m$$
$$I = A_1 \times A_2 \times \cdots \times A_k$$
$$O = Y_1 \times Y_2 \times \cdots \times Y_n$$

Thus each element in S, I, and O is represented by a string of 1's and 0's.

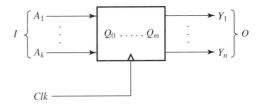

FIGURE 6.15
FSM model of general sequential circuit.

The clock signal defines the time intervals, called clock cycles. If the definition above is adopted, we can model the modulo-4 counter from Example 6.2 as a state-based FSM, where $S = \{s_0, s_1, s_2, s_3\}$, $I = \{i_0, i_1\}$, $O = \{o_0, o_1\}$, and f and h are given by the table in Figure 6.16.

FIGURE 6.16

FSM model of modulo-4 counter from Example 6.2.

PRESENT STATE	NEXT STATE $(S \times I \rightarrow S)$		OUTPUT $(S \rightarrow O)$
	i_0	i_1	
s_0	s_0	s_1	o_0
s_1	s_1	s_2	o_0
s_2	s_2	s_3	o_0
s_3	s_3	s_0	o_1

Similarly, we can model the modulo-4 counter from Example 6.3 as an input-based FSM, in which S, I, O are defined as they were above and f and h are given by the table in Figure 6.17.

FIGURE 6.17

FSM model of modulo-4 counter from Example 6.3.

PRESENT STATE	NEXT STATE $(S \times I \rightarrow S)$ / OUTPUT $(S \times I \rightarrow O)$	
	i_0	i_1
s_0	s_0/o_0	s_1/o_0
s_1	s_1/o_0	s_2/o_0
s_2	s_2/o_0	s_3/o_0
s_3	s_3/o_0	s_0/o_1

Each FSM model can be implemented with flip-flops and logic gates. The content of the flip-flops defines the state of the FSM, while f and h are implemented as combinatorial logic. The general logic block diagrams for state- and input-based FSMs are shown in Figure 6.18. These block diagrams are used in subsequent sections as templates for the synthesis of sequential logic.

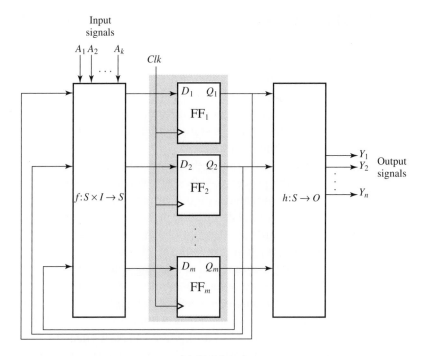

(a) State-based

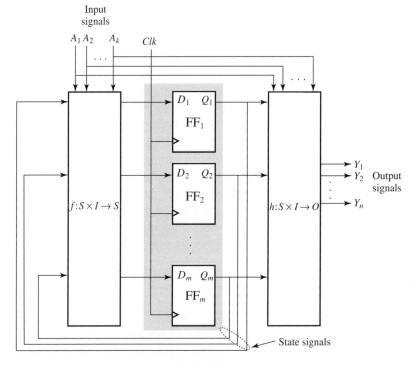

(b) Input-based

FIGURE 6.18

Finite-state-machine implementations.

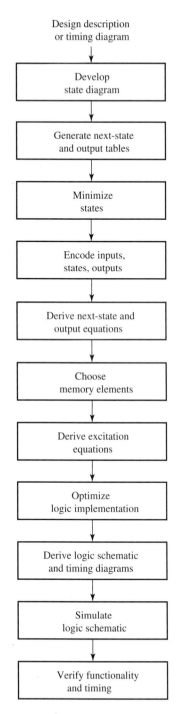

Design description
or timing diagram

Develop
state diagram

Generate next-state
and output tables

Minimize
states

Encode inputs,
states, outputs

Derive next-state and
output equations

Choose
memory elements

Derive excitation
equations

Optimize
logic implementation

Derive logic schematic
and timing diagrams

Simulate
logic schematic

Verify functionality
and timing

F I G U R E 6.19

Synthesis procedure for FSM models.

6.8 SYNTHESIS OF SEQUENTIAL LOGIC

In previous sections we have demonstrated how to analyze various sequential circuits. In this section we turn to the synthesis procedure, which is the inverse of the task of analysis, insofar as analysis starts with the implementation and discovers the function or behavior of the sequential circuit, whereas synthesis starts with a behavioral description and generates an implementation.

A general description of the synthesis procedure is shown in Figure 6.19. As you can see, this process usually starts with an English-language description, possibly augmented with one or more timing diagrams, or sometimes with a more formal description presented in a language such as the IEEE-standard hardware description language known as VHDL. Given this description, the first task in the synthesis procedure consists of developing the state diagram and converting it into next-state and output tables. Next, we try to reduce the number of states by removing redundant states and merging equivalent states, since a smaller number of states will require fewer flip-flops. Ultimately, since each state must be expressed as an n-tuple of its flip-flop values, we need to assign different n-tuples to the various states. This procedure, called encoding, if done properly, will simplify the input and output logic. After encoding, we can generate the binary form of the next-state and output equations.

The next task in the synthesis consists of choosing flip-flop types, keeping in mind the fact that different types require different amounts of logic for implementation of the next-state functions. Having chosen the flip-flop types, we are ready to derive excitation equations for each flip-flop input, at which point we can optimize the logic implementation of the excitation and output equations and draw a logic schematic that serves as a basis for the generation of a timing diagram.

The last task in this series consists of simulating the logic schematic, then comparing the output to the timing diagram derived and checking whether the simulation actually implements the behavior we intended to produce. In the following sections we demonstrate this synthesis procedure in detail by working through a comprehensive example.

6.9 FSM MODEL CAPTURE

The design of sequential logic starts with the generation of a state diagram and/or next-state and output tables. Initially, these diagrams and tables must be derived from a natural language description of the behavior of the sequential circuit. Unfortunately, natural language descriptions can sometimes be ambiguous or in many cases, incomplete, since they often focus exclusively on the main function of the sequential circuit, without enumerating all possible cases of its behavior. For this reason, a natural language description is sometimes supplemented with timing diagrams. Even these timing diagrams, however, can be incomplete, since they do not show circuit responses for every possible input sequence, only for the most important. In most cases, then, it is best to replace the natural language description with a more precise one based on a hardware description language such as VHDL, or with a graphical form such as a flowchart or an ASM chart, introduced in Chapters 7 and 8. Regardless of the form we use, though, the construction of the FSM model is a very creative part of the design process, requiring expertise and experience. In this section we demonstrate construction of the state diagram and state table for a simple example.

> ### ■ **EXAMPLE** *6.4*   Modulo-3 up/down-counter

PROBLEM   Derive the state diagram for a modulo-3 up/down-counter. The counter has two inputs: count enable (C) and count direction (D). When $C = 1$, the counter will count in the direction specified by D, and it will stop counting when $C = 0$. The counter will count up when $D = 0$ and down when $D = 1$. The counter has one output Y, which will be asserted when the counter reaches 2 while counting up or when it reaches 0 while counting down. The counter symbol is shown in Figure 6.20(a).

SOLUTION   On the basis of this description we can conclude that the counter requires at least two flip-flops, since it must remember three digits: 0, 1, and 2. Furthermore, since the counter can count up or down, we need two sequences: up and down. The up sequence consists of three states: u_0, u_1, and u_2, with the counter proceeding from u_0 to u_1 to u_2 and returning to u_0 as long as $CD = 10$. Similarly, when the counter counts down, it again goes through three states, in this case d_0, d_1, and d_2. In the down sequence, however, the counter proceeds from d_0 to d_2 to d_1 and returns to d_0 as long as $CD = 11$. The up and down sequences are shown in Figure 6.20(b).

In developing the state diagram of the counter, we need to account for the possibility that the counter might change direction while it is counting—in other words, we have to allow for the possibility that the value of input D may change

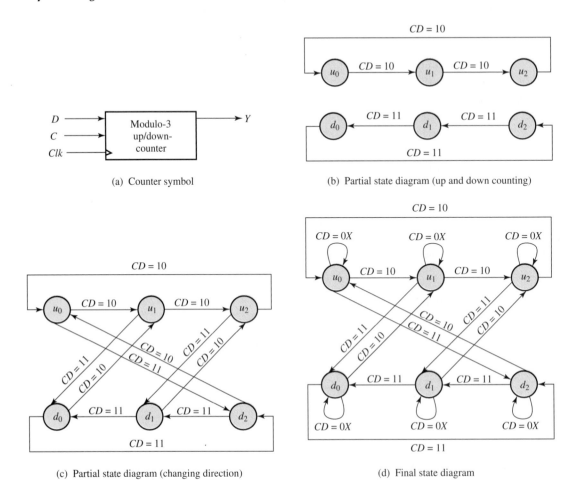

FIGURE 6.20

State diagram for a modulo-3 counter.

while $C = 1$. Although this case is not mentioned in the input description given above, we can accommodate such an occurrence by assuming that the counter would continue counting in a new direction from the peer state in the other sequence—that is, if D changes from 0 to 1, the counter will go from u_i to $d_{(i-1)\bmod 3}$, and if D changes from 1 to 0, the counter will go from d_i to $u_{(i+1)\bmod 3}$, for $i = 0, 1,$ or 2. This case has been added to the state diagram in Figure 6.20(c).

The state diagram will only be complete, however, when we have considered what will happen when the counter is disabled by a change of C from 1 to 0. In this case we assume that the counter will remain in that state until C becomes 1 again. This case is added to the state diagram in

Figure 6.20(d), which now accounts for all possible counter behaviors.   ▪

Although the state diagram derived in Example 6.4 is complete, it is important to note that the diagram does not contain the minimal number of states. Granted, it is easy to understand, since the various cases of the counter's behavior are clearly distinguished and readily apparent in the state diagram. In sequential design, however, clarity is not usually the goal; on the contrary, cost and performance are often the most important factors, and from this perspective, we need to consider minimizing the number of states as part of the design process.

6.10 STATE MINIMIZATION

The purpose of state minimization is to reduce the number of states in a sequential circuit so that the circuit requires fewer flip-flops, which in turn will reduce the cost of its implementation. However, a state reduction will not reduce the required number of flip-flops unless the number of states is reduced below the present power-of-2 level. For a sequential circuit with m states, for example, we would need $\lceil \log_2 m \rceil$ flip-flops. Since reducing the number of states by Δ would require $\lceil \log_2(m - \Delta) \rceil$ flip-flops, Δ must be such a number that $\lceil \log_2 m \rceil$ is greater than $\lceil \log_2(m - \Delta) \rceil$ by at least 1.

Consider, for example, a circuit with six states. Reducing the number of states to five will not reduce the number of flip-flops, because $\lceil \log_2 6 \rceil = \lceil \log_2 5 \rceil = 3$. On the other hand, reducing the number of states to four would reduce the number of flip-flops by 1, because $\lceil \log_2 4 \rceil = 2$.

A second benefit of state reduction is that it can reduce the number of gates and the number of inputs per gate that are needed to implement next-state and output functions. The advantage of such a reduction lies in the fact that gates with fewer inputs are faster; by decreasing the sequential circuit delay, we can improve the clock frequency of the circuit and thereby improve its overall performance.

In general, state minimization is based on the concept of the **behavioral equivalence** of FSMs and, by extension, the equivalence of its states. For example, we would say that two FSMs are equivalent if they produce the same sequence of output symbols for every sequence of input symbols. In some cases, equivalent FSMs may have different numbers of states and may also transition through a different sequence of states for every input sequence; nonetheless, they are considered behaviorally equivalent as long as they produce the same output sequence.

We can conclude from the discussion above that a FSM with the larger number of states will have some states that are equivalent. In cases like this, then, we can reduce the number of states in the FSM by merging those states that are equivalent.

State equivalence can be defined on the basis of the values of state outputs and next states. More formally, two states, s_j and s_k, in an FSM are said to be equivalent, $s_j \equiv s_k$, iff the following two conditions are true.

1. Both states s_j and s_k produce the same output symbol for every input symbol i: that is, $h(s_j, i) = h(s_k, i)$.

2. Both states have equivalent next states for every input symbol i: that is, $f(s_j, i) \equiv f(s_k, i)$.

From this definition of state equivalence, we can derive a simple procedure for obtaining an FSM with the minimal number of states. The procedure requires partitioning all the states in an FSM into equivalence classes and constructing the minimal-state FSM in which each state will represent one equivalence class.

In practice, this procedure consists of two steps. In the first step, we compare output symbols for each state and for each input symbol. The goal of this comparison is to combine states into groups in such a way that all states in the same group generate the same output symbol for each input symbol. In the second step, we determine, for each state in the group and for every input symbol, the next state. Then we can partition the groups into subgroups in such a way that all states in a subgroup have their next states in the same group for every input symbol.

In some cases, all the states that are in the same subgroup after partitioning do not have their next states in the same subgroup although they have their next states in the same group. In such cases, the second step must be repeated until no further partitioning is necessary. Eventually, though, each subgroup will represent an equivalence class that is equal to one state of the minimal FSM. In the following example we demonstrate this procedure on the modulo-3 counter from Example 6.4.

_____ **EXAMPLE 6.5** State reduction

PROBLEM Derive the minimal-state FSM for the modulo-3 counter.

SOLUTION As shown in Figure 6.20(c), the modulo-3 counter has six states. In Figure 6.21(a) we have converted this state diagram into a next-state/output table. Given the information provided by this table, we can now apply the procedure described above to the set of states in Figure 6.21(b). Note

PRESENT STATE	NEXT STATE		
	CD = 0X	CD = 10	CD = 11
u_0	$u_0/0$	$u_1/0$	$d_2/1$
u_1	$u_1/0$	$u_2/0$	$d_0/0$
u_2	$u_2/0$	$u_0/1$	$d_1/0$
d_0	$d_0/0$	$u_1/0$	$d_2/1$
d_1	$d_1/0$	$u_2/0$	$d_0/0$
d_2	$d_2/0$	$u_0/1$	$d_1/0$

(a) Initial state table

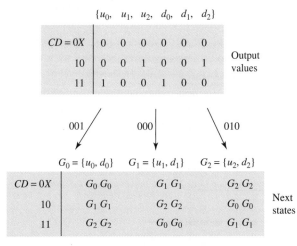

$\{u_0, \ u_1, \ u_2, \ d_0, \ d_1, \ d_2\}$

CD = 0X	0	0	0	0	0	0	Output values
10	0	0	1	0	0	1	
11	1	0	0	1	0	0	

001   000   010

$G_0 = \{u_0, d_0\}$ $G_1 = \{u_1, d_1\}$ $G_2 = \{u_2, d_2\}$

CD = 0X	$G_0\ G_0$	$G_1\ G_1$	$G_2\ G_2$	Next states
10	$G_1\ G_1$	$G_2\ G_2$	$G_0\ G_0$	
11	$G_2\ G_2$	$G_0\ G_0$	$G_1\ G_1$	

(b) Partitioning into equivalence classes

PRESENT STATE	NEXT STATE		
	CD = 0X	CD = 10	CD = 11
s_0	$s_0/0$	$s_1/0$	$s_2/1$
s_1	$s_1/0$	$s_2/0$	$s_0/0$
s_2	$s_2/0$	$s_0/1$	$s_1/0$

(c) Final next-state/output table

FIGURE 6.21

State reduction for modulo-3 counter.

that we start with the set of all states and then determine the output values for each combination of input values. For the input values of $CD = 0X, 10, 11$, we know the value of the output signal to be $Y = 0, 0, 1$ or $0, 0, 0$ or $0, 1, 0$. At this point we can create the following three groups: $G_0 = \{u_0, d_0\}$, $G_1 = \{u_1, d_1\}$, and $G_2 = \{u_2, d_2\}$. Next, we must determine, for each state in each group and for each set of input values, what the next state will be. As you can see, for every value of the input signals, the next states of each state in the group belong to the same group. Therefore, no further partitioning is needed. Since each group represents a class of equivalent states, we can rename the groups G_0, G_1, and G_2 as states s_0, s_1, and s_2 in the minimal-state FSM. The next-state/output table for this minimal FSM is given in Figure 6.21(c).

The equivalence classes of an FSM can also be found by constructing an implication table, which allows us to eliminate nonequivalent states and indicate equivalent states. As shown in Figure 6.22 an implication table is a triangular table in which every entry represents a specific pair of states. Note that the rows have been labeled with all the states but the first, whereas the columns have been labeled with all states but the last. By this means we ensure that every pair of states is assigned one entry in the table.

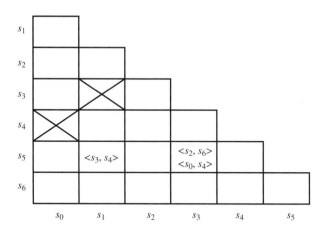

FIGURE 6.22
Implication table.

The procedure for finding equivalence classes follows from the equivalence definition. In the first step we enter an × for every pair of states that differ in their output values for at least one set of input values. In this manner, a pair of states that are not equivalent can be eliminated from consideration, as shown for pair $< s_1, s_3 >$ and $< s_0, s_4 >$ in Figure 6.22. For the remaining pairs of states, we enter into each entry the next-state pairs that would have to be equivalent if the pair of states represented by the entry are to be equivalent. In general, we say that the equivalence of the pair of next states is implied, which gives the name to the implication table. For example, the equivalence of the pair $< s_1, s_5 >$ in Figure 6.22 implies the equivalence of $< s_3, s_4 >$. Similarly, the equivalence of the pair $< s_3, s_5 >$ implies the equivalence of $< s_2, s_6 >$ and $< s_0, s_4 >$ according to condition 2 of the equivalence definition.

In the second step we scan the table from top to bottom one square at a time, and from left to right one column at a time, and enter × into any square having at least one nonequivalent next-state pair. This second step may be iterated several times since nonequivalence of one state pair may cause the nonequivalence of another state pair, and so on. If no ×'s are entered during the entire table scan, we have already found all the nonequivalent pairs, which means that all the noncrossed entries indicate equivalent pairs.

The equivalence classes are formed in the third step by using the transitivity property of the equivalence relation, which states that if $s_i \equiv s_j$ and $s_j \equiv s_k$, then $s_i \equiv s_k$. Thus we can group all the equivalent states into classes by examining the table. We demonstrate this procedure in the following example.

EXAMPLE 6.6   State reduction with implication table

PROBLEM   Find the minimal number of states for the FSM specified by the table in Figure 6.23(a). [Note that this table is a slight modification of the table in Figure 6.21(a).]

SOLUTION   First, we need to create the implication table, as shown in Figure 6.23(b). Next, we cross out all the squares that represent state pairs that have a different output for at least one set of input values. That leaves only pairs $< u_0, d_0 >$, $< u_1, d_1 >$, and $< u_2, d_2 >$ to be checked for the next-state equivalence. The pair $< u_0, d_0 >$ has the same next states for every set of input values. Therefore, they are equivalent and they do not imply the equivalence of any next states. The pair $< u_1, d_1 >$ requires states u_0 and d_2 to be equivalent, so we enter $< u_0, d_2 >$ into the square representing the pair $< u_1, d_1 >$. States u_2 and d_2 are equivalent since they have the same next states for every set of input values. Next, we scan the table and insert an × into the square representing $< u_1, d_1 >$, since u_0 and d_2 are not equivalent, which also implies that u_1 and d_1 are not equivalent. This ends the second step of the procedure.

In the third step we need to group all the equivalent states into equivalence classes. In our example, only u_0 and

PRESENT STATE	NEXT STATE / OUTPUT		
	$CD = 0X$	$CD = 10$	$CD = 11$
u_0	$u_0 / 0$	$u_1 / 0$	$d_2 / 1$
u_1	$u_0 / 0$	$u_2 / 0$	$d_0 / 0$
u_2	$u_2 / 0$	$u_0 / 1$	$d_1 / 0$
d_0	$d_0 / 0$	$u_1 / 0$	$d_2 / 1$
d_1	$d_2 / 0$	$u_2 / 0$	$d_0 / 0$
d_2	$d_2 / 0$	$u_0 / 1$	$d_1 / 0$

(a) Next-state and output table

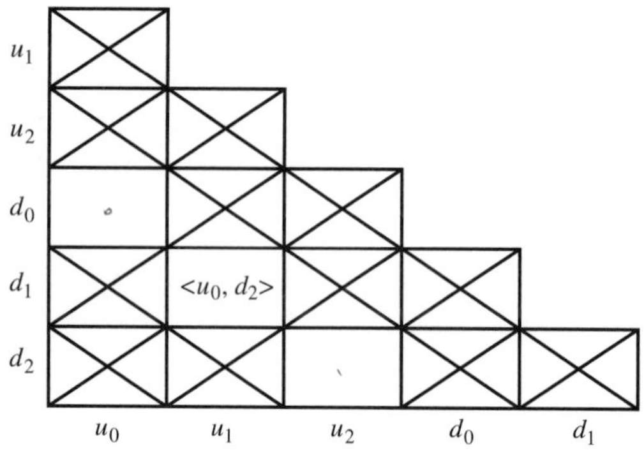

(b) Implication table

FIGURE 6.23
State reduction with implication table.

TABLE 6.4

Twenty-Four Encodings of
Four States

ENCODING NUMBER	s_0	s_1	s_2	s_3
1	00	01	10	11
2	00	01	11	10
3	00	10	01	11
4	00	10	11	01
5	00	11	01	10
6	00	11	10	01
7	01	00	10	11
8	01	00	11	10
9	01	10	00	11
10	01	10	11	00
11	01	11	00	10
12	01	11	10	00
13	10	00	01	11
14	10	00	11	01
15	10	01	00	11
16	10	01	11	00
17	10	11	00	01
18	10	11	01	00
19	11	00	01	10
20	11	00	10	01
21	11	01	00	10
22	11	01	10	00
23	11	10	00	01
24	11	10	01	00

d_0 and u_2 and d_2 are equivalent. Therefore, the minimal FSM turns out to have four states, represented by the following four equivalence classes: $\{u_0, d_0\}$, $\{u_1\}$, $\{d_1\}$, $\{u_2, d_2\}$.

6.11 STATE ENCODING

For any given FSM, the cost and delay inherent in the input and output logic will be largely dependent on what Boolean values are assigned to the symbolic states. For example, a four-state FSM with states s_0, s_1, s_2, and s_3 could be implemented with two flip-flops that contain values 00, 01, 10, or 11. In this case, then, there would be at least $4! = 4 \times 3 \times 2 \times 1 = 24$ possible encodings of the four states to flip-flop values as shown in Table 6.4. In practice, there are generally more than $n!$ encodings for n different states, since we could use more than $\log_2 n$ bits for the encoding of *n* states. For this reason, hand enumeration of all these encodings, as well as cost and delay estimation for the input and output logic, can become tedious, even for a small number of states. To avoid this problem, designers use various strategies or heuristics for state assignment. In the rest of this section we explain the three most popular strategies: minimum bit change, prioritized adjacency, and hot-one encoding.

The **minimum-bit-change** strategy assigns Boolean values to the states in such a way that the total number of bit changes for all state transitions is minimized. In other words, if every arc in the state diagram has a weight that is equal to the number of bits by which the source and destination encodings differ, the optimal encoding would be the one that minimizes the sum of all these weights.

In Figure 6.24(a) and (b) we show two encodings for the same state diagram. The straightforward encoding for this binary counter would have two arcs with a weight of 1 and two arcs with a weight of 2, for a total weight of 6. On the other hand, in the minimum-bit-change encoding, all four arcs would have a weight of 1. In the second encoding, the total weight is minimal, since any two state encodings must differ by at least one bit. This minimum-bit-change strategy is based on the premise that in a two-level implementation, we need at least an extra AND gate and an extra input to the OR gate for setting or resetting a flip-flop, for each bit change.

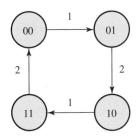
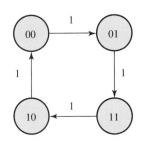

(a) Straightforward encoding   (b) Minimum-bit-change encoding

FIGURE   6.24

Two different encodings for a 2-bit binary counter.

The second strategy for state assignment, the **prioritized-adjacency strategy**, proceeds by assigning adjacent encodings, which differ in one bit only, to all states that have a common destination, source, or output. In this procedure the highest priority is given to states that have the same next state for a given input value. The rationale for this priority derives from the fact that the same next-state encoding will appear in two adjacent entries in the Karnaugh map during the logic minimization, in which case this strategy will lead to a reduction of one literal for each 1 in the next-state encoding. Second priority is given to the next states of the same state, on the assumption that they will also appear adjacent in the Karnaugh map during minimization. Note that this will occur only if the input values, which cause the transition, differ in only one bit. Finally, third priority is given to states that have the same output value for the same input values, on the assumption that adjacent state encodings will create a 1-cube in the Karnaugh map during logic minimization of the output signals.

Figure 6.25(a) shows a state diagram with four states. Note that states s_1 and s_2 satisfy the condition of the first priority; that is, the input value of 0 will move both states into the same state s_3. In addition, they satisfy the condition of the second priority, since they are both next states of the state s_0. In relation to the third priority, note that states s_0 and s_1 have the same output value 0 for the same input value 0 and that states s_2 and s_3 satisfy the same condition. These priorities are listed in Figure 6.25(b), and in Figure 6.25(c) we show a possible encoding that would satisfy the various adjacency priorities.

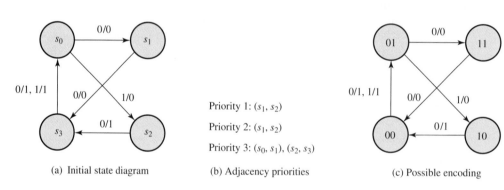

(a) Initial state diagram

Priority 1: (s_1, s_2)

Priority 2: (s_1, s_2)

Priority 3: (s_0, s_1), (s_2, s_3)

(b) Adjacency priorities

(c) Possible encoding

F I G U R E   6.25
Encodings based on prioritized adjacency.

The third strategy for state assignment, **hot-one encoding**, uses redundant encoding in which one flip-flop is assigned to each state. In other words, each state is distinguishable by its own flip-flop having a value of 1 while all the others have a value of 0. In practice, this means that one flip-flop will be set to 1 and another reset to 0 during each transition from state to state. The name of this encoding derives from the fact that the value 1 reminds us of a hot potato being passed from one hand to another. The obvious limitation of hot-one encoding is that it works only for an FSM with a small number of empty states because the number of flip-flops becomes excessive if there are more than a few states.

In general, the best strategy for state encoding is to determine several possible options and then estimate the cost and delay of input and output logic for each candidate encoding. In the rest of this section we demonstrate this procedure using our example of the modulo-3 counter.

■ **EXAMPLE 6.7**   State encodings for modulo-3 counter

PROBLEM   Given the up/down modulo-3 counter that was specified by the minimal next-state/output table in Figure 6.21(c), derive the encoding that will minimize the cost and delay of the counter logic.

SOLUTION   As you can see from the next-state/output table, this counter has only three states, which means that any encoding produces two pairs of states with adjacent encodings and one pair of states whose encodings differ in two bits. Furthermore, since we can encode four states with two variables, Q_1 and Q_0, one combination of values would be redundant. Thus we could omit the combination $Q_1 Q_0 = 11$, since it would allow us to reduce the number of 1's during logic minimization. One possible encoding, then, is encoding A, shown in Figure 6.26. This is the encoding we obtain if we follow the minimum-bit-change strategy.

	ENCODING A	ENCODING B	ENCODING C
STATES	$Q_1 Q_0$	$Q_1 Q_0$	$Q_2 Q_1 Q_0$
s_0	0 0	0 1	0 0 1
s_1	0 1	0 0	0 1 0
s_2	1 0	1 0	1 0 0

FIGURE 6.26
Possible state encodings for modulo-3 counter.

If we use the prioritized-adjacency strategy, we find that no pair of states satisfies the first and second priority rules. According to the third priority rule, we find that states s_0 and s_1, and s_1 and s_2, should be given adjacent encodings, an option already satisfied in encoding A. In this simple problem we could also use a strategy that simplifies state decoding, by assigning combinations $Q_1 Q_0 = 01$ and $Q_1 Q_0 = 10$ to states s_0 and s_2, which are the only states with $Y = 1$. This encoding option is shown as encoding B in Figure 6.26. Its primary advantage is that it reduces the number of AND gate inputs in the implementation of the output logic. Finally, a third strategy is to use hot-one encoding, which yields encoding C in Figure 6.26.

At this point we have established encodings A, B, and C as possible candidate encodings. To evaluate the benefit of each, we must now estimate the cost and delay of their respective input and output logic implementations. For this purpose we need to derive excitation and output equations and estimate the cost and delay of their two-level implementation with NAND gates. To simplify this estimation, we assume that each variable's true and complement values are available at no cost or delay. This assumption is always true for the flip-flop variables, and it is also true for input variables since they require double inverters to increase their input signal strength. The input double inverters add a constant cost and delay to the estimate which can be omitted since it does not affect the comparison of two alternative implementations.

In Figure 6.27 we have shown the cost and delay estimation for encoding A. First, the Karnaugh maps for next-state

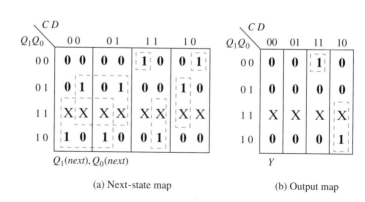

(a) Next-state map   (b) Output map

$$Q_1(next) = Q_1 C' + Q_0 CD' + Q_1' Q_0' CD$$
$$Q_0(next) = Q_0 C' + Q_1 CD + Q_1' Q_0' CD'$$
$$Y = Q_1 CD' + Q_1' Q_0' CD$$

(c) Excitation and output equations

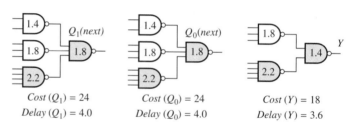

Cost $(Q_1) = 24$ Cost $(Q_0) = 24$ Cost $(Y) = 18$
Delay $(Q_1) = 4.0$ Delay $(Q_0) = 4.0$ Delay $(Y) = 3.6$

(d) Cost and delay estimation

FIGURE 6.27

Cost and delay estimation for encoding A.

and output functions are presented in Figure 6.27(a) and (b), and the excitation and output equations derived from the Karnaugh maps are given in Figure 6.27(c). Finally, each of these equations has been implemented with two-level logic networks of NAND gates. As you can see, the total cost would be equal to $cost(Q_1) + cost(Q_2) + cost(Y) = 24 + 24 + 18 = 66$, and the maximum input delay would be equal to 4.0 ns, while the output delay would be equal to 3.6 ns.

In Figure 6.28 you will find a similar estimation based on encoding B. As we expected in this encoding, the cost and delay of the output logic is slightly improved, since the total cost $cost(Q_1) + cost(Q_2) + cost(Y) = 24 + 24 + 16 = 64$, and the maximum input logic delay is 4.0 ns while the output delay is 3.2 ns.

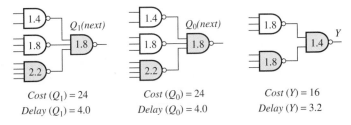

CD

Q_1Q_0	00	01	11	10
00	0 0	0 0	0 1	1 0
01	0 1	0 1	1 0	0 0
11	X X	X X	X X	X X
10	1 0	1 0	0 0	0 1

$Q_1(next)$ $Q_0(next)$

(a) Next-state map

CD

Q_1Q_0	00	01	11	10
00	0	0	0	0
01	0	0	1	0
11	X	X	X	X
10	0	0	0	1

Y

(b) Output map

$$Q_1(next) = Q_1C' + Q_0CD + Q_1'Q_0'CD'$$
$$Q_0(next) = Q_0C' + Q_1CD' + Q_1'Q_0'CD$$
$$Y = Q_0CD + Q_1CD'$$

(c) Excitation and output equations

Cost $(Q_1) = 24$
Delay $(Q_1) = 4.0$

Cost $(Q_0) = 24$
Delay $(Q_0) = 4.0$

Cost $(Y) = 16$
Delay $(Y) = 3.2$

(d) Cost and delay estimation

FIGURE   6.28

Cost and delay estimation for encoding B.

The estimation of encoding C is shown in Figure 6.29. Note that the cost and delay of each excitation equation has been reduced but the total cost is much higher than

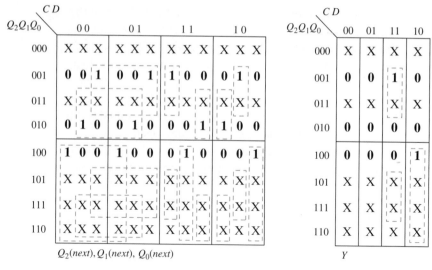

(a) Next-state table

(b) Output table

$$Q_2(next) = Q_2C' + Q_0CD + Q_1CD'$$

$$Q_1(next) = Q_1C' + Q_2CD + Q_0CD'$$

$$Q_0(next) = Q_0C' + Q_2CD' + Q_1CD$$

$$Y = Q_0CD + Q_2CD'$$

(c) Excitation and output equations

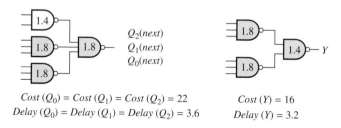

$$Cost\ (Q_0) = Cost\ (Q_1) = Cost\ (Q_2) = 22$$
$$Delay\ (Q_0) = Delay\ (Q_1) = Delay\ (Q_2) = 3.6$$

$$Cost\ (Y) = 16$$
$$Delay\ (Y) = 3.2$$

(d) Cost and delay estimation

FIGURE 6.29
Cost and delay estimation for encoding C.

before, mainly because the implementation has three flip-flops instead of two. As a result, the total cost is equal to $cost(Q_0) + cost(Q_1) + cost(Q_2) + cost(Y) = 22 + 22 + 22 + 16 = 82$, even though the maximum input logic delay is only 3.6 ns and the output delay is the same as for encoding B.

The conclusion to be drawn from this comparison is that encoding C generates the fastest and costliest implementation, while encoding B generates an implementation that is the least expensive of the three alternatives but also slower than that of encoding C. Finally, encoding A generates an implementation that is very similar and only insignificantly inferior to encoding B.

In general, it is very difficult to estimate the impact of each encoding unless we do as we did in Example 6.7, generating an implementation for each encoding and then comparing them on cost, delay, and other quality metrics. In the rest of this chapter, we use encoding A for implementation of the modulo-3 counter, since it is the most natural and easiest to understand.

6.12 CHOICE OF MEMORY ELEMENTS

After we complete the process of state minimization and state encoding, we are ready to choose the proper type of flip-flop for implementation of a given FSM. As shown in Tables 6.1 and 6.2, there are four types of flip-flops. In general, T flip-flops are an excellent match for counter-type sequential circuits in which the flip-flops must flip from 0 to 1 and back from 1 to 0 with great frequency. D flip-flops would usually be used in applications where input information must be stored for some time and then used later. In this sense, D flip-flops can be thought of as temporary storage or information scratch pads. The SR flip-flop is generally used in situations where different signals set and reset the flip-flops. Finally, the JK flip-flop, which is the most complex, is useful whenever we need to combine the behavior of a T and an SR flip-flop.

From the discussion above, we could conclude that the SR and JK types would be most useful. However, although they do tend to reduce the cost of the input logic, they also require twice as many connections as do T and D flip-flops. Generally, since T and D flip-flops require fewer connections, they are better suited for VLSI implementations. To compare the overall efficiency of the various flip-flops, we now derive the input logic for the modulo-3 counter using each of the four types of flip-flops.

EXAMPLE 6.8

PROBLEM   Given the modulo-3 counter with encoding A, as specified in Figure 6.26, select the type of flip-flop that will minimize the cost and/or delay of the input logic.

SOLUTION To accomplish this task, we start with the next-state table shown in Figure 6.27(a), which has been duplicated in Figure 6.30(a). Then, to derive excitation equations for the various types of flip-flops, we use excitation tables for all four flip-flops, shown in Figure 6.30(b). Next, we would take each pair of present and next states from the next-state map and replace their next-state values with the required input values shown in the excitation table. In this way we can

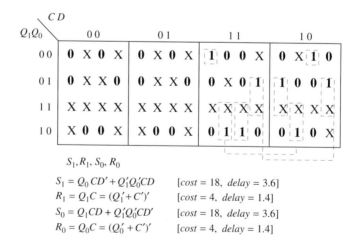

CD

Q_1Q_0	0 0	0 1	1 1	1 0
0 0	0 0	0 0	1 0	0 1
0 1	0 1	0 1	0 0	1 0
1 1	X X	X X	X X	X X
1 0	1 0	1 0	0 1	0 0

$Q_1(next)$ $Q_0(next)$

(a) Next-state table for encoding A

Q (present)	Q (next)	S	R	J	K	T	D
0	0	0	X	0	X	0	0
0	1	1	0	1	X	1	1
1	0	0	1	X	1	1	0
1	1	X	0	X	0	0	1

(b) Flip-flop excitation table

CD

Q_1Q_0	0 0	0 1	1 1	1 0
0 0	0 X 0 X	0 X 0 X	1 0 0 X	0 X 1 0
0 1	0 X X 0	0 X X 0	0 X 0 1	1 0 0 1
1 1	X X X X	X X X X	X X X X	X X X X
1 0	X 0 0 X	X 0 0 X	0 1 1 0	0 1 0 X

S_1, R_1, S_0, R_0

$S_1 = Q_0 CD' + Q_1'Q_0'CD$ [*cost* = 18, *delay* = 3.6]
$R_1 = Q_1C = (Q_1'+C')'$ [*cost* = 4, *delay* = 1.4]
$S_0 = Q_1CD + Q_1'Q_0'CD'$ [*cost* = 18, *delay* = 3.6]
$R_0 = Q_0C = (Q_0' + C')'$ [*cost* = 4, *delay* = 1.4]

(c) Implementation with SR flip-flops

FIGURE 6.30

Modulo-3 counter implementation with various types of flip-flops.

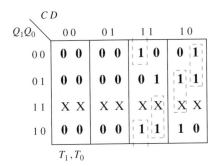

CD

Q_1Q_0	0 0	0 1	1 1	1 0
0 0	0 X 0 X	0 X 0 X	1 X 0 X	0 X 1 X
0 1	0 X X 0	0 X X 0	0 X X 1	1 X X 1
1 1	X X X X	X X X X	X X X X	X X X X
1 0	X 0 0 X	X 0 0 X	X 1 1 X	X 1 0 X

J_1, K_1, J_0, K_0

$J_1 = Q_0CD' + Q_0'CD = (C' + Q_0D + Q_0'D')'$ $[cost = 12, \ delay = 2.4]$
$K_1 = C$ $[cost = 0, \ delay = 0]$
$J_0 = Q_1CD + Q_1'CD' = (C' + Q_1D' + Q_1D')'$ $[cost = 12, \ delay = 2.4]$
$K_0 = C$ $[cost = 0, \ delay = 0]$

(d) Implementation with JK flip-flops

CD

Q_1Q_0	0 0	0 1	1 1	1 0
0 0	0 0	0 0	1 0	0 1
0 1	0 0	0 0	0 1	1 1
1 1	X X	X X	X X	X X
1 0	0 0	0 0	1 1	1 0

T_1, T_0

$T_1 = Q_1C + Q_0'CD + Q_0CD'$ $[cost = 22, \ delay = 3.6]$
$T_0 = Q_0C + Q_1CD + Q_1'CD'$ $[cost = 22, \ delay = 3.6]$

(e) Implementation with T flip-flops

CD

Q_1Q_0	0 0	0 1	1 1	1 0
0 0	0 0	0 0	1 0	0 1
0 1	0 1	0 1	0 0	1 0
1 1	X X	X X	X X	X X
1 0	1 0	1 0	0 1	0 0

D_1, D_0

$D_1 = Q_1C' + Q_0CD' + Q_1'Q_0'CD$ $[cost = 24, \ delay = 4.0]$
$D_0 = Q_0C' + Q_1CD + Q_1'Q_0CD'$ $[cost = 24, \ delay = 4.0]$

(f) Implementation with D flip-flops

F I G U R E   6.30
Continued.

create input maps for the SR, JK, T, and D flip-flops, which
are shown in Figure 6.30(c), (d), (e), and (f), respectively.
Note that the input maps really combine four maps in the
case of the SR and JK flip-flops, or two maps in the case
of T and D flip-flops. From these input maps we can now
derive minimal expressions for each flip-flop input, shown
underneath each map, along with cost and delay estimates
for each expression. These cost and delay estimates do not
include the input drivers (inverters) or the cost and delay of
the flip-flops.

From these estimates we can see that an implementation with JK flip-flops has the lowest cost and least delay, mainly because in this case we can use one AOI gate for implementation of the J_1 and J_0 input logic instead of two levels of NAND gates. In many cases, though, when sequential circuits with many states are being implemented, JK flip-flops will not have such a great advantage over other types of flip-flops. We can also see from this example that the T, D, and SR flip-flops generate implementations with very similar costs and delays.

6.13 OPTIMIZATION AND TIMING

The next-to-last step in a sequential logic synthesis would consist of mapping the input and output logic to the components in the given library. In the case of the modulo-3 counter, we had already used AOI gates when we computed the delay and cost of the implementation with JK flip-flops.

After the technology mapping is completed, we can draw the schematic to visualize all the counter's gates and connections. As an example, the logic schematic for the JK implementation of the modulo-3 counter is shown in Figure 6.31. (The output logic was derived in Figure 6.27(c).) In this figure you can see that double inverters are used at the input to deliver more current, which decreases the delay caused by the charging and discharging of wire capacitances. Note that this logic schematic is generated for human consumption and will have to be converted into a component netlist expressed in a hardware description language before it can be used by the simulation and testing software.

The final step in the process of sequential synthesis consists of deriving a timing diagram from the schematic and the given gate and flip-flop delays. The timing diagram for the modulo-3 counter is shown in Figure 6.32. Note that the delays in the timing diagram correspond to the delays given in Figure 6.31(b). In Figure 6.32 the modulo-3 counter is enabled at t_0 but does not change the state until the rising edge of the *Clk* signal. It enters state $s_1(Q_1Q_0 = 01)$ at $t_1 + 4.0$ ns. After the second rising edge it enters state $s_2(Q_1Q_0 = 10)$ at $t_2 + 4.0$ ns. The output signal Y becomes 1 at $t_2 + 7.6$ ns since Y must be 1 in s_2 if $CD = 10$. When at the next rising edge modulo-3 counter enters state $s_0(Q_1Q_0 = 00)$ output Y returns to 0 at $t_3 + 7.6$ ns. When D is disasserted

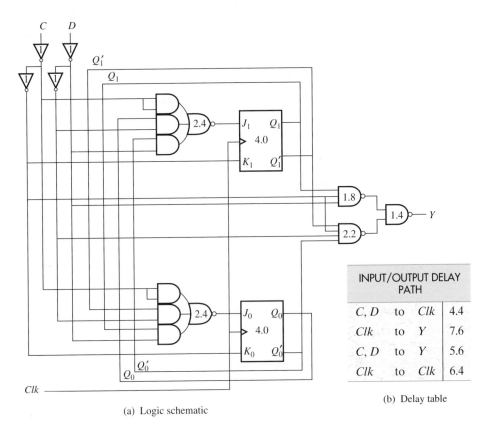

(a) Logic schematic

INPUT/OUTPUT DELAY PATH			
C, D	to	Clk	4.4
Clk	to	Y	7.6
C, D	to	Y	5.6
Clk	to	Clk	6.4

(b) Delay table

F I G U R E   6.31
Modulo-3 counter schematic.

at t_4 the output Y becomes 1 again at $t_4 + 5.6$ ns since output Y must be 1 in state s_0 if $CD = 11$. After that modulo-3 counter enters state $s_2(Q_1Q_0 = 10)$ at $t_5 + 4.0$ ns and Y returns to 0 at $t_5 + 7.6$ ns since Y must be 0 in s_2 if $CD = 11$. Finally, after $t_6 + 4.0$ modulo-3 counter enters state $s_1(Q_1Q_0 = 01)$. This is the last state shown in this timing diagram.

   This and other timing diagrams will be used to verify the input and output behavior of the synthesized circuit and to generate input and output waveforms for simulation. Given as a set of input waveforms, a simulator will generate the waveforms for the outputs, which must be compared to the expected output waveforms obtained from the schematics, circuit specification, or behavioral description. These input and output waveforms are sometimes called test vectors since they will also be used for testing the circuit after it has been manufactured.

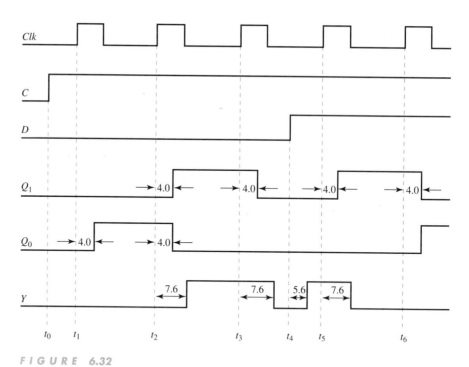

Timing diagram of a modulo-3 counter for a sequence of input values.

6.14 CHAPTER SUMMARY

In this chapter we have explained how to construct the basic memory elements that are used in the design of sequential logic. To this end we have introduced several different types of latches and flip-flops and described them with characteristic equations, characteristic tables, and state diagrams. We have also introduced the concept of sequential logic, as well as the finite-state-machine model, which is used to represent the sequential logic during the design process. We have provided step-by-step procedures for the analysis and synthesis of sequential logic and demonstrated these procedures on examples of modulo-4 and modulo-3 counters. In Chapter 7 we use these procedures to analyze and synthesize sequential components.

6.15 FURTHER READINGS

DeMicheli, G. *Synthesis and Optimization of Digital Circuits.* New York: McGraw-Hill, 1994.

Describes logic and sequential synthesis concepts and algorithms in detail. Requires expert knowledge in design and in CAD tool development.

Katz, R. H. *Contemporary Logic Design.* Redwood City, CA: Benjamin-Cummings, 1994.

Introductory text on logic design, with explanations of how to use UC–Berkeley CAD tools in the design process.

Kohavi, Z. *Switching and Automatic Theory*, 2nd ed. New York: McGraw-Hill, 1978.

Thorough theoretical treatment of finite-state machines and sequential logic.

McCluskey, E. *Logic Design Principles.* Englewood Cliffs, NJ: Prentice Hall, 1986.

Provides detailed explanations of the basic concepts in sequential logic analysis, synthesis, and testing.

6.16 PROBLEMS

6.1 (Clock signal) Compute the clock frequency and duty cycle for a clock signal with a width and period of:
  (a) 5 ns and 20 ns
  (b) 10 ns and 100 ns
  (c) 100 ns and 1 ns

6.2 (SR latch) Draw the output timing diagram of (a) NOR and (b) NAND implementation of an SR latch for the input signals depicted in Figure P6.2.

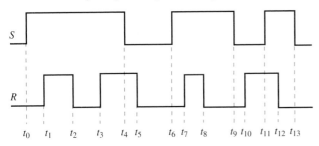

FIGURE P6.2

6.3 (SR latch) Derive an implementation of a clocked SR latch using only:
  (a) NOR gates
  (b) NAND gates
  (c) AND, OR, and INVERT gates

6.4 (Clocked D latch) Design a D latch using only (a) NAND gates and (b) NOR gates, and then compute D-to-Q and Clk-to-Q delays for positive and negative output transitions.

6.5 (Flip-flops) Design a master–slave (a) SR flip-flop, (b) JK flip-flop, (c) D flip-flop, and (d) T flip-flop using clocked SR latches and AND, OR, and INVERT gates.

6.6 (JK flip-flops) Derive the output waveforms of a master–slave JK flip-flop for the input waveforms depicted in Figure P6.6.

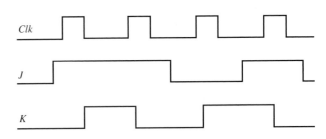

FIGURE P6.6

6.7 (Flip-flops) Using Karnaugh maps, derive the characteristic equations from the characteristic tables of the four flip-flops shown in Table 6.1.

6.8 (Flip-flops) Implement SR, JK, D, and T flip-flops using only AND, OR, and INVERT gates, and:
  (a) SR flip-flops
  (b) JK flip-flops
  (c) D flip-flops
  (d) T flip-flops

6.9 (Sequential analysis) Derive a (a) state table and (b) state diagram for the sequential circuit shown in Figure P6.9.

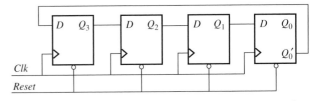

FIGURE P6.9

6.10 (Sequential analysis) Derive the (a) state/output table and (b) FSM representation of the circuit shown in Figure P6.10. What is the function of this sequential circuit?

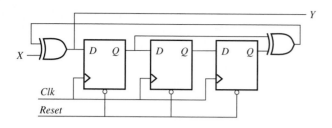

FIGURE P6.10

6.11 (Sequential analysis) Derive (a) excitation equations, (b) a next-state equation, (c) a state/output table, and (d) a state diagram for the circuit shown in Figure P6.11.

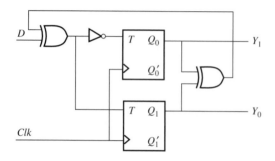

FIGURE P6.11

6.12 (State minimization) Derive the minimal-state FSM from the state/output table shown in Figure P6.12.

PRESENT STATE	NEXT STATE	
	$x = 0$	$x = 1$
s_0	$s_0 / 1$	$s_4 / 0$
s_1	$s_0 / 0$	$s_4 / 0$
s_2	$s_1 / 0$	$s_5 / 0$
s_3	$s_1 / 0$	$s_5 / 0$
s_4	$s_2 / 0$	$s_6 / 1$
s_5	$s_2 / 0$	$s_6 / 1$
s_6	$s_3 / 0$	$s_7 / 1$
s_7	$s_3 / 0$	$s_7 / 1$

FIGURE P6.12

6.13 (State minimization) Minimize the states for the FSM given in Figure P6.13, using:

(a) State partitioning

(b) An implication table

PRESENT STATE	NEXT STATE / OUTPUT		
	$AB = 00$	$AB = 01$	$AB = 10$
s_0	$s_4 / 1$	$s_2 / 0$	$s_1 / 1$
s_1	$s_2 / 0$	$s_5 / 1$	$s_4 / 1$
s_2	$s_1 / 1$	$s_0 / 0$	$s_3 / 1$
s_3	$s_2 / 0$	$s_5 / 1$	$s_4 / 1$
s_4	$s_0 / 0$	$s_5 / 1$	$s_1 / 1$
s_5	$s_2 / 0$	$s_4 / 1$	$s_2 / 1$

FIGURE P6.13

6.14 (State encoding) For the state diagram shown in Figure P6.14, derive the state encodings using:

(a) The minimum-bit-change heuristic

(b) The prioritized-adjacency heuristic

(c) Hot-one encoding

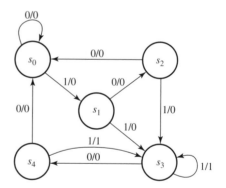

FIGURE P6.14

6.15 (State encoding) Find the state encoding that minimizes the output logic for a counter that counts in the following sequence: $0, 1, 3, 6, 10, 15, 0, \ldots$.

6.16 (Sequential synthesis) Design a counter that counts in the sequence $0, 1, 3, 6, 10, 15$, using four (a) D, (b) SR, (c) JK, and (d) T flip-flops as memory elements, and natural binary encoding.

6.17 (Sequential synthesis) Design a counter that counts in the sequence $0, 1, 2, 3, 4, 5, 6, 7, 8, 9, 0, \ldots$, using natural binary encoding and D flip-flops.

6.18 (Sequential synthesis) Design a parity checker that counts the number of 1's in the input stream. This checker asserts its output Y if it has received an odd number of 1's on the input X. An asynchronous *Reset* signal returns the parity checker into its initial state. As storage elements use only (a) D, (b) JK, and (c) T flip-flops.

6.19 (Sequential synthesis) Design a recognizer that recognizes an input sequence that has at least three 1's. The recognizer has a single input X and a single output Y, in addition to an asynchronous *Reset* signal. The recognizer sets the output Y to 1 if the input signal X equals 1 at least three clock cycles after *Reset* was disasserted. For the recognizer described above:

    (a) Devise the state diagram.

    (b) Minimize the number of states.

    (c) Encode the states to minimize the combinatorial logic.

    (d) Draw a schematic diagram using D flip-flops.

6.20 (Sequential synthesis) Redo Problem 6.19, designing a recognizer that will recognize all the input sequences that have three or more consecutive 1's, or three or more consecutive 0's.

6.21 (Sequential synthesis) Implement a sequential circuit that can complement a 16-bit two's-complement number, $X = x_{15}x_{14}\cdots x_1x_0$. The circuit has one input, X, which has the value x_i in the clock cycle i, and another input *Reset*, which resets the circuit into the initial state after 16 clock cycles. The output Y is the two's-complement of X. In the initial state a flag is set to 0. The circuit works as follows: For every $x_i, 0 \le i \le 15$. If *flag* $= 0$, then $y_i = x_i$ and *flag* $= x_i$; else $y_i = x_i'$. Develop a state diagram and logic schematic using D-type flip-flops.

6.22 (Sequential synthesis) Design a simplified traffic-light controller that switches traffic lights on a crossing where a north-south (NS) street intersects an east-west (EW) street. The input to the controller is the *WALK* button pushed by pedestrians who want to cross the street. The outputs are two signals *NS* and *EW* that control the traffic lights in the NS and EW directions. When *NS* or *EW* are 0, the red light is on, and when they are 1, the green light is on. When there are no pedestrians, $NS = 0$ and $EW = 1$ for 1 minute, followed by $NS = 1$ and $EW = 0$ for 1 minute, and so on. When a *WALK* button is pushed, *NS* and *EW* both become 1 for a minute when the present minute expires. After that the *NS* and *EW* signals continue alternating. For these traffic-light controller:

    (a) Develop a state diagram and a state/output table.

    (b) Minimize the number of states.

    (c) Encode the states

    (d) Derive a logic schematic.

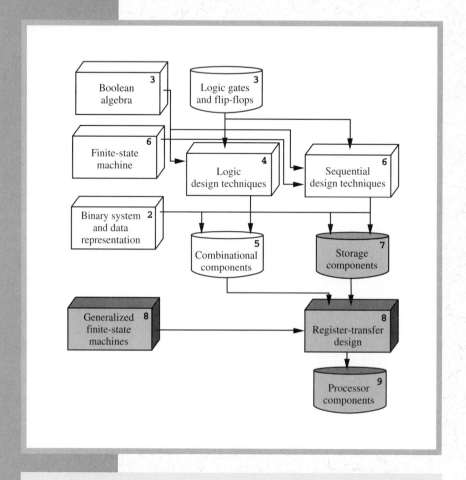

In Chapter 6, we introduced and studied various techniques for the design of sequential logic, which is characterized by the use of latches and flip-flops. Using these sequential logic techniques, in this chapter we design some of the basic storage components that, together with combinatorial components, make up the microarchitecture of standard microprocessors as well as application-specific microchips.

CHAPTER

7

Storage Components

The basic purpose of a storage component is to store data and perform simple data transformations, such as counting and shifting. In this chapter we define and design various types of storage components, such as registers, counters, memories, stacks, and queues. In addition, we define several types of datapaths and controllers that are used as the computing engines of many microchips. To simplify our explanation of these components, we use only generic gates and flip-flops and do not try to optimize the design for a particular technology or gate library.

7.1 REGISTERS

The simplest of the storage components is a **register** which can be thought of as a bitwise extension of a flip-flop. Each register consists of n flip-flops driven by a common clock signal. In other words, each flip-flop in a given register stores its own data on every rising edge of the clock signal. Thus a simple register has n inputs and n outputs in addition to the clock signal.

In Figure 7.1 we show an example of a 4-bit register. Its graphic symbol, which we use throughout this book, is shown in Figure 7.1(a). The register consists of four D flip-flops connected in parallel as shown in Figure 7.1(b).

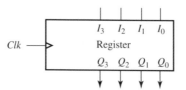

(a) Graphic symbol

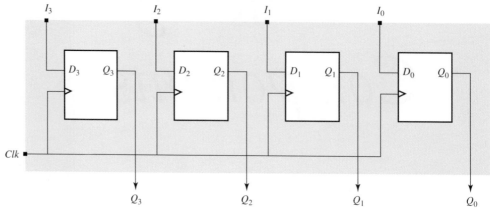

(b) Register schematic

FIGURE 7.1
4-bit register.

The functionality of the basic register in Figure 7.1 can be enhanced by adding different control signals. For example, if the register must be set or reset independent of the clock signal either during power-up or on the occurrence of a special event, we can add an **asynchronous preset** and **clear signals**. Such an enhancement is achieved by replacing the simple flip-flops shown in Figure 7.1 with setable/resetable flip-flops, as shown in Figure 7.2.

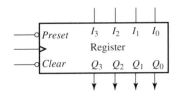

(a) Graphic symbol

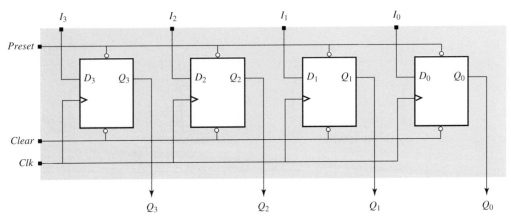

(b) Register schematic

FIGURE 7.2

4-bit register with asynchronous *preset* and *clear.*

As you can see from Figure 7.2(b), the register could be reset to an all-0's content by pulling the *Clear* input to 0 for a short period of time. Similarly, an all-1's content could be introduced by pulling the *Preset* input to 0. Note that these set and reset inputs are independent of the clock signal and have priority over it, which means that if the *Preset* or *Clear* inputs are equal to 0 during the rising edge of the clock signal, the input I will be ignored and the register will be set or reset. Throughout the rest of this book, we will assume that every register or counter could have asynchronous set, reset, or both. In general, we do not indicate this explicitly except where it is essential for an explanation of the component's behavior.

In both registers shown in Figures 7.1 and 7.2, we store any new data automatically on every rising edge of the clock. However, in most digital systems, the data is stored for several clock cycles before it is rewritten. For this reason it is useful to be able to control when the data will be entered into a register. This is achieved by the use of a control signal, usually called *Load* or *Enable*, which allows loading of data into a register known as a **parallel-load register**.

In Figure 7.3 a register with such a control signal is shown. Note that register design contains a 2-to-1 selector, which selects either input

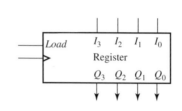

(a) Graphic symbol

PRESENT STATE	NEXT STATE			
Load	Q_3	Q_2	Q_1	Q_0
0	No change			
1	I_3	I_2	I_1	I_0

(b) Operation table

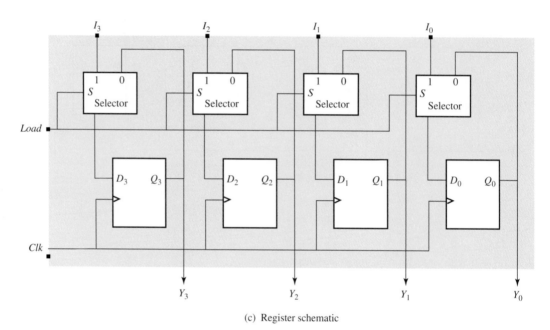

(c) Register schematic

FIGURE 7.3
Register with parallel load.

data or data already in the register. The *Load* signal controls the selector, so that when the *Load* signal is equal to 1, new data is entered into the register. On the other hand, when *Load* is equal to 0, the data that was stored previously is loaded back into the register on each rising edge of the clock signal.

7.2 SHIFT REGISTERS

In Section 7.1 we have shown how a selector can be placed in front of the flip-flops to allow controlled loading of a register. We could also use a selector to enable us to shift the data stored in the register. This kind of register, called a **shift register**, shifts its contents one bit in the specified direction when the control signal *Shift* is equal to 1. As an example, a 4-bit shift-right register is presented in Figure 7.4. The serial input I_L is used to enter the new 1-bit data into the leftmost flip-flop in the design. A shift register like the one in Figure 7.4 would usually be used to convert a serial data stream into a parallel stream. For this reason it is sometimes called a serial-in/parallel-out shift register.

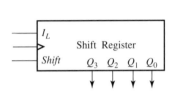

(a) Graphic symbol

PRESENT STATE	NEXT STATE			
Shift	Q_3	Q_2	Q_1	Q_0
0	No change			
1	I_L	Q_3	Q_2	Q_1

(b) Operation table

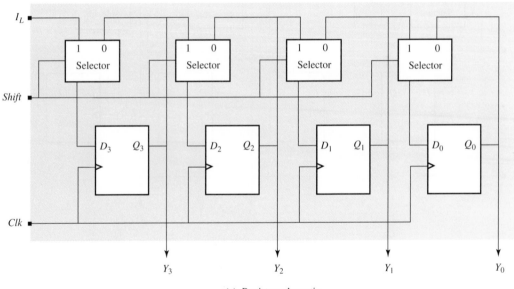

(c) Register schematic

FIGURE 7.4
4-bit serial-in/parallel-out shift-right register.

To increase the versatility of a register, we might also use a 4-to-1 selector, which allows us to combine shift and loading functions. For example, the shift register in Figure 7.5 could either shift its contents or load new data. Furthermore, it could shift one-bit either left or right while at the same time shifting in the data available at the right serial input I_R or the left serial input I_L. Figure 7.5(a) and (b) show the graphic symbol and table of operation and Figure 7.5(c) shows the schematic for this multifunctional register.

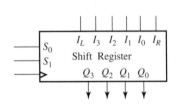

(a) Graphic symbol

PRESENT STATE			NEXT STATE			
S_1	S_0	OPERATION	Q_3	Q_2	Q_1	Q_0
0	0	No change	Q_3	Q_2	Q_1	Q_0
0	1	Load input	I_3	I_2	I_1	I_0
1	0	Shift left	Q_2	Q_1	Q_0	I_R
1	1	Shift right	I_L	Q_3	Q_2	Q_1

(b) Operation table

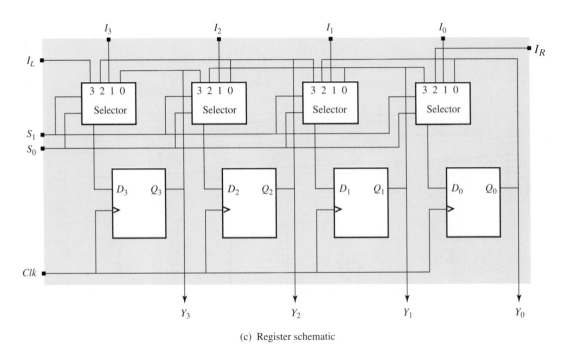

(c) Register schematic

FIGURE 7.5

4-bit shift register with parallel load.

Note that in the shift register schematic, as with the ALU schematic, we can distinguish the most-significant, middle, and least-significant bit slices. Each of these bit slices must be designed separately since their functions are slightly different. Since the middle slices are more natural to grasp, they are usually designed first. For example, the flip-flop input equation for these three slices for the shift register in Figure 7.5 can be obtained from its operation table:

$$D_0 = S_1'S_0'Q_0 + S_1'S_0I_0 + S_1S_0'I_R + S_1S_0Q_1$$
$$D_i = S_1'S_0'Q_i + S_1'S_0I_i + S_1S_0'Q_{i-1} + S_1S_0Q_{i+1}, \ 1 \le i \le 2$$
$$D_3 = S_1'S_0'Q_3 + S_1'S_0I_3 + S_1S_0'Q_2 + S_1S_0I_L$$

The shift register with parallel load can be used to convert a serial data stream to parallel and a parallel data stream to serial with options to output the MSB or LSB first. These registers are frequently used to convert computer data for serial communications and assemble the serially transmitted data for processing inside a processor.

7.3 COUNTERS

A **counter** is a special type of register that incorporates an incrementer, which allows it to count upward or downward. In Figure 7.6, for example, we have shown an up-counter that has two control signals: an enable signal, E, that will enable counting when it is equal to 1; and a *Clear* signal that will reset the counter to 0. The graphic symbol for this 4-bit

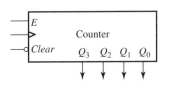

(a) Graphic symbol

E	OPERATIONS
0	No change
1	Count

(b) Operation table

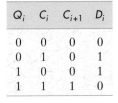

Q_i	C_i	C_{i+1}	D_i
0	0	0	0
0	1	0	1
1	0	0	1
1	1	1	0

(c) HA truth table

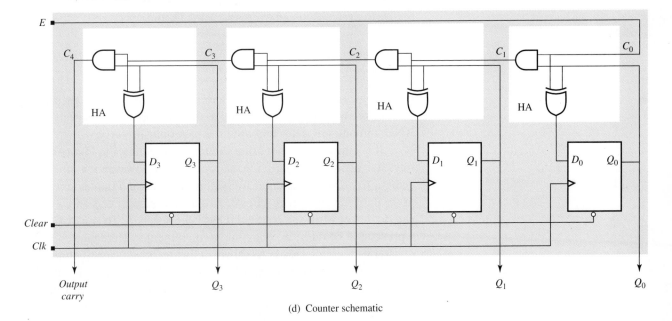

(d) Counter schematic

FIGURE 7.6
4-bit binary counter.

binary up-counter is shown in Figure 7.6(a) and its operation table in Figure 7.6(b). In Figure 7.6(d) you can see that the incrementer consists of a series of **half-adders** (HA) arranged such that an HA in bit position i will have two inputs connected to the output of the ith flip-flop Q_i and the carry C_i from the HA in position $i - 1$. Note that the new value of the flip-flop D_i will be equal to 1 if either Q_i or C_i, but not both, is equal to 1. In contrast, the output C_{i+1} will be equal to 1 only if Q_i and C_i are both equal to 1. The truth table for an HA is given in Figure 7.6(c), from which we can derive the following Boolean expressions for D_i and C_{i+1}:

$$D_i = Q_i \oplus C_i$$
$$C_{i+1} = Q_i C_i$$

As long as the E signal is equal to 1, this counter will count up modulo 16, adding 1 to its content on every rising edge of the clock.

This basic up-counter could also be extended to an **up/down-counter** if we replace the half-adder with a half-adder/subtractor (HAS), which can increment or decrement under the control of a direction signal. In Figure 7.7, for example, we show an up/down-counter that resembles the up-counter of Figure 7.6 in most ways, with the exception that this counter has a third control input, D. As indicated by the operation table in Figure 7.7(b), the purpose of this additional input is to allow counting up when its value is 0 and counting down when its value is 1. The truth table for an HAS is shown in Figure 7.7(c), from which it is easy to derive Boolean expressions for D_i and C_{i+1}:

$$D_i = Q_i \oplus C_i$$
$$C_{i+1} = D' Q_i C_i + D Q_i' C_i$$

In the logic schematic shown in Figure 7.7(d), you see that each HAS consists of an XOR gate connected to the flip-flop inputs, as well as two AND and one OR gates that are used to propagate carry.

It is important to note that the up/down-counter in Figure 7.7 always starts counting from 0. On many occasions, however, it is more convenient to preset the counter to a different value and then count down or up until the counter reaches 0. In such a case we need only a NOR gate to detect when the count of 0 has been reached. To construct such a **presetable counter**, we combine an incrementer/decrementer with a register with parallel load. As shown in Figure 7.8(a), such a counter has three control signals: E, D, and $Load$. The E signal will enable counting in the direction specified by the D signal, and the $Load$ signal will load a new input and disable counting whenever its value is equal to 1. On the other hand, whenever the $Load$ signal is equal to 0, the counter will behave exactly like the up/down-counter of Figure 7.7. The operational

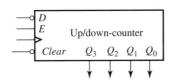

E	D	OPERATIONS
0	X	No change
1	0	Count up
1	1	Count down

(a) Graphic symbol

(b) Operation table

E	D	Q_i	C_i	C_{i+1}	D_i
1	0	0	0	0	0
1	0	0	1	0	1
1	0	1	0	0	1
1	0	1	1	1	0
1	1	0	0	0	0
1	1	0	1	1	1
1	1	1	0	0	1
1	1	1	1	0	0

(c) HAS truth table

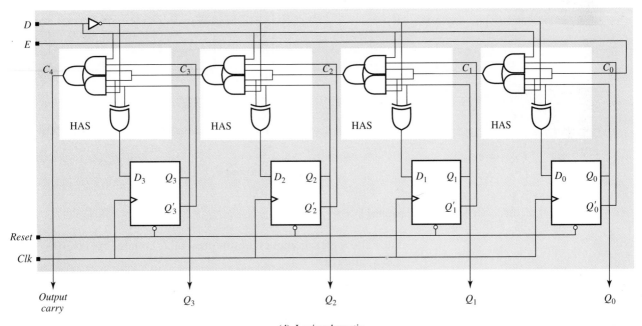

(d) Logic schematic

FIGURE 7.7

4-bit up/down binary counter.

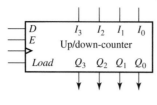

LOAD	E	D	OPERATIONS
0	0	X	No change
0	1	0	Count up
0	1	1	Count down
1	X	X	Load the input

(a) Graphic symbol   (b) Operation table

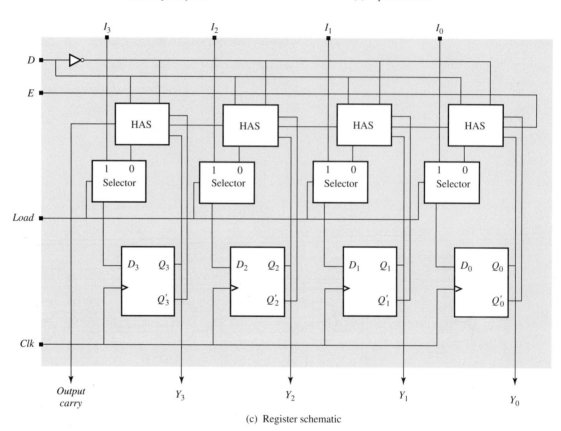

(c) Register schematic

FIGURE 7.8
4-bit up/down-counter with parallel load.

table and logic schematics for this presetable counter are given in Figure 7.8(b) and (c).

7.4 BCD COUNTER

The presetable counter described in Section 7.3 can be used in the construction of other counters. One such application is the design of **BCD counters** that count in the sequence $0, 1, 2, 3, 4, 5, 6, 7, 8, 9, 0 \ldots$ As shown in Figure 7.9(a), we can construct such a counter by detecting when the counter reaches a count of 9 and loading 0 instead of 10 in the next clock cycle. The detection is accomplished by an AND gate whose output is equal to 1 when the content of the counter is equal to 1001. The output of the AND gate is connected to the counter's *Load* input, which allows the counter to load 0 at the next rising edge of the clock signal.

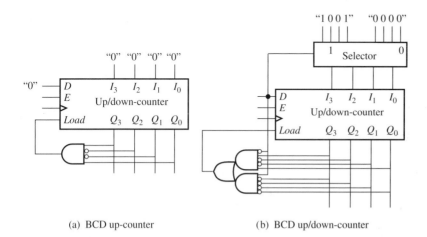

(a) BCD up-counter

(b) BCD up/down-counter

FIGURE 7.9
BCD counters.

We can construct a BCD up/down-counter similarly. In the up direction, we must load 0 into the counter when it reaches a count of 9, while in the down direction, we must load 9 when the counter reaches a count of 0. As shown in Figure 7.9(b), we need a selector that selects between the loading of 0 or 9 when the counter must be reset, as well as an AND–OR gate, which asserts the *Load* input when the counter reaches a count of 0 or 9.

In a similar manner, we can construct counters that start at any point and count in almost any sequence. Note, however, that any out-of-sequence jump requires one additional gate for detection and one additional selector input for loading.

7.5 ASYNCHRONOUS COUNTER

In previous sections we have described several different versions of a binary counter, all of which require an incrementer, a decrementer, or both. In some cases, however, we can lower the cost of the counter by constructing it without an incrementer or decrementer. Such a counter is called an **asynchronous counter**, since its flip-flops are not all clocked by the same signal.

Counting without an incrementer/decrementer is achieved by toggling each flip-flop at half the frequency of the preceding flip-flop. In other words, the flip-flop in position i will change states only half as often as the flip-flop in position $i - 1$, or to put this another way, the flip-flop in position i will change its state when flip-flop in position $i - 1$ goes from 1 to 0 but not when it goes from 0 to 1.

Given these general observations, we would construct such an asynchronous counter by connecting the complementary output of the flip-flop in position $i - 1$ to the clock input of the flip-flop in position i, while connecting the other flip-flop inputs in such a way that the flip-flop will change its state on every 0-to-1 transition of its clock input. A T flip-flop is very convenient for such an asynchronous design because the value 1 at its input will make the flip-flop change its state on the rising edge of the clock signal. In Figure 7.10 we show a 4-bit counter using T-type flip-flops. Note that it has two control signals, the enable signal E, which enables counting, and the *Clear* signal, which resets the counter to 0. The logic schematic of this counter is shown in Figure 7.10(b), where you can see how the complementary output of each flip-flop has been connected to the clock input of the flip-flop in the next higher-significant position. As a result, the clock signal *Clk* has been used to only clock the flip-flop in the least-significant position. The operation of the 4-bit asynchronous counter is demonstrated in Figure 7.10(c), which shows the output waveforms of each flip-flop. As you can see, the least-significant flip-flop (FF_0) will change its state with Δ delay on every rising edge of the clock—that is, at times $t_0 + \Delta, \ldots, t_7 + \Delta$. However, the next-most-significant flip-flop, FF_1, will change its state only when FF_0 goes from 1 to 0—that is, at times $t_1 + 2\Delta, t_3 + 2\Delta, t_5 + 2\Delta$, and $t_7 + 2\Delta$. Note that the delay has increased to 2Δ, since the change has had to propagate through two flip-flops. Similarly, the next flip-flop, FF_2, will change only when both FF_0 and FF_1 go from 1 to 0—that is, at times $t_3 + 3\Delta$ and $t_7 + 3\Delta$. Finally, the most-significant flip-flop, FF_3, will change states only when FF_2, FF_1, and FF_0 go from 1 to 0—that is, at time $t_7 + 4\Delta$.

From the preceding analysis we can conclude that the clock-to-output delay of the ith flip-flop will be equal to $i\Delta$, and consequently, that the maximum counting frequency of an n-bit asynchronous counter will be equal to $1/n\Delta$. In contrast, the counting frequency of a synchronous counter would be limited only by the carry propagation in the incrementer. In other words, since the carry propagation (carry-in to carry-out delay) through the series of HAs is much faster than the state-change propagation (clock-to-Q delay) through an equal number of flip-flops, the asynchronous counter described above would seem to be slower than a synchronous counter even without using carry-look-ahead techniques to speed up the carry propagation.

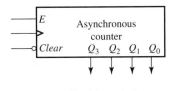

(a) Graphic symbol

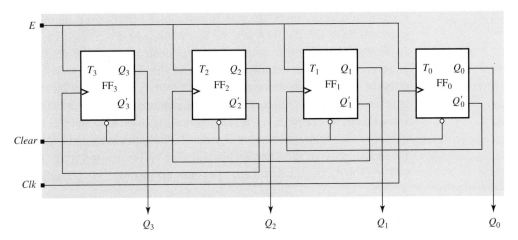

(b) Logic schematic

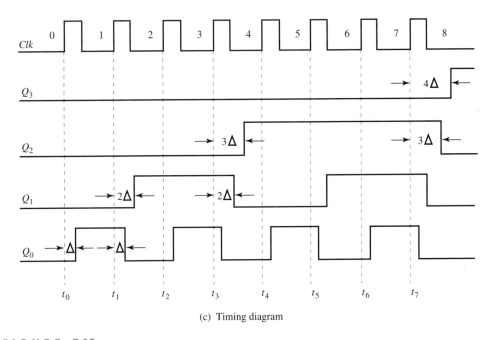

(c) Timing diagram

FIGURE 7.10

4-bit asynchronous up-counter.

To speed up an asynchronous counter, we must make it partly synchronous. To do this, we would divide a large counter into n-bit slices so that the operations within each slice are asynchronous, while the propagation between slices is synchronous, or vice versa. As an example of this technique, consider the 8-bit **mixed-mode counters** shown in Figure 7.11. In Figure 7.11(a) we have constructed a synchronous counter with 4-bit asynchronous slices. Note that in such a counter, all slices would be driven by the same clock signal, but the more significant slice will be enabled only when the less significant slice is in state 1111. In Figure 7.11(b), by contrast, we have constructed an asynchronous counter with 4-bit synchronous slices. In this version of the counter, only the flip-flops within each slice are driven by the same clock signal, whereas the more significant slice will be clocked with a signal that indicates when the less significant slice is entering or leaving state 1111. In other words, whenever the less-significant slice goes from 1111 to 0000, the clock signal of the more-significant slice will transition from 0 to 1, causing the more-significant slice to count up by one.

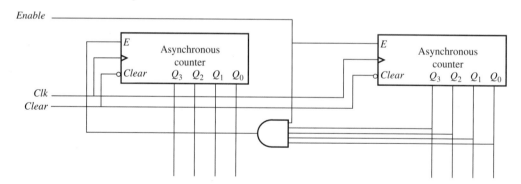

(a) Synchronous counter with 4-bit asynchronous slices

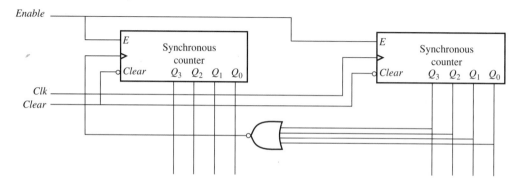

(b) Asynchronous counter with 4-bit synchronous slices

FIGURE 7.11
8-bit mixed-mode up-counter.

7.6 REGISTER FILES

In previous sections we have described different types of registers and counters, each of which consists of m flip-flops and some combinatorial logic at their inputs. It is also possible, however, to combine flip-flops into a two-dimensional array that would consist of 2^n rows of m flip-flops each. In such a two-dimensional arrangement, called a **register file**, each row of flip-flops can be thought of as one register. In general, a register file will store the same amount of information as would 2^n registers having m bits each, but the primary advantage to using a register file is that because of its regularity, it requires less wiring in the final design. Furthermore, each flip-flop in a register file can be implemented with many fewer transistors, as only one flip-flop in each column is accessed at any one time.

On a more concrete level, a register file consists of a two-dimensional array of **register-file cells** (RFCs), read and write decoders, and an output-driving logic. As shown in Figure 7.12(a), a typical RFC may be represented by a D flip-flop and two gates. Note that, in addition to the clock signal, the cell has three inputs and one output: *Write select*, *Read select*, *Input*, and *Output* signals. Within this cell the D flip-flop will store the value of the *Input* signal whenever *Write select* is equal to 1; consequently, whenever the *Read select* signal is equal to 1, this D flip-flop will pass its stored value to the output through a tristate driver.

In Figure 7.12(b) we present the graphic symbol for a $2^n \times m$ register file and, as an example, the organization for a 4×4 register file in Figure 7.12(c), in which the clock signal has been omitted for the sake of clarity. From these illustrations you can see that a $2^n \times m$ register file has m inputs, $I_{m-1}, \ldots, I_0$, m outputs, $O_{m-1}, \ldots, O_0$, and 2^n rows of flip-flops. In application, the write decoder would select one of the rows for storing the input values at the rising edge of the clock signal. The inputs to write the decoder consist of n address lines, $WA_{n-1}, \ldots, WA_0$, and the write enable signal WE. When WE is equal to 0, the input values are not stored at all.

Like the write decoder, the read decoder will select the row whose stored values appear at the register file outputs. The read decoder has n read address lines, $RA_{n-1}, \ldots, RA_0$, and a read enable signal RE. When RE is equal to 1, the values stored in the row selected will appear at the outputs, after a slight delay. On the other hand, when RE is equal to 0, all output signals will have a high-impedance value.

The primary limitation of a register file is that they allow us only limited access to the registers in the file—that is, at any given time, data can be written into only one register (row) and read from only one register (row). To some extent this situation can be remedied by constructing register files with more than one read or write port. Unfortunately, the

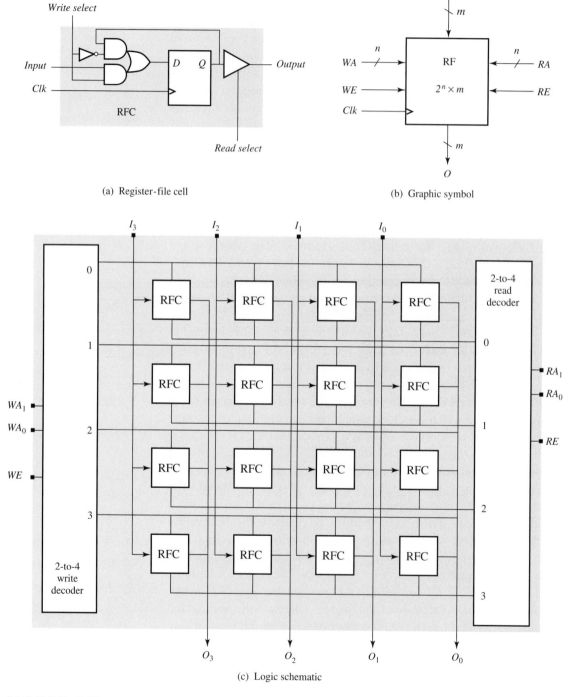

(a) Register-file cell

(b) Graphic symbol

(c) Logic schematic

FIGURE 7.12
Register file with one write port and one read port.

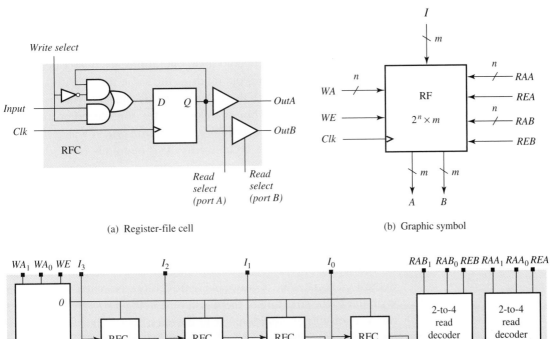

(a) Register-file cell

(b) Graphic symbol

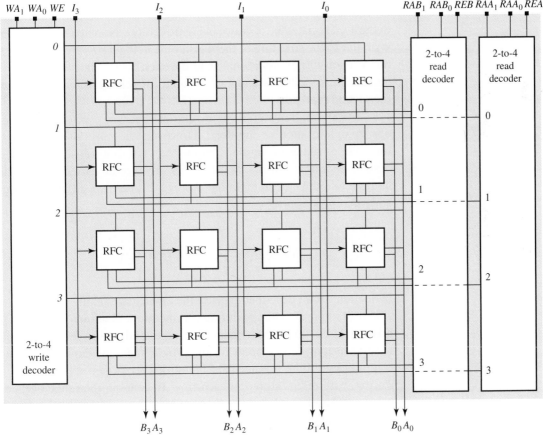

(c) Logic schematic

Register file with one write port and two read ports.

cost of the register will increase in proportion to its number of ports. For this reason, the most popular types of register files have one or two write ports and two read ports. The main justification for the two read ports being that most arithmetic and logic operations are binary operations that require us to use two operands at the same time. With two read ports it is possible to fetch these two operands and store the result back into the register file within one clock cycle. On the other hand, the justification for using two write ports lies in the rate at which operands are consumed: On each cycle, we use two operands to produce one result. Consequently, if we are to perform one operation every clock cycle, we must be able to bring a new operand into the register file and store the result from the operation at the same time.

In Figure 7.13 we show an example of a register file with one write and two read ports. As shown in Figure 7.13(a), the RFC has been modified to accommodate two read ports, and the graphic symbol presented in Figure 7.13(b) reflects these additional ports. The complete structure of the 4×4 register file is shown in Figure 7.13(c). Note that this diagram is similar to the structure of the register file in Figure 7.12(c) except that this version has an additional read decoder, which, in turn, adds one more wire to each row and each column for reading the data through the second read port.

In general, register files are very fast because every cell includes one complete latch or flip-flop. However, they are also expensive, since these latches or flip-flops require half a dozen transistors in their design. For this reason, register files are typically used to provide limited amounts of temporary storage in high-speed applications and microprocessors.

7.7 RANDOM-ACCESS MEMORIES

In Section 7.6 we described register files, which are small, fast, and suitable for temporary storage during computation. **Random-access memories** (RAMs), on the other hand, are larger and slower, but well suited to serve as long-term storage for the program and the data used during computation. Like register files, memories are organized as arrays of 2^n rows with m bits stored in each row. In general, the range of n lies between 16 and 32, while m is usually 1, 4, 8, 16, or 32. A typical memory would be like the one shown in Figure 7.14(a). Note that since each memory has 2^n rows, we need n address lines to identify each row uniquely. In addition to these n address lines, we would also need a *Chip-select* (*CS*) line, to be used when we are constructing large, multichip memories. Whenever *CS* is equal to 1, the memory will operate in its normal mode.

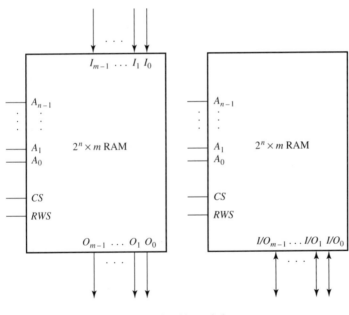

MEMORY ADDRESS		MEMORY CONTENT
Binary	Decimal	
$0...000$	0	$011...0100$
$0...001$	1	$011...0100$
$0...010$	2	$101...1100$
$0...011$	3	$101...0001$
$0...100$	4	$011...0101$
$0...101$	5	$010...0101$
$0...110$	6	$110...0011$
$0...111$	7	$101...0001$
$\vdots$	$\vdots$	$\vdots$
$1...110$	$2^n - 2$	$000...0010$
$1...111$	$2^n - 1$	$111...0110$
		$\overleftrightarrow{m \text{ bits}}$

(a) Memory address and content

$I_{m-1} \cdots I_1\, I_0$

A_{n-1}

A_1 $2^n \times m$ RAM

A_0

CS

RWS

$O_{m-1} \cdots O_1\, O_0$

A_{n-1}

A_1 $2^n \times m$ RAM

A_0

CS

RWS

$I/O_{m-1} \cdots I/O_1\; I/O_0$

(b) Graphic symbols

FIGURE 7.14
Random-access memory.

However, when CS is 0, memory operation will be disabled. Note also that each memory chip has one control line, *Read/write select* (*RWS*), which selects the memory's operation. When *RWS* is equal to 0, the memory will read its content at the location specified by the address lines and make it available at its output ports. On the other hand, when *RWS* is equal to 1, the memory will write the content presented on its input ports into the location specified by the address lines.

Each memory will also have *m* input and *m* output ports. For a small value of *m* (1 or 4), a given memory chip could have separate input and output ports. Usually, however, input and output ports are combined, to reduce the number of pins on the memory package. In general, the number of pins on the memory package determines the size of the package and therefore the amount of area on the printed-circuit board occupied by memory chips. The graphic symbols for both types of packages are shown in Figure 7.14(b).

At a more concrete level, a RAM is organized as an array of memory cells together with an address decoder and I/O drivers. As shown in Figure 7.15(a), a **memory cell** (MC) can be represented symbolically with a clocked D latch, an AND gate, and an output driver. When the *Row select* signal is equal to 1, the bit stored in the latch will be output. If the *Write enable* signal is also 1, the value of *Input* will be stored in the latch. The *Write enable* signal serves as a clock signal for the latch.

Although this MC has been represented by a latch and two gates, you should realize that in reality, it can be implemented with far fewer transistors. The implementation style of a MC classifies memories as either static or dynamic RAM. In the case of **static RAM** (SRAM), we construct a memory cell with four to six transistors, using cross-coupled inverters to serve as a latch, and implementing the input AND gate and the output drivers with one transistor each. This kind of SRAM memory cell will retain its content indefinitely as long as it is not rewritten and power is not disconnected. In the case of **dynamic RAM** (DRAM), however, the memory cells are implemented with only one transistor. The disadvantage of DRAM is that the content of the cell is lost during each read operation, and has to be rewritten afterward. To make things worse, due to manufacturing imperfections, the content of each cell disappears permanently after a time. To avoid this problem, each memory location must be accessed with a certain frequency, or alternatively, the content must be rewritten or refreshed periodically. During refreshing, all other read or write operations must be suspended, which can be a nuisance. Nonetheless, DRAMs' superior density and reduced cost make them very popular in the design of electronic products. SRAMs, on the other hand, although more costly, are faster and therefore suitable when used in smaller quantities and in places where faster memory access is required.

Both SRAMs and DRAMs are called **volatile memories**, since their content is lost if the power source is removed. For this reason, we must include batteries in equipment such as telephones and answering machines to prevent memory loss in case of short, temporary electricity blackouts. On the other hand, ROMs and PROMs are called **nonvolatile memories** since their content is preserved even if the power supply is cut off. In that case, however, we cannot read the memory content until the power is restored.

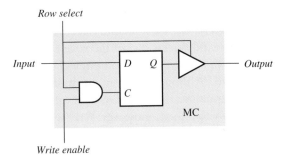

(a) Memory cell

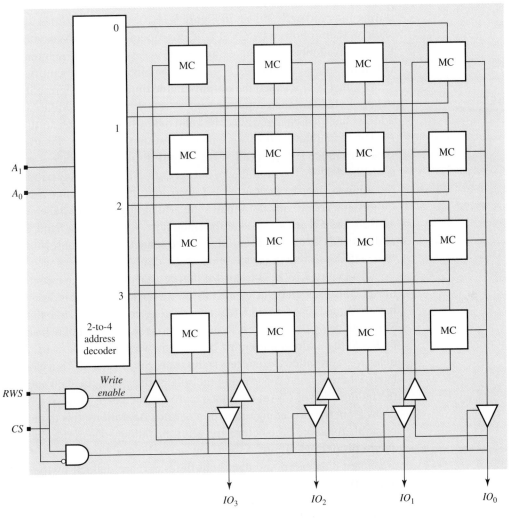

(b) Memory schematic

F I G U R E   7.15
RAM organization.

In Figure 7.15(b) we show an example of a 4×4 memory consisting of 16 MCs. For each memory access, the address decoder decodes the address and selects one of the rows. At that point, if RWS and CS are both equal to 1, the new content will be written into each cell of the row selected. Although the content of each cell in that row is available on the output line, the output drivers will be disabled to allow the new data to be written in. If, however, $RWS = 0$ and $CS = 1$, the data from the row selected will be passed through the tristate drivers to the IO pins.

The RAM organization determines input and output timing constraints for memory read and write operations. For example, since the critical path from input to output goes through the address decoder, the address lines must be stable before any other signal. This means that during the read cycle shown in Figure 7.16(a), the address lines will be set at t_0 then followed by CS at t_1. Consequently, the RAM's data will become available at t_2. The delay time $t_2 - t_0$ is called the **memory access time**, since it would take $t_2 - t_0$ ns to obtain data from memory. The delay time $t_2 - t_1$ is called the **output-enable time**, since it represents the delay in enabling the output drivers. Note that after the value of the address lines has changed at t_3, the valid data will be available until time t_5. This time interval $t_5 - t_3$ is called the **output-hold time**. Finally, the time difference $t_5 - t_4$ is called the **output-disable time**, since it represents the delay in the disabling of output data. Since the delay path from the address lines to the output is longer than the path from CS to the output, the access time determines the availability of data whenever the address and CS are asserted at the same time. On the other hand, if the address and the CS are disasserted at the same time, the output-disable time will determine the availability of the data.

In Figure 7.16(b) you can see that certain other timing constraints must be also satisfied during a RAM write operation. In this design we have assumed that CS and RWS have been asserted at the same time, t_1. Since the delay from address to output is longer than the delay from CS or RWS, the address lines must be set somewhat earlier, say at t_0. The delay $t_1 - t_0$ is called the **address setup time**. Since each MC is a clocked latch, where signal CS is playing the role of the clock, the data value at the falling edge of CS (at t_3) will be stored in the latch. However, as we know from the preceding discussion of latch operations, this data must be stable for some time before and after the falling edge of the clock, to assure proper operation. As you can see in Figure 7.16(b), these times are called **data setup** and **data hold times** and are defined by the time intervals $t_3 - t_2$ and $t_4 - t_3$.

We also learned from the latch discussion in Chapter 6 that the clock width must be of a certain duration for data to be latched properly. The same constraint is also imposed on the CS or RWS signals, which have to be asserted for a duration equal to or longer than the **write-pulse**

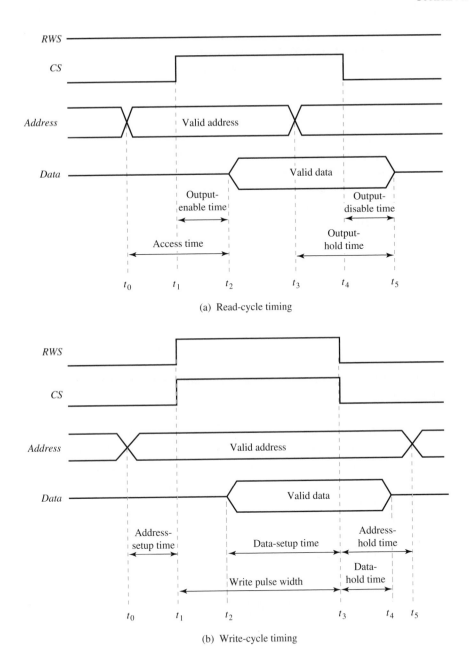

FIGURE 7.16

RAM timing.

width, defined by the time $t_3 - t_1$. Furthermore, an address must stay valid for some time after the falling edge of *CS* or *RWS*. This time, called the **address-hold time**, is defined by the time interval $t_5 - t_3$.

As we mentioned earlier, memory components are always manufactured in sizes $2^n \times m$, where n and m can vary over a wide range of numbers. In general, though, the product $2^n \times m$ will be constant for a particular technology and a particular year of manufacturing. Given these circumstances, the need for larger memories must be satisfied by constructing them from smaller memory chips that are available at the time of design. In the rest of this section we describe how to build wider and larger memories showing how to extend m and n beyond the capacity offered by a single chip.

To obtain wider bit widths, we can connect several memory chips in parallel. This process is shown in Figure 7.17, where a 16K $\times$ 32 RAM was obtained by connecting, in parallel, four 16K $\times$ 8 RAMs, $M_3, M_2, M_1,$ and M_0. In this case, the address line, A, as well as the CS and RWS signals, are connected to all the memory chips. Note that the input and output data buses are partitioned into four bytes, ranging from least significant to most significant, and each byte is connected to its corresponding memory. Using this procedure, we could construct a memory of any width.

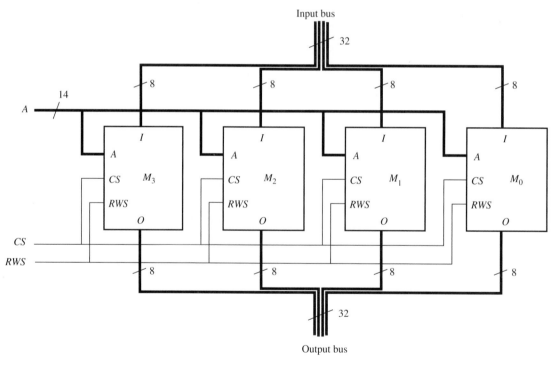

FIGURE 7.17
16K $\times$ 32 RAM design with 16K $\times$ 8 RAMs.

To obtain a larger memory, however, we would need to connect several memory chips in series, so that each chip could contain a portion of memory words. This procedure has been shown in Figure 7.18, where

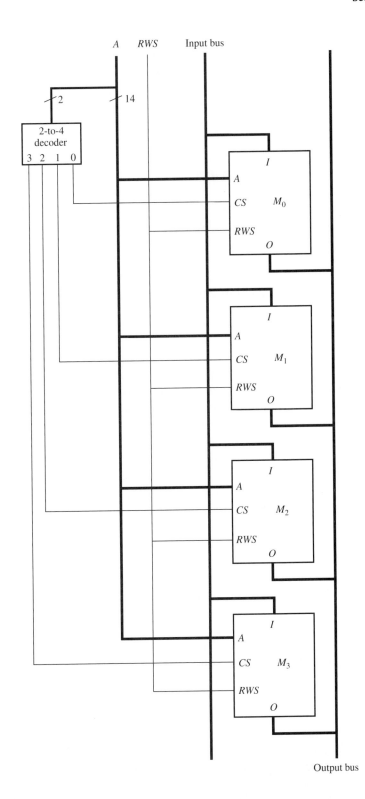

FIGURE 7.18

Output bus   64K × 8 RAM design with 16K × 8 RAMs.

a 64K × 8 RAM has been constructed by connecting in series four 16K × 8 RAMs, M_0, M_1, M_2, and M_3. Note that in this case, all the RAMs share the same input and output buses, as well as the common control signal *RWS*. During memory access, the chip-select signal *CS* is used to distinguish which memory chip contains the proper data. Assume that M_0 will contain all the data with addresses 0 to $2^{14}-1$, M_1 from 2^{14} to $2^{15}-1$, M_2 from 2^{15} to $2^{15}+2^{14}-1$, and M_3 from $2^{15}+2^{14}$ to $2^{16}-1$. We divide the 16-bit address bus into two parts so that the two most-significant bits are used to select the appropriate chip and the 14 least-significant bits are used to select a particular location in that memory chip. To accomplish this, the least-significant 14 bits of the address bus have been connected to the address ports of all the memory chips, and the two most-significant bits are connected to a 2-to-4 decoder, which determines which of the four chips should be selected for read or write operations. This selection is implemented by connecting each decoder output to the *CS* input of the appropriate memory chip, as indicated in Figure 7.18.

7.8 PUSH-DOWN STACKS

Push-down stacks are frequently used in software and hardware designs. By definition, a **push-down stack** is a memory component that has limited access. While any data stored in a RAM can be accessed at any time, the data stored in a push-down stack can be accessed through only one location: the top of the stack. In other words, when data is pushed on the stack, it is stored in the top and all the rest of the data is pushed one location down into the stack. Conversely, when data is popped from the stack, it is removed from the top and all the data in the stack is moved one location up. In the case of the 4-word push-down stack in Figure 7.19, the stack initially contains two numbers: 34 in the location *Top* and 23 in the location *Top* − 1. In Figure 7.19(b) you can see that pushing the number 45 on the stack requires that numbers 34 and 23 be pushed down to locations *Top* − 1 and *Top* − 2. On the other hand, when 45 is popped from the top of the stack, 34 and 23 are moved up again and now occupy *Top* and *Top* − 1, as shown in Figure 7.19(c). In this particular case, of course, we can push no more than four numbers onto the stack before it becomes full. Beyond this point, pushing additional numbers results in loss of the number at the bottom of the stack.

When designing a push-down stack, the important point to recall is that the stored data is shifted one position up or down during the push and pop operations. This observation leads us to use shift registers for the stack implementation, along with an up-down counter to detect

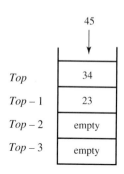

(a) Stack content before 45 is pushed down

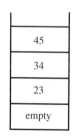

(b) Stack content after 45 is pushed down

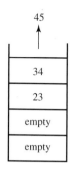

(c) Stack content after 45 is popped up

FIGURE 7.19

Push-down stack operations.

when the stack is full or empty. These components are used in the design of the 4-word, m-bit push-down stack shown in Figure 7.20. Note that this stack has m input lines IN_i and m output lines OUT_i, where $0 \leq i \leq m - 1$. It also has three control signals, *Push/pop*, *Enable*, and *Reset*.

The *Push/pop* signal controls pushing and popping in such a manner that when it is equal to 0, the data will be pushed on the stack, and when it is equal to 1, the data will be removed from the top of the stack. The *Enable* signal enables the stack operation, and the *Reset* signal will reset the shift registers and the counter whenever it is equal to 0. The stack's synchronous operations are shown in the operation table in Figure 7.20(a). Note also that the stack has two output signals, *Empty* and *Full*, which indicate the status of the stack as follows: When *Empty* has a value of 1, this indicates that the stack is empty; on the other hand, when *Full* has a value of 1, the stack is full.

In Figure 7.20(d) you can see that the stack implementation contains one 4-bit shift register with parallel load from Figure 7.5 (SRwPL) for every input/output pair—all together, that is, the stack contains m shift registers. These shift registers will shift to the right whenever a push operation is requested and to the left whenever a pop operation is needed. Any new data is pushed on the stack through the I_L input in the shift register, and stored in the Q_3 output, which represents the top of the stack. Since the counter contains the number of entries in the stack, we know that on every rising edge of the clock the shift register will either shift to the right with the counter counting up (if $Push/pop = 0$ and $Enable = 1$), or it will shift to the left with the counter counting down (if $Push/pop = 1$ and $Enable = 1$).

The values of the control signals for the shift registers and counter can be derived from the control table shown in Figure 7.20(b). From this control table we can also derive the following Boolean equations for various control signals:

$$S_1 = Enable$$
$$S_0 = (Push/pop)' \, Enable$$
$$D = (Push/pop) \, Enable$$
$$E = Enable$$

The implementation of these equations represents the control logic of the push-down stack.

From the output table shown in Figure 7.20(c), the output logic would decode the counter states of 000 and 100. Simply put, whenever the counter content is 0, the value of the *Empty* signal will be equal to 1; at any other time, it is 0. Conversely, whenever the counter's content is 4, the value of the *Full* signal will be 1, although at any other time it

PUSH/POP	ENABLE	OPERATIONS
X	0	No change
0	1	*Push*
1	1	*Pop*

(a) Operation table

		SHIFT REGISTER CONTROLS		COUNTER CONTROLS	
PUSH/POP	ENABLE	S_1	S_0	D	E
X	0	0	0	X	0
0	1	1	1	0	1
1	1	1	0	1	1

(b) Control table

COUNTER OUTPUTS				
Q_2	Q_1	Q_0	EMPTY	FULL
0	0	0	1	0
0	0	1	0	0
0	1	0	0	0
0	1	1	0	0
1	0	0	0	1

(c) Output table

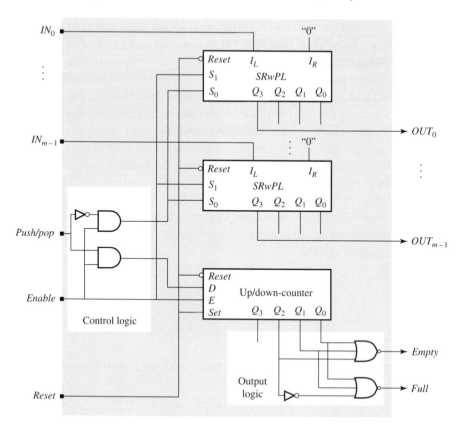

(d) Stack schematic

FIGURE 7.20
4-word push-down stack.

will be 0. Thus we can derive the following Boolean equations for the output logic:

$$Empty = Q_2'Q_1'Q_0'$$
$$Full = Q_2Q_1'Q_0'$$

The main weakness of the shift-register implementation is in the large number of costly shift registers when a larger push-down stack is needed. For this reason, large push-down stacks are usually implemented with RAMs. On the other hand, since RAMs are not capable of shifting their contents, the push and pop operations in these larger stacks must be implemented in a slightly different way, by changing the location of the top of the stack. In other words, as we push data on the stack, the address of the top will be incremented with every push, and conversely, with every pop, the address will be decremented. Consider, for example, a stack that is empty: The top of the stack is at address 0. Then, as data is written in the top of the stack, the address of the stack's top is incremented with every push operation so that the stack's top is always an empty location into which new data can be written whenever a new push operation is requested. On the other hand, whenever a pop operation is requested, the data is read from the location just below the the top, whose address is one less than that of the stack's top. Following this logic, we know that for a RAM with 2^n words, the stack is empty when the top is at location 0 and full whenever the top is at location $2^n - 1$. Note that the location with address $2^n - 1$ is never used for storing data, only for determining if the stack is full. Although it is true that this approach sacrifices one word out of the 2^n words in the RAM, it nonetheless simplifies the output logic.

In Figure 7.21 we show this kind of stack implementation with a 1K RAM and two counters pointing to the location on the top of the stack and the location just below the top. Note that the input and output signals and the stack operations are the same as in Figure 7.20, and that for convenience, the operation table from Figure 7.20(a) has been reproduced in Figure 7.21(b). As you can see, this stack has two 10-bit counters, one 10-bit selector, a 1K RAM, a control, and an output logic. The two counters, called *Top* and *Top* − 1, contain the address of the top, which represents the lowest unused location and of the location immediately below the top, which represents the data most recently pushed on the stack. As you should expect, the content of the counters *Top* and *Top* − 1 differs by 1, and both will be incremented during the push operation and decremented during the pop operation. Whenever a push operation is requested, the content of the counter *Top* will be selected as the RAM address, whereas the content of *Top* − 1 will be selected whenever a pop operation is requested.

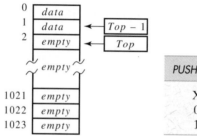

0	*data*	
1	*data*	← Top − 1
2	*empty*	← Top
	empty	
1021	*empty*	
1022	*empty*	
1023	*empty*	

(a) Symbolic design

PUSH/POP	ENABLE	OPERATIONS
X	0	No change
0	1	*Push*
1	1	*Pop*

(b) Operation table

		SELECTOR CONTROL	MEMORY CONTROLS		COUNTER CONTROLS	
PUSH/POP	ENABLE	S	CS	RWS	D	E
X	0	X	0	0	X	0
0	1	1	1	1	0	1
1	1	0	1	0	1	1

(c) Control table

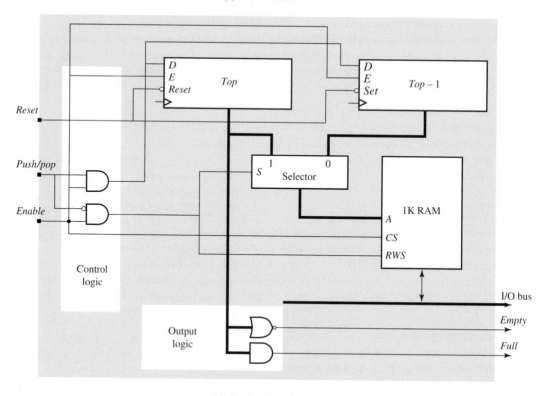

(d) Stack schematic

FIGURE 7.21

Push-down stack implemented with a 1K RAM.

From the preceding description we have constructed the control table shown in Figure 7.21(c), which specifies the values of all the signals controlling the counters, the selector, and the RAM for either push and pop operations. From this table we can also derive the following Boolean equations for the control logic:

$$E = CS = Enable$$

$$S = RWS = (Push/Pop)'\,Enable$$

$$D = (Push/Pop)\,Enable$$

The output logic consists of two gates that indicate when the stack is empty or full. Since the stack is empty whenever the content of counter *Top* is 0, we have used a 10-input NOR gate whose inputs are connected to the output of the counter *Top* to detect an empty stack. Similarly, we declare that the stack is full when the counter *Top* contains all 1's, which is detected by a 10-input AND gate when its output becomes equal to 1. The complete stack schematic is shown in Figure 7.21(d).

7.9 FIRST-IN-FIRST-OUT QUEUE

A **first-in-first-out** (FIFO) **queue** is frequently used to smooth bursts in the requests for a service. Consider, for example, the people who queue for movie tickets, to enter a bus, or to get on a ride at Disneyland, who must wait in a line until it is their turn to receive service. Similar situations can arise with different processors, ASICs, or any products that send data to each other, in the sense that when the data production momentarily exceeds the data consumption, we must insert a FIFO queue between the producer and the consumer. Of course, in such cases the data production rate cannot exceed the consumption rate indefinitely, since that would require an infinite queue. On the contrary, on average, both rates must be the same. However, production and consumption bursts do occasionally occur, and the size of the queue determines how large a burst can be tolerated.

The purpose of a FIFO queue is to store the surplus data, which will eventually be read out of the queue in the same order in which it was written in. Thus the first data stored is read first, and so on, as illustrated in Figure 7.22. In Figure 7.22(a) we show the content of the queue after the numbers 23 and 34 were queued but before the number 45 has arrived. In Figure 7.22(b) you see the queue's content after the number 45 was queued. Note that when the queue is read, the number 23 is output and discarded, which causes the content of the queue to be shifted one position down. The queue content after the shift is shown in Figure 7.22(c).

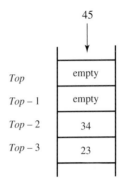

(a) Queue content before 45 is stored

(b) Queue content after 45 is stored

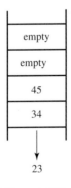

(c) Queue content after 23 is read

FIGURE 7.22
FIFO queue operations.

In general, a queue has m input lines IN_i, and m output lines OUT_i, where $0 \leq i \leq m - 1$. It also has three control signals: *Read/write*, *Enable*, and *Reset*. When the *Read/write* signal is equal to 0, the queue will output the data that has been stored longest, taking it from the front of the queue. Consequently, when the *Read/Write* signal is equal to 1, the data will be added to the back of the queue.

The typical FIFO queue would also have two control outputs which are used to control the producer and consumer circuits. When the queue is full, for example, the signal *Full* will have a value of 1, which will warn the producer that any further data sent to the queue will be discarded. When the queue is empty, the signal *Empty* becomes 1, which warns the consumer that new data has not yet arrived.

Since the arrival order of the data is preserved within the queue, we can construct the queue using shift registers together with a counter to count the amount of valid data that it contains. Such a queue implementation is shown in Figure 7.23, and its operation table is shown in Figure 7.23(a). Whenever data is queued, the shift register shifts data to the right and the counter is incremented. On the other hand, whenever data is read out, the data at the bottom of the queue is selected by the selector and the counter is decremented. Notice that data is not really discarded at that time, but rather, is invalidated by decrementing the counter. In Figure 7.23(b) we have translated the operation table in Figure 7.23(a) into a control table, which shows the values of the various control signals. During a read operation, the content of the shift register will not change and the counter will count down by 1. During the write operation, however, the shift register will shift one position to the right and the counter will count up by 1. The counter also controls selection of the proper data during the read operation. As a rule it would be set to 1111 during the initialization so that its content will be zero when the first data is in the queue. This negative bias of 1 in counting is necessary to accommodate the selector control, which requires a value of 00, 01, 10, or 11 in order to select one of the shifter outputs.

The Boolean equations for the other control signals can be derived from the control table as follows:

$$S_0 = S_1 = (Read/Write)Enable$$

$$D = (Read/Write)'Enable$$

$$E = Enable$$

The purpose of the output logic is to specify the value of *Full* and *Empty* signals, indicating that the queue is empty whenever the counter content is all 1's, and that the queue is full whenever the counter content is equal

READ/WRITE	ENABLE	OPERATIONS
X	0	No change
0	1	Read
1	1	Write

(a) Operation table

READ/WRITE	ENABLE	S_1	S_0	D	E
X	0	0	0	X	0
0	1	0	0	1	1
1	1	1	1	0	1

(b) Control table

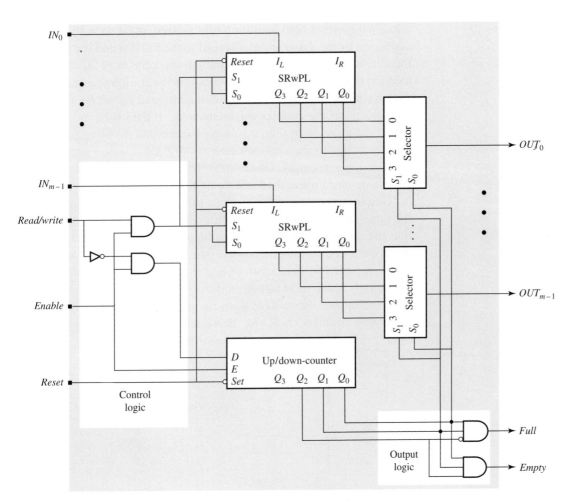

(c) Queue schematic

F I G U R E   7.23
4-word FIFO queue.

to 011. Therefore, we can say that

$$Full = Q_2'Q_1Q_0$$

$$Empty = Q_2Q_1Q_0$$

The complete schematic of the 4-word FIFO queue is shown in Figure 7.23(c).

As with push-down stacks, larger queues are usually implemented with a RAM rather than a shift register, and incorporate two counters, pointing at the front and the back of the queue. Such an implementation is known as a circular queue and shown symbolically in Figure 7.24(a). Note that it uses 1K RAM and two counters designated as *Front* and *Back*. The *Front* counter contains the address of the earliest written data. Whenever a read operation is requested, the data in the location addressed by the *Front* counter is read to the I/O bus and the counter is incremented. The *Back* counter contains the address of the first empty location in the queue, and whenever a write operation is requested, the data is written into the empty location addressed by the *Back* counter, at which point the counter is incremented. If data is being read from the queue more often than it is being written into the queue, the *Front* counter points to the same location as the *Back* counter, which means that the queue is empty. On the other hand, if data is being written into the queue more often than it is being read out, the *Back* counter that is being incremented in the modulo 1024 fashion eventually points to the same location as the *Front* counter, although in this case this means that the queue is full. To avoid ambiguity we can use 11-bit (modulo 2048) counters, which will indicate that the queue is empty when both counters have the same content and that it is full when their content differs only in the most significant bit.

In Figure 7.24 we have shown a queue implementation that uses two counters and a 1K RAM. This queue uses a selector to select the

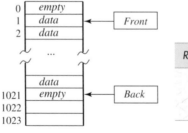

(a) Symbolic design

READ/WRITE	ENABLE	OPERATIONS
X	0	No change
0	1	Read
1	1	Write

(b) Operation table

READ/WRITE	ENABLE	S	CS	RWS	E (Front)	E (Back)
X	0	X	0	X	0	0
0	1	1	1	0	1	0
1	1	0	1	1	0	1

(c) Control table

FIGURE 7.24
FIFO queue implemented with a 1K RAM.

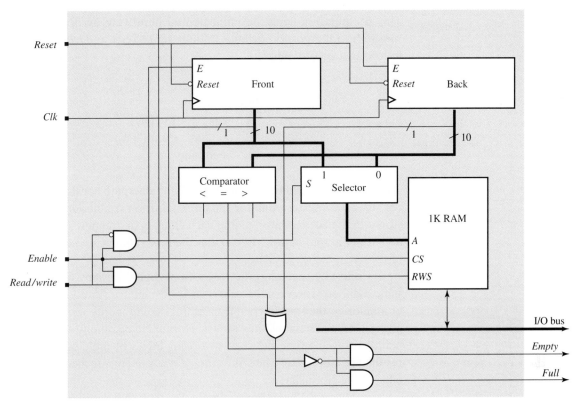

(d) Schematic

FIGURE 7.24
Continued.

content of the *Front* or *Back* counters, as well as a comparator to compare their contents. Its operation table is shown in Figure 7.24(b), its
control table in Figure 7.24(c), and finally, the complete schematic is
shown in Figure 7.24(d).

7.10 SIMPLE DATAPATHS

Datapaths are used in all standard processor and ASIC implementations
to perform complex numerical computation or data manipulations. A
datapath consists of some temporary storage in addition to arithmetic,
logic, and shift units. Let's consider, for example, how we might perform
the summation of 100 numbers:

$$sum = \sum_{i=1}^{100} x_i$$

This computation could be implemented iteratively by declaring the *sum* to be a temporary variable, initially set to zero, and executing the following loop statement:

$$sum = 0$$

loop:
    for $i = 1$ **to** 100
        $sum = sum + x_i$
    end loop

This loop body could be executed on a 32-bit datapath consisting of one register called an **accumulator** and an ALU. The variable *sum* would be stored in the accumulator, and in each clock cycle the new x_i would be added to the *sum* in the ALU so that the new value of *sum* could again be stored in the accumulator.

Generally speaking, the majority of digital designs work in the same manner. The variable values and constant are stored in registers or memories, they are fetched from storage components after the rising edge of the clock signal, they are transformed in combinatorial components during the time between two rising edges of the clock, and the results are stored back into the storage components at the next rising edge of the clock signal.

In Figure 7.25 we show a simple datapath that could perform the summation above. This datapath contains a selector, which selects either 0 or some outside data as the left operand for the ALU. The right operand will always be the content of the accumulator, which could also be output through a tristate driver. The accumulator is a shift register with a parallel load. This datapath's schematic is shown in Figure 7.25(a), and in Figure 7.25(b) we show the 9-bit control word that specifies the values of the control signals for the selector, the ALU, the accumulator, and the output drivers. All the components in the datapath are 32 bits wide.

On each clock cycle, a specific control word would define the operation of the datapath. To compute the sum of 100 numbers, we would need 102 clock cycles. In this case the control words would be the same for all clock cycles except the first and last. In the first clock cycle, we must clear the accumulator; in the next 100 clock cycles we add the new data to the accumulated sum; finally, in the last clock cycle, we output the accumulated sum.

Although the datapath above would be useful for simple arithmetic expressions, more complicated expressions require several temporary variables as well as a more elaborate datapath that requires a register file instead of an accumulator. In Figure 7.26(a) we show an example of a more complex datapath, consisting of a selector, an 8-register 3-port register file, an ALU, a shifter, and tristate drivers. In this case it

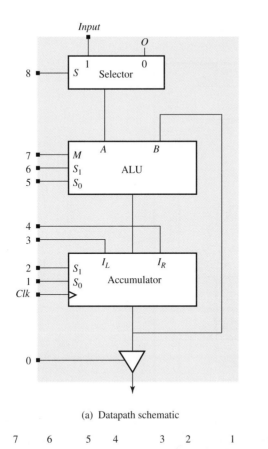

(a) Datapath schematic

8	7	6	5	4	3	2	1	0
Input select	ALU controls			Shift values		Accumulator controls		Out enable

(b) Control word

FIGURE 7.25
Simple datapath with one accumulator.

would be the register file that supplies the two operands, in addition to storing one result on every clock cycle. For completeness, we have included the tables of ALU and shifter operations, shown in Figure 7.26(b) and (c), and the control word, shown in Figure 7.26(d). Note that the datapath is controlled by a 20-bit control word, which determines all the destinations, sources, and operations in the datapath. For a better understanding of datapath operation, we use it next in implementation of a one's-count algorithm.

EXAMPLE 7.1 One's-counter implementation

PROBLEM Using a datapath with a 3-port register file, design a one's counter that will count the number of 1's in an input data word and return the result after completion.

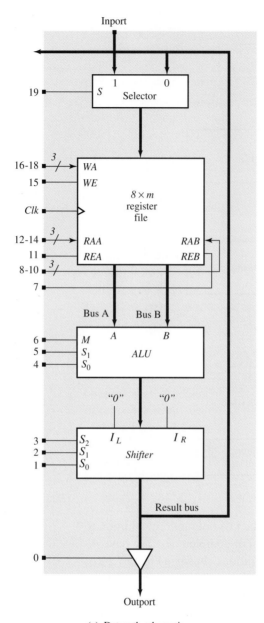

Inport

M	S_1	S_0	ALU OPERATIONS
0	0	0	Complement A
0	0	1	AND
0	1	0	EX-OR
0	1	1	OR
1	0	0	Decrement A
1	0	1	Add
1	1	0	Subtract
1	1	1	Increment A

(b) ALU operations

S_2	S_1	S_0	SHIFT OPERATIONS
0	0	0	Pass
0	0	1	Pass
0	1	0	Not used
0	1	1	Not used
1	0	0	Shift left
1	0	1	Rotate left
1	1	0	Shift right
1	1	1	Rotate right

(c) Shifter operations

(a) Datapath schematic

19	18 17 16 15	14 13 12 11	10 9 8 7	6 5 4	3 2 1	0
IE	Write address	Read address A	Read address B	ALU operation	Shifter operation	OE

(d) Control word

FIGURE 7.26
Datapath with 3-port register file.

SOLUTION   In solving this problem we assume that the data-word is provided from the outside environment and is available as an input to the datapath. We use the variables *Data*, *Ocount*, *Mask*, and *Temp* to describe this algorithm for counting ones. The variable *Data* will store the dataword, which consists of 0's and 1's. The algorithm will then scan the *Data*, from LSB to MSB, and add 1 to the *Ocount* for each 1 it encounters in the *Data*. *Mask* will store the constant 1, and *Temp* will be used to store temporarily the LSB of the *Data*. After the initialization, the algorithm will isolate the LSB of *Data*, store it in *Temp*, add *Temp* to *Ocount*, and finally, shift *Data* one position to the right. This sequence would be repeated until *Data* contains nothing but 0's. Note that for different data words, this algorithm will repeat the sequence of operations above a different number of times.

In Figure 7.27(a) we show the basic algorithm for counting the number of 1's in a data word. Statements 1, 2, and 3 are used to initialize the variables, while in statements 4, 5, one is added to the *Ocount* whenever the LSB of the *Data* is

1. *Data* := *Inport*
2. *Ocount* := 0
3. *Mask* := 1
   while *Data* :≠ 0 **repeat**
   4. *Temp* := *Data* AND *Mask*
   5. *Ocount* := *Ocount* + *Temp*
   6. *Data* := *Data* >> 1
   end while
7. *Outport* := *Ocount*

(a) Basic algorithm for one's count

R_1:   Data
R_2:   Mask
R_3:   Ocount
R_4:   Temp

(b) Register assignment

CONTROL WORDS	IE	WRITE ADDRESS	READ ADDRESS A	READ ADDRESS B	ALU OPERATION	SHIFTER OPERATION	OE	
1	1	R_1	X	X	X	X	0	
2	0	R_3	0	0	Add	Pass	0	
3	0	R_2	0	X	Increment	Pass	0	
4	0	R_4	R_1	R_2	AND	Pass	0	Repeated while Data ≠ 0
5	0	R_3	R_3	R_4	Add	Pass	0	
6	0	R_1	R_1	0	Add	Shift right	0	
7	0	None	R_3	0	Add	Pass	1	

(c) Control words for one's counter

FIGURE 7.27
One's-count algorithm.

equal to 1, and then in statement 6 *Data* is shifted one place to the right while 0 is shifted into the MSB of *Data*. Statement 7 is used to output the *Ocount*. Note that we use the symbols $>>$ and $<<$ to indicate shifting of data to the right or left, with the shift amount following the symbol.

In implementing this algorithm, we must first assign the variables to registers in the register file. As shown in Figure 7.26(b), the variables *Data*, *Mask*, *Ocount*, and *Temp* are assigned to registers R_1, R_2, R_3, and R_4. Once we have assigned these variables to the registers, we are ready to derive proper control words for each statement, as shown in Figure 7.27(c), where the mnemonics are used in each control field to indicate the proper operations and the addresses of operand and result registers. To control the datapath, we assume that the one's counter is a separate module, which will start its one's count whenever a *Start* signal equals 1, and that it will set the signal *Done* to 1 as soon as the result becomes available.

As you can see in Figure 7.28, the FSM representation of the one's counter would consist of eight states. Note that the one's counter will stay in state s_0 while it is waiting for the *Start* signal to become 1, and then, in the next seven states, $s_1, \ldots, s_7$, it will execute the algorithm that was shown in Figure 7.27(a). Finally, in state s_7, it would output the result, set the signal *Done* to 1, and then return to its original state, s_0.

The one's-counter controller has two input signals, *Start* and *Data* = 0, and one output signal, *Done*. *Start* and *Done* are used to communicate the starting and completing times to the rest of the system. The signal *Data* = 0 is basically a status signal provided by the datapath. Finally, on each clock cycle, the controller must also supply 20 control signals in the control word. Note that to implement its eight states, we need three D flip-flops, designated as Q_2, Q_1, and Q_0. In Figure 7.29(a), (b), and (c), we have shown the next-state table, maps, and next-state equations.

The output logic of this counter would be derived from the control words given in Figure 7.27(c). In Figure 7.30(a) we show an output logic table that was derived from Figure 7.27(c) by substituting the proper binary values for all the mnemonics. Note that the minimal expressions for each control signal could have been derived from the output logic table in Figure 7.27(a) using any of the logic minimization techniques. The control equations have been given in Figure 7.30(b). Finally, in Figure 7.31, we show the schematic for the one's counter that uses the datapath introduced in Figure 7.26.

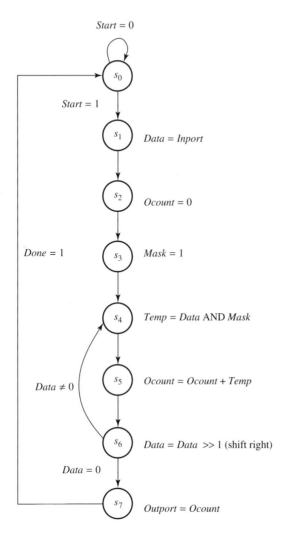

$Start = 0$

$Start = 1$

s_0

s_1 $Data = Inport$

s_2 $Ocount = 0$

$Done = 1$ s_3 $Mask = 1$

s_4 $Temp = Data$ AND $Mask$

$Data \neq 0$ s_5 $Ocount = Ocount + Temp$

s_6 $Data = Data \gg 1$ (shift right)

$Data = 0$

s_7 $Outport = Ocount$

F I G U R E   7.28

FSM representation of one's counter.

				Start, (Data = 0)			
STATES	Q_2	Q_1	Q_0	00	01	10	11
s_0	0	0	0	0 0 0	0 0 0	0 0 1	0 0 1
s_1	0	0	1	0 1 0	0 1 0	0 1 0	0 1 0
s_2	0	1	0	0 1 1	0 1 1	0 1 1	0 1 1
s_3	0	1	1	1 0 0	1 0 0	1 0 0	1 0 0
s_4	1	0	0	1 0 1	1 0 1	1 0 1	1 0 1
s_5	1	0	1	1 1 0	1 1 0	1 1 0	1 1 0
s_6	1	1	0	1 0 0	1 1 1	1 0 0	1 1 1
s_7	1	1	1	0 0 0	0 0 0	0 0 0	0 0 0

(a) Next-state table

F I G U R E   7.29

Next-state logic for one's counter.

	$Q_2 = 0$				$Q_2 = 1$			
$Q_1 Q_0$	00	01	11	10	00	01	11	10
Start (Data = 0) 00	0 0 0	0 1 0	1 0 0	0 1 1	1 0 1	1 1 0	0 0 0	1 0 0
01	0 0 0	0 1 0	1 0 0	0 1 1	1 0 1	1 1 0	0 0 0	1 1 1
11	0 0 1	0 1 0	1 0 0	0 1 1	1 0 1	1 1 0	0 0 0	1 1 1
10	0 0 1	0 1 0	1 0 0	0 1 1	1 0 1	1 1 0	0 0 0	1 0 0

Q_2(next), Q_1(next), Q_0(next)

(b) Karnaugh map

$$Q_2(next) = Q_2'Q_1Q_0 + Q_2Q_1' + Q_2Q_0'$$

$$Q_1(next) = Q_1'Q_0 + Q_2'Q_1Q_0' + (Data = 0)Q_1Q_0'$$

$$Q_0(next) = Q_2'Q_1Q_0' + Q_2Q_1'Q_0' + Start\ Q_1'Q_0' + (Data = 0)Q_2Q_0$$

FIGURE 7.29
Continued.

(c) Next-state equations

STATE	$Q_2 Q_1 Q_0$	IE	WRITE ADDRESS $WA_2\ WA_1\ WA_0\ WE$				READ ADDRESS A $RAA_2\ RAA_1\ RAA_0\ REA$				READ ADDRESS B $RAB_2\ RAB_1\ RAB_0\ REB$				ALU OPERATIONS $M\ S_1\ S_0$			SHIFT OPERATIONS $S_2\ S_1\ S_0$			OE
s_0	0 0 0	0	X	X	X	0	X	X	X	0	X	X	X	0	X	X	X	X	X	X	0
s_1	0 0 1	1	0	0	1	1	X	X	X	0	X	X	X	0	X	X	X	X	X	X	0
s_2	0 1 0	0	0	1	1	1	X	X	X	0	X	X	X	0	1	0	1	0	0	0	0
s_3	0 1 1	0	0	1	0	1	X	X	X	0	X	X	X	0	1	1	1	0	0	0	0
s_4	1 0 0	0	1	0	0	1	0	0	1	1	0	1	0	1	0	0	1	0	0	0	0
s_5	1 0 1	0	0	1	1	1	0	1	1	1	1	0	0	1	1	0	1	0	0	0	0
s_6	1 1 0	0	0	0	1	1	0	0	1	1	X	X	X	0	1	0	1	1	1	0	0
s_7	1 1 1	0	X	X	X	0	0	1	1	1	X	X	X	0	1	0	1	0	0	0	1

(a) Output logic table

$IE = Q_2'Q_1'Q_0$

$WA_2 = Q_1'Q_0'$
$WA_1 = Q_2Q_0 + Q_2'Q_1$
$WA_0 = Q_1'Q_0 + Q_1Q_0'$
$WE = Q_2Q_1' + Q_2'Q_0 + Q_1Q_0'$

$RAA_2 = 0$
$RAA_1 = Q_0$
$RAA_0 = 1$
$REA = Q_1$

$RAB_2 = Q_0$
$RAB_1 = Q_0'$
$RAB_0 = 0$
$REB = Q_2Q_1'$

$M = Q_1 + Q_0$
$S_1 = Q_2'Q_0$
$S_0 = 1$
$S_2 = S_1 = Q_2Q_1Q_0'$
$S_0 = 0$
$OE = Q_2Q_1Q_0$

(b) Output equations

FIGURE 7.30
Output logic for one's-counter controller.

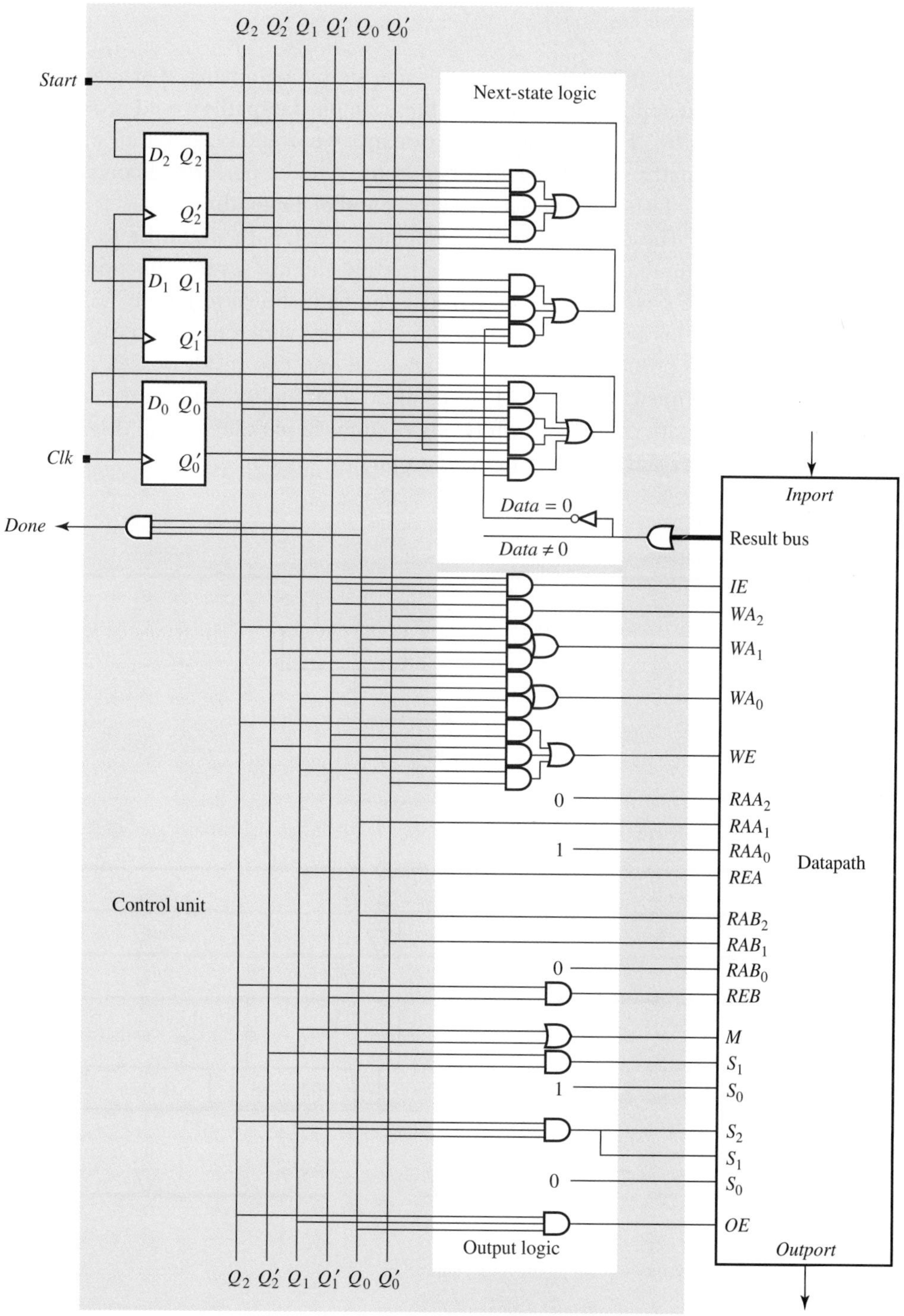

FIGURE 7.31
One's-counter schematic.

7.11 GENERAL DATAPATHS

In Section 7.10 we described some simple datapaths. For many high-speed applications, however, these simple datapaths would probably be too slow. To increase the performance we would need to redesign these datapaths so that several operations could be performed concurrently. These faster datapaths are called **parallel datapaths**.

The obvious way to parallelize a datapath would be to increase the number of ports in the register file and use several functional units, as we have done in the parallel datapath shown in Figure 7.32. Note that this datapath has a 6-port register file (with four read ports and two write ports), six buses (four operand and two result buses), and four functional units (an ALU, a shifter, a multiplier, and a divider). This datapath could perform two operations in parallel, one in the ALU or shifter and the other in the multiplier or divider.

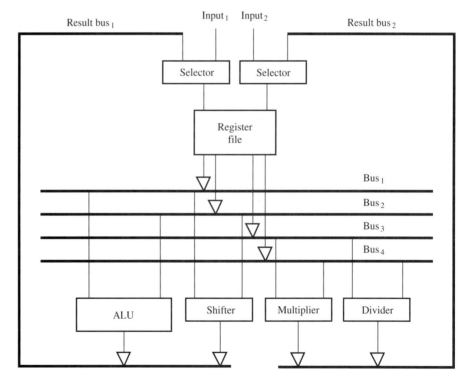

Parallel datapath.

On the other hand, this datapath still could not perform two additions or two multiplications in parallel; in this sense, the datapath in

Figure 7.32 provides only limited parallelism. In other words, if the algorithm being computed does not require this type of parallelism, this datapath would not double the performance of the simple datapath as we had expected. Furthermore, the components in this datapath are not fully connected, which means that some types of parallelism will not be exploited. For example, this datapath could not execute multiply and divide operations in parallel, or perform add and shift operations in parallel, even though they may be available in the algorithm. As you can see, the problem with this datapath is that the multiplier and divider, as well as the ALU and shifter, must use the same buses for their operands and results, which limits its capacity for parallel operations.

From the preceding discussion we can conclude that the performance increase in a parallel datapath will depend not just on the number and type of units in the datapath, but also on their connectivity and the amount of parallelism that is available in the algorithm which is executing on that datapath. In other words, for the best performance/cost ratio, the types of units and their connectivity must match the parallelism in the algorithm. We should keep in mind also the fact that a given algorithm does not offer the same amount of parallelism at all times, since the amount of parallelism will vary during the algorithm's execution.

In general, to achieve the best possible match between an algorithm and a custom datapath, we should use a different number of counters, registers, register files, and memories, with a varied number of ports that are connected with several buses. Note that these buses can be used to supply operands to functional units as well as to supply results back to storage units. It is also possible for the functional units to obtain operands from several buses, although this would require the use of a selector in front of each input. It is also possible for each unit to have input and output latches which are used to store the input operands or results temporarily. Such latching can significantly shorten the amount of time that the buses will be used for operand and result transfer and thus can increase the traffic over these buses.

On the other hand, input and output latching requires a more complicated control unit since each operation requires more than one clock cycle to execute. At least one clock cycle is required to fetch operands from registers, register files, or memories and store them into input latches, at least one clock cycle to perform the operation and store a result into an output latch, and at least one clock cycle to store the result from an output latch back to a register or memory.

An example of such a custom datapath is shown in Figure 7.33. Note that it has a counter, a register, a 3-port register file, and a two-port memory. It also has four buses and three functional units: two ALUs and a multiplier. As you can see, ALU_1 does not have any latches, while ALU_2 has latches at both the inputs and outputs and the single multiplier has only the inputs latched. With this arrangement, ALU_1 can receive its left operand from buses 2 and 3, while the multiplier can receive its right operand from buses 1 and 4. Similarly, the storage units can also receive data from several buses. Such custom datapaths are frequently used in application-specific design to obtain the best performance/cost ratio.

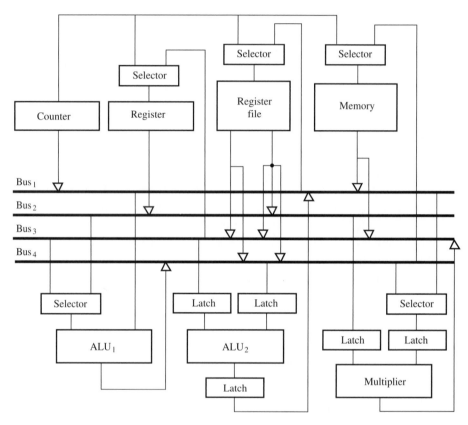

FIGURE 7.33
Example of a custom datapath.

7.12 CONTROL UNIT DESIGN

In previous sections we have assumed that the design of a control unit follows the FSM model, consisting of a next-state logic, a state register, and an output logic. An example of this is shown in Figure 7.34(a), where the state register consists of D flip-flops, and the next- state and output logic have been implemented as either two-level AND–OR or multilevel logic networks. This type of control unit was used in Example 7.1. In some cases, however, a control unit can have thousands of states and hundreds of input, output, and control signals, in which case the straightforward approach to implementation suggested above would become far too complex. Therefore, in this section we describe several alternative design styles that help to simplify implementation of these complex control units.

To begin with, we can simplify the next-state and output logic implementation by using a state register and a decoder, as shown in Figure 7.34(b). In this design each state is identified by a state signal, which

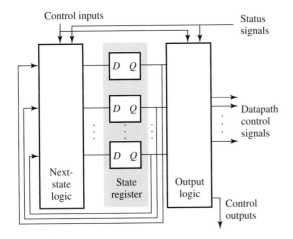

(a) Control unit model

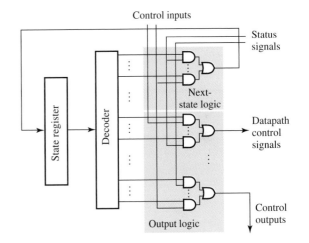

(b) Control unit with state-register and decoder

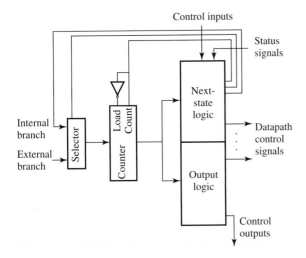

(c) Control unit with counter

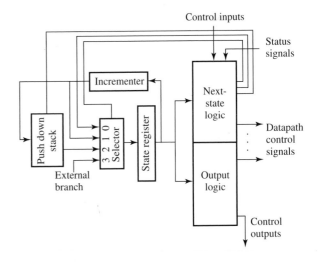

(d) Control unit with state-register and push-down stack

F I G U R E   7.34

Control-unit implementation styles.

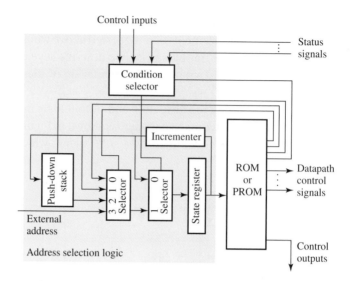

FIGURE 7.34

Continued.

(e) Control unit with stateregister, ROM, and push-down stack

is 1 when the state register is in that particular state, and 0 otherwise. The additional decoder simplifies implementation of the next-state and output logic by simplifying the Boolean expressions for the state register inputs, datapath control signals, and control outputs. In those cases where these signals are dependent only on the state register values, they could be implemented with n-input OR gates, where n represents the number of states in which each signal is asserted. Alternatively, those cases where these signals are also dependent on the status or input signals they could be implemented with an AND–OR logic in which the AND gates would usually have only two inputs, one being the state signal and the other being the status or input signals, as shown in Figure 7.34(b).

We can reduce the amount of next-state logic if we observe that most FMSs contain unconditional state sequences in which each state has only one successor. Furthermore, if the states in such a sequence are encoded such that each state encoding can be obtained by incrementing the state encoding of its predecessor, we replace the state register with a counter. This alternative design style is shown in Figure 7.34(c). In this case, two more signals are added to the next-state logic, a load/count signal and a selector control signal. Note that the load/count signal can increment the counter or load a branch state to branch out of the sequence. In the latter case, the value of the branch state is provided internally by the next-state logic or supplied externally through the control inputs. The proper value of the branch state is selected through the selector.

Another way to modularize control implementation is to encode frequently used tasks as subroutines. For example, instead of repeating the same sequence several times, we could replace that sequence with a call to a subroutine and then return from that subroutine when it is complete. For this purpose we need a push-down stack, which saves the state that follows the subroutine call. This design is shown in Figure 7.34(d). As you can see, the push-down stack stores the successor of the present state, which is loaded into the state register when the subroutine terminates. Note that we have also added a new signal to the next-state logic, designed to control the pushing and popping of the push-down stack.

A final strategy in simplifying control unit designs requires that we replace the next-state logic with a control memory, usually implemented by a ROM or PROM. When we use this strategy, the state register serves as an address register for the control memory. This design style is shown in Figure 7.34(e). In this style it is important that we limit the number of control and status signals used in the next-state selection, since the cost of the control memory doubles for each additional control input or status signal. For this reason we use only one input or status signal to select the next state, which limits the branching capability to two-way branching. In other words, the next address is either an incremented present address or one of the branching addresses. The two-way branching is implemented by a series of two address selectors, and introducing a condition selector, which selects one of control inputs or status signals to be used in selection of the next address. The next address is chosen from the incremented present address or the branch address supplied by ROM, a push-down stack, or the external environment. The control style in Figure 7.34(e) is usually called **microprogrammed control**, and the task of converting ASM charts into ROM words is sometimes called **microprogramming**. The most popular control design styles are the straightforward implementation shown in 7.34(a), used in application-specific custom designs and simple processors, and microprogrammed control, frequently used in complex processors.

7.13 CHAPTER SUMMARY

In this chapter we defined and designed some of the basic sequential components that are used in the design of microprocessors and custom ASICs. First, we described the different types of registers that are used for storing and shifting data. We also defined several types of counters and presented some rules for constructing a larger counter from smaller ones. Next, we described some array-storage components, such as register files and memories that are used for the temporary and permanent storage of data. As we have shown, register files are fast but are also more costly in comparison to memories. Next, we defined specific storage components such as stacks and queues, used in many designs because of their efficiency in implementing well-known storage functions. For these stacks and queues, we also described possible implementations that used shift registers as well as RAMs.

Finally, we introduced the concept of a datapath and showed how to use it for the hardware implementation of specific algorithms, focusing on the example of the one's counter. We also discussed briefly the datapaths that are used in microprocessors and other high-performance ASICs. We also explained briefly different styles of implementing control units. In the next chapter we formalize this concept of the custom datapath and their control units and present techniques for the design synthesis on register-transfer level.

7.14 FURTHER READINGS

Mick, J. and S. Brick. *Bit-Slice Microprocessor Design*. New York: McGraw-Hill, 1980.

> Professional book that explains, in detail, datapath and control unit concepts as well as how to construct a microprocessor from register-transfer components. Requires a good understanding of the principles of computer design.

An 2900 Family Data Book. Sunnyvalle, CA: Advanced Micro Devices, 1985.

> Data book for the first 4-bit datapath and associated support components.

7.15 PROBLEMS

7.1 (Registers) Working from the input waveforms shown in Figure P7.1, draw the output waveform of a setable/resetable D flip-flop.

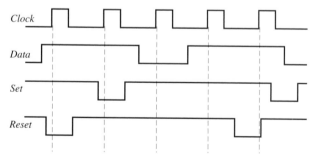

FIGURE P7.1

7.2 (Registers) Design a register with two load signals that enable the loading of data from two different sources.

7.3 (Registers) Explain the difference between resetting the register and loading an all-0's input into the register.

7.4 (Registers) Design a 16-bit register that can load new data and rotate or shift its content left or right.

7.5 (Shift registers) Using a 4-bit shift register, construct a 4-bit register that can rotate its content one position to the left or right.

7.6 (Shift registers) Design a 16-bit register that can perform two operations: (1) load a new data and (2) swap the most-significant and least-significant bytes.

7.7   (Shift registers) Using 16-bit shift registers, design a serial comparator that will compare two 16-bit numbers after loading them into the shift registers. The serial comparator should have three outputs, which indicate whether the first number was greater than, equal to, or smaller than the second number.

7.8   (Counters) Design a binary counter that counts up only in:

    (a)   Even numbers $(0, 2, 4, 6, 8, \ldots)$

    (b)   Odd numbers $(1, 3, 5, 7, 9, \ldots)$

7.9   (Counters) Design a logic circuit that will detect when a 4-bit binary counter has reached a value of:

    (a)   7

    (b)   14

    (c)   15

    (d)   0

7.10   (Counters) Design a modulo (a) 15, (b) 17, (c) 31, and (d) 32 counter.

7.11   (Counters) Design a decimal counter that counts modulo 1000.

7.12   (Counters) Design a counter that counts in the following sequence: $1, 5, 9, 11, 13, 15, 1, 5, \ldots$.

7.13   (Asynchronous counters) Construct a 4-bit asynchronous counter using:

    (a)   D flip-flops

    (b)   J-K flip-flops

7.14   (Asynchronous counters) Design a decimal modulo-100 asynchronous counter.

7.15   (Register files) Design an 8×4 register file with:

    (a)   One write and two read ports

    (b)   Two write and one read ports

    (c)   Two write and two read ports

7.16   (Memories) Design:

    (a) $256K \times 8$ RAM using $256K \times 1$ RAM chips

    (b) $64K \times 32$ RAM using $64K \times 8$ RAM chips

    (c) $1M \times 1$ RAM using $256K \times 1$ RAM chips

    (d) $256K \times 8$ RAM using $64K \times 8$ RAM chips

7.17   (Stack) Design a push-down stack with 1K RAM that uses all (1024) words of the 1K RAM.

7.18   (Queues) Design a FIFO queue with 1K RAM that will be empty when the front and back counters point to the same location, and full when the front and back differ by 1.

7.19   (Datapaths) Design a simple datapath that can compute the expression:

    (a) $\sum_{i=1}^{n} a_i x_i$

    (b) $\sum_{i=1}^{n} a_i x_i + b_i$

    (c) $\sum_{i=1}^{n} x_i^2 + x_i + c_i$

7.20   (Datapaths) For the datapath in Figure 7.26, develop a field-insertion algorithm and control words for all the statements. Assume that the datapath is 8 bits wide and that the field-insertion algorithm inserts the four least-significant bits of the source word into the middle of the destination word: for example, your field-insertion algorithm should take two words, $A = a_7 a_6 a_5 a_4 a_3 a_2 a_1 a_0$ and $B = b_7 b_6 b_5 b_4 b_3 b_2 b_1 b_0$, and generate the resultant word $C = b_7 b_6\ a_3 a_2 a_1 a_0 b_1 b_0$ by replacing $b_5 b_4 b_3 b_2$ with $a_3 a_2 a_1 a_0$.

7.21   (Datapaths) Using the field-insertion algorithm developed in Problem 7.20, define and implement a controller for the datapath that could execute it.

7.22   (Datapaths) Using the 8-bit-wide datapath given in Figure 7.26, develop an algorithm to add two positive 8-bit integers and generate a 9-bit result. Derive the control word for each statement in your algorithm.

7.23   (Datapaths) Define and implement the controller for the datapath that could execute the algorithm developed in Problem 7.22.

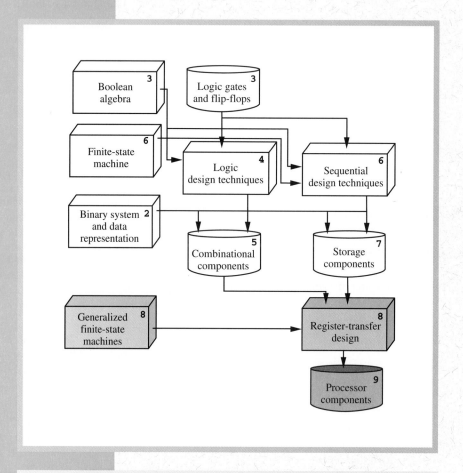

In previous chapters we developed register-transfer combinatorial and storage components. In this chapter we generalize the finite-state-machine model and on the basis of this model, learn how to describe, design, and optimize register-transfer implementations of arbitrary algorithms.

CHAPTER

8

Register-Transfer Design

*I*n Chapter 7 we designed various storage components, such as registers, counters, memories, stacks, and queues; in Chapter 5 we designed combinatorial components such as ALUs, comparators, shifters, selectors, buses, ROMs and PLAs. In designing application-specific integrated circuits (ASICs) and standard processors, we group those components into control units and datapaths. Each ASIC or processor consists of at least one control unit and one datapath, although many ASICs contain multiple control units and datapaths. To synthesize register-transfer designs we introduce the model of an FSM with a datapath (FSMD) and present several different ways to specify register-transfer designs, including popular algorithmic-state-machine (ASM) charts. We then explain the techniques for converting such an ASM chart into an design implementation consisting of a control unit and a datapath. We also describe design techniques for cost and performance optimization of these implementations. While register-transfer design is the focus of this chapter, we cover the design of standard processors in Chapter 9 as a special case of register-transfer design. Since the processor instruction set can be described by a restricted type of ASM chart, the processor architecture can also be thought of as a special case of the FSMD model.

8.1 DESIGN MODEL

In Example 7.1 we implemented the one's-count algorithm with a standard datapath and a custom control unit. The control unit had eight states, two input signals, and 14 output signals. The input signals were the external signal *Start* and a status signal from the datapath ($Data = 0$). The output signals were the external signal *Done* and datapath control-signals. The datapath contained a register file, an ALU, and a shifter, and had an input port and an output port. The 16-bit operand *Data* was entered into the datapath through the input port at the beginning of the operation, and the result *Ocount* was outputted at the end, through the output port.

Similar to the one's counter, each digital design consists of a control unit and a datapath. As shown in Figure 8.1(a), the datapath has two types of I/O ports. One type of I/O ports are data ports, which are used by the outside environment to send and receive data to and from the microchip. The data could be of type integer, floating point, or characters, and it is usually packed into one or more words. The data ports are usually 8, 16, 32, or 64 bits wide. The other type of I/O ports are control ports, which are used by the control unit to control the operations performed by the datapath and receive information about the status of selected registers in the datapath.

As shown in Figure 8.1(b), the datapath consists of storage units such as registers, register files, and memories, and combinatorial units such as ALUs, multipliers, shifters, and comparators. These units and the input and output ports are connected by buses. The datapath takes the operands from storage units, performs the computation in the combinatorial units, and returns the results to storage units during each state, which is usually equal to one clock cycle. The selection of operands, operations, and the destination for the result is controlled by the control unit by setting proper values of datapath control signals. The datapath also indicates through status signals when a particular value is stored in

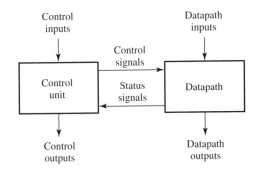

(a) High-level block diagram

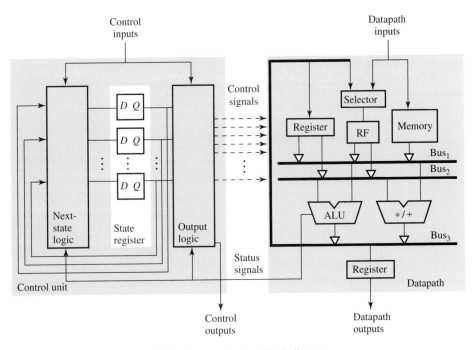

(b) Register-transfer-level block diagram

FIGURE 8.1
Design model.

a particular storage unit or when a particular relation between two data values stored in the datapath is satisfied.

Similar to the datapath, a control unit has a set of input and a set of output signals. Each signal is a Boolean variable that can take a value of 0 or 1. There are two types of input signals: external signals and status signals. External signals represent the conditions in the external environment on which an ASIC must respond. The *Start* signal in Example 7.1, which starts the one's counter, is such an input signal. On the other hand, the status signals represent the state of the datapath. Their value is obtained by comparing values of selected variables stored in the datapath. For example, $Data = 0$ in Example 7.1 was such a signal whose value was equal to 1 when the value of Data was equal to 0 and 0 when $Data$ value was not equal to 0.

There are also two types of output signals: external signals and datapath control signals. External signals identify to the environment that an ASIC has reached a certain state or finished a particular computation. The datapath controls select the operation for each component in the datapath.

Each ASIC implementation follows this general architecture, although two ASICs may differ in the number of control units and datapaths, the number of components and connections in the datapath, the number of states in the control unit, and the number of I/O ports. To generate such a design, we must first learn how to define its architecture and specify its behavior.

8.2 FSMD DEFINITION

In Section 8.1, we discussed in general terms the architecture and the implementation model of a digital design. In this section we discuss how to specify its functionality. For this purpose we modify the style and format used for specifying the one's counter from Example 7.1.

The one's counter was specified by an FSM, representing the control unit and a set of variable assignments representing transformations in the datapath. For convenience, this specification is repeated in Figure 8.2.

The FSM has eight states and transitions from one state to another under the control of the external signal $Start$ and the status signal $(Data = 0)$. In each state the FSM assigns values to a set of datapath control signals which completely specifies the behavior of the datapath. However, when there are too many control signals it is difficult to realize what and how the datapath will operate. To improve the comprehension of such a specification, in Example 7.1 we have used variable assignment statements to indicate changes in variable values stored in the datapath.

A variable assignments statement gives an expression to be used for computation of the new variable value. In each state and for each variable assignment associated with that state the datapath evaluates the expression on the right-hand side of the assignment and loads the result on the next rising edge of the clock signal into the register that stores the variable on the left-hand side of the assignment. It is worth noting that although expression evaluation is performed in one state, the

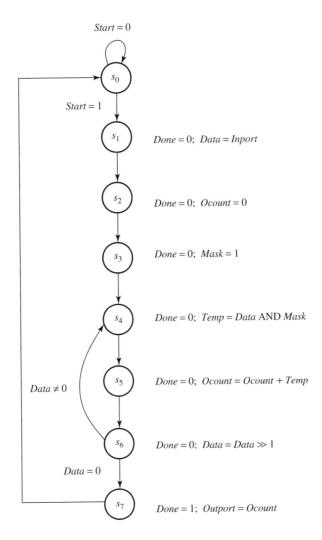

$Start = 0$

s_0

$Start = 1$

s_1 $Done = 0$; $Data = Inport$

s_2 $Done = 0$; $Ocount = 0$

s_3 $Done = 0$; $Mask = 1$

s_4 $Done = 0$; $Temp = Data$ AND $Mask$

s_5 $Done = 0$; $Ocount = Ocount + Temp$

$Data \neq 0$

s_6 $Done = 0$; $Data = Data \gg 1$

$Data = 0$

s_7 $Done = 1$; $Outport = Ocount$

FIGURE 8.2
One's-counter specification.

new variable value could not be used until the next state, at the earliest. Generalizing from the one's-counter specification, we may say that an FSM model with assignment statements added to each state, usually called an **FSM with a datapath**, or FSMD, can completely specify the behavior of an arbitrary digital design.

To define an FSMD formally, we must extend the definition of a FSM by introducing sets of datapath variables, inputs, and outputs that will complement the sets of FSM states, inputs, and outputs. In Chapter 6 we defined an FSM as a quintuple

$$< S, I, O, f, h >$$

where S is a set of states, I and O are the sets of input and output symbols, and f and h are functions that define the next state and the FSM output. More formally, f and h were defined as mappings

$$f : S \times I \rightarrow S$$

$$h : S \times I \rightarrow O$$

They are usually specified by a table in which the next state and output symbols are given for each state and each input symbol. Each state, input, and output symbol is defined by a cross-product of Boolean variables. More precisely,

$$I = A_1 \times A_2 \times \cdots \times A_k$$
$$S = Q_1 \times Q_2 \times \cdots \times Q_m$$
$$O = Y_1 \times Y_2 \times \cdots \times Y_n$$

where $A_i, 1 \leq i \leq k$, is an input signal, $Q_i, 1 \leq i \leq m$, is the flip-flop output, and $Y_i, 1 \leq i \leq n$, is an output signal.

To include a datapath, we must extend the FSM definition above by adding the set of datapath variables, inputs, and outputs. More formally, we define a variables set

$$V = V_1 \times V_2 \times \cdots \times V_q$$

which defines the state of the datapath by defining the values of all variables in each state. In the same fashion we can separate the set of FSMD inputs into a set of FSM inputs I_C and a set of datapath inputs I_D. Thus

$$I = I_C \times I_D$$

where $I_C = A_1 \times A_2 \times \cdots \times A_k$ as before and $I_D = B_1 \times B_2 \times \ldots \times B_p$.

Similarly, the output set consists of FSM outputs O_C and datapath outputs O_D. In other words,

$$O = O_C \times O_D$$

where $O_C = Y_1 \times Y_2 \cdots \times Y_n$ as before and $O_D = Z_1 \times Z_2 \times \cdots \times Z_r$. However, note that A_i, Q_j, and Y_k represent Boolean variables, while B_i, V_i, and Z_i represent Boolean vectors, which in turn represent integers, floating-point numbers, and characters. For example, in a 16-bit datapath, B_i, V_i, and Z_i would be 16 bits wide, and if they were positive integers, they would be able to assume values from 0 to 2^{16-1}.

Except for very trivial cases, the size of the datapath variables and ports makes specification of functions f and h in tabular form very

difficult. To be able to specify variable values in an efficient and under-
standable way in the definition of an FSMD, we specify variable values
with arithmetic expressions.

We define the set of all possible expressions, *Expr*, over the set of
variables V to be the set of all constants K of the same type as variables in V, the set of variables V itself, and all the expressions obtained
by combining two expressions with arithmetic, logic, or rearrangement
operators. More formally,

$$Expr(V) = K \cup V \cup \{(e_i \square e_j) \mid e_i, e_j$$
$$\in Expr, \square \text{ is an acceptable operator}\}$$

Using $Expr(V)$, we can define the values of the status signals as well
as transformations in the datapath. Let $STAT = \{stat_k = e_i \triangle e_j \mid e_i, e_j, \in$
$Expr(V), \triangle \in \{\leq, <, =, \neq, >, \geq\}\}$ be the set of all status signals that
are described as relations between variables or expressions of variables.
Examples of status signals are $Data = 0$, $(a-b) > (x+y)$, and $(counter =$
$0)$ AND $(x > 10)$. The relations defining status signals are either true,
in which case the status signal has value 1, or false, in which case it has
value 0.

With formal definition of expressions and relations over a set of
variables, we can simplify function $f : (S \times V) \times I \to S \times V$ by separating
it into two parts: f_C and f_D. The function f_C defines the next state of
the control unit,

$$f_C : S \times I_C \times STAT \to S$$

while the function f_D defines the values of datapath variables in the next
state,

$$f_D : S \times V \times I_D \to V$$

In other words, for each state $s_i \in S$ we compute a new value
for each variable $V_j \in V$ in the datapath by evaluating an expression
$e_j \in Expr(V)$. Thus the function f_D is represented by a set of simpler
functions, in which each function in the set defines variable values for
the state s_i:

$$f_D := \{f_{Di} : V \times I_D \to V :$$
$$\{V_j = e_j | V_j \in V, e_j \in Expr(V \times I_D)\}\}$$

In other words, function f_D is decomposed into a set of functions
f_{Di}, where each f_{Di} assigns one expression e_k to each variable V_j in
the datapath in state s_i. Therefore, new values for all variables in the
datapath are computed by evaluating expressions e_j, for all j such that
$1 \leq j \leq q$.

Similarly, we can decompose the output function $h : S \times V \times I \rightarrow O$ into two different functions, h_C and h_D, where h_C defines the external control outputs O_C as in the definition of an FSM and h_D defines external datapath outputs. Therefore,

$$h_C : S \times I_C \times STAT \rightarrow O_C$$

$$h_D : S \times V \times I_D \rightarrow O_D$$

Note again that variables in O_C are Boolean variables and that variables in O_D are Boolean vectors.

An FSMD can be specified in tabular form as shown in Figure 8.3(a) for the case of the one's counter, which was defined in Figure 8.2. The first three columns define the present state, the next state, and external control outputs, whereas the next two columns define the datapath outputs and variable values. As usual, the symbol X is used for don't-care conditions. From the table in Figure 8.3(a) we see that a new value is assigned to each of the control outputs, datapath variables, and datapath outputs in each state.

We know that a practical datapath may store hundreds of different variables and that many of those variables seldom change their values. Therefore, it would be more efficient if we could assume that variables retain their old values if no new value is specified in a particular state. Therefore, the fifth column in Figure 8.3(a) could be rewritten as a set of assignment statements, reminding us of straight-line code in most programming languages, as shown in Figure 8.3(b).

The same format can also be used in the next-state column in Figure 8.3(b). In this case we do not have to specify the next state for every control input and every status signal, but only for those that affect the next state selection. Therefore, we can simplify the next-state column by specifying in each state only the condition and the next state that the control unit will enter if the condition is true.

In much the same way that we represented variable assignments, we can use assignment statements for datapath and control unit output ports. However, unlike variables in the datapath, output ports do not retain their value beyond the present state since the values are not stored in registers or memory. Therefore, the control unit or the datapath must resupply the last assigned value to the output ports in each state, although not specified explicitly in the table. With this in mind, we can obtain a reduced table, usually called a **state-action table**, containing only three columns. As before, the first column specifies set of present states, and the second column specifies the next states and the conditions under which the control unit will move to those states. The third column specifies the assignments of new values to selected variables in the datapath and conditions under which these assignments occur. The assignments to output ports are also included in this column.

As an example, we show a state-action table for the one's counter in Figure 8.3(c). Such a table is easy to understand and provides all the necessary information for the implementation of a control unit and a datapath. It can be used to construct the state diagram for the control unit, synthesize next-state and output logic, and define the datapath components and their connections as we will explain later in this chapter.

PRESENT STATE	NEXT STATE (Start, Data = 0)				CONTROL OUTPUT	DATAPATH OUTPUT	DATAPATH VARIABLES			
	00	01	10	11	Done	Outport	Data	Ocount	Temp	Mask
s_0	s_0	s_0	s_1	s_1	0	Z	X	X	X	X
s_1	s_2	s_2	s_2	s_2	0	Z	Inport	X	X	X
s_2	s_3	s_3	s_3	s_3	0	Z	Data	0	X	X
s_3	s_4	s_4	s_4	s_4	0	Z	Data	Ocount	X	1
s_4	s_5	s_5	s_5	s_5	0	Z	Data	Ocount	Data AND Mask	Mask
s_5	s_6	s_6	s_6	s_6	0	Z	Data	Ocount+Temp	X	Mask
s_6	s_4	s_7	s_4	s_7	0	Z	Data>>1	Ocount	X	Mask
s_7	s_0	s_0	s_0	s_0	1	Ocount	Data	Ocount	X	X

(a) State and output table

PRESENT STATE	NEXT STATE (Start, Data = 0)				CONTROL OUTPUT	DATAPATH OUTPUT	DATAPATH VARIABLES
	00	01	10	11	Done	Outport	
s_0	s_0	s_0	s_1	s_1	0	Z	
s_1	s_2	s_2	s_2	s_2	0	Z	Data = Inport
s_2	s_3	s_3	s_3	s_3	0	Z	Ocount = 0
s_3	s_4	s_4	s_4	s_4	0	Z	Mask = 1
s_4	s_5	s_5	s_5	s_5	0	Z	Temp = Data AND Mask
s_5	s_6	s_6	s_6	s_6	0	Z	Ocount = Ocount + Temp
s_6	s_4	s_7	s_4	s_7	0	Z	Data = Data>>1
s_7	s_0	s_0	s_0	s_0	1	Ocount	

(b) State and output table with variable assignments

F I G U R E 8.3
FSMD specification of one's counter.

PRESENT STATE	NEXT STATE		CONTROL AND DATAPATH ACTIONS	
	CONDITION,	STATE	CONDITION,	ACTIONS
s_0	$\begin{bmatrix} Start = 0, \\ Start = 1, \end{bmatrix}$	$\begin{matrix} s_0 \\ s_1 \end{matrix}$	$\Bigg[$	$\begin{bmatrix} Done = 0 \\ Output = Z \end{bmatrix}$
s_1		s_2		$Data = Inport$
s_2		s_3		$Ocount = 0$
s_3		s_4		$Mask = 1$
s_4		s_5		$Temp = Data$ AND $Mask$
s_5		s_6		$Ocount = Ocount + Temp$
s_6	$\begin{bmatrix} Data \neq 0, \\ Data = 0, \end{bmatrix}$	$\begin{matrix} s_4 \\ s_7 \end{matrix}$		$Data = Data \gg 1$
s_7		s_0	$\Bigg[$	$\begin{bmatrix} Done = 1 \\ Output = Ocount \end{bmatrix}$

FIGURE 8.3
Continued.

(c) State–action table

8.3 ALGORITHMIC-STATE-MACHINE CHARTS

In Section 8.2, we defined the FSMD model and explained how to develop a state-action table for specifying FSMDs. In this section we introduce an alternative graphic form for specifying FSMDs, referred to as an **algorithmic-state-machine** (ASM) **chart**. In general, an ASM chart is fully equivalent to the state-action tables described above: that is, for every state-action table, there is at least one ASM chart that describes the same functionality. In many cases, however, ASM charts can have a slight advantage for human consumption, since they explicitly show the paths from one state to another that are less visible in a state-action table. The following definition makes these advantages apparent.

As shown in Table 8.1, the ASM chart represents the FSMD in terms of four basic components: a state box, a decision box, a conditional output box, and the ASM block. Each state in the ASM chart is indicated by a **state box**, which contains the set of unconditional assignments to variables and output ports in the datapath. This state box has its name placed on the top of the box on the left side. If known, the state code can be placed on the top of the box on the right side. However, the state code is not usually known when the ASM chart is first drawn, as it must be added later during the process of state assignment described in Chapter 6.

The **decision box** describes the condition under which the FSMD will execute specific actions in the datapath and select the next state. These conditions can refer either to external control inputs or to status

TABLE 8.1
ASM Symbols

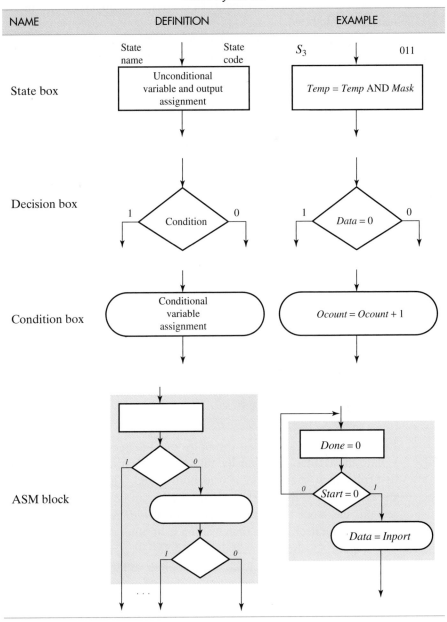

NAME	DEFINITION	EXAMPLE

signals. Note that each decision box has two exit paths, one path that will be taken when the enclosed condition is true, and the other when it is false. These two paths are usually indicated by a 1 for true and a 0 for false.

The **conditional output box** describes variable or output assignments that are executed under conditions specified by one or more decision boxes. The rounded corners of a condition output box differentiate it from a state box.

Finally, the **ASM block** is the complex structure that incorporated one state box and a serial–parallel network of decision boxes and conditional output boxes. The ASM block is usually represented with dashed lines around it. As you can see in Table 8.1, it has one input and can have any number of output paths that are generated by its particular network of decision boxes.

In general, an **ASM chart** will consist of one or more interconnected ASM blocks, arranged so that each output path from an ASM block connects to a single state box. Each ASM block describes the operations executed in one state. In other words, each block is equivalent to a row in the state-action table described in Section 8.2, the only difference being the way they present their conditions: In the state-action table, the conditions for the selection of the next state and the execution of the datapath operations were separated, whereas the ASM block combines them into a binary tree of decision and condition boxes.

When specifying an FSMD with a ASM chart, there are two rules we must follow:

1. The chart must define a unique next state for each state and set of conditions.

2. Every path defined by the network of condition boxes must lead to another state.

In Figure 8.4, we show two examples of ill-defined ASM charts that violate these rules. Specifically, the chart in Figure 8.4(a) violates the first rule, since when $Cond2$ is true, both s_2 and s_3 are specified as next states. Similarly, the chart in Figure 8.4(b) can be seen to violate the second rule, since the path defined when $Cond1$ is true and $Cond2$ is false loops on itself rather than leading to another state.

Figure 8.5 shows a well-defined ASM chart which is equivalent to the state-action table of the one's counter in Figure 8.3(c). As you can see, this chart clearly specifies all the states, next-state transitions, and datapath actions (variable assignments) that were represented in the state-action table. Note also that this ASM chart clearly shows the loops which were less visible in the state-action table, as well as showing all the conditional paths as a tree rather than specifying each path by a conditional expression. We should realize, of course, that an ASM chart may become too bulky when the FSMD in question has a large number of states and conditions.

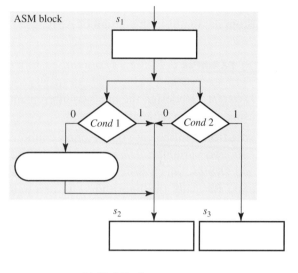

(a) Undefined next state

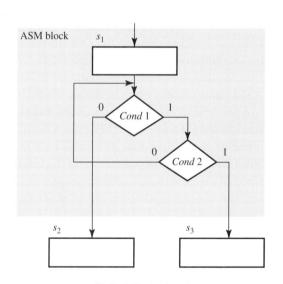

(b) Undefined exit path

FIGURE 8.4
Ill-defined ASM charts.

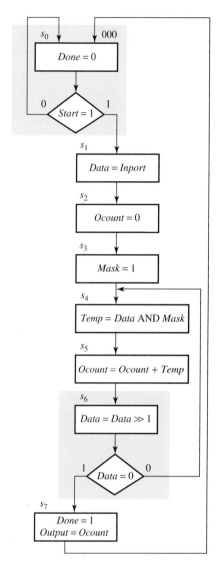

FIGURE 8.5
ASM chart for one's counter.

To understand the role of ASM charts and state-action tables in the design process, we redesign the one's counter given in Example 7.1, this time using a custom datapath instead of the standard one. In comparison with a standard datapath, a custom datapath would be tuned to a particular algorithm and might therefore require fewer components and interconnections. Since it uses fewer components, the custom datapath may also exhibit higher performance. For these reasons, designers use custom datapaths in the design of ASICs.

■ **EXAMPLE 8.1**   One's counter: custom design

PROBLEM   Redesign the one's counter given in Example 7.1 using a custom datapath.

SOLUTION   In the case of the one's counter, we really need only two variables: *Data*, which stores the incoming data, and *Ocount*, which stores the number of 1's counted in that data. Basically, the algorithm is written to look at the least-significant bit of data, $Data_{LSB}$, and add 1 to the *Ocount* whenever $Data_{LSB} = 1$. At this point, *Data* will be shifted one position to the right and the same sequence will be repeated as long as $Data \neq 0$. As before, the one's counter waits for *Start* to become 1 to input the data from the input port *Inport*. Whenever $Data = 0$, though, the one's counter will signal that it has counted all the 1's by setting the *Done* signal to 1 and outputting the *Ocount* through the *Outport* for the duration of one clock cycle.

To design a custom datapath, we must first develop an ASM chart for this one's counter. In Figure 8.6 we show two versions of the same one's counter that is modeled as a state-based (Moore) FSMD [Figure 8.6(a)], and one that is modeled as an input-based (Mealy) FSMD [Figure 8.6(b)]. Note that the state-based version of the FSMD has six states, since all the variable assignments must be executed unconditionally and only next states are to be selected conditionally. In the input-based model, by contrast, the number of states has been reduced to four since the variable assignments are to be executed conditionally together with the conditional selection of next states.

Either one of these ASM charts can easily be converted to a state-action table, which enables us to derive Boolean equations for the next-state and output logic in the control unit. In Figure 8.7(a) and (b), we show the state-action tables that correspond to the state-based and input-based versions of the one's counter.

The implementation of this same one's counter is shown in Figure 8.8. Note that the datapath is the same in both versions since both counters store only two variables and perform only two operations—that is, both versions shift the value in the variable *Data* and increment the value in the

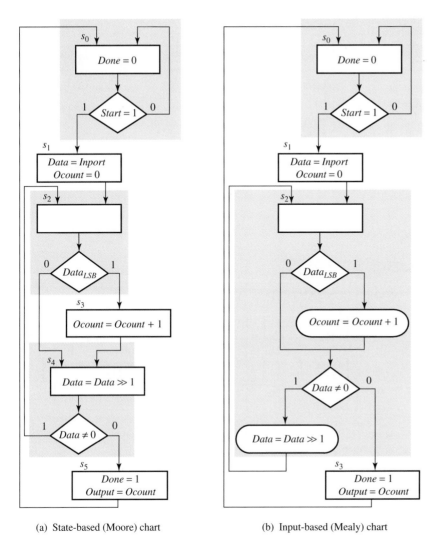

(a) State-based (Moore) chart   (b) Input-based (Mealy) chart

FIGURE 8.6

ASM charts for one's counter (custom design).

variable *Ocount*. Given these two operators, the datapath
needs only a shift register with parallel load, which loads data
from the *Inport* and an up/down-counter with parallel load,
which loads 0 at the start of one's counting and increments
its content whenever $Data_{LSB}$ is equal to 1.

The control unit of this one's counter consists of a state
register and the next-state and output logic. For the state-
based version, we would need a 3-bit state register, whereas
the input-based version would require a 2-bit register. The
encoding of states is also given in the state-action tables,

PRESENT STATE				NEXT STATE		DATAPATH ACTIONS	
Q_2	Q_1	Q_0	NAME	CONDITION,	STATE	CONDITION,	OPERATIONS
0	0	0	s_0	$\begin{bmatrix} Start = 0, \\ Start = 1, \end{bmatrix}$	$\begin{matrix} s_0 \\ s_1 \end{matrix}$		$Done = 0$
0	0	1	s_1		s_2		$\begin{bmatrix} Data = Inport \\ Ocount = 0 \end{bmatrix}$
0	1	0	s_2	$\begin{bmatrix} Data_{LSB} = 1, \\ Data_{LSB} = 0, \end{bmatrix}$	$\begin{matrix} s_3 \\ s_4 \end{matrix}$		
0	1	1	s_3		s_4		$Ocount = Ocount + 1$
1	0	0	s_4	$\begin{bmatrix} Data \neq 0, \\ Data = 0, \end{bmatrix}$	$\begin{matrix} s_2 \\ s_5 \end{matrix}$		$Data = Data \gg 1$
1	0	1	s_5		s_0		$\begin{bmatrix} Done = 1 \\ Output = Ocount \end{bmatrix}$

(a) State-based table

PRESENT STATE			NEXT STATE		DATAPATH ACTIONS	
Q_1	Q_0	NAME	CONDITION,	STATE	CONDITION,	OPERATIONS
0	0	s_0	$\begin{bmatrix} Start = 0, \\ Start = 1, \end{bmatrix}$	$\begin{matrix} s_0 \\ s_1 \end{matrix}$		$Done = 0$
0	1	s_1		s_2		$\begin{bmatrix} Data = Inport \\ Ocount = 0 \end{bmatrix}$
1	0	s_2	$\begin{bmatrix} Data \neq 0, \\ Data = 0, \end{bmatrix}$	$\begin{matrix} s_2 \\ s_3 \end{matrix}$	$\begin{bmatrix} Data_{LSB} = 1, \\ Data \neq 0, \end{bmatrix}$	$\begin{matrix} Ocount = Ocount + 1 \\ Data = Data \gg 1 \end{matrix}$
1	1	s_3		s_0		$\begin{bmatrix} Done = 1 \\ Output = Ocount \end{bmatrix}$

(b) Input-based table

FIGURE 8.7

State-action tables for one's counter.

where we have used a natural binary encoding to simplify understanding of the control logic schematic.

When implementing the control logic, we could reduce the number and size of the gates if we note that in the state-based version, states s_2, s_3, s_4, and s_5 can be defined uniquely by Q_1Q_0', Q_1Q_0, Q_2Q_0', and Q_2Q_0. With this in mind we can derive the next-state equations for the state-based version in Figure 8.8(a) directly from the state-action table.

$$D_2 = Q_2(next) = s_2Data'_{LSB} + s_3 + s_4(Data = 0)$$
$$= Q_1Q_0'Data'_{LSB} + Q_1Q_0 + Q_2Q_0'(Data = 0)$$
$$D_1 = Q_1(next) = s_1 + s_2Data_{LSB} + s_4(Data \neq 0)$$
$$= Q_2'Q_1'Q_0 + Q_1Q_0'Data_{LSB} + Q_2Q_0'(Data \neq 0)$$
$$D_0 = Q_0(next) = s_0Start + s_2Data_{LSB} + s_4(Data = 0)$$
$$= Q_2'Q_1'Q_0'Start + Q_1Q_0'Data_{LSB} + Q_2Q_0'(Data = 0)$$

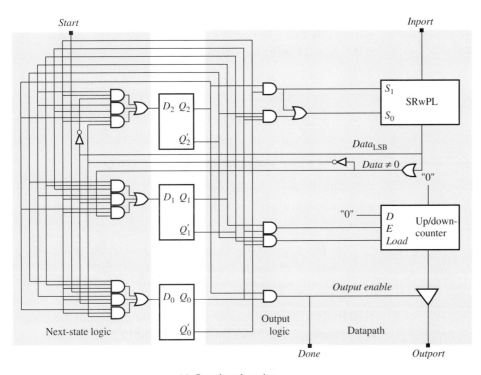

(a) State-based version

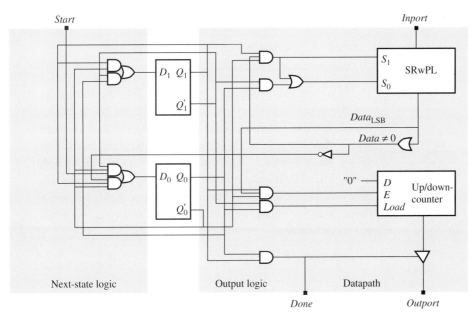

(b) Input-based version

F I G U R E   8.8

Logic schematics for one's counter.

Similarly, we can derive the output-logic equations remembering from Section 7.3 that $S_1 S_0 = 01$ loads the data and $S_1 S_0 = 11$ shifts the data to the right:

$$S_1 = s_4 = Q_2 Q_0'$$
$$S_0 = s_1 + s_4 = Q_2' Q_1' Q_0 + Q_2 Q_0'$$
$$E = s_3 = Q_1 Q_0$$
$$Load = s_1 = Q_2' Q_1' Q_0$$
$$Done = Output\ enable = s_5 = Q_2 Q_0$$

For the input-based version of the one's counter, the same procedure generates the following next-state equations:

$$D_1 = Q_1(next) = s_1 + s_2 = Q_1' Q_0 + Q_1 Q_0'$$
$$D_0 = Q_0(next) = s_0 Start + s_2 (Data \neq 0)'$$
$$= Q_1' Q_0' Start + Q_1 Q_0' (Data \neq 0)'$$

Note that for the input-based version, the output logic is more complex, since it includes conditional execution of datapath operations:

$$S_1 = s_2 (Data \neq 0) = Q_1 Q_0' (Data \neq 0)$$
$$S_0 = s_1 + s_2 (Data \neq 0) = Q_1' Q_0 + Q_1 Q_0' (Data \neq 0)$$
$$E = s_2 Data_{LSB} = Q_1 Q_0' Data_{LSB}$$
$$Load = s_1 = Q_1' Q_0$$
$$Done = Output\ enable = s_3 = Q_1 Q_0$$

As you can see from Figure 8.8, while the datapaths are the same in both cases, the state register in the state-based version has more bits, since this version has more states. Similarly, the next-state logic of the state-based version is more complex. The output logic, on the other hand, is simpler, since it is dependent only on the present state. By contrast, the input-based version has fewer states but has a more complex output logic that includes external and internal conditions.

8.4 SYNTHESIS FROM ASM CHARTS

In previous sections we have defined the FSMD model and explained the ASM charts that are used to describe these models. Furthermore, as we demonstrated in Example 8.1, an ASM chart can also be used to derive a register-transfer (RT)-level implementation that will execute the behavior specified in the chart. At this point, however, no attempt has been made to optimize these RT-level implementations for any design metric. In the following three sections, then, we describe several techniques used to optimize the implementations that we derive from ASM charts.

Since each RT implementation defines both a control unit and a datapath, we can approach the optimization of these parts separately. In Chapter 6, for example, we discussed specific techniques for minimizing control units, showing first how the number of states can be reduced by merging equivalent states, then how the size of the next-state and output logic can be reduced by encoding these states properly. Furthermore, we have shown how the size of the control unit can be reduced through the Boolean minimization and technology mapping techniques described in Chapter 4.

In minimizing the datapath, there are three general techniques based on the three major component types used in the datapath: storage components, functional units, and buses. In an FSMD model, the datapath is defined by the variable assignments that are executed in its various states. In each state, that is, selected variables will be assigned new values through arithmetic, logic, and shift operations that are performed by functional units. To execute each variable assignment statement, then, the datapath must take data from a storage component that stores the variables in the right-hand side of the assignment, pass this data to the functional units that compute the new value, and then pass it back to the storage component, which stores the variables on the left-hand side of the equation. Given these procedures, it follows that we can approach datapath optimization by minimizing the storage components, the functional units, or the buses that connect these components.

By focusing on the storage components, for example, we note that the variables in the datapath must be stored in registers, register files, and memories. However, since not all variables are alive at the same time, it is possible for certain variables to share the same register or the same location in a register file or a memory. In other words, we can merge the datapath variables in a way that reduces the number of storage locations in the datapath. Furthermore, even if certain variables are alive at the same time, they may not be accessed at the same time, which means that we could combine them into a register file or memory so that they can share the same register file or memory ports. In this manner, by combining storage locations we minimize the number of storage ports in the datapath and thus reduce the number of connections needed.

Alternatively, certain optimization techniques can focus on minimizing the number of functional units in the datapath. As mentioned above, in each state, selected variables are to be assigned new values

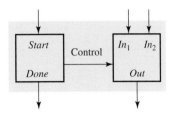

(a) Block diagram

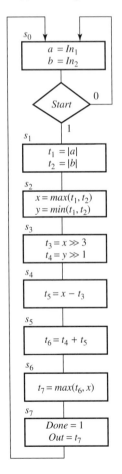

(b) ASM chart

FIGURE 8.9

Square-root approximation.

through various arithmetic, logic, or shift operations, each of which can be performed by a separate functional unit. However, since most of these operations are executed in different states, they could share the same functional unit. In other words, we can reduce the number of units in the datapath by combining different operations into groups, allowing each group of operations to be executed in a single functional unit.

The third basic technique for optimization focuses on the datapath connectivity. As mentioned above, the execution of an assignment statement requires that data pass from one storage component to the functional unit that computes the new value and then back to another storage component. The data, in other words, is passed through connections between storage and functional units. However, since different connections will be used in different states, we can group connections into buses, which enables us to reduce the number of wires in the datapath.

These three basic optimization techniques can be demonstrated for the small custom ASIC shown in Figure 8.9, which is designed to compute the square-root approximation (SRA) of two signed integers, a and b, by the following formula:

$$\sqrt{a^2 + b^2} \approx max((0.875x + 0.5y), x)$$

where $x = max(|a|, |b|)$ and $y = min(|a|, |b|)$. According to Figure 8.9(a), this ASIC has two input ports, In_1 and In_2, which are used to read integers a and b, and one output port Out. As you can see in the ASM chart in Figure 8.9(b), the ASIC reads the input ports and starts the computation whenever the input control signal $Start$ becomes equal to 1. In state s_1 it computes the absolute values a and b, and in s_2 it assigns the maximum of these two values to x and the minimum to y. In state s_3 it shifts x three positions to the right to obtain $0.125x$ and shifts y one position to the right to obtain $0.5y$. The ASIC calculates $0.875x$ by subtracting $0.125x$ from x in state s_4. In state s_5 it adds $0.875x$ and $0.5y$, while in state s_7 it computes the maximum of x and the expression $0.875x + 0.5y$. In state s_7, the ASIC produces the result and makes it available through the Out port for one clock cycle. At the same time, it sets the control signal $Done$ to 1, to signal to the environment that the data that has appeared at the Out port is a valid result.

To determine resource requirements from this ASM chart, we would need to generate the variable and operation use tables shown in Figure 8.10(a) and (b). In the variable-use table, each row represents one variable found in the ASM chart and each column represents one state. For each variable, then, we would enter an × in the column(s) that correspond to the state(s) in which the variable is alive. A variable is considered to be alive in the first state that follows the rising edge of the

	s_1	s_2	s_3	s_4	s_5	s_6	s_7
a	×						
b	×						
t_1		×					
t_2		×					
x			×	×	×	×	
y			×				
t_3				×			
t_4				×	×		
t_5					×		
t_6						×	
t_7							×
Number of live variables	2	2	2	3	3	2	1

(a) Variable usage

	s_1	s_2	s_3	s_4	s_5	s_6	s_7	MAX NUMBER OF UNITS
abs	2							2
min		1						1
max		1			1			1
>>			2					2
–				1				1
+					1			1
Number of operations	2	2	2	1	1	1		

(b) Operation usage

FIGURE 8.10
Resource use in square-root approximation.

clock signal which assigns its new value and also in all states inclusively between the first and final states in which this new value is used for the last time. In Figure 8.10(a), for example, variables a and b are assigned their values at the rising edge of the clock signal indicating the beginning of state s_1, but they are not used in any other states. Therefore, they are alive only in state s_1. By contrast, variable x is assigned its new value at the beginning of state s_3, but the value of x is also used in states s_4 and s_6, indicating that the variable x is alive in states s_3, s_4, s_5, and s_6. On the basis of this table, then, we can see which variables are alive in which states.

More important, however, Figure 8.10(a) also shows the maximum number of variables alive in a single state—that is, it shows us that in states s_4 and s_5 there are three live variables. We would therefore conclude that we will need at least three registers in the datapath of this SRA design. Because of this, we must combine variables from Figure 8.10(a) into three groups so that each group that is to be stored in one of the registers contains only variables that are not alive at the same time. On the basis of this example, then, you can see that one of the major tasks in RT synthesis consists of **merging or grouping variables** and assigning the groups to registers or memory locations in a way that will minimize the number of storage components or some other design metric, such as performance, power, or testability. Since each group of variables shares a register or memory location this task is also frequently called **register/memory sharing**.

In a similar fashion, we might determine the minimal number of units needed to execute all the operations in the ASM chart. For this purpose we would use the table shown in Figure 8.10(b), in which the rows represent the different operator types found in the ASM chart and the columns represent the states, as before. From this table we can conclude that we need two units that can compute absolute value (indicated by || in the ASM chart) and shift data (indicated by $\gg$ in the ASM chart) and one unit that can perform *max*, *min*, +, and − operations. Given these requirements, the straightforward approach in designing the datapath for the SRA is to allocate two units for computation of absolute value, two shifters, one unit each for the computation of maximums and minimums, one adder, and one subtractor. From Figure 8.11, which shows the design of each unit, we can see that this straightforward implementation requires one adder, five subtractors, four selectors, and several gates. Note that the two shifters are implemented by signal rearrangement and do not require a logic circuit.

The problem with this straightforward implementation, however, is that we do not necessarily need one functional unit per operation: Since no state uses all of these operations simultaneously, the implementation with one unit per operation will have functional units idling most of the time. In fact, we do not need more than two operations in any one state, so it is more efficient to construct functional units that can perform more than one operation, as this allows a substantial hardware saving.

For example, in the SRA description, addition and subtraction are never performed at the same time, which means that we can merge these operations into one functional unit called an adder/subtractor. In this case we gain one adder and a complementer at the expense of an additional EX-OR logic, as shown in Figure 8.11(k). On the other hand, merging the 1-bit shifter and the 3-bit shifter does not save hardware but requires an additional selector, as shown in Figure 8.11(h). On the basis of these examples, you can see how we perform the second major

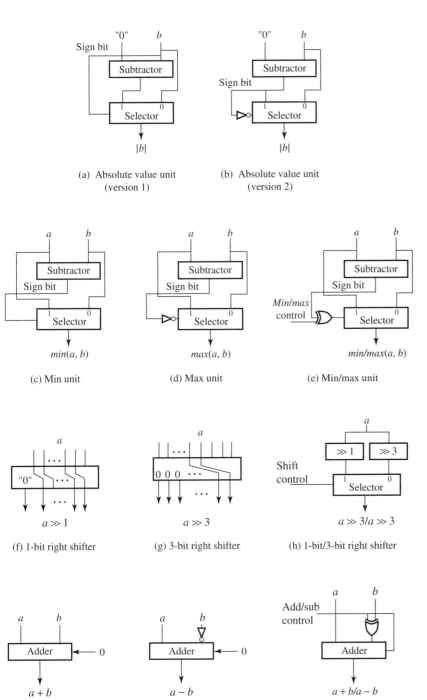

(a) Absolute value unit
(version 1)

(b) Absolute value unit
(version 2)

(c) Min unit

(d) Max unit

(e) Min/max unit

(f) 1-bit right shifter

(g) 3-bit right shifter

(h) 1-bit/3-bit right shifter

(i) Adder

(j) Subtractor

(k) Adder/Subtractor

FIGURE 8.11

Simple library components.

task in RT synthesis, which consists of **merging or grouping operators** and designing a functional unit for each group, thereby minimizing a given design metric such as area, the number of gates or transistors, or the number of functional units in the datapath. This task is also called **functional-unit sharing**.

If our primary goal is to minimize wiring, we should also consider merging connections into buses, since each single connection between any two units would be used in very few states and would mostly remain idle. As an example, let us consider the connections in an SRA datapath that uses one register per variable and single-operation functional units. The connections for such a datapath are given in the connectivity table shown in Figure 8.12, in which each row corresponds to one functional unit and each column represents one register. To complete the table, we enter an I for every connection between a register and the input of a functional unit, and for every connection between the output of the functional unit and a register, we enter the letter O. As you can see in Figure 8.12, such an SRA requires 14 input connections and 9 output connections, for a total of 23 connections.

	a	b	t_1	t_2	x	y	t_3	t_4	t_5	t_6	t_7
abs1	I		O								
abs2		I		O							
min			I	I	O						
max			I	I	I	O				I	O
>>3				I			O				
>>1					I			O			
−					I		I		O		
+								I	I	O	

Of these 23 connections, however, very few are needed in any one state. From the ASM chart, in fact, we know that the maximum number of connections is used in state s_2, when we need four input connections, linking the registers storing the variables t_1 and t_2 to the *min* and *max* units as well as two output connections, linking *min* and *max* units to the registers that store the variables x and y. In other words, the maximum number of connections needed concurrently is six.

From this example, you can see that the third major task in RT synthesis consists of **merging or grouping connections** and assigning one bus to each group so as to minimize the connection cost. Note that this connection cost includes the cost of bus drivers, which are required for every connection of a unit to a bus, and the cost of input selectors, which are required whenever two or more buses are connected to the same input of a storage or functional unit. This task is also frequently called **bus sharing**.

8.5 REGISTER SHARING (VARIABLE MERGING)

As we mentioned in Section 8.2, one of the major tasks in datapath optimization involves grouping variables so that they share a common register or memory location. The advantage of such grouping lies in the fact that it reduces the number and size of storage components, which in turn reduces the silicon area and therefore the cost of ASIC manufacture. Since a register can be shared only by those variables with nonoverlapping lifetimes, this technique requires us to determine the lifetimes of each variable.

The **lifetime** of a variable is defined as the set of states in which that variable is alive, which includes the state following the state in which it is assigned a new value (write state), every state in which it is used on the right-hand side of an assignment statement (read state), and all the states on each path between the write state and a read state. Note also that each variable may have multiple assignments and that each assigned value may be used several times. Once the lifetime of each variable has been determined, we can group variables that have nonoverlapping lifetimes and assign each group to a single register.

When we group variables, one of the common goals is to try to have as few registers as possible, which means that we would try to partition variables into the smallest number of groups while ensuring that every variable belongs to one of these groups. This goal can be accomplished by a **left-edge algorithm**, which tries to pack as many variables as possible into each register. As you can see in Figure 8.13, this algorithm begins by creating a priority list in which all the variables are sorted by their write state. If two variables have the same write state, the priority is given to the variable with the longer lifetime. If two variables have the same write state and the same lifetime, the priority will be assigned at random. When all the variables have been sorted, the algorithm allocates a new register, assigns to it the variable at the top of the list, and scanning the sorted list from top to bottom, keeps assigning the first nonoverlapping variable that it encounters to the same register. When the algorithm can not find any nonoverlapping variables, it ends the assignment of variables to that particular register. If at this point the priority list is not empty, the algorithm will allocate a new register and repeat the entire assignment procedure until all the variables have been removed from the priority list.

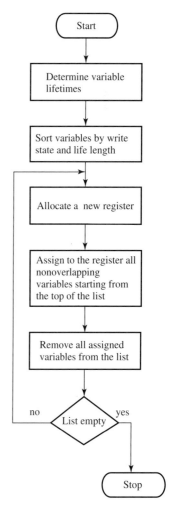

FIGURE 8.13
Left-edge algorithm.

To clarify the workings of the left-edge algorithm, we use it to merge variables and assign them to registers in the SRA datapath. First, we sort all the variables by their write states and lifetimes, as shown in Figure 8.14(a). Then we can allocate R_1 and assign to it variable a, as

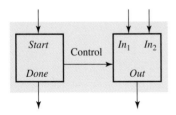

(a) Block diagram

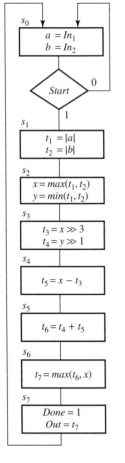

(b) ASM chart

FIGURE 8.9
Square-root approximation.

	s_0	s_1	s_2	s_3	s_4	s_5	s_6	s_7
a	×							
b	×							
t_1			×					
t_2			×					
x				×	×	×	×	
y				×				
t_4					×	×		
t_3					×			
t_5						×		
t_6							×	
t_7								×

(a) Sorted list of variables

$$R_1 = [a, t_1, x, t_7]$$
$$R_2 = [b, t_2, y, t_4, t_6]$$
$$R_3 = [t_3, t_5]$$

(b) Register assignments

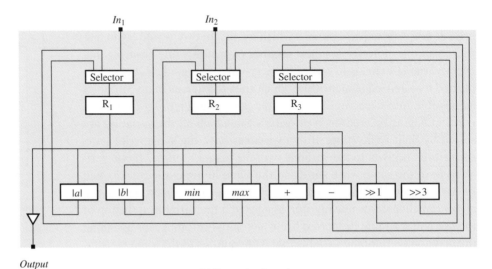

(c) Datapath schematic

FIGURE 8.14
Register sharing generated by left-edge algorithm.

well as the next nonoverlapping variable t_1 followed by x and t_7. At this point, since there are no more nonoverlapping variables left on the list, we would remove the assigned variables and conclude the assignment to register R_1. Next, we allocate register R_2 and, in the same way, assign to it variables b, t_2, y, t_4, and t_6. Finally, we assign the remaining variables, t_3 and t_5, to register R_3, as indicated in Figure 8.14(b). Using these assignments, we can then design an SRA datapath that requires three registers, as shown in Figure 8.14(c).

As we demonstrated in Figure 8.10(a), we cannot reduce the number of registers in the datapath to fewer than three. However, since there are many possible datapath designs with three registers, we would like to select one that minimizes a second design metric, such as connectivity cost. For example, the cost of connecting I/O ports, registers, and functional units can be measured in number of selector inputs assuming that the cost per selector input is constant. In the case of the SRA datapath shown in Figure 8.14(c), the total number of selector inputs is 10.

To develop an algorithm that will minimize the number of registers as well as connectivity cost, we give priority to the combining of certain variables. Priority is given to two variables that are used as the left or right operands for the same operator type and to variables whose value is generated by the same operator type, since merging such variables can potentially save one selector input. This concept is demonstrated in Figure 8.15(a) for two additions ($x = a + b$ and $y = c + d$) performed in different states on different operands and assigned to different variables. If we assume that both additions may be executed in the same functional unit, merging operands and results may result in the saving of selector inputs. For example, if we assign each variable to a separate register, we may obtain the design shown in Figure 8.15(b), which requires 10 selector inputs. However, if we merge variable a with c, b with d, and x

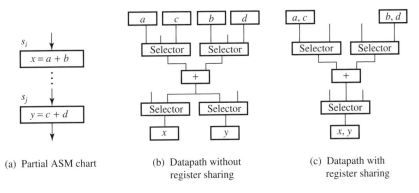

(a) Partial ASM chart   (b) Datapath without   (c) Datapath with
                               register sharing   register sharing

FIGURE 8.15
Merging variables with common sources and destinations.

with y, then assign each pair to the same register, we reduce number of selector inputs by three, as shown in Figure 8.15(c).

In general, for any n variables that are used as a source or a destination to the same operator or functional unit, there is a potential saving of $n - 1$ selector inputs when these n variables share the same register. To consider this potential saving during variable merging, we present a new algorithm which partitions a variable compatibility graph. Such a **compatibility graph** consists of nodes and edges in which each node represents a variable and each edge between two nodes represents compatibility or incompatibility in merging variables represented by these two nodes. There are two types of edges in the graph: An **incompatibility edge** (represented by a dashed line) between two nodes indicates variables with overlapping lifetimes, while a **priority edge** between two nodes indicates variables with nonoverlapping lifetimes that serve as the source or destination to the same functional units. Each priority edge has a priority weight indicating the number of selector inputs that can be saved. The priority weight has the form s/d, where s is equal to the number of different functional units that use both nodes as left or right operands, and d is equal to the number of different functional units that generate results for both nodes.

In what follows we describe a **graph-partitioning algorithm** that merges compatible nodes into supernodes until all nodes in the graph are incompatible. More precisely, the algorithm always merges two nodes that are connected with a priority edge with largest weight and creates from them a supernode. Next, it deletes all the edges within the supernode and creates new edges between the supernode and other nodes. For example, it creates an incompatibility edge to any node that is incompatible with at least one node in the supernode, or conversely, it creates a priority edge to any node that is used as a common source or destination with at least one node in the supernode and that is compatible with all the nodes in the supernode. The weight of the new priority edge is computed as before. This procedure is summarized in Figure 8.16.

If we apply this algorithm to the SRA example, we obtain a grouping of variables that is slightly different from the grouping we obtained with the left-edge algorithm. First, we need to create a compatibility graph, as shown in Figure 8.17(a). Note that all the variables that have overlapping lifetimes have been connected with a dashed line, indicating that they cannot be merged. To create priority edges that indicate compatibility, we assume the simple library given in Figure 8.10, which includes units for computing absolute value, minimum, maximum, shift, sum, and difference, in addition to functional units capable of performing a combination of operations, such as an adder/subtractor, a min/max unit, or a two-way shifter. Assuming that the units defined in this library

FIGURE 8.16
Graph-partitioning algorithm.

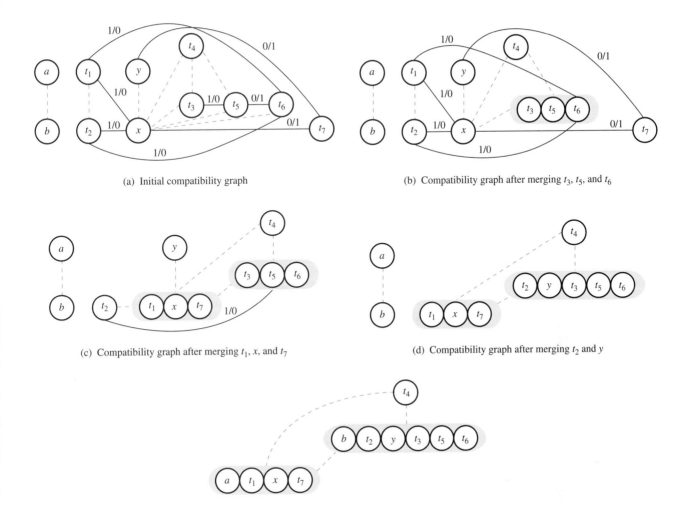

(a) Initial compatibility graph

(b) Compatibility graph after merging t_3, t_5, and t_6

(c) Compatibility graph after merging t_1, x, and t_7

(d) Compatibility graph after merging t_2 and y

(e) Final compatibility graph

F I G U R E   8.17
Graph-partitioning algorithm for SRA.

will be used in the final design, we find that there are priority edges between the variables t_1, t_2 and x, and t_1, t_2 and t_6 since they are all inputs of the same *max* unit; there are priority edges between the variables x, y, and t_7 because they are possible destinations of a *min/max* unit; and there are priority edges between t_3 and t_5 and t_5 and t_6 because they all are possible inputs and outputs of an adder/subtractor.

After creating this compatibility graph, we can start merging variables and creating supernodes. In this case all priority edges have the same weight, so we first select those nodes whose merging will not remove any priority edges from the compatibility graph. In other words, we merge the variables t_3, t_5, and t_6 for a possible gain of two selector inputs, thereby creating the supernode $[t_3, t_5, t_6]$, as shown in Figure 8.17(b). Next, we select the node that has a maximum number of priority edges—namely x—and merge it with t_7 and then t_1 as shown in Figure 8.17(c). Note that by merging x, t_7, and t_1, we have removed three priority edges from the compatibility graph, between y and t_7, t_2 and x, and t_1 and t_6. At this point we can merge t_2 and then y with the supernode $[t_3, t_5, t_6]$, as shown in Figure 8.17(d). Finally, we can assign a randomly to the supernode $[t_1, x, t_7]$ and b to the supernode $[t_2, y, t_3, t_5, t_6]$ to further reduce the number of registers needed, so that the supernode $[a, t_1, x, t_7]$ can be assigned to register R_1, $[b, t_2, y, t_3, t_5, t_6]$ to register R_2, and $[t_4]$ to register R_3.

To compare connectivity cost for solutions generated by left-edge and graph-partitioning algorithms, we use the same eight functional units that we used in Figure 8.14(c), where we designed the datapath for the register assignment generated by the left-edge algorithm. From the datapath shown in Figure 8.18, constructed for the register assignment generated by the graph-partitioning algorithm, we see that the number of selector inputs is 9, or one less than in Figure 8.14(c). The difference would be larger if we had used multifunctional units for the design in Figure 8.18 instead of single-function units, since there would be fewer units and therefore fewer connections. The observation above suggests that we should combine operations into multifunction units to further minimize the cost of datapath resources and connections, which is discussed in Section 8.6.

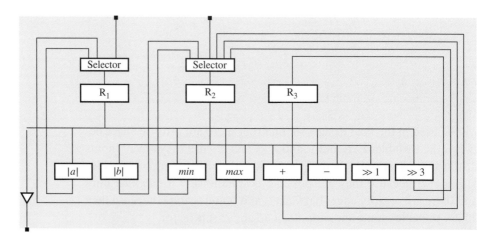

$R_1 = [a, t_1, x, t_7]$
$R_2 = [b, t_2, y, t_3, t_5, t_6]$
$R_3 = [t_4]$

(a) Register assignments   (b) Datapath

F I G U R E   8.18
Register assignment generated by the graph-partitioning algorithm.

8.6 FUNCTIONAL-UNIT SHARING (OPERATOR MERGING)

The main goal behind functional-unit sharing or operator merging is to minimize the number of functional units in a datapath. Like register sharing, functional-unit sharing is possible because within any given state, a datapath will not perform every operation. Therefore, similar operators can be grouped into a single multifunction unit, which will be used more frequently, thus increasing the unit utilization. In some cases, of course, grouping operations in this manner may not reduce the cost of the datapath; since dissimilar operators often require structurally different designs, grouping them can sometimes result in no gain or even in a higher cost. In many cases, however, operator merging can yield cost reductions that are not negligible, as demonstrated in Figure 8.19.

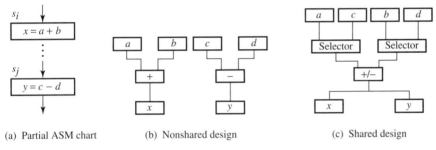

(a) Partial ASM chart   (b) Nonshared design   (c) Shared design

FIGURE 8.19
Functional-unit sharing.

In this example we have assumed that the datapath will perform two different operations, addition and subtraction, on different operands in different states, as indicated in Figure 8.19(a). If we implemented the ASM chart using single-function units, we would get the design shown in Figure 8.19(b), in which the datapath requires both an adder and a subtractor. We could, however, obtain the same functionality by using only one adder/subtractor and two selectors, as shown in Figure 8.19(c). Obviously, the second design would be preferable when the cost of an adder/subtractor and two selectors is less than the cost of a separate adder and subtractor. It is in cases like this that functional-unit sharing would be advantageous. Thus we would like to develop an algorithm that will combine operators into functional units in such a way that the total cost of all multifunction units and necessary selectors is minimal. For this purpose we can use the graph-partitioning algorithm presented in Section 8.5. We demonstrate the algorithm for operator merging by the example of the SRA given by the ASM chart in Figure 8.9. For this example we assume the availability of the simple and complex component libraries shown in Figures 8.11 and 8.20. Note that the complex library in Figure 8.20 includes several multifunction units that can each compute three of more of the following operations: absolute value, minimum, maximum, sum, and difference. Each of these units uses an adder, one or two selectors, AND and/or EX-OR logic units, and a few control gates. For simplicity, however, we omit their control gates from our cost computation.

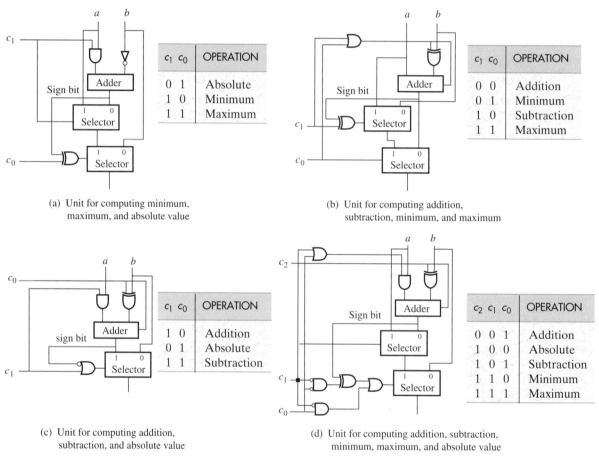

(a) Unit for computing minimum, maximum, and absolute value

c_1 c_0	OPERATION
0 1	Absolute
1 0	Minimum
1 1	Maximum

(b) Unit for computing addition, subtraction, minimum, and maximum

c_1 c_0	OPERATION
0 0	Addition
0 1	Minimum
1 0	Subtraction
1 1	Maximum

(c) Unit for computing addition, subtraction, and absolute value

c_1 c_0	OPERATION
1 0	Addition
0 1	Absolute
1 1	Subtraction

(d) Unit for computing addition, subtraction, minimum, maximum, and absolute value

c_2 c_1 c_0	OPERATION
0 0 1	Addition
1 0 0	Absolute
1 0 1	Subtraction
1 1 0	Minimum
1 1 1	Maximum

FIGURE 8.20
Complex library components.

To merge the operators called for in the ASM chart, we must first construct a compatibility graph that indicates which operators can be combined. Each node in the compatibility graph represents one operator type from the ASM chart, although each graph may have several nodes for each operator type. As a rule, the number of nodes will be equal to the maximum number of occurrences of a particular operator type in any single state. To indicate the compatibility of the various operators, we need to connect the nodes in the graph with priority edges or incompatibility edges. As you would expect, an incompatibility edge indicates that its two operators cannot be merged under any circumstances, since they are to be used concurrently in the same state. By contrast, the priority edges indicate preferences for merging, because of the operator's similarity in construction or because they can substantially reduce the cost of the datapath's connections. In the following explanation of operator merging, we consider both of these types of cost metrics.

In creating the compatibility graph shown in Figure 8.21(a), we excluded shift operators, because their cost is zero and grouping them with other operators would only increase the cost of the SRA datapath. As you can see, we included two absolute-value operators in the graph, since the absolute values of a and b are to be computed simultaneously in state s_1. Including the remaining operators, we find that the graph has six nodes and two incompatibility edges: One connects the two absolute-value operators since they are to be used in the same state, while the second edge connects the maximum and minimum operators since they are incompatible for the same reason.

If we used single-function units, then, implementing the SRA datapath would require two absolute-value units and one unit each for maximum, minimum, addition, and subtraction. As we show in Figure 8.21(b), the total cost of these units would be five invert-logic units, six adders, and four selectors.

By merging operators in the compatibility graph we can reduce the datapath cost in several different ways. Two of these ways are shown in Figure 8.21(c) and (e), with their corresponding datapath costs in Figure 8.21(d) and (f). Note that either one of these alternatives would require two AND-logic units, one invert-logic and EX-OR logic unit, two adders, and two selectors, for a total cost that is much less than the original implementation using single-function units. The datapath connections for these two alternatives are shown in Figure 8.22(a) and (b). In these figures you can see that either design would require nine selector inputs, as did the datapath shown in Figure 8.18(b). On the other hand, the designs in Figure 8.22 have much lower functional-unit costs, which means that as a whole, these designs are more cost-efficient.

It is also possible to reduce the datapath cost further by minimizing connectivity cost while merging operators. For this purpose we must use the priority edges in the compatibility graph, as we did in the case of the variable merging. Again, the weight of these priority edges is based on the number of common sources and common destinations.

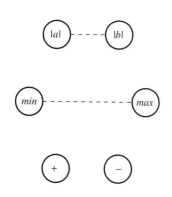

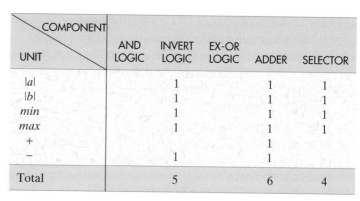

(a) Compatibility graph

COMPONENT UNIT	AND LOGIC	INVERT LOGIC	EX-OR LOGIC	ADDER	SELECTOR
|a|			1	1	1
|b|			1	1	1
min			1	1	1
max			1	1	1
+				1	
−			1	1	
Total			5	6	4

(b) Cost table

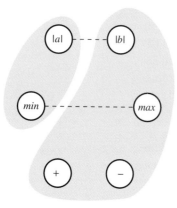

COMPONENT UNIT	AND LOGIC	INVERT LOGIC	EX-OR LOGIC	ADDER	SELECTOR
[|a|/min]	1	1		1	2
[|b|/max/+/−]	1		1	1	2
Total	2	1	1	2	2

(c) Merging alternative

(d) Cost table

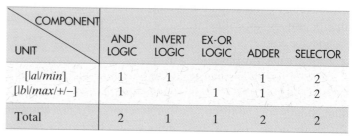

COMPONENT UNIT	AND LOGIC	INVERT LOGIC	EX-OR LOGIC	ADDER	SELECTOR
[|a|/min/+]	1		1	1	2
[|b|/max/−]	1	1		1	2
Total	2	1	1	2	2

(e) Merging alternative

(f) Cost table

FIGURE 8.21

Operator merging for SRA implementation.

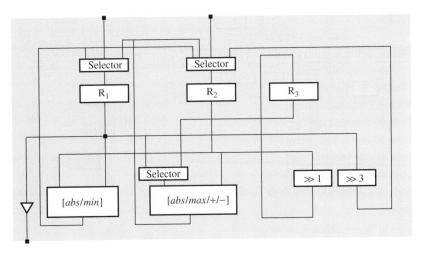

(a) Datapath schematic for unit allocation from Figure 8.21(c)

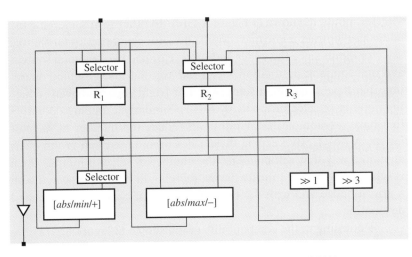

(b) Datapath schematic for unit allocation from Figure 8.21(e)

FIGURE 8.22
Datapath connectivity.

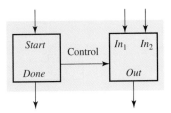

(a) Block diagram

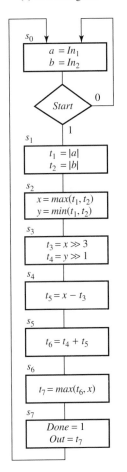

(b) ASM chart

FIGURE 8.9
Square-root approximation.

To demonstrate the computation of priority weights, consider, for example, the partial ASM chart shown in Figure 8.23(a), in which an addition and a subtraction operation are performed in different states on different sets of operands, while the results are assigned to different variables. Furthermore, if variables a and c, b and d, and x and y share the same registers, a datapath design with a separate adder and subtractor would require four 2-input selectors and one 3-input selector, for a total of 11 selector inputs, as shown in Figure 8.23(b). On the other hand, a datapath design that used one adder/subtractor would require

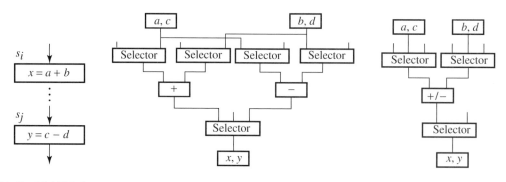

(a) Partial ASM chart   (b) Design without merged units   (c) Design with merged units

FIGURE 8.23

Priorities in unit merging.

only two 3-input selectors and one 2-input selector, for a total of eight selector inputs, as shown in Figure 8.23(c). In other words, merging the adder and subtractor into one adder/subtractor generated a gain of three selector inputs since the adder and subtractor had two common sources and one common destination. As a rule we find that grouping operators that have n common sources as left (right) operands will reduce the number of selector inputs by $n - 1$. Similarly, grouping operators that have n common destinations will reduce the number of selector inputs by $n - 1$. By keeping these rules in mind, we can group operators in a way that will minimize the number of selector inputs, which is achieved by giving priority during merging to nodes connected with a priority edge and with the highest number of common sources and destinations.

Returning to the compatibility graph shown in Figure 8.21(a), we can now add priority edges and redesign the SRA datapath so as to reduce the number of selector inputs while merging operators. In Figure 8.24(a), for example, we have labeled each priority edge with a weight s/d, in which s indicates the number of common sources and d indicates the number of common destinations. As you can see, the edge between the $+$ and $-$ operators is labeled 1/1, since two source variables (right operands), t_3 and t_5, and two destination variables, t_5 and t_6, share register R_2. Similarly, the edge between the min and $-$ operators is labeled 2/1, since min and $-$ have two common sources and one common destination—that is, the left operands, t_1 and x, share register R_1, the right operands, t_2 and t_3, share register R_2, and the results, y and t_5, share register R_2.

At this point we can use the graph-partitioning algorithm presented in Figure 8.16 to group these operators into the appropriate

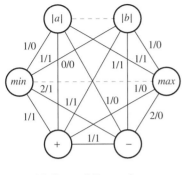

(a) Compatibility graph

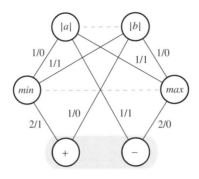

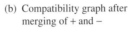

(b) Compatibility graph after
merging of + and −

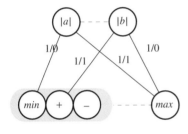

(c) Compatibility graph after
merging of min, +, and −

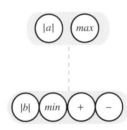

(d) Final graph partitions

F I G U R E   8.24

Graph partitioning for SRA datapath with $R_1 = [a, t_1, x, t_7]$, $R_2 = [b, t_2, y, t_3, t_5, t_6]$, and $R_3 = [t_4]$.

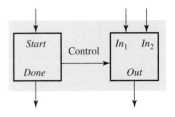

(a) Block diagram

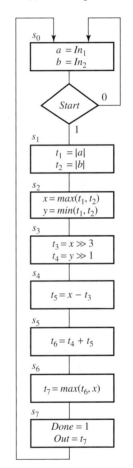

(b) ASM chart

F I G U R E   8.9

Square-root approximation.

functional units. According to this algorithm, we first try to group those operators that have a similar design structure, such as addition and subtraction, *min* and *max*, and left shift and right shift. In general, grouping similar operators in this manner will produce the largest cost reduction. In the case of the SRA algorithm, for example, we could group the + and − operators into a single supernode and then redraw the compatibility graph as shown in Figure 8.24(b). Next, we add the *min* operator to this supernode, since it has the largest number of common sources (two) and destinations (one) of all the nodes in the graph. This next version of the compatibility graph is shown in Figure 8.24(c). Finally, we add to this supernode the absolute-value operator for variable *b*, for the same reason, and then merge the *max* operator with the absolute-value operator for variable *a*. At this stage we have arrived at the graph partition shown in Figure 8.24(d), which cannot be reduced further.

As you can see from this partitioned graph, we should be able to construct a datapath for the SRA algorithm by using three registers and four functional units. The final assignment of the variables and operators to their registers and functional units is given in Figure 8.25(a), and the datapath schematic is shown in Figure 8.25(b). Note that this datapath design requires only seven selector inputs, in comparison with the nine selector inputs required by the previous design solutions, which did not take merging priorities into account.

$$R_1 = [a, t_1, x, t_7] \qquad AU_1 = [|b|/min/+/-]$$
$$R_2 = [b, t_2, y, t_3, t_5, t_6] \qquad AU_2 = [|a|/max]$$
$$R_3 = [t_4] \qquad SH_1 = [\gg 1]$$
$$SH_2 = [\gg 3]$$

(a) Register and functional unit allocation

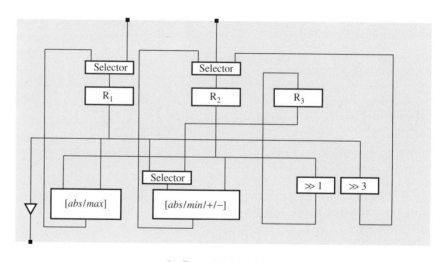

(b) Datapath schematic

FIGURE 8.25
SRA datapath obtained by using prioritized partitioning.

8.7 BUS SHARING (CONNECTION MERGING)

In previous sections we have seen how to merge variables and operators and assign them to registers and functional units. After the assignment, however, we still need to connect these registers and functional units into a datapath, wiring each register output to the input of a functional unit and each functional-unit output to the input of a register. The outputs of registers and functional units are called **connection sources**, and their inputs are called **connection destinations**. Since several connections can

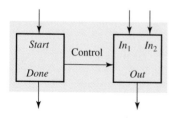

(a) Block diagram

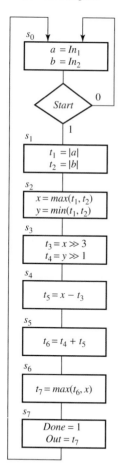

(b) ASM chart

FIGURE 8.9
Square-root approximation.

have the same destination, a datapath often includes selectors that are designed to provide the proper connection at the proper time.

Since the connections of a datapath usually occupy a substantial silicon area in a microchip, we generally try to reduce the number of connections by merging several connections into a bus, which occupies less area. As was the case when we were merging variables and operators, we do this by grouping all those connections that are not being used at the same time, and assigning each of these groups to a bus. Each connection source in the group is connected to a bus through a tristate bus driver which drives the bus in those states in which that source sends data to its destination; otherwise, the source is disconnected from the bus.

The technique for merging connections is similar to the techniques we used for merging variables and operators. First, we create a connection use table, which indicates the states in which each connection is to be used. Second, we create from this use table a compatibility graph in which each connection is represented by a node and any two nodes can be connected by a priority edge or an incompatibility edge. As the name implies, two nodes are connected by an incompatibility edge whenever their corresponding connections do not originate from the same source but are to be used at the same time. Conversely, the nodes are connected by priority edges whenever their corresponding connections have a common source or a common destination. Once we have constructed this compatibility graph, we use a graph-partitioning algorithm to group connections in a way that will maximize the number of priority edges included in all groups.

In Figure 8.26 we show how we merge the connection for the SRA datapath presented above, which has been duplicated and clarified in Figure 8.26(a). From this diagram and the ASM chart shown in Figure 8.9, we have created a connection-use table, shown in Figure 8.26(b). In this table an × has been used to designate the state in which each connection is to be used. Note that this table contains both input connections, which link register outputs to functional unit inputs, and output connections, which link functional unit outputs to the appropriate register inputs. To simplify the partitioning task, it is useful to separate these two types of connections and partition each type separately. By separating these two types of connections, we create separate input and output buses, which simplifies the datapath architecture.

Once we have completed the use table, we can then transform it into compatibility graphs by assigning one node for each connection and adding the appropriate edges between these nodes. Compatibility graphs for the input and output buses have been shown in Figure 8.26(c) and (d). Note that incompatibility edges also exist between all those nodes that are not electrically connected but are used at the same time. In Figure 8.26(c), for example, input connection B is incompatible with C and D, F incompatible with C, D, and E, and G incompatible with H. We have also added priority edges for those connections that have the same source or destination, indicating, for example, that connections

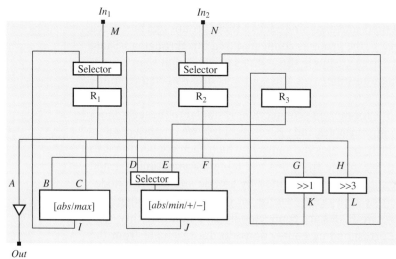

(a) Datapath for SRA

	s_0	s_1	s_2	s_3	s_4	s_5	s_6	s_7
A								×
B			×			×		
C		×	×			×		
D			×		×			
E						×		
F		×	×		×	×		
G				×				
H				×				
I		×	×				×	
J		×	×		×	×		
K				×				
L				×				
M	×							
N	×							

(b) Connection use table

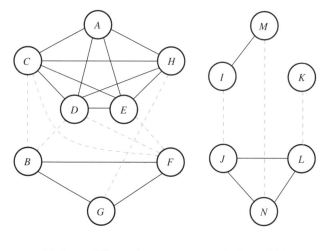

(c) Compatibility graph for input buses

(d) Compatibility graph for output buses

FIGURE 8.26

Connection merging in SRA datapath.

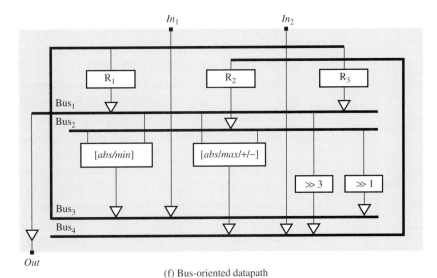

Bus$_1$ = [A, C, D, E, H]
Bus$_2$ = [B, F, G]

Bus$_3$ = [I, K, M]
Bus$_4$ = [J, L, N]

(e) Bus assignment

(f) Bus-oriented datapath

FIGURE   8.26
Continued

A, C, D, and H all originate from register R_1, and that connections B, F, and G all originate from register R_2. Nodes D and E in the graph have also been connected with a priority edge because they both have the same destination—the left input of the functional unit, AU$_2$.

In Figure 8.26(d) we have determined the priority edges for the output connections, proceeding in a similar fashion. At this point, when we have determined all the priority and incompatibility edges, we can partition the connections, trying to cut all the incompatibility edges while cutting as few priority edges as possible. As shown in Figure 8.26(e), the fewest possible partitions can be achieved by grouping connections A, C, D, E, and H into Bus$_1$ and connections B, F, and G into Bus$_2$, which accounts for all of the input connections. Similarly, we group I, K, and M into Bus$_3$ and J, L, and N into Bus$_4$, which merges all the output connections. In Figure 8.26(f), then, you can see that the SRA datapath can be connected with a total of four buses, which substantially reduces the cost of its implementation.

8.8   REGISTER MERGING

In Section 8.5 we described a procedure for variable merging which resulted in several variables sharing the same register. As we explained, a number of variables share the same register whenever they have nonoverlapping lifetimes. In the same fashion, registers with nonoverlapping access times can be merged into register files to share the register input and output ports, which in turn reduces the number of connections in the datapath, because there will be fewer ports. Unfortunately, it also increases the register-to-register delay because an extra delay is incurred for the address decoding that occurs in the register file. Nonetheless, this additional delay is frequently acceptable given the cost reductions obtained by replacing many registers with a single register file.

In register merging we can use the same approach that we described for variable, operator, and connection merging. Initially, we create a register access table, on the basis of which we can then generate a compatibility graph. Finally, we use a graph-partitioning algorithm to group compatible registers into register files. Since each register file can have more than one port, we can generally group registers so that at no time does the total number of read or write accesses to the registers in the group exceed the number of read or write ports in the register file.

In Figure 8.27 we demonstrated the procedure for register merging using the example of the SRA datapath. First, we created a register access table, using one row for each register in the datapath and one column for each state in the ASM chart. In this table a dividing line between the states represents the rising edge of the clock signal, which loads the data into the registers. An open triangle pointing toward a dividing line means that new data will be written into the register at that particular rising edge of the clock signal. We have also drawn a black triangle pointing away from a dividing line when we need to indicate the state in which the data will be used.

From the register access table shown in Figure 8.27(b), we can then generate a compatibility graph. In the case of the SRA datapath, we can see that registers R_1 and R_2 are not compatible because they are written or read concurrently in states s_0, s_1, s_2, s_3, s_4, and s_6. Similarly, R_2 and R_3 are not compatible because both are written in state s_3 and read in state s_5. On the other hand, registers R_1 and R_3 are compatible simply because they are never accessed at the same time. These conclusions are reflected in the compatibility graph shown in Figure 8.27(c), which shows that we can merge registers R_1 and R_3 into a single register file with one read and one write port. The final datapath using such a register file is shown in Figure 8.27(d).

From this schematic we can also see that by merging registers R_1 and R_3, we have been able to reduce the number of bus drivers in the datapath because R_1 and R_3 share the same read port and we need only one bus driver instead of two. In general, merging n registers that drive m

$R_1 = [a, t_1, x, t_7]$
$R_2 = [b, t_2, y, t_3, t_5, t_6]$
$R_3 = [t_4]$

(a) Register assignment

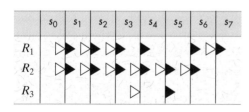

(b) Register access table

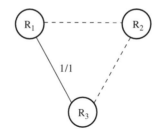

(c) Compatibility graph

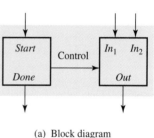

(a) Block diagram

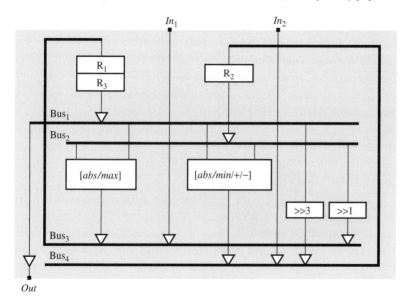

(d) Datapath schematic

FIGURE 8.27
Register merging.

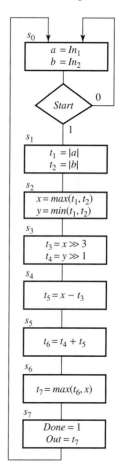

(b) ASM chart

FIGURE 8.9
Square-root approximation.

buses into a single register file with one read port will reduce the number of drivers by $n - m$. However, if we merge n registers that are loaded from m different buses into a single register file with one input port, we have to introduce an m-input selector in front of the input port. Because of potential savings in bus drivers and input selectors, the priority in merging registers is generally given to registers with a common source or destination—that is, to registers that are loaded from the same bus or that drive the same bus.

8.9 CHAINING AND MULTICYCLING

In Section 8.8, we presented techniques for datapath synthesis that are based on a simple datapath model. For example, in these datapaths the registers were connected by one or more buses to the functional units, and the functional units in turn were connected by one or more buses to the registers. In some cases selectors were used whenever a register or a functional unit received data from more than one bus. In this kind of datapath, the registers are clocked by a clock signal whose cycle is equal to the worst register-to-register delay. Since the worst register-to-register delay path goes through the slowest functional unit, this means that other functional units are busy for only part of the clock cycle and remain idle for the rest of the cycle. If, however, the total delay of any two of these functional units is shorter than the clock cycle, it is possible to connect them in series and thereby perform two operations in a single clock cycle. This same principle can be extended to more than two functional units if the datapath has a longer clock cycle. This technique of connecting units in series is called **chaining**, since two or more units would be chained together without a register between them, thus creating a larger combinatorial unit that can compute assignments with two or more operations. Whenever we use this technique, a variable assignment statement in the ASM chart will contain two or more operators on the right-hand side of the statement.

To demonstrate chaining we use the ASM chart shown in Figure 8.28(a), which illustrates the SRA algorithm. Note that this chart has been modified from the chart in Figure 8.9, insofar as it merges two states (s_2 and s_3) into one state (s_2). As you can see, this means that three assignment statements will be executed in state s_2 of Figure 8.28(a): the first of these statements requires one binary operation (maximum), while the other two statements require two operations each. More specifically, the new value would be assigned to t_3 by computing the maximum of t_1 and t_2 and then shifting the result to the right by three positions. At the same time, the new value for t_4 will be obtained by computing the minimum of t_1 and t_2 and then shifting the result one position to the right. Since shifting to the right by three or one positions incurs no delay as demonstrated in Figure 8.11(f) and (g), the clock cycle for this chained datapath would be no longer than the original clock cycle. On the other hand, since this ASM chart has only seven states instead of the eight states in the original chart, we would conclude that this modified datapath can perform the SRA algorithm 12.5% faster. The new datapath schematic with the chained units is shown in Figure 8.28(b). Note that we had to create an additional connection from right

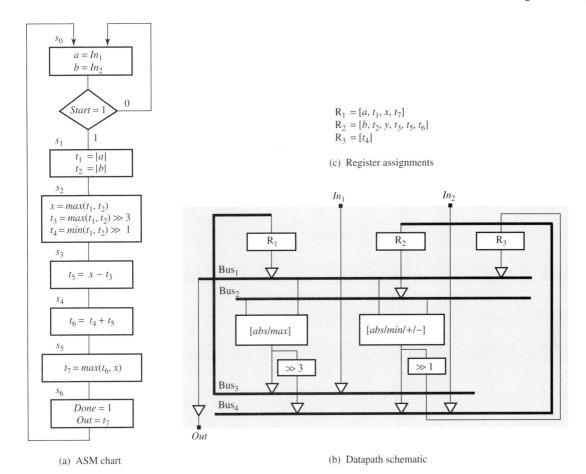

$R_1 = [a, t_1, x, t_7]$
$R_2 = [b, t_2, y, t_3, t_5, t_6]$
$R_3 = [t_4]$

(c) Register assignments

(a) ASM chart   (b) Datapath schematic

F I G U R E   8.28
SRA datapath with chained units.

shifter indicated by $\gg 1$ to register R_3 in order to store concurrently three new values for variables x, t_3 and t_4 that were generated in state s_2.

In addition to chaining, which allows us to use faster units, we may sometimes want to use slower but less expensive units that take more than one clock cycle to generate their results. This technique is called **multicycling**, and these slower units are called **multicycle units**. For obvious reasons such units can be used only on the noncritical paths through the ASM chart. For example, in the ASM chart in Figure 8.28(a), variable t_4 will be assigned a new value $(min(t_1, t_2)) \gg 1$ in state s_2, but this new value will not be used until state s_4. In this case, then, we could use a unit that takes two clock cycles to compute the minimum value, and chain this unit with a right shifter that takes no time to generate its result.

This multicycling arrangement is shown in Figure 8.29. As you can see in Figure 8.29(a), the ASM chart has been modified by the introduction of square brackets, used to indicate that the result will only be available in some successor state or that the computation of an expression was already started in one of the predecessor states. For example, the variable assignment $[t_4] = (min(t_1, t_2)) \gg 1$ indicates that the new value will be assigned to t_4 in one of the successor states. Similarly, the expression $t_4 = [(min(t_1, t_2)) \gg 1]$ indicates that the new value is assigned to t_4 in the present state but that computation of the expression in brackets has started in one of the previous states. As illustrated in Figure 8.29(b), such an ASM chart is easily translated into a datapath with multicycle units. Note that we had to introduce an additional state

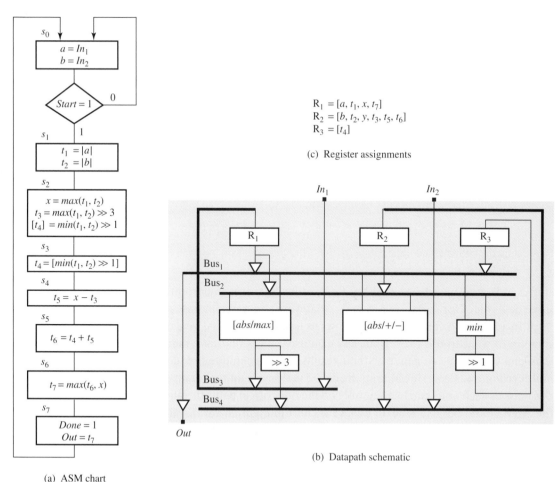

$$R_1 = [a, t_1, x, t_7]$$
$$R_2 = [b, t_2, y, t_3, t_5, t_6]$$
$$R_3 = [t_4]$$

(c) Register assignments

(b) Datapath schematic

(a) ASM chart

FIGURE 8.29
SRA datapath with multicycle units.

since assignment $t_4 = (\min(t_1, t_2)) \gg 1$ takes two states during which both **Bus**$_1$ and **Bus**$_2$ are used to supply operands t_1 and t_2, which in turn delays the execution of the assignment $t_5 = x - t_3$ to state s_5.

At this point we have shown how datapath performance can be improved by chaining fast functional units and how datapath cost can be reduced by using multicycle units. As you would expect, the techniques described previously for variable, operator, and connection merging can be extended to include chained and multicycle units. For the sake of brevity, however, we omit their discussion in this book.

8.10 FUNCTIONAL UNIT PIPELINING

In previous sections we introduced various techniques for reducing data-path cost, mainly by reducing the number of registers, functional units, and connections. In this section we shift focus by introducing techniques that increase the performance of a datapath. The single most effective technique for performance improvement is **pipelining**. A pipelined datapath is similar to a factory assembly line where a product moves from station to station. In other words, at a given station, the same operation is being performed on every product, but each station performs a different task in product assembly, which significantly speeds up product manufacturing.

Pipelining technique can be applied to functional units, datapaths, or control. In case of functional units, we divide a functional unit into two or more stages, each separated by latches so that each stage can operate on a different set of operands. At any time, then, there are several sets of operands in the pipeline—more precisely, the number of sets in the pipeline equals the number of stages. Using pipelined functional units does not affect the time taken to generate result for the first set of operands, which is the same as the time in a nonpipelined unit. However, for every additional set of operands, a result is available in a time equal to the delay of only one stage. For example, for a 2-stage pipelined unit, whose non-pipelined delay is 100 ns, the result for the first set of operands is still generated in 100 ns, but the result for the second set of operands is available only 50 ns later, and so on for every subsequent set of operands. In general, if there are n stages in the pipeline, we can reduce the time taken to generate results to $1/n$ times the nonpipelined execution time, with the exception of the first result.

As an example of a pipelined unit, consider the 2-stage arithmetic unit (AU) shown in Figure 8.30, which was obtained by inserting three data latches and one control latch in the middle between the input and output ports of the nonpipelined AU in Figure 8.20(d). We could have

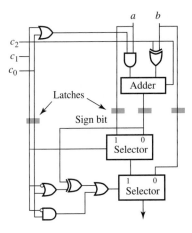

FIGURE 8.30
Pipelined arithmetic unit.

inserted latches through the middle of the ALU instead of between the ALU and the selectors in order to cut the critical path in two equal parts. If these latches are exactly in the middle of the critical delay path, each stage takes only half as long as the nonpipelined unit to generate its results. Thus the pipelined unit can operate with a clock cycle that is approximately equal to half the clock cycle of the nonpipelined unit. As mentioned before, it still takes two clock cycles (or states) for the pipeline to produce a result; in the first clock cycle, the partial result is stored into latches; in the second clock cycle, the final result is generated in the second stage of the pipeline, while the first stage is generating partial results for the next set of operands, and so on for each set of operands.

To compare the results of pipelined and nonpipelined units, let us consider an SRA datapath with only one nonpipelined AU which performs absolute value, minimum, maximum, sum, and difference. This datapath and its corresponding ASM chart are shown in Figure 8.31. Note that this datapath requires nine states, or nine clock cycles, to compute a square-root approximation. On the other hand, we could redesign the datapath in Figure 8.31(b), replacing its nonpipelined AU with a 2-stage pipelined AU, as shown in Figure 8.32(a). This new datapath with the pipelined AU requires 13 states or clock cycles to compute a square-root approximation, as shown in the timing diagram in Figure 8.32(b).

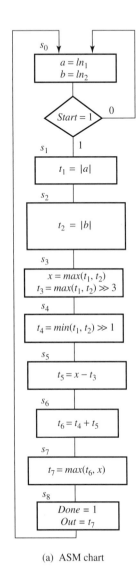

(a) ASM chart

FIGURE 8.31

SRA datapath with single AU.

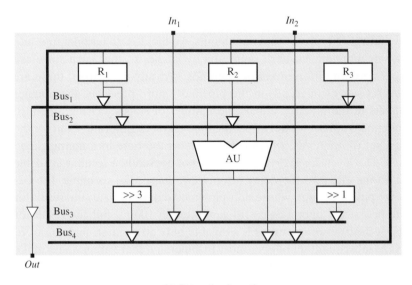

(b) Datapath schematic

In this timing diagram, the loading and reading of each register and the operation of each functional unit are shown on a state-by-state

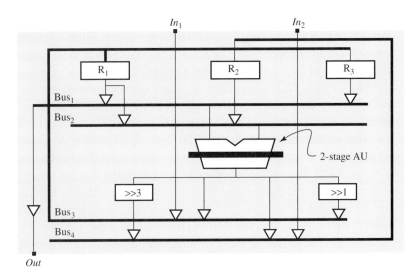

(a) Datapath with pipelined AU

	s_0	s_1	s_2	s_3	s_4	s_5	s_6	s_7	s_8	s_9	s_{10}	s_{11}	s_{12}
Read R_1		a			t_1	t_1	x				x		t_7
Read R_2			b		t_2	t_2	t_3		t_5		t_6		
Read R_3									t_4				
AU stage 1		$\lvert a\rvert$	$\lvert b\rvert$		max	min	$-$		$+$		max		
AU stage 2			$\lvert a\rvert$	$\lvert b\rvert$		max	min	$-$		$+$		max	
Shifters						$>>3$	$>>1$						
Write R_1	a	t_1			x							t_7	
Write R_2	b			t_2		t_3		t_5		t_6			
Write R_3							t_4						
Out													t_7

(b) Timing diagram

FIGURE   8.32
Datapath with pipelined functional units.

basis. The timing diagram has one row for each register read or write access as well as one row for each stage of the *AU* and shift units. Each column represents one state of the control unit. As you can see, then, in state s_0 the datapath reads the values of variables a and b from the input ports and stores them in registers R_1 and R_2. Next, in state s_1, it reads the value of variable a from register R_1 and partially computes the absolute value of a. This partial result is then stored in the AU pipeline latches between two stages. Then, in state s_2, the datapath finishes the computation of $|a|$ and assigns this value to variable t_1, which is stored in register R_1. At the same time, in state s_2 the datapath also initiates the computation of $|b|$, storing the partial result of this computation in the pipeline latches. Thus in state s_2 both stages of the pipelined AU are active, although they process different operands. In state s_3 the datapath finishes computation of $|b|$ and assigns it to variable t_2 stored in register R_2. Note that at this point the datapath cannot yet initiate the next operation because it requires the value of t_2, which has not yet been loaded in register R_2. Therefore, no operation is scheduled to start in s_3. In a similar fashion, the datapath starts execution of maximum, minimum, and subtraction operations in states s_4, s_5, and s_6, and completes these operations, together with the shifts, in states s_5, s_6, and s_7. It cannot start the addition until state s_8, since it must wait for the availability of the value assigned to t_5. Similarly, it starts the maximum operation in state s_{10} but does not finish it until state s_{11}. Finally, the datapath uses state s_{12} to output the result.

According to this timing diagram, this SRA algorithm requires 13 states or clock cycles to complete. As mentioned above, however, two of these clock cycles are equal to one clock cycle of the nonpipelined design, which means that the datapath with the pipelined AU computes the square-root approximation in six and a half clock cycles instead of the nine needed by the nonpipelined design. Note that this pipelined datapath can outperform any other nonpipelined design that has been described in previous sections.

8.11 DATAPATH PIPELINING

In Section 8.10, we demonstrated how to improve datapath performance by pipelining functional units within the datapath. In the case of a datapath that performs the same computation on different sets of operands, however, we can improve performance even more by pipelining the entire ASM chart. To do this we divide the entire ASM chart into several equal-size parts and then use a separate datapath stages to execute each part. With this design, all the stages could work on different sets of operands simultaneously, each generating a partial result that could be used by the next datapath in the sequence.

As an example of this ASM pipelining, consider the ASM chart shown in Figure 8.33(a), which describes the SRA algorithm. In this chart we assume that the loop will execute indefinitely and that a new set of operands will be available on the input ports every 10 clock cycles. In this case we can easily divide the ASM chart into two parts: The first part would consist of states s_0 through s_4, and the second part would consist of states s_5 through s_8. In Figure 8.33(a) this division is indicated by a heavy line between states s_4 and s_5, which shows that the SRA algorithm will be computed in two parts with two separate datapath stages.

In Figure 8.33(b) you can see that the first datapath stage includes registers R_1 and R_2, one AU and two shifters, while the second stage

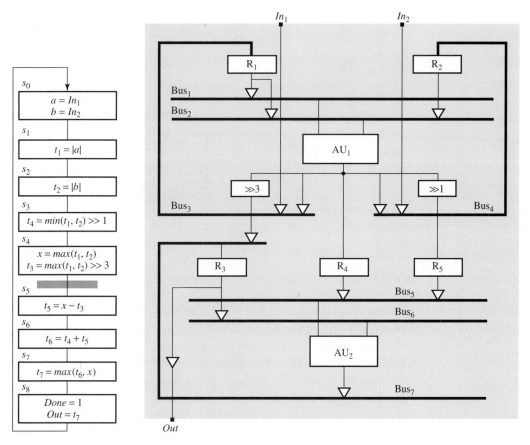

(a) ASM chart

(b) Pipelined datapath

$R_1 = [a, t_1]$ $R_3 = [t_3, t_5, t_6, t_7]$
$R_2 = [b, t_2]$ $R_4 = [x]$
$AU_1 = [abs/min/max]$ $R_5 = [t_4]$
                       $AU_2 = [+/-/max]$

(c) Register and functional
unit assignment

F I G U R E   8.33
Datapath pipelining.

	nth pair					(n + 1)th pair					
	s_0	s_1	s_2	s_3	s_4	s_5	s_6	s_7	s_8	s_9	
Read R_1		a		t_1	t_1						STAGE 1
Read R_2			b	t_2	t_2						
AU stage 1		$\lvert a \rvert$	$\lvert b \rvert$	min	max						
Shifters				$\gg 1$	$\gg 3$						
Write R_1	a	t_1									
Write R_2	b		t_2								
Read R_3						t_3	t_5	t_6	t_7		STAGE 2
Read R_4						x		x			
Read R_5							t_4				
AU stage 2						$-$	$+$	max			
Write R_3						t_3	t_5	t_6	t_7		
Write R_4						x					
Write R_5				t_4							

nth pair

(d) Timing diagram

FIGURE 8.33
Continued

includes registers R_3, R_4, and R_5, as well as another AU. The assignment of variables to registers is given in Figure 8.33(c).

In Figure 8.33(d) we present a timing diagram for the pipelined datapath. As before, this timing diagram shows all the read and write accesses to registers R_1 through R_5 as well as all the operations performed in the functional units in each state. As you can see, the first stage will take five cycles to complete the first part of the ASM chart; that is, the first stage takes five cycles to read a and b from the input ports, to assign the appropriate values to the variables t_1, t_2, t_3, x, and t_4, and to store the last three variables in registers R_3, R_4, and R_5, which can be thought of as latches between the two datapath stages. Furthermore, the second part of the ASM chart takes only four cycles since registers R_3, R_4, and R_5 are already loaded by the first stage. Overall, it takes nine cycles to execute one iteration of the SRA loop; however, it is important to realize that the first stage is ready to input a new set of operands every five clock cycles since both datapath stages will be executing concurrently. More precisely, the first datapath will compute partial results for the $(n + 1)st$ set of operands at the same time that the second datapath is computing the final results for the nth set of operands. Thus for n pairs of operands it takes $5n + 4$ clock cycles to compute the SRA. In comparison, a nonpipelined datapath with one AU and two shifters takes $9n$ clock cycles to obtain the same results.

If we combine this pipelined datapath with pipelined functional units, we could improve its performance even further. For example, we can use 2-stage pipelined AUs in the datapath we just developed, which would give us a datapath that corresponds to the timing diagram shown in Figure 8.34. In this diagram we indicate that each stage of this new datapath pipeline would need seven states to compute its result; however, since each state in this diagram is only half as long as the states in Figure 8.33, our new datapath will compute the SRA in $(7/2)n + (7/2) = 3.5n + 3.5$ clock cycles compared with the $5n + 4$ clock cycles required when nonpipelined units are used. In other words, by pipelining the datapath into two stages and using 2-stage pipelined functional units in each of these stages, we reduced this datapath's execution time to approximately one-third of its original time, improving its performance by a factor of 3.

	s_0	s_1	s_2	s_3	s_4	s_5	s_6	s_7	s_8	s_9	s_{10}	s_{11}	s_{12}	s_{13}
Read R_1		a			t_1	t_1								
Read R_2			b		t_2	t_2								
AU_1 stage 1		$|a|$	$|b|$		min	max								
AU_1 stage 2			$|a|$	$|b|$		min	max							
Shifters						$\gg 1$	$\gg 3$							
Write R_1	a		t_1											
Write R_2	b			t_2										
Read R_3								t_3		t_5		t_6		t_7
Read R_4								x				x		
Read R_5										t_4				
AU_2 stage 1								$-$		$+$		max		
AU_2 stage 2									$-$		$+$		max	
Write R_3							t_3		t_5		t_6		t_7	t_3
Write R_4							x							x
Write R_5					t_4								t_4	
Out														t_7

FIGURE 8.34

Timing diagram for datapath pipeline with pipelined units.

8.12 CONTROL-PIPELINING

In Section 8.11, we discussed two methods for improving performance through pipelining techniques. As we have shown, datapath pipelining allows us to compute different sets of operands concurrently, thus reducing the total time required to execute a given algorithm. In addition, component pipelining allows us to increase the utilization of the datapath's various components, and to shorten the clock cycle, by reducing the register-to-register delay. It is important to note, however, that the longest register-to-register delay generally goes through the control unit, as shown in Figure 8.35(a), where the longest or critical-path register-to-register delay is from state register to state register. To some extent, of course, this delay will vary depending on whether the control signals depend on status signals or not, as shown by the dashed status line in Figure 8.35(a). If the status signals are used only for the selection of the next state, the critical path goes from clock signal to output of the *state register* and then through *output logic*, *RF, ALU*, and via status signal through *next-state logic*, back to *state register*, including *state-register* setup time. On the other hand, if some status signals are used for controlling a part of the datapath, the critical path is longer since it goes twice through the datapath: first time to compute status signals, and second time to perform an operation on values stored in the datapath registers. In this case the critical path goes from clock signal to the output of the *state register* and then through *output logic*, *RF, ALU, output logic* again, *RF or memory, multiplier/divider*, and back to *register* or *RF*, including *register* or *RF* setup time.

In any case it is the critical path through the control that determines the length of the clock cycle (clock period). Consequently, if we want to improve performance by shortening the clock cycle, it would make sense to divide the critical path into pieces and insert registers between them. In Figure 8.35(b), for example, registers are inserted in three difference places. First, we introduce a **status register** between the datapath and the control unit so that all status signals leaving the datapath are latched in that register, which has one flip-flop for each status signal. Second, we insert a **control register** between the control unit and the datapath so that all control signals generated by the *output logic* are latched in that register, which has one flip-flop for each control signal. Finally, we pipeline the datapath itself by inserting **pipeline latches** between the storage units (register, RF, and memory) and the functional units (ALU, multiplier/divider), as shown in Figure 8.35(b) and explained in Section 8.11.

In general, when we plan to use control and datapath pipelining in the FSMD implementations, we need to construct our ASM charts

Control inputs   Datapath inputs

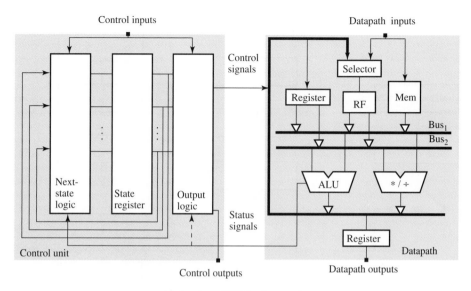

(a) Standard FSMD implementation

Control inputs   Datapath inputs

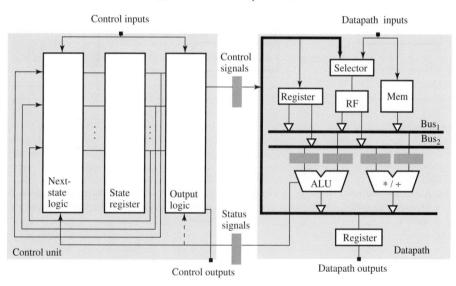

(b) FSMD implementation with control and datapath pipelining

FIGURE 8.35
Pipelined FSMD implementation.

so that they reflect our pipelining decisions. To demonstrate this, let us consider the ASM chart in Figure 8.36(a), which in its original form has three states. In the first state, s_1, we test whether $a > b$, then go to s_2 if this inequality is not true or to s_3 if it is true. In state s_2 we execute the assignment $x = c * d$, and in state s_3 we would execute the

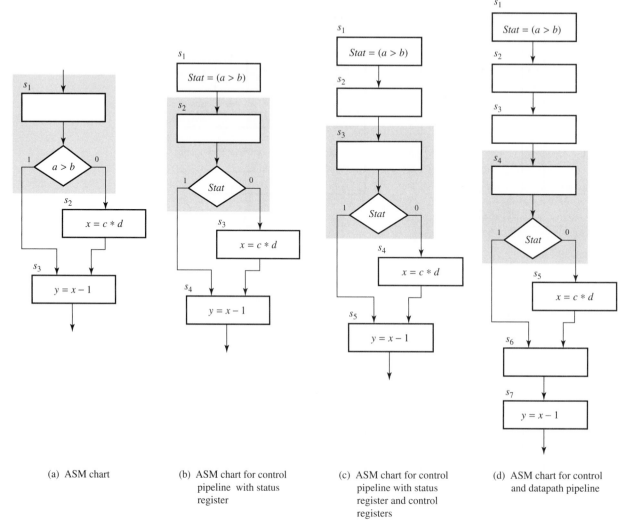

(a) ASM chart

(b) ASM chart for control pipeline with status register

(c) ASM chart for control pipeline with status register and control registers

(d) ASM chart for control and datapath pipeline

FIGURE 8.36
ASM charts for pipelined implementations.

assignment $y = x - 1$. This ASM chart does not assume any pipelining in its implementation.

If, however, we introduce a status register for control pipelining in the FSMD implementation, we need to modify this ASM chart accordingly, introducing a new status variable, *Stat*, as well as the assignment statement, $Stat = (a > b)$. Furthermore, we could not, in a single state, assign a value to a status variable and branch on it, since we need one clock cycle to compute the value of the status variable and load it into the status register, and a second clock cycle to test it and select the next state. These additional requirements are reflected in Figure 8.36(b), where the status register is to be loaded in s_1 but the branch on the status is not executed until state s_2. Similarly, if we introduce control and status registers, we have to insert two new states as shown in Figure 8.36(c), where we would use two clock cycles to load the status registers before we branch on the status signal.

Finally, if we introduce control and status registers and pipeline the datapath as we did in Figure 8.35(d), we have to add four new states. More specifically, we first need three clock cycles to load the status register, since we cannot branch on the status until state s_4, as shown in Figure 8.36(d). Second, we must introduce another empty state, s_6, between states s_5 and s_7 since the computation $y = x - 1$ to be performed in s_7 requires the new value of x, which in turn requires now two clock cycles to be computed. As you can see from these examples, ASM charts may require a number of modifications when they are used to describe pipelined FSMD implementations.

8.13 SCHEDULING

In previous sections we have demonstrated how to synthesize an ASM chart into a custom design that consists of a datapath and a control unit. In general, the synthesis of these ASM charts is based on the FSMD model, which explicitly specifies states, state transitions, and the variable assignments to be performed in each state. Unfortunately, custom designs are usually based on algorithms that have not been specified by ASM charts but have been described in some programming language or represented by a flowchart, neither of which supports the concept of a state, although they provide the order in which variable assignments are to be executed. Therefore, the main difference between programming languages or flowcharts and ASM charts is that the former do not specify state boundaries or bind variable assignments to particular states.

To transform an ordinary algorithm or a flowchart into an ASM chart, we would have to partition its execution time into a series of time intervals called states and assign each variable assignment operation to a particular state. In other words, we must schedule the variable access and operations into states under either resource or time constraints. In this section we demonstrate both types of scheduling, resource-constrained (RC) and time-constrained (TC) scheduling, and give one scheduling algorithm for each type.

To perform scheduling we must first convert a program or a flowchart into a **control/dataflow graph** (CDFG), which shows explicitly the control dependencies among statements and data dependencies among variable values. In other words, a CDFG should retain the control structure of a flowchart but must also represent variable assignments as dataflow graphs, in which each node represents an operator while each edge between two nodes represents the result that is generated by the first operator and is then used as an operand by the second operator.

Since a flowchart is a recursive structure of serial–parallel connections of assignment and decision boxes, a CDFG differs from a flowchart only in the representation of the assignment box: While a flowchart assignment box contains a sequence of assignment statements, the CDFG contains the same sequence as a dataflow graph. In Figure 8.37 we compare a flowchart and its corresponding CDFG: Figure 8.37(a) shows the flowchart for the SRA algorithm, and Figure 8.37(b) shows the corresponding CDFG.

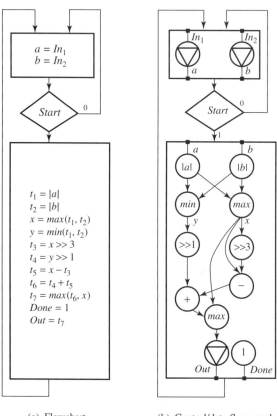

$$a = In_1$$
$$b = In_2$$

$$Start \qquad 0$$

$$t_1 = |a|$$
$$t_2 = |b|$$
$$x = max(t_1, t_2)$$
$$y = min(t_1, t_2)$$
$$t_3 = x \gg 3$$
$$t_4 = y \gg 1$$
$$t_5 = x - t_3$$
$$t_6 = t_4 + t_5$$
$$t_7 = max(t_6, x)$$
$$Done = 1$$
$$Out = t_7$$

(a) Flowchart (b) Control/data flow graph

FIGURE 8.37
Control/dataflow graph for SRA.

A CDFG representation of a flowchart or a program is frequently used by scheduling algorithms, since a scheduled CDFG is equivalent to an ASM chart. As we mentioned earlier, a CDFG can be scheduled using resource or timing constraints. The resource constraints are specified by the number and type of functional and storage units used in the datapath, whereas the time constraints are specified as the number of states the datapath will take to execute all the operations on the longest path through CDFG. Before we explain RC and TC scheduling algorithms, we introduce as-soon-as-possible (ASAP) and as-late-as-possible (ALAP) scheduling algorithms, which are frequently used by other scheduling algorithms to determine operation priority and range for scheduling.

ASAP and ALAP algorithms assume, first, that each operation will take exactly one clock cycle to execute, and second, that an unlimited number of functional units or resources are available for each operation in each state. Because of the assumption above we may consider both algorithms as being constrained only by data dependencies. Within this context, the **ASAP algorithm** schedules each operation into the earliest state in which all its operands are available. In other words, it scans the control/data flow graph from the top to the bottom and assigns to each state all the nodes in the graph whose predecessor or parent nodes have been already assigned into previous states. Thus the ASAP algorithm generates a schedule that has the minimum number of states or, in other words, the shortest execution time.

In contrast to the ASAP approach, the **ALAP algorithm** schedules each operation into the last possible state before its result is needed if it is given the length of the final schedule in the number of states as a constraint. In other words, it scans the control/data flow graph from the bottom to the top and assigns to each state all the nodes whose successor or children nodes have been already assigned into later states. If the given schedule length is equal to the number of states obtained by the ASAP algorithm, the ALAP algorithm schedules all the operations on the longest or critical path through the dataflow graph into the same states as the ASAP algorithm. The operations that are not on the critical path are executed earlier than needed in the ASAP schedule and later than possible in the ALAP schedule.

In Figure 8.38 we have applied ASAP and ALAP scheduling to the larger of two assignment boxes in Figure 8.37, limiting this application to a single assignment box for the sake of simplicity. Both schedules in Figure 8.38 require seven states. We also see that all operations except min and $\gg 1$ are on the critical path. These two operations are scheduled as early as possible (states s_2 and s_3) in the ASAP schedule and as late as possible (states s_3 and s_4) in the ALAP schedule.

The fact that ASAP and ALAP algorithms schedule operations on the critical path to the same states can be used to separate critical from

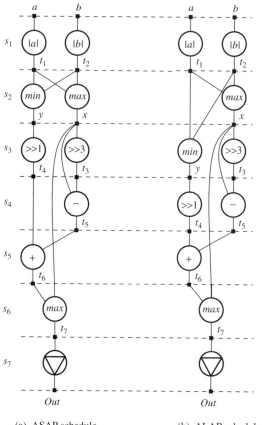

FIGURE 8.38
Basic schedules.

(a) ASAP schedule (b) ALAP schedule

noncritical operations in general scheduling algorithms. The priority is always given to those operations that are on the critical path, since delaying one of these operations by one state would extend the schedule by one state and increase the execution time. On the other hand, lower priority can be given to operations that are not on the critical path since they have greater flexibility of being scheduled in different states and can be delayed without affecting the execution time of the entire CDFG.

An operation's priority during scheduling can be measured by several different metrics. One of these metrics is the operation's mobility, which is equal to the distance in number of states between the states assigned to that particular operation in ASAP and ALAP schedules. In other words, if an operation, op, is scheduled in state s_i in the ASAP schedule and in state s_k in the ALAP schedule, its mobility, $M(op)$, will be equal to $k - i$. Thus **mobility** defines the operation's ability to be postponed without an impact on the total execution time, and it can be used for prioritizing operations. In other words, states with higher mobility can therefore be given lower priority.

As an alternative measure of priority, we can use the criterion of **operation urgency**, which is equal to the distance in number of states between the state in which the operation is available for scheduling and the state in which the operation occurs in its ALAP schedule. In other words, if an operation, op, is available in state s_j but is not scheduled until state s_k in its ALAP schedule, that state's urgency $U(op)$ will be equal to $k - j$. As a third measure of operation's priority, we could consider how many other operations use its result as an operand. This measure gives priority to operations that increase the number of operations available for scheduling in the future. There are several other priority measures in addition to these, but none of them works perfectly in all cases. In theory, we could use any number of priority metrics in any order.

One of the most popular algorithms for RC scheduling is the **list-scheduling algorithm**, which derives its name from its use of a ready list of operations that are available for scheduling. In this algorithm the operations on the ready list are sorted by their mobilities, so that the operations with zero mobility will be placed at the top of the list while those operations with the greatest mobility will be placed at the bottom of the list. In those cases where two operations have the same mobility, priority is given to the operation with the lower urgency number. If these are the same, too, the priority is assigned randomly. In applying this list-scheduling algorithm, we take the following steps in each state: assign the highest-priority operations from the ready list to the available functional units, one at a time, then delete all the assigned operations from the list, and insert new operations, that become schedulable, into the list in the positions that correspond to their mobilities and urgencies. This list-scheduling algorithm is summarized in Figure 8.39.

We demonstrate this list-scheduling algorithm on the dataflow graph of the assignment box in Figure 8.37(b) under the assumption that we have only one arithmetic unit, which can perform absolute value, minimum, maximum, addition, and subtraction, in addition to two shifter units. First, we generate ASAP and ALAP schedules, as shown in Figure 8.40(a) and (b). Then we create a ready list for the first state as shown in Figure 8.40(c) and compute the mobilities for the operations in that ready list. In our case, only operations $|a|$ and $|b|$ are available in the first state. Since these operations have the same mobility $[M(|a|) = M(|b|) = 0]$, we select their order randomly and schedule $|a|$ first. Since scheduling $|a|$ does not free any more operations for scheduling, we do not change the ready list at this time. Therefore, we must schedule $|b|$ in state s_2, which allows us to add *max* and *min* operators to the ready list. Since the *max* operator is on the critical path, it has a mobility $M(max) = 0$, which gives it priority over the *min* operator, which has mobility $M(min) = 1$. Therefore, we would schedule *max* into state s_3, which allows us to add $\gg 3$ to the ready list. Since its mobility

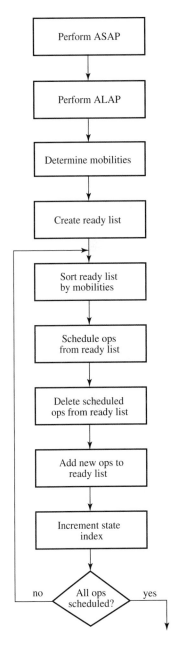

FIGURE   8.39

List-scheduling algorithm.

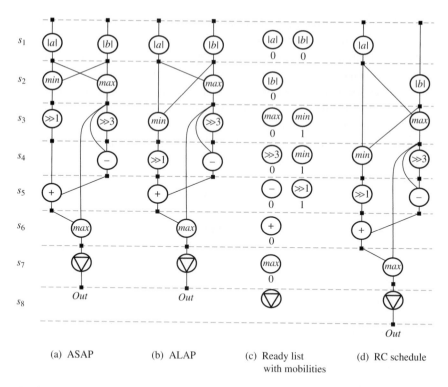

(a) ASAP   (b) ALAP   (c) Ready list   (d) RC schedule
                            with mobilities

F I G U R E   8.40
Resource-constrained scheduling.

$M(\gg 3) = 0$, this operator should be placed at the top of the ready list. At this point we have have one AU and two shifters available, so we can now schedule both the ($\gg 3$) and the *min* operations in state s_4. We then update the ready list, adding $-$ and $\gg 1$, which can then be both scheduled into state s_5. At this point we can schedule $+$ into state s_6 and *max* into state s_7, and finally, output the result in state s_8. The final RC schedule is shown in Figure 8.40(d).

As we have shown, the goal of the RC scheduling algorithm is to schedule in each state as many operations as it can given the fixed number of available functional units. When more operations are available than there are functional units, we must use a priority metric, such as mobility or urgency. In our example we obtained a schedule that requires one more state than the ASAP or ALAP schedules but at lower cost since we used only one AU and two shifters, while the ASAP and ALAP schedules required two AUs and two shifters.

In many cases the primary goal of a design optimization is not the cost but the performance, since a datapath must execute a given algorithm in a fixed amount of time. When execution time is constrained we use **time-constrained** (TC) **scheduling**, which generates a schedule comprising a particular number of states while attempting at the same time to minimize the number of functional units it requires in the datapath. This goal is achieved by creating a probability-distribution graph, and scheduling operations, one at the time, into states, so that the largest sum of probabilities for each operator and each state is minimal.

To use TC scheduling as indicated in Figure 8.41, we first apply the ASAP and ALAP scheduling algorithms to determine the mobility range for each operation. Having established these ranges, we then assign to each operation an equal probability of being scheduled in each state of its range. Obviously, for each operation, the sum of all these probabilities over the entire range equals 1.

Once we have calculated these probabilities, we can then create probability distribution graphs, which define the probability sums in each state for each set of compatible operations. In other words, these probability sums determine the number of functional units of each type required in each state. At this point we can attempt to minimize the number of functional units by selecting an operation and scheduling it in the state that will reduce the largest probability sum for this operation type in the distribution graph. If reduction is not possible, we can select an operation and schedule it in the state in which it will minimally increase the probability sum. The algorithm terminates only when all operations have been scheduled, as indicated in Figure 8.41.

We demonstrate TC scheduling on the dataflow graph of the assignment box in Figure 8.37(b), and for comparison purposes we set a goal of eight states for the complete schedule, as this was the schedule length that we obtained with RC scheduling using one AU and two shift units. In our first step we create ASAP and ALAP schedules, as shown in Figure 8.42(a) and (b).

From these schedules we can compute mobility ranges, concluding that the mobility range for all the operators except $\gg 1$ and min would be 2. In other words, the probability of each of these operators being scheduled in any particular state in its range would be 0.5. Since the operators min and $\gg 1$ each have a range of three states, the probability of their being scheduled in any particular states within that range would be 0.33. These individual probabilities are combined in Figure 8.43(a) into two distribution graphs that we use for minimizing the number of AUs and shift units.

As you can see from the distribution graphs for AUs and shift units, scheduling any operation into a particular state increases the probability sum in that state, and therefore the number of units required except in state s_7, where the probability sum is only 0.5. Therefore, we schedule the *max* operator in state s_7, which increases the probability sum to 1.0. For the same reason we schedule + in state s_6 and − in state s_5. At this point we have the option of scheduling *max* or *min* in state s_3. As you

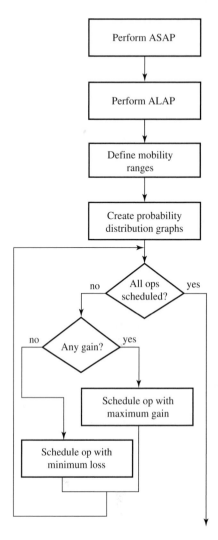

FIGURE 8.41
Time-constrained scheduling.

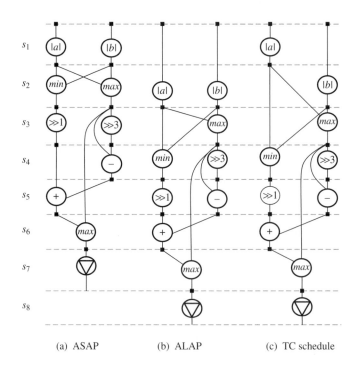

FIGURE 8.42
TC schedule for SRA algorithm.

(a) ASAP   (b) ALAP   (c) TC schedule

can see, however, scheduling *max* there decreases the probability sum in state s_2 to 1.33, while scheduling *min* would decreases the probability sum to 1.5, so we schedule *max* in state s_3 and decrease this probability sum as much as possible. Once *max* has been scheduled in state s_3 we have to schedule $\gg 3$ into state s_4 since $\gg 3$ has to use the result of the *max* operation as its input. In Figure 8.43(b) you can see the distribution graphs that correspond to the partial schedule that we have developed by this point in the algorithm. Using the same criteria as before, we then schedule the *min* operation into state s_4 and $\gg 1$ into state s_5, producing the distribution graph shown in Figure 8.43(c).

As you can see, when we try to schedule either |a| or |b| we have to increase the probability sum of either s_1 or s_2, but this increase is only temporary, since when both have been scheduled, the probability sum in each state equals 1.0 for the AU as well as for the shifter unit. In other words, we have shown that the CDFG from Figure 8.37(b) can be scheduled into nine states using only one AU and one shift unit, although we will eventually use two separate shifters instead of one shift unit, since their cost and delay is equal to zero.

Although in this case, the TC algorithm has produced the same schedule as the RC algorithm, in more complex cases these two algorithms will generally produce different schedules. As a rule we would usually select the algorithm that better matches the primary goal of our

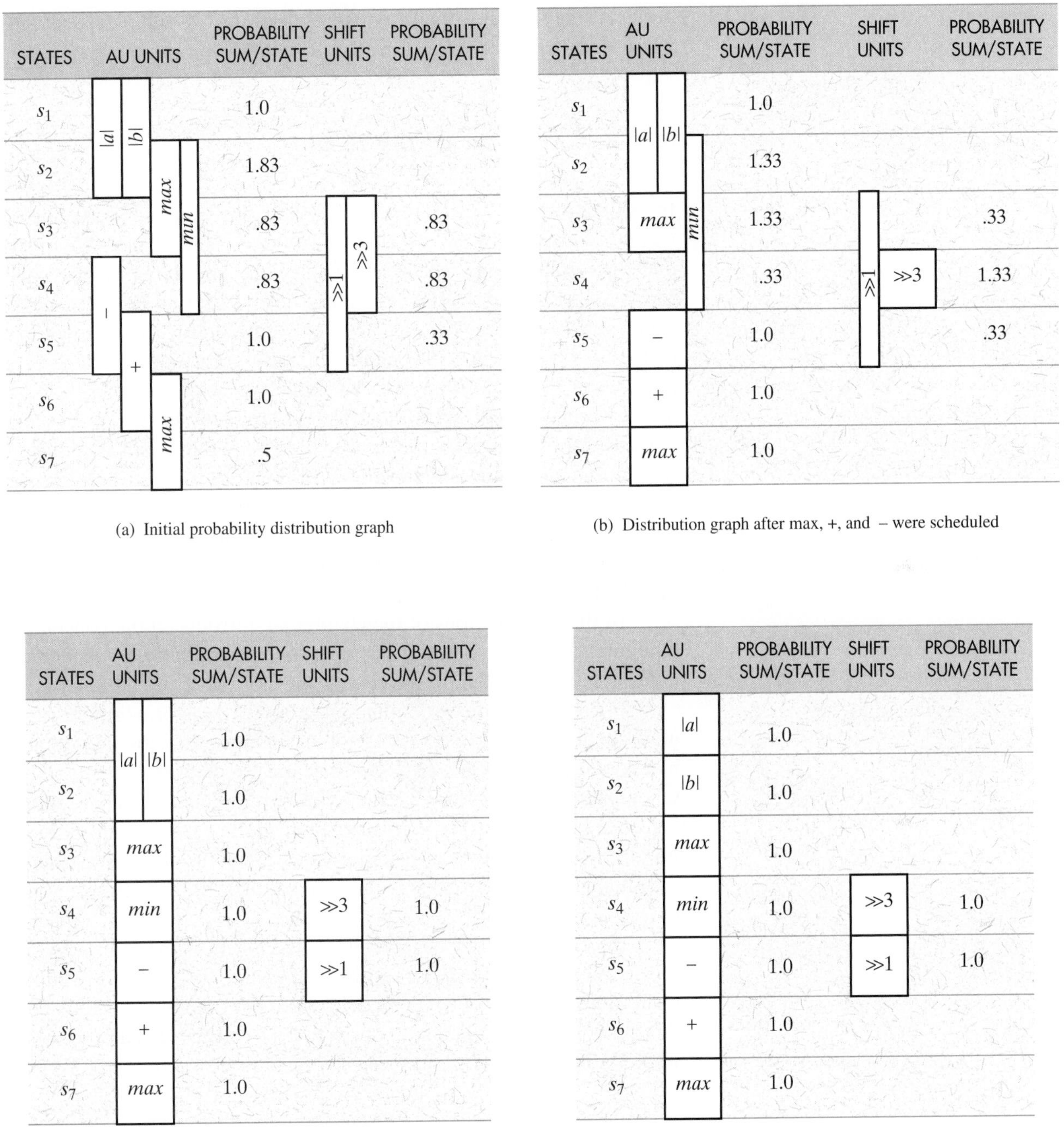

STATES	AU UNITS		PROBABILITY SUM/STATE	SHIFT UNITS	PROBABILITY SUM/STATE
s_1	|a|	|b|	1.0		
s_2			1.83		
s_3	*max*	*min*	.83		.83
s_4			.83	|<<	>>3	.83
s_5			1.0		.33
s_6		+	1.0		
s_7	*max*		.5		

(a) Initial probability distribution graph

STATES	AU UNITS		PROBABILITY SUM/STATE	SHIFT UNITS	PROBABILITY SUM/STATE
s_1	|a|	|b|	1.0		
s_2			1.33		
s_3	*max*	*min*	1.33		.33
s_4			.33	|<<	>>3	1.33
s_5	−		1.0		.33
s_6	+		1.0		
s_7	*max*		1.0		

(b) Distribution graph after max, +, and − were scheduled

STATES	AU UNITS		PROBABILITY SUM/STATE	SHIFT UNITS	PROBABILITY SUM/STATE
s_1	|a|	|b|	1.0		
s_2			1.0		
s_3	*max*		1.0		
s_4	*min*		1.0	>>3	1.0
s_5	−		1.0	>>1	1.0
s_6	+		1.0		
s_7	*max*		1.0		

(c) Distribution graph after max, min, +, −, >>3, and >>1 were scheduled

STATES	AU UNITS	PROBABILITY SUM/STATE	SHIFT UNITS	PROBABILITY SUM/STATE
s_1	|a|	1.0		
s_2	|b|	1.0		
s_3	*max*	1.0		
s_4	*min*	1.0	>>3	1.0
s_5	−	1.0	>>1	1.0
s_6	+	1.0		
s_7	*max*	1.0		

(d) Distribution graph for final schedule

FIGURE 8.43

Probability distribution graph before, during, and after TC scheduling.

design, using RC scheduling to satisfy cost constraints and TC scheduling when we need to satisfy performance constraints.

8.14 CHAPTER SUMMARY

In this chapter we have explained how to specify and generate implementations for arbitrary descriptions given by ASM charts. We introduced a formal design model called an FSMD and then described two forms for specifying ASICs on the register-transfer level, called state-action tables and ASM charts. We also showed how to derive an implementation from an ASM chart. In addition, we described several procedures for optimizing such an implementation, showing how to merge variables and assign them to registers, how to merge registers into register files or memories, how to merge operators and assign them to multifunction units, and how to merge connections and create buses for each group of connections. We also demonstrated how to optimize these implementations for functional units of different speed by chaining fast functional units and multicycling slow units that take more than one clock cycle to produce results.

In the later sections of the chapter we introduced the concept of pipelining and showed how we can improve performance by pipelining either the functional units, the control units or the entire datapaths.

In the last section we demonstrated how to transform ordinary programs or flowcharts into ASM charts by scheduling the assignment statements into specific states. For this purpose we described two types of scheduling algorithms which reflect different optimization goals, showing how to use resource-constrained scheduling to minimize execution time for a given set of resources and how to use time-constrained scheduling to minimize the required resources for a given execution time.

In conclusion, this chapter presented a general methodology for specifying arbitrary behaviors with ASM charts and generating implementations fitting the FSMD model. In the next chapter, we will apply this methodology to the design of specific microchips called processors, whose behavior is described succinctly by their instruction sets.

8.15 FURTHER READINGS

Clare, C. R. *Designing Logic Systems Using State Machines.* New York: McGraw-Hill, 1973.

Introduces algorithmic-state-machine charts and demonstrates the essential steps in the design of different types of FSMDs.

DeMicheli, G. *Synthesis and Optimization of Digital Circuits.* New York: McGraw-Hill, 1994.

Presents a good survey of the results in scheduling and synthesis of ASIC behavioral descriptions.

Gajski, D. D., N. Dutt, A. C-H. Wu, and S. Lin *High-Level Synthesis: Introduction to Chip and System Design.* Boston: Kluwer Academic Publishers, 1992.

Describes models and algorithms for ASM optimization and scheduling. Knowledge of algorithms and data structures is required for reading the material.

8.16 PROBLEMS

8.1 (FSMD model) Determine the minimum clock cycle (rising edge to rising edge) for the FSMD model in Figure 8.2, when it is operating as an:

    (a) State-based FSMD

    (b) Input-based FSMD

Hint: The minimum clock cycle is equal to the longest register-to-register delay. Thus in Figure 8.2 you need to identify the path with the longest delay, usually called the critical path.

8.2 (FSMD description) Rewrite the one's-counter description in Figure 8.1 without using the *Mask* and *Temp* variables. Use the least significant bit of *Data* to increment *Ocount*. The implementation should use the datapath shown in Figure 7.25.

Hint: The least-significant bit is available on the result bus when *Data* has been read from the register file and passed through the ALU and Shifter.

8.3 (FSMD description) Derive an (a) ASM chart and (b) state-action table for the solution in Problem 8.2.

8.4 (ASM charts) Derive an ASM chart description for a decade counter that has three outputs, indicating counts of less than five ($L5$), equal to five ($E5$), and greater than five ($G5$).

8.5 (ASM charts) Derive an ASM chart for a counter that will count modulo 4 whenever the control signal *range* equals 0 and modulo 7 when it is equal to 1.

8.6 (ASM charts) Derive an (a) state-based and (b) input-based ASM chart that can simulate a Black Jack dealer, assuming that the cards are valued 2 through 10 and aces are valued at either 1 or 11. Follow the dealer as he performs the following actions:

    1. Set the *score* to zero and reset the 11-point ace *flag*.

    2. Accept the card and add its value to the *score*.

    3. Add 10 more to the *score* if the card is an ace and the 11-point ace *flag* is reset. Set the 11-point ace *flag*.

    4. Go to 2 if the *score* is 16 or less.

    5. Indicate a *stand* and go to 1 (start a new game) if the *score* is 21 or less.

    6. Subtract 10 from the *score*, reset the *flag*, and go to 4 if the *flag* is set.

    7. Indicate a *broke* and go to 1 (start a new game).

8.7 (ASM charts) Develop an ASM chart for the following:

```
loop
    while x < a do
        x₁ = x + dx
        u₁ = u − 3xudx − 3ydx
        y₁ = y + udx
        x = x₁
        u = u₁
        y = y₁
    end while
```

$$\text{loop}$$
$$\quad \textbf{while } x < a \textbf{ do}$$
$$\qquad x_1 = x + dx$$
$$\qquad u_1 = u - 3xudx - 3ydx$$
$$\qquad y_1 = y + udx$$
$$\qquad x = x_1$$
$$\qquad u = u_1$$
$$\qquad y = y_1$$
$$\quad \textbf{end while}$$

8.8 (ASM charts) Develop an ASM chart for a shift-and-add multiplier that will look at the least-significant bit of the multiplier (MR), add the multiplicand (MD) to the partial product (PP) if the bit is 1, and then shift the partial product and the multiplier one bit position to the right.

8.9 (Library components) Design units that can perform the following operations.

    (a) Absolute value and shift right by three positions

    (b) Absolute value and shift right by one and three positions

    (c) Add and shift right by three positions

    (d) Add and shift right by one and three positions

8.10 (Left-edge algorithm) Assign the variables t_1 through t_8 to the minimum number of registers using the left-edge algorithm. The variable lifetimes are given in Figure P8.10.

	s_0	s_1	s_2	s_3	s_4	s_5	s_6	s_7
t_1	×	×	×	×				
t_2	×	×	×					
t_3			×	×	×	×		
t_4				×	×			
t_5					×	×	×	
t_6					×	×		
t_7						×	×	
t_8							×	×

FIGURE P8.10

8.11 (Graph partitioning) Group the nodes specified by the compatibility graphs shown in Figure P8.11. Assume that weight on a priority edge to a supernode is equal to the sum of the weights on the priority edges to each node in the supernode.

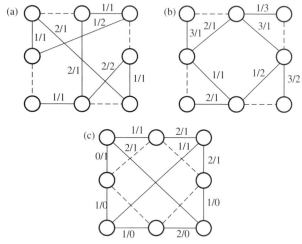

FIGURE P8.11

8.12 (Chaining) Derive an ASM chart for an SRA algorithm in which:
   (a) Any two operators can be chained.
   (b) $+$ and $-$ can be chained, and $\gg$ can be chained with any other operation.
   (c) Any three operations can be chained.

8.13 (Multicycling) Create an ASM chart for an SRA algorithm in which:
   (a) *min, max,* and *absolute-value* operations take two clock cycles.
   (b) *max* takes two clock cycles.
   (c) *min* takes two clock cycles.

8.14 (Unit pipelining) Give an ASM chart and timing diagram for an SRA algorithm with two pipelined units, in which:
   (a) The $[abs/min/max]$ unit has two stages, and the $[+/-/\gg 1/\gg 3]$ unit has three stages.
   (b) The $[min/max/\gg 1/\gg 3]$ unit has two stages, and the $[abs/+/-]$ unit has two stages.
   (c) The $[abs/max/\gg 3/-]$ unit has two stages, and the $[min/+/\gg 1/]$ unit has two stages.

8.15 (Datapath pipelining) Construct a pipelined datapath by dividing a SRA algorithm into (a) three, and (b) four stages. Give timing diagrams for each. What is the performance gain?

8.16 (Control pipelining) Using the one's counter described by the ASM chart in Figure 8.6, derive the timing diagram for a datapath with a pipelined control consisting of:
   (a) A status register
   (b) A control register
   (c) A status and a control register

8.17 (Control pipelining) Derive ASM charts for (a) a state-based and (b) an input-based one's counter with a pipelined control that uses control and status registers.

8.18 (Control design) For the state-based version of the one's counter in Figure 8.9(a), design the control unit using:
   (a) A state register and a decoder
   (b) A counter and a decoder
   (c) A microprogrammed control (also give the ROM content)

8.19 (Control design) Repeat Problem 8.18 for the input-based version of the one's counter given in Figure 8.9(b).

8.20 (Scheduling) Derive (a) the ASAP and (b) the ALAP schedules for the loop body in Problem 8.7.

8.21 (Scheduling) Derive the TC schedule with (a) four states, (b) five states, and (c) six states for the loop body in Problem 8.7.

8.22 (Scheduling) Derive a RC schedule for the loop body in Problem 8.7 given:
   (a) Three multipliers and two adder/subtractors
   (b) Two multipliers and two adder/subtractors
   (c) Two multipliers and one adder/subtractor

(*Hint*: Use a subtractor to compare of two variable values.)

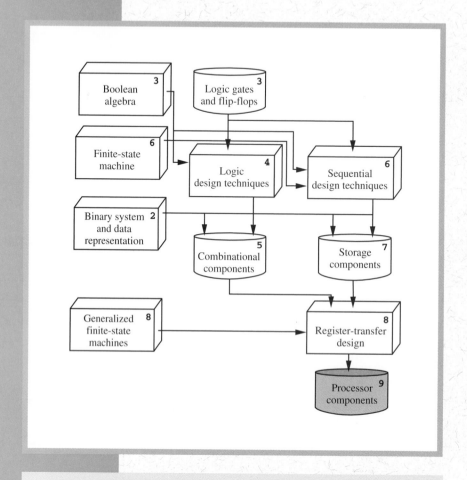

In Chapter 8 we presented techniques for the design of custom processors that can execute arbitrary algorithms. In this chapter we apply these design techniques to the standard general-purpose processors used in all personal computers, engineering workstations, and other computer products. These general-purpose processors execute a specific set of instructions, which means that any software program written in a high-level programming language such as C must be converted into a sequence of instructions from this set. The performance of such software programs depends primarily on the design of the processor and its instruction set. In this chapter we show how to optimize a processor design and its corresponding instruction set for performance.

CHAPTER 9

Processor Design

*I*n Chapter 8, we presented techniques for synthesizing ASICs. In this chapter we focus on the design of general-purpose processors, which, along with memories, and ASICs, are the main components in the majority of computer systems and consumer electronic products. Within such a system, a processor controls the overall system operation, supervising input/output (I/O) devices such as keyboards, disks, tapes, displays, and others, and synchronizes the data communication among the system's various components. In addition, the processor performs most of the computational tasks, with the exception of certain computationally intensive tasks that require performance beyond the processor's capability and must be relegated to application-specific components.

Compared with a processor, an **application-specific integrated circuit** (ASIC) can perform a single task or algorithm very well, but it lacks the generality and programmability that characterizes a processor. Along with processors and ASICs, most computer systems include **main memory**, which stores the data that is needed immediately by the processor or the ASICs. The remainder of the data is stored in **I/O devices** such as disks, CD ROMs, or tapes and is brought to the memory whenever it is needed for computation. These computer components are usually connected into a system with a bus, as shown in Figure 9.1.

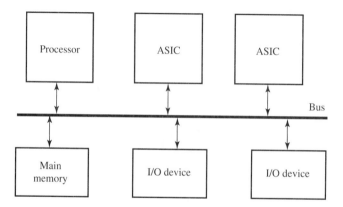

As indicated in Chapter 8, ASICs are specified with behavioral descriptions that are presented in the form of algorithms, programs, or flowcharts. A processor, on the other hand, is specified completely by its **instruction set** (IS), in which each instruction represents the smallest indivisible unit of computation. A sequence of such instructions are needed to compute a mathematical expression or any other computational task. Each task is usually specified in one of the programming languages which can be translated by a **compiler** into such an instruction sequence. Thus an instruction set must be general enough to support efficient compilation from different programming languages, but simple enough to yield a fast and manufacturable processor design.

In this chapter we discuss the relationship between instruction sets and processor design and show how we would design a processor for a given instruction set. We also use some of the techniques presented in Chapter 8 and show how to design a small, 16-bit, complex instruction-set computer (CISC) as well as its counterpart, a reduced instruction-set computer (RISC).

9.1 INSTRUCTION SETS

As mentioned above, a processor is designed to execute a sequence of instructions, called a **program**. Each instruction performs a small amount of computation, such as storing data into the memory, loading data from memory into the processors and I/O devices, performing a single arithmetic, logic, or shift operation, or deciding which instruction to execute next. Each instruction set will have a variety of instructions and instruction formats, which will be interpreted by the processor's control unit and executed in the processor's datapath. The **instruction** itself is a string of bits, which are grouped into different numbers and sizes of substrings or fields.

The fields we encounter most frequently are **operation code** (op-code), which specifies the operation to be performed, and the **address field**, which specifies where we can find the operands needed for that operation. To represent each instruction, we usually use a type of programming notation that first specifies the opcode, followed by the necessary addresses. For example, consider an instruction that would perform $a = b + c$, where a, b, and c are stored in memory at locations A, B, and C, respectively. To represent this instruction, we would write

$$Add\ A, B, C$$

Alternatively, we could represent the same instruction by means of a mathematical notation that is similar to the variable assignment used in programming languages. In this case we write

$$Mem[A] \leftarrow Mem[B] + Mem[C]$$

in which Mem is assumed to be an array and a, b, and c are array elements $Mem[A]$, $Mem[B]$, and $Mem[C]$, in which the symbols in brackets indicate array indices.

It is also possible that variables a, b, and c could be stored in a register file in the datapath, in which case we write

$$Add\ RA, RB, RC$$

to indicate that the addresses RA, RB, and RC are register file addresses. In mathematical notation, the same instruction would be represented with the expression

$$RF[A] \leftarrow RF[B] + RF[C]$$

In addition to the opcode and address fields, in each instruction we frequently find an *instruction-type field*. The most common instruction types are **register instructions**, which operate on values stored in registers, **move instructions**, which move data between the memory and the registers, and **branch instructions**, which select one of the two possible next instructions to be executed on the basis of the datapath status.

Typical register instructions, such as the *Add* instruction discussed above, perform arithmetic, logic, or shift operations on operands stored in the register file. The examples of frequently used move instructions are **load instructions**, such as

$$Load \; R2, A \quad (RF[2] \leftarrow Mem[A])$$

which would load data stored in the memory at location A, into the register $RF[2]$, in the register file, and **store instructions** such as

$$Store \; A, R2 \quad (Mem[A] \leftarrow RF[2])$$

which would store the value in register $RF[2]$ into the memory at location A.

A typical **branch instruction** compares the values in two registers and decides what to do next on the basis of this comparison. For example, a branch-on-equal instruction, *Beq*, determines whether the two values are equal and then decides, if so, to execute the instruction located at the memory address specified in the instruction's address field, or if they are not equal, execute the next instruction in the sequence. Thus the instruction

$$Beq \; R2, R3, A$$

indicates that if the values in $RF[2]$ and $RF[3]$ are equal, the processor should execute the instruction located in $Mem[A]$.

In addition to type fields, an instruction may include a **mode field** that would specify how we are to derive the data's effective address from the information given in the address field. For example, if the mode field indicates that the instruction contains an indirect address, we know that the address field in the instruction specifies a location in memory where we can find the real address of the operand. Consider, for example, the following instruction:

$$Lind \; R2, A \quad (RF[2] \leftarrow Mem[Mem[A]])$$

According to the mode field in the instruction, we will be loading data from memory at the location specified by the value in $Mem[A]$, and not at the address specified by A.

Finally, an instruction can also include a **constant field**, which contains the value of a constant that is to be used as an operand. For example, the instruction

$$Add \; R2, R3, 1 \quad (RF[2] \leftarrow RF[3] + 1)$$

indicates that the processor will add 1 to the value in the third register of the register file and store it into the second register. The constant field can also be used to specify an array index whenever we are accessing array elements.

When defining an instruction set, one of the most important factors to keep in mind is how many address fields its instructions will contain, because the number of address fields strongly affects the program size and the performance of the processor. In other words, the more address fields an instruction has, the longer the instruction width but the shorter the program will be for computing a given task, since it will contain fewer instructions. Conversely, instruction with fewer address fields are shorter but require a longer program to execute a given task. When using longer instructions, the processor makes more memory accesses per instruction for fetching instructions and operands. However, the total number of memory accesses may not be different for shorter instructions, since a program would require more short instructions than longer instructions. If the total number of memory accesses is used as a crude performance measure, we must design the instruction set in such a way that the minimal number of memory accesses is needed in an average program. We demonstrate several options on one simple example.

Let us consider instructions with a different type and number of addresses for computing the expression $c = a^2 - b^2 = (a + b) * (a - b)$. In general, three-address instructions are the most powerful since they can execute a complete variable assignment containing a single binary operation. Specifically, a **three-address instruction** would contain the location of both the operands and the result in addition to specifying the binary operation to be performed. For example, the computation of $(a + b) * (a - b)$ could be specified by the following three hypothetical instructions, in which we assume that variables a, b, c and a temporary variable x are stored in memory at locations A, B, C, and X, respectively:

1. *Add* X, A, B $(Mem[X] \leftarrow Mem[A] + Mem[B])$
2. *Sub* C, A, B $(Mem[C] \leftarrow Mem[A] - Mem[B])$
3. *Mul* C, X, C $(Mem[C] \leftarrow Mem[X] * Mem[C])$

The example above demonstrates a weakness of three-address instructions: Although they are very convenient, they are also very long, by the standards of present-day memory and processor technology. If we assume that memory sizes currently run from 16 to 256 million words, each address would require 24 to 28 bits, and a three-address instruction would require 80 to 90 bits, including the opcode field. If we further assume that such three-address instructions execute on 32-bit processors with 32-bit memory words, each three-address instruction would occupy three words in memory. In other words, a processor would require three memory accesses to fetch the instruction and three more memory accesses to execute it. All together, then, to execute the program above, the processor would have to access memory nine times to fetch instructions, and another nine times to get the operands and store the result.

One strategy that can improve the performance of a program is to reduce the number of addresses from three to two, using **two-address instructions** which assume that the first operand and the result share the same memory location. For example, if we used two-address instructions, the program to compute $c = (a + b) * (a - b)$ would require five instructions, as follows:

1.	Move	X, A	$(Mem[X] \leftarrow Mem[A])$
2.	Add	X, B	$(Mem[X] \leftarrow Mem[X] + Mem[B])$
3.	Move	C, A	$(Mem[C] \leftarrow Mem[A])$
4.	Sub	C, B	$(Mem[C] \leftarrow Mem[C] - Mem[B])$
5.	Mul	C, X	$(Mem[C] \leftarrow Mem[C] * Mem[X])$

Assuming again that each address would require 24 to 28 bits, each of the two-address instructions would now fit into only two memory words, as opposed to three. At the same times, however, we would now need five instructions to compute the same result. In other words, the processor would, in this case, access memory 10 times to fetch instructions, and another 13 times to get the operands and store the results. This being the case, the program above would result in a longer execution time than did the program containing three-address instructions, because we now require two extra *Move* instructions to load the data into the proper locations, for use by subsequent two-address instructions.

We could, however, reduce the number of addresses to one if we created a dedicated register in the datapath, which would store the result of each operation as well as containing one of the operands. Such a register is usually called the **accumulator** (ACC). Using an accumulator in the preceding example, we could compute $c = (a + b) * (a - b)$ with the following seven instructions:

1.	Load A	$(ACC \leftarrow Mem[A])$
2.	Add B	$(ACC \leftarrow ACC + Mem[B])$
3.	Store X	$(Mem[X] \leftarrow ACC)$
4.	Load A	$(ACC \leftarrow Mem[A])$
5.	Sub B	$(ACC \leftarrow ACC - Mem[B])$
6.	Mul X	$(ACC \leftarrow ACC * Mem[X])$
7.	Store C	$(Mem[C] \leftarrow ACC)$

Under the same assumptions as before, each instruction would now require only one memory word, which means that the processor would need to access memory seven times to fetch the instructions and another seven times to get the operands and store the results. Altogether, then, this program would result in a shorter execution time than in any of the previous cases, because the accumlator enables us to hold the operands and results temporarily so that the processor does not have to access memory.

This concept of temporary storage can also be extended to apply to more than one register and thus brings us to a second strategy for improving program performance: We can increase the number of registers in the datapath by introducing a register file. Since this register file will comprise several registers, we would have to include additional address fields for these registers in our instructions. To execute the program above, then, we use two-address instructions, in which one address specifies a particular location within the register file. If, for example, we were using a register file (RF) with three or more registers, we could compute $c = (a + b) * (a - b)$ with the following series of two-address instructions:

1.	*Load R1, A*	$(RF[1] \leftarrow Mem[A])$
2.	*Load R2, B*	$(RF[2] \leftarrow Mem[B])$
3.	*Move R3, R1*	$(RF[3] \leftarrow RF[1])$
4.	*Add R1, R2*	$(RF[1] \leftarrow RF[1] + RF[2])$
5.	*Sub R3, R2*	$(RF[3] \leftarrow RF[3] - RF[2])$
6.	*Mul R1, R3*	$(RF[1] \leftarrow RF[1] * RF[3])$
7.	*Store C, R1*	$(Mem[C] \leftarrow RF[1])$

As you can see from the program above, the processor would still have to access the memory seven times to fetch instructions but would access it only three times to fetch the operands and store the result. Since the processor would have to load the variables a and b and store c in any program, this figure of three memory accesses would be the minimum for computing $c = (a + b) * (a - b)$.

An important feature of this modified program is the fact that only the load and store instructions need to access the memory, while the arithmetic instructions will only access the registers, which have a shorter address field. Because of this modification, we could use three-address instructions for those operations whose operands and result are in the registers, and use two-address instructions for loading the data from the memory to register file and storing it back to the memory. In fact, the majority of the processors on the market today use this strategy, because it yields shorter instructions and a lower frequency of memory accesses. For example, if we used this strategy, we could compute $c = (a+b)*(a-b)$ with only six instructions, as in the following program:

1. *Load R1, A* $(RF[1] \leftarrow Mem[A])$
2. *Load R2, B* $(RF[2] \leftarrow Mem[B])$
3. *Add R3, R1, R2* $(RF[3] \leftarrow RF[1] + RF[2])$
4. *Sub R4, R1, R2* $(RF[4] \leftarrow RF[1] - RF[2])$
5. *Mul R5, R3, R4* $(RF[5] \leftarrow RF[3] * RF[4])$
6. *Store C, R5* $(Mem[C] \leftarrow RF[5])$

Using the preceding program, a processor could execute it by accessing the memory six times to fetch instructions and three times to load and store data. We use this strategy in designing instruction sets in the rest of this chapter.

In the example above, we demonstrated several solutions in satisfying contradictory goals of having the maximum possible number of addresses per instruction to make programs faster. As the last option demonstrates, the comprise is found by using a small register file as a temporary storage, which allows us to use three-address instructions for operations on data in the temporary storage since register file addresses require only a few bits and then use load and store instructions with one memory address to move data between the register file and the main memory. This strategy of dividing the instruction into register and load/store instructions is supported by the fact that each variable in the program is used more than once, and that accessing those variables from a fast register file with short addresses reduces main memory accesses. Since all contemporary commercial processors use this strategy, we also use this strategy in designing instruction sets in the rest of this chapter.

9.2 ADDRESSING MODES

As we described in Section 9.1, while the opcode of an instruction specifies the operation to be performed, it is the address field that contains the information we need to determine the location of the operands and the result of that operation. Within this address field, the addressing mode specifies how to interpret the information given in the address field, showing, in other words, how to compute the **actual** or **effective address** of the data we need. Different types of addressing modes can be used to reduce the size of the address field, allowing us to specify only part of the address while the mode field defines the technique for computing the entire address. In general, we need different addressing modes to support various programming language constructs, data structures, and operating system tasks, such as loops, if statements, array indexing, data pointers, program reallocation, and context switching. Thus the availability of a variety of addressing modes lets a programmer write programs that will be efficient in the number of instructions and the execution time. In the rest of this section we describe the most frequently used addressing modes, which are illustrated in Figure 9.2.

In the **implied addressing mode** shown in Figure 9.2(a), we find that an instruction does not need an explicit addressing field because the location of the operand or the result is specified within the opcode. An instruction that sets or resets a particular register, such as the status register or the accumulator in a datapath, does not need an address field because these registers are unique and therefore implied by the opcode. This kind of implied-mode instruction was commonly used by early stack-organized computers, in which all the operands could always be found on the top of the stack and the result was automatically pushed to the top of the stack.

In the **immediate addressing mode** shown in Figure 9.2(b), it is the operand that is specified in the address field, so we might say that an immediate-mode instruction has an operand field instead of an address field. This operand field is used to specify any constants that are to be used as operands for the operation that is specified by the opcode. This addressing mode is particularly useful when we are incrementing or decrementing loop or array indices, or computing expressions that have many coefficients, since indices and coefficients can be given in the address field instead of being stored in the memory, which in turn saves the processor from making unnecessary memory accesses.

In the **direct addressing mode** shown in Figure 9.2(c), the address field specifies the location of an operand or the result, which may be located in the memory or in the register file. Note that a memory address is much longer than a register address, just because memory sizes currently vary from 16 million words to 256 million words, whereas register file sizes vary from 8 to 128 words, meaning that we need 24 to 28 bits for a memory address instead of only 3 to 7 bits needed for a register address.

In the **indirect addressing mode**, which corresponds to Figure 9.2(d), the address field specifies the location of the address of an operand or the result. Thus the processor has to access the memory twice in memory-indirect mode: once to fetch this address, and again to fetch the operand or store the result. In the register-indirect mode the address field contains the address of the particular register in the register file that contains the operand's or result's address. Thus to use a register-indirect mode instruction, the programmer needs to ensure that the memory address is placed in the proper register before it is accessed. The primary

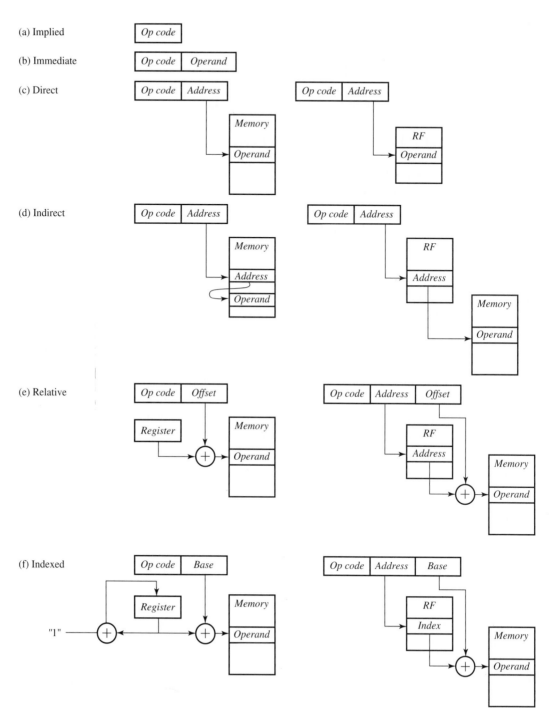

FIGURE 9.2
Addressing modes.

advantage of using this kind of register indirect mode of addressing is that a register address requires fewer bits than is required by a memory address and that register file access is much faster, as discussed in the preceding paragraph.

In the **relative addressing mode** shown in Figure 9.2(e), the content of the address field, frequently called the offset, is added to the content of a specified register, such as the program counter or a register in the register file. This offset is usually a small integer that can be positive or negative. When this integer is added to the content of the program counter, the sum is the address of an instruction in the neighborhood of the next instruction pointed to by the program counter. Consequently, such relative-mode addressing is used in branch instructions, because the branch address is usually in the neighborhood of the branch instruction itself. In addition, relative addressing can also be used with respect to any given register in a register file, as shown on the right in Figure 9.2(e). In this case it is being used to perform table look-ups, in which the register will contain the table origin and the offset will be used to point to a specific element in the table. Relative addressing can also be used for relocating code, in which case the register contains the first instruction and the offset is used to point to the next instruction to be executed. Code relocation allows computers to move programs in the memory, switch from one program to another, and interleave execution of several programs at the same time. The primary advantage of this mode of addressing is that it results in a shorter address field in the instruction format, since the offset usually requires fewer bits than would the entire memory address.

The **indexed addressing mode**, shown in Figure 9.2(f), is generally used when we need to access data that is stored in arrays, stacks, and queues. The address field of the instruction specifies a starting address, called the base, while the index of a particular data is specified in a dedicated index register or in one of the registers in the register file. To compute the effective address, we add the value of the base and index registers. In some instructions, moreover, the value in the index register is then incremented or decremented automatically to access the next element in the array, the stack or the queue. This particular type of instruction, in which the index register is incremented or decremented automatically, is called an **autoincrement** or an **autodecrement** instruction. This indexed addressing also helps to reduces the number of bits needed in the address field, since the base addresses are usually multiples of 2^n which contain $(n-1)$ 0's. Since these $(n-1)$ 0's need not be stored in the address field, the instruction requires fewer bits.

We note that indexed addressing is similar to relative addressing, since the two values contained in the address field and specific register are to be added to obtain the effective address. These two addressing modes differ only in the locations of the base and the index or offset: in relative addressing, the base is in a dedicated register and the offset is located in the address field, whereas in indexed addressing, the base is in the address field and the index is located in a dedicated register. Generally speaking, the availability of various indexing modes in an instruction set makes programs executing on a processor shorter, but it also makes the processor implementation more complex, as we will see in the remainder of this chapter.

9.3 PROCESSOR DESIGN

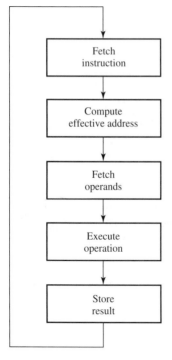

Instruction-execution cycle.

Although any given instruction set can contain a variety of instructions with different addressing fields and modes, every processor nonetheless performs the same five general steps when executing an instruction. These five steps, shown in Figure 9.3, constitute the processor's **instruction-execution cycle**. The cycle begins when the processor fetches an instruction from the memory and loads it into an **instruction register** (IR), which stores the instruction while it is being executed in the processor's datapath. In this first step, the processor also increments the content of another register, called the **program counter** (PC), which stores the address of the next instruction to be executed. In the second step, after the instruction has been fetched, the processor must consider the mode and address fields in the instruction and then determine the effective address of all the operands and the result involved in the computation. In the third step, the processor must fetch these operands from the memory and store them temporarily in a register file or in some other register in the datapath. After the operands have been fetched, the processor will then execute the operation that is specified in the opcode, which constitutes the fourth step of the instruction cycle. Finally, in the fifth step, the processor stores the result of this operation in the memory, or stores it temporarily in the register file for use by subsequent instructions.

Although we can identify all five of these steps in a typical instruction, different instructions require slightly different actions within some of these steps, and some instructions may even skip some of these steps. Therefore, to design a processor, we must first design its instruction set, by specifying the operations taken by each instruction. As indicated in Figure 9.4, instruction-set design is the first step in the design of a processor. Once the instruction set has been defined, we can describe it succinctly with an **instruction-set** (IS) **flowchart**, which describes precisely all the operations that are performed in each instruction. The

IS flowchart is then used as a starting point for allocating components for the datapath that executes all these instructions. However, since the datapath design depends on the instruction set, and the instruction-set design depends on the final datapath, we may repeat the process of instruction-set design, flowcharting, and component allocation several times. Then, once the basic components for the processor datapath have been determined, we can derive the **processor's ASM chart**, which divides each instruction into clock cycles and specifies all the register transfers that take place in each clock cycle. At this point we can easily deduce the datapath connections to complete the datapath design. Finally, the last step in processor design consists of designing the control unit. It is crucial to realize, though, that this sequence of steps will always be somewhat iterative since the design of the instruction set and processor datapath are mutually dependent and we will not know the processor performance until we are finished. We must repeat the entire design process, or some of its steps, several times before a fully satisfactory design can be obtained.

9.4 INSTRUCTION SET DESIGN

When designing an instruction set, we have to consider several different aspects and make trade-offs between programming efficiency and program size on the one hand, and processor cost and performance on the other. The instruction types and formats in an instruction set will always represent a compromise between the program size and the processor size. On one hand, for example, we would like to have a versatile set of powerful instructions with multiple instruction types, addressing fields, addressing modes, and a variety of operations. Such an instruction set, usually called a complex instruction set, makes programs smaller, since fewer instructions are needed for computing each expression or task in a program. However, this kind of complex instruction set also requires a complex datapath, with multiple units, registers, and complex connections for instruction execution. By contrast, a simple instruction set, usually called a reduced instruction set, is easier to implement because it requires fewer datapath components. At the same time, though, its programs are larger since each program requires a longer sequence of these simpler instructions.

   Another aspect to consider when we design instruction sets is the execution time of a typical program. Specifically, we need to keep in mind that programs using complex instructions are shorter, but alternatively, they may not execute any faster than programs using simpler instructions because each complex instruction may take more clock cy-

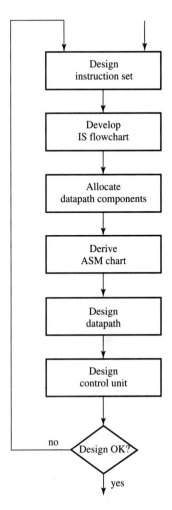

F I G U R E   9.4
Design process.

cles to execute. In most cases, in fact, simple instructions require fewer clock cycles, so the processor is able to execute several simple instructions in the same number of clock cycles that it takes to execute only one complex instruction. In addition, the clock cycle for simple datapaths is usually shorter than for complex datapaths, since the register-to-register delays would be shorter. The shorter clock cycle allows an even larger number of simple instructions to be executed in the same amount of time as one complex instruction.

The third and final aspect to consider in the design of an instruction set is the possibility for pipelining the instruction-execution cycle in order to improve a processor's performance. This pipelining of the instruction-execution cycle is difficult to implement in the case of complex instructions because each step requires a different number of clock cycles for each instruction, so that the instruction-execution pipeline moves at the speed of the slowest step, which is determined by the instruction requiring the greatest number of clock cycles in that step. Simple instructions, however, can be made to execute each step in the instruction cycle in the same number of clock cycles, usually one clock cycle, and thus allow for the pipelined implementation of the datapath.

We demonstrate the differences described in the preceding paragraphs by two examples. In Example 9.1 we design a complex instruction set for a 16-bit processor; in Example 9.5 we convert this complex instruction set into a reduced instruction set for a 32-bit processor.

EXAMPLE 9.1   Complex instruction set

PROBLEM   Design an instruction set for a 16-bit processor.

SOLUTION   A 16-bit processor can access 64K of memory with one word of data. To reduce the number of memory accesses during the instruction fetch, we limit the instruction size to at most two memory words, which means that we can only use one-address instructions when accessing memory. Therefore, each instruction would consist of one or two 16-bit words; the second word, if used, would be a memory address, while the first word would specify the instruction type, the operation code, and the register file addresses. To accommodate three register file addresses, we have to divide the 16-bit instruction into five fields: the *Type* field (2 bits), the *Op* field (5 bits), and three register file addresses identified as *Dest* (3 bits), *Src1* (3 bits), and *Src2* (3 bits).

Several examples of instructions from the instruction set derived from these premises are shown in Figure 9.5. This instruction set includes four different types: register, mem-

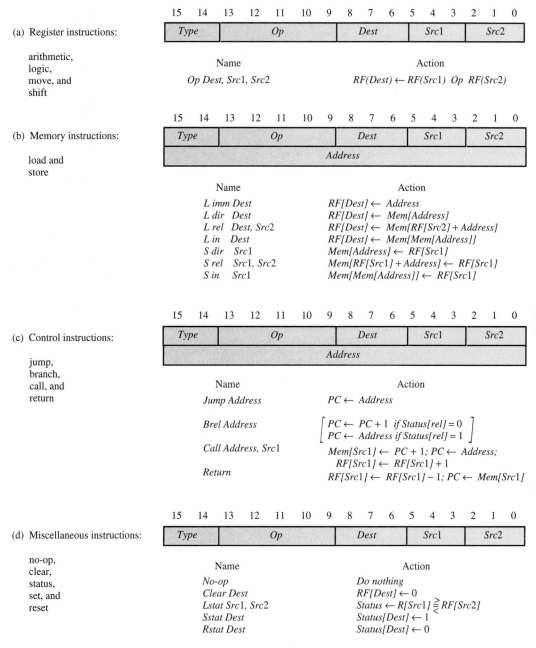

(a) Register instructions:

arithmetic,
logic,
move, and
shift

Name	Action
Op Dest, Src1, Src2	RF(Dest) ← RF(Src1) Op RF(Src2)

(b) Memory instructions:

load and
store

Name	Action
L imm Dest	RF[Dest] ← Address
L dir Dest	RF[Dest] ← Mem[Address]
L rel Dest, Src2	RF[Dest] ← Mem[RF[Src2] + Address]
L in Dest	RF[Dest] ← Mem[Mem[Address]]
S dir Src1	Mem[Address] ← RF[Src1]
S rel Src1, Src2	Mem[RF[Src1] + Address] ← RF[Src1]
S in Src1	Mem[Mem[Address]] ← RF[Src1]

(c) Control instructions:

jump,
branch,
call, and
return

Name	Action
Jump Address	PC ← Address
Brel Address	$\begin{bmatrix} PC \leftarrow PC + 1 & \text{if } Status[rel] = 0 \\ PC \leftarrow Address & \text{if } Status[rel] = 1 \end{bmatrix}$
Call Address, Src1	Mem[Src1] ← PC + 1; PC ← Address; RF[Src1] ← RF[Src1] + 1
Return	RF[Src1] ← RF[Src1] − 1; PC ← Mem[Src1]

(d) Miscellaneous instructions:

no-op,
clear,
status,
set, and
reset

Name	Action
No-op	Do nothing
Clear Dest	RF[Dest] ← 0
Lstat Src1, Src2	Status ← R[Src1] $\gtreqless$ RF[Src2]
Sstat Dest	Status[Dest] ← 1
Rstat Dest	Status[Dest] ← 0

FIGURE 9.5

Instruction set of a 16-bit processor.

ory, control, and miscellaneous instructions. The register
type of instruction, which is shown in Figure 9.5(a), is a one-
word instruction designed to perform an arithmetic, logic,
or shift operation, which is indicated by the opcode, on two

operands, each of which is stored in the registers indicated by the *Src*1 and *Src*2 fields. The result of this operation is returned to the register indicated by the *Dest* field of the instruction.

The memory instructions, shown in Figure 9.5(b), are load and store instructions, which are designed to move data between a given register in the register file and memory. Note that the memory address is specified by the second instruction word, whereas the register address can be specified either by the *Dest* field in the case of load instructions, or by the *Src*1 field in the case of store instructions. Note also that the memory instructions can support four different addressing modes, including immediate, direct, relative, and indirect addressing. In relative mode, the offset is stored in the register indicated by the *Src*2 field of the instruction.

As shown in Figure 9.5(c), control instructions also comprise two words and can specify either jump, branch, subroutine call, or subroutine return instructions. When the processor executes the jump instruction, for example, it loads the *PC* with the jump address specified in the second word of the jump instruction and executes the instruction at the jump address in the next instruction cycle. The branch instruction has the same effect if the appropriate bit in the status register is 1; otherwise, the processor executes the next instruction in sequence. The six **relation bits** correspond to the six relational operations: equal, greater than, greater than or equal to, less than, less than or equal to, and not equal. These bits are set or reset by miscellaneous instructions after comparing the contents of two registers.

When the processor executes a call instruction, it jumps to the subroutine whose first instruction is at the location that is specified by the address field. In addition, it also increments and stores the value of the *PC*, pushing it on top of the stack whose address is in the stack pointer indicated by the *Src*1 field. As you would expect, the call instruction will also increment the value in the stack pointer. By contrast, the return instruction is the opposite of the call instruction—it loads the return address back into the *PC* and decrements the stack pointer that is stored in the register indicated by the *Src*1 field.

Finally, miscellaneous instructions, which are shown in Figure 9.5(d), include the *No-op* instruction as well as those instructions necessary for setting and resetting particular registers in the datapath. The most important instruction in this group is the *Lstat* instruction, which is designed to compare the values in the registers indicated by the *Src*1 and *Src*2 fields and to set the six relational bits in the status register accordingly. As mentioned earlier, each branch instruction tests a specific bit after it has been set by the *Lstat* instruction.

9.5 CISC DESIGN

As mentioned before, an instruction set, defined in Section 9.4, completely specifies the behavior of a processor, and in this sense, it can be thought of as a behavioral description of that processor. One of the frequently used forms for representing such a behavior is an **instruction set (IS) flowchart**, which describes the execution cycles of all instructions. We should note that the IS flowchart specifies nothing but the behavior of the processor and that no architectural details are implied beyond the existence of a memory (*Mem*), a register file (*RF*), a program counter (*PC*), an instruction register (*IR*), and a status register (*Status*). We demonstrate the construction of an IS flowchart in the following example.

EXAMPLE 9.2 Instruction-set flowchart

PROBLEM Derive an instruction-set flowchart for the instruction set presented in Figure 9.5.

SOLUTION As mentioned above, an instruction-set flowchart does not presume any architectural details or any particular processor datapath. Furthermore, it does not consider any timing constraints or clock cycle duration. The sole purpose of the flowchart is to give the order in which the operations specified by each instruction will be executed.

In Figure 9.6 we have presented the instruction-set flowchart for the instruction set given in Figure 9.5. Note that each instruction has been specified in two parts. In the first part, which applies to all instructions, the processor fetches the instruction into the *IR* and increments the *PC*. In the second part, the processor decodes the type field to determine the instruction type and then executes the instruction by computing an effective address (EA), performing the operation specified by the opcode, and incrementing the *PC* in the case of memory and control instructions.

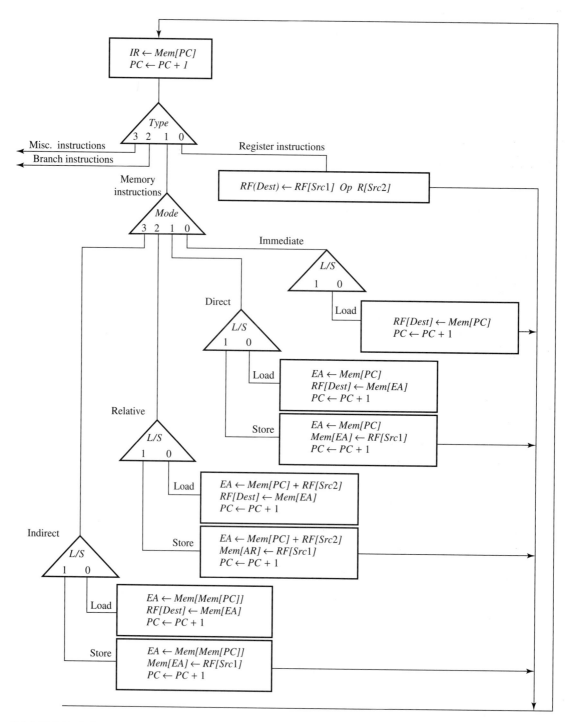

Instruction-set flowchart.

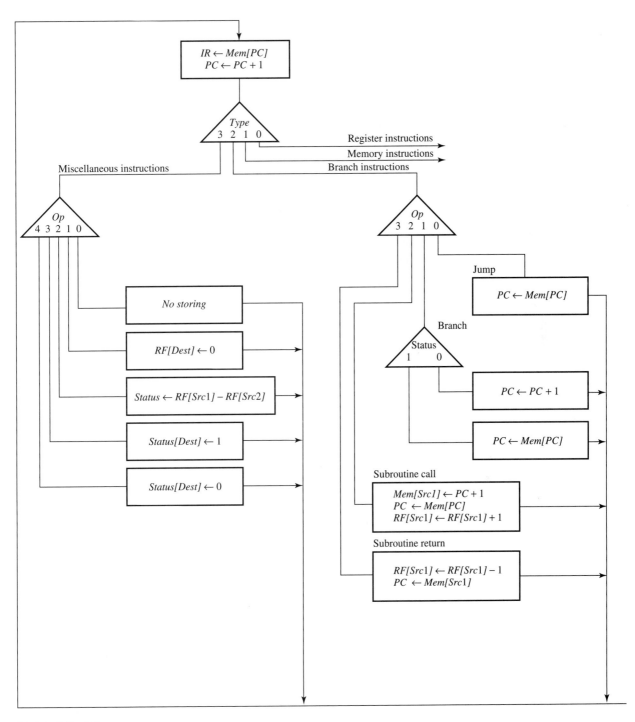

FIGURE 9.6
Continued.

Once we have developed an IS flowchart, the next step in designing a processor is to allocate its main components by selecting the proper number and type of functional units to be included in its datapath. For a single processor we need to include at least one ALU with the ability to shift data one position to the right or left (ALSU). For high-performance processors, however, we might want to add a barrel shifter, a multiplier, and a floating-point adder/subtractor and multiplier/divider. In the latter case, we may also include a separate unit for computing the effective address.

At this allocation stage, we also have to determine how many memories are necessary and how they might best be organized. Then we have to determine how many buses are necessary, including their bit width and the appropriate protocol to be used. Furthermore, we need to select an interface implementation that will allow communication with the memory and other ASICs. Finally, we consider adding several special-purpose registers, such as stack pointers, base registers, loop counters, and interface registers, which can simplify the movement of data and improve the performance of a processor. The allocation step is demonstrated in the following example.

EXAMPLE 9.3 Component allocation for a 16-bit processor

PROBLEM Allocate the datapath components for the instruction set given in Figures 9.5 and 9.6.

SOLUTION During the instruction set design, we assumed the existence of a 64K memory *Mem*, an 8-register register file *RF*, and the special-purpose registers *PC*, *IR*, and *Status*. If our only goal is to have a low-cost processor, we might not add any extra components to this basic set.

However, if we are to take performance into account, we can improve the efficiency of this processor by adding two more registers. In this processor, the memory will be the slowest component, so we do not want to chain the memory access with an operation in any other component, as this requires long clock cycles. For this reason we must add an address register (*AR*) and a data register (*DR*), as shown in Figure 9.7. With the addition of these registers, we are able to compute the effective address in one clock cycle, storing it in the *AR*, and then to fetch the corresponding operand in a second clock cycle during execution of a load instruction. Similarly, we can load the effective address into the *AR* and its corresponding data into the *DR* in one clock cycle, and then store the data into the memory in the next clock cycle during execution of a store instruction. Thus, by adding these two registers, we shorten the required clock period and improve the performance of the processor.

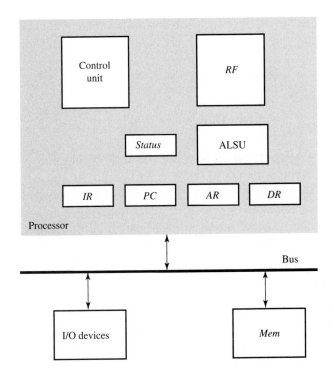

FIGURE 9.7
Component allocation for the 16-bit processor.

After deciding which components will be included in the datapath, the next step in designing a processor is the development of an ASM chart based on the information present in the IS flowchart. For this task we could use the scheduling methods presented in Section 8.14. On the other hand, we might also schedule the flowchart manually, since each instruction cycle in the IS chart is described with very few assignment statements.

During manual scheduling, it is crucial that we detect any data and resource conflicts and make sure that we resolve them by assigning any conflicting operations or data transfers to different states or different clock cycles. For example, it is possible to read an old value from some register and write a new value into that register during the same clock cycle, since register reads can occur any time in the clock cycle after the rising edge of the clock signal, whereas writing occurs only at the end of the clock cycle on the next rising edge of the clock signal. However, it is not possible to write a value into a register and read a new value from that register in the same clock cycle, since writing can occur only at the end of each clock cycle. Similarly, within a single cycle, we can either read or write into a given memory location, but we cannot do both, since the memory has only one address decoder. By the same token, we can use each functional unit or bus only once in each clock cycle. By following these guidelines properly, we should find the process of converting the instruction flowchart into an ASM chart to be relatively straightforward one.

■ **EXAMPLE 9.4**   Processor ASM chart

PROBLEM   Develop an ASM chart from the IS flowchart given in Figure 9.6.

SOLUTION   The ASM chart is shown in Figure 9.8. Note that it is similar to the flowchart except for the fact that the instruction execution has been broken into several clock cycles to eliminate resource dependencies.

As shown in Figure 9.8, register instructions execute in two clock cycles. In the first clock cycle, the processor fetches the instruction and stores it in the IR, while in the second clock cycle it performs the operation specified in the opcode field.

The memory instructions require three or four clock cycles. Consider, for example, the load-indirect instruction Lin, which requires four clock cycles to execute. In the first clock cycle, the processor fetches the first instruction word and stores it in the IR, whereas in the second clock cycle, it fetches the second instruction word and loads it in the AR. Then, in the third clock cycle, it fetches the real data address and loads it into the AR. Finally, in the fourth clock cycle, the processor fetches the data from the memory and loads it into the RF.

The control instructions take two or three clock cycles to execute. For example, a branch instruction would take two clock cycles. In the first clock cycle, the processor fetches the instruction, and in the second clock cycle it tests the specific status bit and increments the PC if the status bit is equal to 0, or loads the second instruction word into the PC if the status bit is equal to 1.

Similarly, the miscellaneous instruction takes two clock cycles to execute. In the first clock cycle, the instruction is fetched as usual, whereas the second clock cycle is used to set

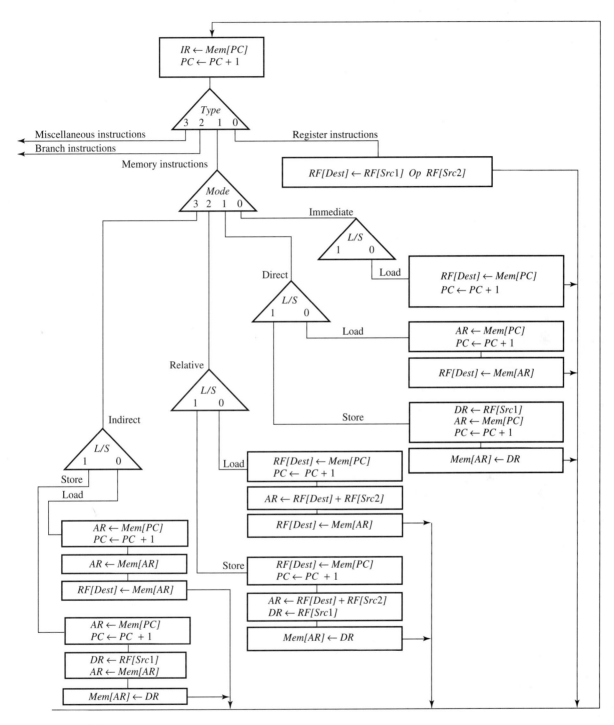

F I G U R E   9.8
ASM chart for the 16-bit processor.

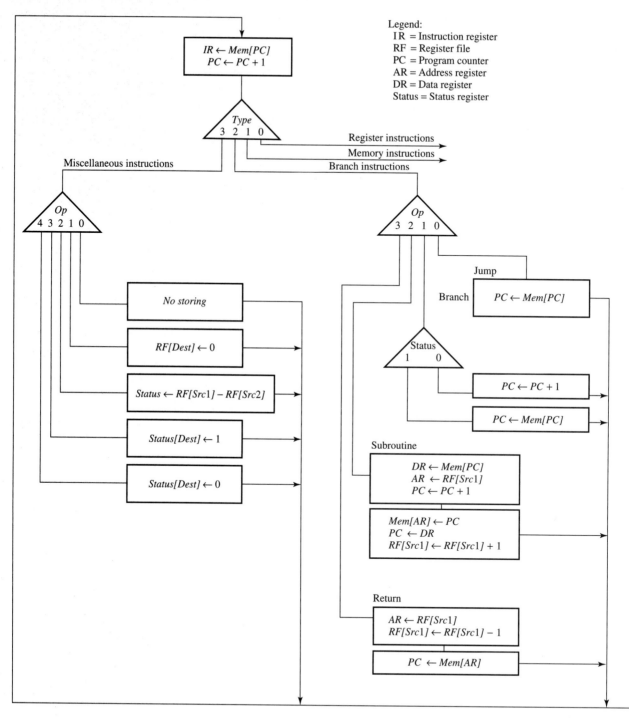

FIGURE 9.8
Continued.

a particular register or a bit in that register. As an example, let us consider the *Lstat* instruction. In the second clock cycle, the processor compares two values that are stored in the *RF* by first subtracting one of the values from the other and then setting the six status bits in the status register accordingly. For example, if the value in *RF*[*Src1*] is greater than the value in *RF*[*Src2*], the *Lstat* instruction will set the bits, which correspond to the relations greater than, greater than or equal to, and not equal, to 1 and all the remaining bits, which represent less than, less than or equal to, and equal relations, to 0.

In conclusion, we can see from the ASM chart that the processor requires two to four clock cycles to execute any instruction. Furthermore, we can easily derive the datapath and control unit from this ASM chart, as demonstrated in Chapter 8.

Once we have developed an ASM chart, the final step in designing a processor is to interconnect all its resources by inserting selectors and bus drivers as necessary and deriving the control logic for the control unit. Figure 9.9 shows a completed processor schematic based on the ASM chart presented in Figure 9.8. It was obtained by adding the necessary connections to allow execution of each assignment statement in the ASM chart.

For this purpose, we added data, address, and control buses. The data bus is used for moving data between memory and other registers in the processor. It is used to load data from memory into the *IR*, *PC*, *AR*, *DR*, and the register file. It is also used to store data from the *PC* or *DR* into memory. The specific memory address for storing and loading data to memory is supplied from the *PC* or *AR* through the address bus. The control bus contains control signals for controlling the memory. Note that we assume in this design and the ASM chart of Figure 9.8 that memory load or store will take only one clock cycle. If memory access time is longer than one clock cycle, the ASM chart has to be adjusted but the basic design in Figure 9.9 will not change, except that it will take two or more clock cycles to store data from the *DR* into memory or load data from memory into the *DR*.

In addition to three buses, we also added connections from the *ALSU* to the *PC*, *AR*, *DR*, and the register file as well as connections from the *ALSU* to the status register and status register and *IR* to the control logic, which generates control signals for the operation of the *ALSU*, all registers, register file, and memory.

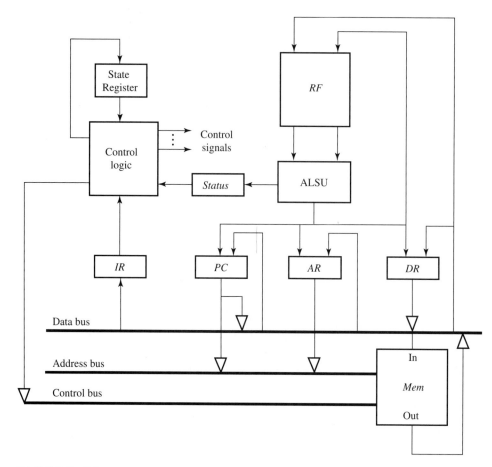

FIGURE 9.9
Processor schematic.

Note that the control unit shown in this schematic contains a state register and control logic and that it can be implemented using any of the control styles shown in Figure 7.34(a), (b), or (c). The most natural style would be to implement the state register as a modulo n counter, where n represents the maximal number of states on any path that we might take through the ASM chart. For the 16-bit processor we can see from the ASM chart shown in Figure 9.8 that we would need no more than four states on any path, including the state for the instruction fetch. Therefore, we can assume that the state register in Figure 9.9 would be a modulo-4 counter, which is capable of returning to state 0 from states 1, 2, and 3, depending on the instruction being executed.

The control logic can be specified by using one sum-of-products Boolean expression for each control line. In turn, each control expression contains one product term for each state and for each instruction in which that particular control line is activated. Thus, each product term consists of bits defining the instruction type, the instruction opcode, and the processor state. Since the derivation of these control expressions is straightforward, we have left it as an exercise for the reader at the end of the chapter.

9.6 REDUCED INSTRUCTION SET

In Section 9.5 we designed a complex instruction set processor (CISC), in which the instructions required a different number of memory words and a different number of clock cycles for their execution. To increase the performance of this processor, we could use either one of the following strategies:

1. Faster technology, which would allow us to shorten the clock cycle
2. A redesigned instruction set, which would make it possible to pipeline the instruction cycle.

As you might expect, the first strategy does not call for any conceptual changes but requires only a tighter logic design and a more compact physical design. The second strategy, however, requires that the instruction-execution cycle be redefined, by dividing the entire cycle into a set of stages of equal length and ensuring that each instruction goes through each stage at the same speed so that an uninterrupted instruction stream is maintained during execution of a program.

When we try to divide the instruction cycle shown in Figure 9.3, we observe that although it consists of five different steps, none of the instructions in Figure 9.5 call for effective address computation as well as ALSU operations. Specifically, memory and control instructions both require effective address computation, but neither performs any ALSU operations on any operands. On the other hand, neither register nor the miscellaneous instructions need effective address computation, but they do perform an ALSU operation as specified in the opcode field. On the basis of this observation, it makes sense to combine the effective address computation and the execution of the ALSU operation into a single stage. Furthermore, if both share a single stage, we can use the same ALSU to perform both tasks. As you can see in Figure 9.10(a), by combining these two tasks into one, we obtain an instruction-execution cycle, which could easily be executed by a pipelined datapath with four stages.

Such a pipelined execution is shown in the timing diagram in Figure 9.10(b), in which each row represents one stage of the instruction pipeline and each column represents a clock cycle. We see that each

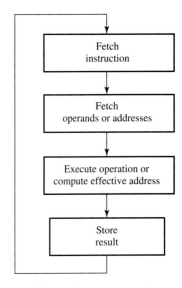

(a) Instruction-execution cycle

Clock cycle	0	1	2	3	4	5
Fetch instruction	I_1	I_2	I_3	I_4	I_5	I_6
Fetch operands or addresses		I_1	I_2	I_3	I_4	I_5
Execute operation or compute effective address			I_1	I_2	I_3	I_4
Store result				I_1	I_2	I_3

(b) Pipelined execution

FIGURE 9.10

Reduced instruction-set cycle.

instruction requires four clock cycles to execute. For example, instruction I_1 is fetched from memory in cycle 0, an operand or address fetch is performed in cycle 1, an operand or effective address is computed in cycle 2, and the result is stored in cycle 3. Instruction I_2 follows the same sequence with a one clock cycle delay, as do instructions I_3, I_4, and so on. Since four instructions are executed concurrently in four different stages of the instruction-execution cycle pipeline, we can expect a fourfold increase in performance from this four-stage pipeline, assuming that one instruction can be started in every clock cycle. On the other hand, when one instruction needs data generated by the previous instruction, we must delay the start of this instruction by three clock cycles until the required data are stored in the memory. This interrupt in the pipeline execution is called the pipeline stall. To minimize the number of pipeline stalls, we can reorder instruction so that no instruction requires data from any of the previous three instructions. When this is not possible, we must insert no-op instructions in the instruction sequence to secure proper operation.

In order to use a pipelined instruction execution, we also need to redesign the instruction set in such a way that all instructions are alike and each instruction consumes approximately the same amount of time in each stage. We have to ensure, in other words, that each instruction contains the same type and number of instruction fields. To satisfy this requirement, however, we need to extend the processor width to 32 or more bits and limit its addressing modes, using only the immediate and relative modes, which require fewer bits in the instruction words than do direct or indirect addresses. In addition, you will recall that the indirect addressing mode automatically violates the second requirement—that all instructions take the same amount of time in each stage. For these reasons, other addressing modes have to be implemented by a sequence of available instructions. In the following example, we demonstrate the design of this reduced instruction set.

▌ **EXAMPLE 9.5** Reduced instruction set

PROBLEM Design a reduced instruction set for a 32-bit processor using the pipelined instruction-execution cycle shown in Figure 9.10.

SOLUTION Since we are to use 32-bit instructions instead of 16-bit instructions, we can solve the problem by extending the 16-bit format presented in Figure 9.5 with a 16-bit offset field that can also hold the immediate operands for the register instructions. In Figure 9.11 we have illustrated this extension. Presently each instruction has two 16-bit parts. As you can

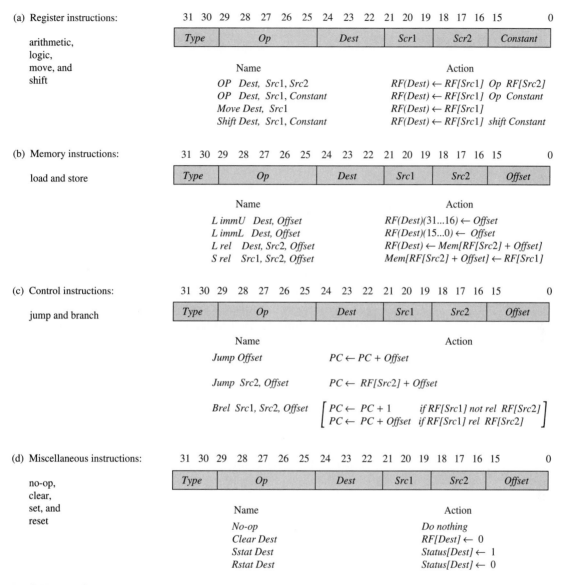

(a) Register instructions:

arithmetic, logic, move, and shift

31 30	29 28 27 26 25	24 23 22	21 20 19	18 17 16	15 0
Type	Op	Dest	Scr1	Scr2	Constant

Name	Action
OP Dest, Src1, Src2	RF(Dest) ← RF[Src1] Op RF[Src2]
OP Dest, Src1, Constant	RF(Dest) ← RF[Src1] Op Constant
Move Dest, Src1	RF(Dest) ← RF[Src1]
Shift Dest, Src1, Constant	RF(Dest) ← RF[Src1] shift Constant

(b) Memory instructions:

load and store

31 30	29 28 27 26 25	24 23 22	21 20 19	18 17 16	15 0
Type	Op	Dest	Src1	Src2	Offset

Name	Action
L immU Dest, Offset	RF(Dest)(31...16) ← Offset
L immL Dest, Offset	RF(Dest)(15...0) ← Offset
L rel Dest, Src2, Offset	RF(Dest) ← Mem[RF[Src2] + Offset]
S rel Src1, Src2, Offset	Mem[RF[Src2] + Offset] ← RF[Src1]

(c) Control instructions:

jump and branch

31 30	29 28 27 26 25	24 23 22	21 20 19	18 17 16	15 0
Type	Op	Dest	Src1	Src2	Offset

Name	Action
Jump Offset	PC ← PC + Offset
Jump Src2, Offset	PC ← RF[Src2] + Offset
Brel Src1, Src2, Offset	$\begin{bmatrix} PC \leftarrow PC + 1 & \text{if } RF[Src1] \text{ not rel } RF[Src2] \\ PC \leftarrow PC + Offset & \text{if } RF[Src1] \text{ rel } RF[Src2] \end{bmatrix}$

(d) Miscellaneous instructions:

no-op, clear, set, and reset

31 30	29 28 27 26 25	24 23 22	21 20 19	18 17 16	15 0
Type	Op	Dest	Src1	Src2	Offset

Name	Action
No-op	Do nothing
Clear Dest	RF[Dest] ← 0
Sstat Dest	Status[Dest] ← 1
Rstat Dest	Status[Dest] ← 0

FIGURE 9.11
Reduced instruction set.

see, the least-significant 16 bits contain the constant that will be used as an operand or an address offset, and the most-significant 16 bits contain a 2-bit instruction type field, a 5-bit opcode, a 3-bit result-register address (*Dest*), and two 3-bit operand-register addresses (*Src1* and *Src2*).

Note that this instruction set has the same four instruction types as the CISC instruction set in Figure 9.5. The register instructions shown in Figure 9.11(a) perform various operations on the operands stored in an 8-register register file and then return the result to a register in the same register file. Each instruction may use the value in the constant field as one of the operands.

The memory instructions, which are shown in Figure 9.11(b), load the memory values into the register file and store register values in memory. In this set of instructions, the main addressing mode is the relative mode wherein the base address can be found in the register whose address is indicated by the *Src2* field, and the offset is indicated by the *Offset* field. Since this *Offset* field is only 16 bits, we are able to address any of the 64K memory locations around the base address. When we need to switch the base, we have to use two different load instructions, which load the upper and lower 16 bits of the new base into a register in the register file. Specifically, the instruction *LimmU* is used to load the value in the offset field into the upper 16 bits of the register indicated by the *Dest* field, and the instruction *LimmL* is used to load the lower 16 bits of that register.

The control instructions are presented in Figure 9.11(c), which shows both jump and branch instructions. The jump instructions can transfer control to a location that is relative to the *PC* or to any other base indicated in the *Src2* field. Similarly, the branch instructions can transfer control to a location relative to the *PC*. In reality, there are six possible branch instructions in the instruction set: *Beq*, *Bgre*, *Bgoeq*, *Bless*, *Bloeq*, and *Bneq*, which are denoted in this figure by *Brel*. Each branch instruction compares the values in the registers indicated in the *Src1* and *Src2* fields and then, if the specific relationship holds, branches to the memory location that is obtained by adding the value in the *Offset* field to the present value of the *PC*. If, however, this relationship does not hold, the processor executes the next instruction. As before, the miscellaneous instructions, shown in Figure 9.11(d), are used to initialize different registers and perform certain specialized functions.

9.7 RISC DESIGN

In general, the design flow for a reduced instruction set processor (RISC) follows the flow presented in Figure 9.4, the primary difference being the fact that in this case, the datapath and control are pipelined. By using this pipelining technique, however, we introduce the following changes in the processor's architecture:

1. Separation of instruction and data memories
2. Addition of a control register in each stage, instead of a single control unit
3. Pipeline flushing for the control instructions

The separation of instruction and data memories is necessary if we are to keep the instruction pipeline full by executing one instruction in every clock cycle. In other words, the processor must be able to fetch one instruction each clock cycle. However, since some of these instructions will also need to access the memory in order to load or store data, we need separate instruction and data memories to allow concurrent instruction fetch and data fetch or store.

The incorporation of a control register in each stage is a natural result of a pipelined instruction execution, simply because in such a cycle, each pipelined stage executes a different instruction, so we have to divide the control unit into four control units. Each control unit has only one state in which it receives a decoded instruction, or a part of one, from the previous stage, then uses some portion of the supplied instruction to control the execution in its own stage, and then passes the unused portion of the instruction to the control unit in the next stage. In other words, the control unit is reduced to a series of control registers and small decode logic in the second stage.

The final change in the processor's structure results from its pipelined execution. Whenever a jump or branch instruction is encountered, the processor must wait for several clock cycles to determine where to jump or whether to branch at all. Therefore, no instructions should be issued during those clock cycles, or if they are issued, they must be discarded if the branch is taken. This process, called **pipeline stalling**, is explained in greater detail in later sections.

■ **EXAMPLE** *9.6*   RISC processor design

PROBLEM   Design a 32-bit processor for the instruction set given in Figure 9.11.

SOLUTION   In solving this problem we can follow the same design procedure as before, beginning by constructing a flow-chart, allocating datapath resources, and deriving an ASM chart for the processor. At this point, we omit these steps since they are very similar to those outlined in the 16-bit processor presented earlier. The only significant difference lies in the ASM chart, in that in this case, each instruction takes exactly four clock cycles to execute. From this revised ASM chart we can derive the RISC schematic shown in Figure 9.12, in which the connections indicated by dotted lines are discussed in Section 9.8.

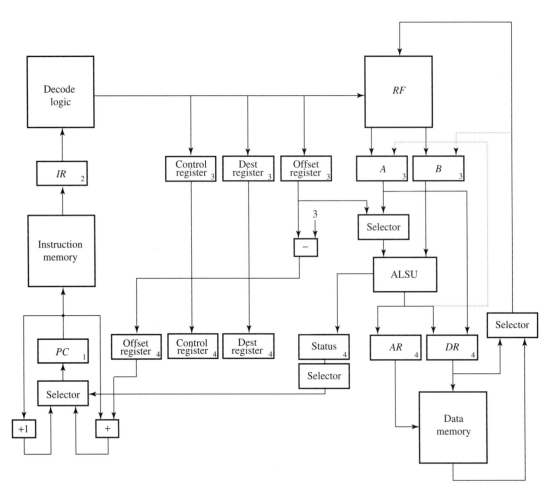

RISC schematic.

In this schematic you can see that this 32-bit processor has an *IR*, a *PC*, an *AR*, a *DR*, a *Status* register, and a *RF*, as did the 16-bit processor. Unlike the 16-bit processor, however, it also has an instruction and a data memory. We have also added two registers, *A* and *B*, which will store the operands after they have been read from the register file and before we input them to the ALSU. This processor also has a control register, a destination register, and an offset register between the second and third and between the third and fourth pipeline stages. These additional registers contain the destination register address, the offset amount for the computation of the effective address, and the values of the control signals for the third and fourth pipeline stages.

In operation, the processor in Figure 9.12 executes each instruction in four steps, which correspond to its four pipeline stages. Each pipeline stage takes data from one set of registers and delivers its results into the next set of registers. In this figure the input register(s) for each stage is(are) identified by its(their) stage number in the lower right corner of the register symbol. By following these stage indicators, you can see that in the first stage, the content of the *PC* is used to address the instruction memory, and a new instruction is then stored in the *IR*. The *PC* is also incremented in this stage.

In the second stage, the instruction in the *IR* is first decoded by the decode logic and then its two operands are fetched from the *RF* and stored in registers *A* and *B*. In addition, the values from the *Dest* and *Offset* fields of the instruction are copied to the destination register and offset register for later use. Similarly, the part of the decoded opcode that will be used for control in the third and fourth pipeline stages is stored in the control register.

The third stage of the pipeline performs various operations for different instruction types. In the case of register instructions, for example, it performs the operation specified in the opcode, using the operands in registers *A* and *B*, and then stores the result in the *DR*. In the case of memory instructions, the third stage adds the base value in register *B* to the offset value in the offset register and stores the effective address in the *AR*. In addition, if the memory instruction is a store instruction, this stage transfers the data to be stored from register *A* to the *DR*. In the case of a control instruction, the third stage subtracts the constant 3 from the offset value since the *PC* will be incremented three times before the jump or branch addresses are computed in the fourth pipeline stage.

Finally, the fourth stage of the pipeline either reads the data from the data memory and stores it in the *RF* in the register whose address is in the destination register or stores the data from the *DR* in data memory. At the same time, the fourth stage also computes the jump or branch addresses, by adding the values in the *PC* and the offset register. In addition, this stage increments the *PC* and loads it with the branch address, depending on the value of the particular bit in the status register. The proper status bit is selected through a selector that is controlled by the value in the control register, which was initially derived from the instruction opcode.

To demonstrate the workings of this RISC processor, we now show its cycle-by-cycle operation on a sequence of three instructions:

$$x = a + b$$
$$y = b - c$$
$$z = c + d$$

In Figure 9.13(a) we show the symbolic assembly language for the program above. For the sake of simplicity we have used the symbols $a, b, c, d, x, y, z, base$, and *off* to replace real addresses. In Figure 9.13(b) we show a cycle-level timing diagram, which has been divided horizontally into four pipelined stages and vertically into a series of clock cycles or states. In this design each vertical line indicates the rising edge of the clock signal, which causes the loading of data into the processor's registers and the register file. Thus each entry in the diagram indicates the register or memory value that is written at the end of that particular clock cycle and that will be available in the next clock cycle.

As you can see, this timing diagram begins with four *Load* instructions, which load the values a, b, c, and d into the register file. Note that these values a, b, c, and d will then be available for reading four clock cycles after their instruction addresses have been loaded into the *PC*, that is, in clock cycles 4, 5, 6, and 7, respectively. In clock cycles 4, 5, and 6, the processor issues arithmetic instructions which will store the results x, y, and z into the *RF* four clock cycles later. Finally, the processor issues three *Store* instructions to store the values of x, y, and z into memory. Thus the value of z is available 13 clock cycles after the instruction at address 100 has been loaded into the *PC*.

On the basis of this timing diagram, we can see how a pipelined processor, which executes four instructions concurrently, can attain a performance that is almost four times the performance of a processor that executes instructions sequentially, even though each instruction by itself would still need four clock cycles to finish. In general, this processor will take $n + 3$ clock cycles to execute n instructions, in comparison with the $4n$ clock cycles it would take if they were executed sequentially. Note, however, that in the calculation above, we have assumed

ADDRESS	INSTRUCTION
100	Load a, base, off
101	Load b, base, off
102	Load c, base, off
103	Load d, base, off
104	Add x, a, b
105	Sub y, b, c
106	Add z, c, d
107	Store x, base, off
108	Store y, base, off
109	Store z, base, off
110	—

(a) Assembly program

CLOCK CYCLE	0	1	2	3	4	5	6	7	8	9	10	11	12	13
Read PC	100	101	102	103	104	105	106	107	108	109	110			
Write IR	Load	Load	Load	Load	Add	Sub	Add	Store	Store	Store				
Write A					a	b	c	x	y	z				
Write B		base	base	base	base	b	c	d	base	base	base			
Write AR			base + offa	base + offb	base + offc	base + offd				base + offx	base + offy	base + offz		
Write DR						a + b	b − c	c + d	x	y	z			
Write RF				a	b	c	d	x	y	z				
Write Mem											x	y	z	
Write PC	101	102	103	104	105	106	107	108	109	110	111	112	113	114

(b) Timing diagram

FIGURE 9.13
Cycle-by-cycle RISC operation.

that each instruction does not use the results of either of the preceding two instructions. When this assumption does not hold, the processor's performance will actually decrease, as we show in the next section.

9.8 DATA FORWARDING

In previous sections we have designed a RISC processor and demonstrated its pipelined execution on a small program. It is important to note, however, that this program had no data or control dependencies, as the performance of this processor is somewhat different if this condition is changed. More precisely, a **data dependence** occurs whenever one instruction generates a value that is used by one or more successive instructions. In the case of our RISC processor, then, this kind of data dependence between an instruction and either of the two previous instructions prevents the processor from producing the correct results, since the proper data would not be available by the time it is needed. In other words, we cannot execute such dependent instructions one after the other as specified, because the necessary data cannot be returned to the *RF* in time to be read by the next dependent instruction.

In such cases the problem can be rectified by postponing the dependent instruction for one or two clock cycles through the insertion of *No-op* instructions into the instruction stream. These *No-op* instructions can be inserted by the compiler during compile time or the control unit can initialize necessary stalls during instruction execution after detecting a data dependence between two instructions. Consider, for example, how we would deal with a data dependence within a short program that computes the sum of the three variables a, b, and c, and then stores the sum in the variable *total* while using the register *temp* in the *RF* for temporary storage:

$$temp = a + b$$
$$total = temp + c$$

In Figure 9.14(a) we show the assembly program for this computation. Note that one *No-op* instruction has been inserted after the third instruction, because the value b could not be fetched out of the *RF* until two instructions later. Similarly, two *No-op* instructions have been inserted after each *Add* instruction as well, because the values of *temp* and *total* will not be available for two clock cycles.

The performance loss caused by these *No-op* instructions is readily apparent in the timing diagram presented in Figure 9.14(b). According to this diagram, three *Load* instructions are fetched in the first three clock cycles. However, since the value b is not written into the *RF* until the end of clock cycle 4, it cannot be read from the *RF* until clock cycle 5. Thus we insert a *No-op* instruction to start in clock cycle 3. Similarly, the value of *temp* and *total* is written into the *RF* at the end of clock cycles 7 and 10. Therefore, we have to insert two *No-op* instructions after each of the *Add* instructions, allowing the processor to wait for the values of *temp* and *total* to become available in clock cycles 8 and 11, respectively. Taken all together, this diagram indicates that we will need a total of 11 instructions and 14 clock cycles to add a, b, and c. However, since five (or 45%) of those 11 instructions are *No-op* instructions, it is apparent that the data dependencies have substantially decreased the performance of our pipelined processor. We

ADDRESS	INSTRUCTION
100	Load a, base, offa
101	Load b, base, offb
102	Load c, base, offc
103	No-op
104	Add sum, a, b
105	No-op
106	No-op
107	Add total, c, sum
108	No-op
109	No-op
110	Store total, base, offt

(a) Assembly program

CLOCK CYCLE	0	1	2	3	4	5	6	7	8	9	10	11	12	13
Read PC	100	101	102	103	104	105	106	107	108	109	110			
Write IR	Load	Load	Load	No-op	Add	No-op	No-op	Add	No-op	No-op	Store			
Write A						a			temp			total		
Write B		base	base	base		b			c			base		
Write AR			base + offa	base + offb	base + offc								base + offt	
Write DR							a + b			temp+c			total	
Write RF				a	b	c		temp			total			
Write Mem														total
Write PC	101	102	103	104	105	106	107	108	109	110	111	112	113	114

(b) Timing diagram

FIGURE 9.14
Execution of instructions with data dependence.

can improve the performance by reordering instructions in such a way that insertion of *No-op* instructions is avoided as much as possible. In other words, we insert other independent instructions in place of *No-op* instructions.

To increase the processor's performance we can introduce **data-forwarding** paths into the processor's datapath, allowing data to skip one or more pipeline stages and "jump" ahead into a future stage. For example, in Figure 9.12, the first of these paths (indicated by dotted lines) forwards data from the output of the ALSU into the *A* register, shortening data transfer by two pipeline stages: one stage that transfers data from the *DR* to the *RF*, and another that transfers it from the *RF* to the *A* register. By using this path, we ensure that the results generated by one instruction can be used by the next instruction. The second path transfers data directly from the *DR* or data memory to the *B* register, skipping the pipeline stage that writes data into the *RF*, from which it is then moved to the *B* register. By using this path, we ensure that the data generated by one instruction can be used two instructions later.

To demonstrate the usefulness of data forwarding, we return to the example program that computes the sum of *a*, *b*, and *c*. As shown in Figure 9.15(a), its assembly program now consists of only six instructions, without the additional *No-op* instructions that extended the previous program. In this figure you can see that the first three instructions load *a*, *b*, and *c* into the *RF* as before. However, in clock cycle 4, the value of *b* is loaded into the *RF* and concurrently into the register *B* via the second forwarding path. Similarly, in clock cycle 5, both forwarding paths are used, as the value *c* is loaded into the *RF* and into register *B*

ADDRESS	INSTRUCTION
100	Load a, base, off
101	Load b, base, off
102	Load c, base, off
103	Add sum, a, b
104	Add total, c, sum
105	Store total, base, off

(a) Assembly program

CLOCK CYCLE	0	1	2	3	4	5	6	7	8
Read *PC*	100	101	102	103	104	105			
Write *IR*	Load	Load	Load	Add	Add	Store			
Write *A*					a	a + b	temp+c		
Write *B*		base	base	base	b	c	base		
Write *AR*			base + off	base + off	base + off			base + off	
Write *DR*						a + b	temp+c	temp+c	
Write *Status*									
Write *RF*				a	b	c	temp	temp+c	
Write *Mem*									total
Write *PC*	101	102	103	104	105	106	107	108	109

(b) Timing diagram

FIGURE 9.15
RISC processor operation with data forwarding.

(via the second forwarding path), and $a + b$ is loaded into the DR and into register A (via the first forwarding path). Next, in clock cycle 6, the value $a + b$ is stored into the RF in the register containing the *temp* variable, while *temp* is added to the variable c in the ALSU and then stored in both the DR and the A register. In clock cycle 7, the value of *temp* $+c$ is stored in the RF and, at the same time, moved from register A to the DR. Then, in the next clock cycle, this value is finally stored in data memory at the location assigned to the variable *total*.

As you can see from this example, it is apparent that data forwarding keeps the pipeline working at full speed, by eliminating the need for the insertion of *No-op* instructions that delay data-dependent instructions. Typically, data forwarding is used in some form in all modern commercial processors.

9.9 BRANCH PREDICTION

In general, we can pipeline all but control instructions successfully using data forwarding. When we use control instructions such as branch instructions, the processor cannot determine the address of the next instruction until the fourth pipeline stage, when the decision will be made whether to take a branch or not. Similarly, whenever we use jump instructions, it will also take four clock cycles to load the PC with a new address. In both these cases, we need to insert three *No-op* instructions after each control instruction.

The necessity for this insertion is demonstrated in Figure 9.16, where we present timing diagrams for a program that computes the

ADDRESS	INSTRUCTION
100	*Bgoeq a, b, +10*
101	*No-op*
102	*No-op*
103	*No-op*
104	*Move max, b*
105	*Move min, a*
106	*Jump +6*
107	*No-op*
108	*No-op*
109	*No-op*
110	*Move max, a*
111	*Move min, b*
112	—

(a) Assembly program

FIGURE 9.16
RISC operation with simple branching.

CLOCK CYCLE	0	1	2	3	4	5	6	7	8	9	10
Read *PC*	100	101	102	103	104	105	106	107	108	109	112
Write *IR*	*Bgoeq*	*No-op*	*No-op*	*No-op*	*Move*	*Move*	*Jump*	*No-op*	*No-op*	*No-op*	
Write *A*		*a*				*b*	*a*				
Write *B*		*b*									
Write *AR*											
Write *DR*							*b*	*a*			
Write *Status*			$a \geq b$								
Write *RF*								*max*	*min*		
Write *Mem*											
Write *PC*	101	102	103	104	105	106	107	108	109	112	

(b) Timing diagram when branch is not taken

CLOCK CYCLE	0	1	2	3	4	5	6	7	8	9	10
Read *PC*	100	101	102	103	110	111	112				
Write *IR*	*Bgoeq*	*No-op*	*No-op*	*No-op*	*Move*	*Move*					
Write *A*		*a*				*a*	*b*				
Write *B*		*b*									
Write *AR*											
Write *DR*							*a*	*b*			
Write *Status*			$a \geq b$								
Write *RF*								*max*	*min*		
Write *Mem*											
Write *PC*	101	102	103	110	111	112					

(c) Timing diagram when branch is taken

FIGURE 9.16
Continued.

maximum and minimum of two values that are stored in variables *a* and *b*. In Figure 9.16(a) you can see the assembly program, which compares *a* and *b*, and if *a* is greater than or equal to *b*, will set *max* = *a* and *min* = *b*; otherwise, it will set *max* = *b* and *min* = *a*. Since this processor cannot determine the address of the next instruction for three clock cycles, we have to insert three *No-op* instructions after the branch instruction, *Bgoeq*. Similarly, we have inserted three more *No-op* instructions after the *Jump* instruction at location 106. Figure 9.16(b) shows the timing diagram of the program's execution when the branch is not taken, and Figure 9.16(c) demonstrates what happens when the branch is taken.

Consider first the case when the branch is not taken, in which the processor executes the instruction *Bgoeq*, followed by three *No-op* instructions. As you can see, it is not until clock cycle 3 that the processor determines that the branch is not taken, at which time it loads address 104 into the *PC*. Two *Move* instructions and one *Jump* instruction are executed next. Like the branch instruction, however, the *Jump* instruction is also followed by three *No-op* instructions, since the earliest time when the processor can load the jump address 112 is clock cycle 9. In this case, then, it takes 10 clock cycles to perform the computation because the processor must execute six *No-op* instructions.

In the case when the branch is taken, the processor executes the instruction *Bgoeq*, which is followed by three *No-op* instructions. Then, in clock cycle 3, the processor is able to load the branch address into the *PC* and execute the two *Move* instructions and the rest of the program. As in the preceding case where the branch was not taken, this processor executes six instructions, including three *No-op* instructions. If we assume that there is an equal probability that either branch could be taken, we would expect the processor to execute the foregoing program in eight clock cycles, on average.

We can improve the processor's performance by replacing the *No-op* instructions in both branches by instructions outside the branch that are always executed. Alternatively, we can avoid the need to insert *No-op* instructions after every control instruction, by modifying the processor design and introducing **branch prediction**, which allows the processor to execute instructions that follow the branch instruction as it would if the branch is not taken. If and when the processor finds that the branch should have been taken, the instructions that were started in this speculative manner will simply be abandoned and the pipeline is flushed.

We demonstrate this technique of branch prediction in Figure 9.17, beginning with the sequence of assembly instructions from Figure 9.17(a). Note that this assembly program is equivalent to the program in Figure 9.16(a) except that it excludes the *No-op* instructions. The timing diagram presented in Figure 9.17(b) shows how the program executes if the branch is not taken, while Figure 9.17(c) shows the alternative case in which the branch is to be taken. As you can see, in the former case, the processor executes the instructions at addresses 101, 102, and 103, assuming that the branch will not be taken. Then, in clock cycle 3, when this prediction is confirmed, the processor proceeds to load the next instruction at address 104, not knowing that the previous instruction was a *Jump* instruction. When in clock cycle 6, the processor finds that the value of the jump address is 106, it will load this value into the *PC* and fetch that instruction into the *IR* in clock cycle 7. At this point, the previous three instructions started in clock cyles 4, 5, and 6, including the instruction at location 106, are flushed out of the pipeline by preventing data to be stored in the registers or the memory. In this case the

ADDRESS	INSTRUCTION
100	Bgoeq a, b, +4
101	Move max, b
102	Move min, a
103	Jump +3
104	Move max, a
105	Move min, b
106	—

(a) Assembly program

CLOCK CYCLE	0	1	2	3	4	5	6	7	8
Read PC	100	101	102	103	104	105	106	106	
Write IR	Bgoeq	Move	Move	Jump	Move	Move			
Write A		a	b	a		a	b		
Write B		b							
Write AR									
Write DR				b	a		a		
Write Status			$a \geq b$						
Write RF					max	min			
Write Mem									
Write PC	101	102	103	104	105	106	106		

⌐— Pipeline flush

(b) Timing diagram when branch is not taken

CLOCK CYCLE	0	1	2	3	4	5	6	7	8
Read PC	100	101	102	103	104	105	106		
Write IR	Bgoeq	Move	Move	Jump	Move	Move			
Write A		a	b	a		a	b		
Write B		b							
Write AR									
Write DR				b			a	b	
Write Status			$a \geq b$						
Write RF								max	min
Write Mem									
Write PC	101	102	103	104	105	106			

⌐— Pipeline flush

(c) Timing diagram when branch is taken

FIGURE 9.17
RISC processor operation with branch prediction.

processor would need seven clock cycles to compute the minimum and maximum of a and b.

In the second diagram we see what happens when the branch is taken. To begin with, the processor executes the first four instructions as before. However, when in clock cycle 3 it finds that the branch must be taken, it loads the branch address 104 into the PC and flushes the pipeline—that is, it abandons execution of the instructions at addresses 101, 102, and 103. Note that the address 104 would be loaded anyway, as it is the next address in the sequence. The processor then continues to execute the instructions at addresses 104, 105, and 106. For this case the processor needs six clock cycles to finish the same computation. Again, assuming an equal branch probability, the processor using branch prediction would need, on average, 6.5 clock cycles to compute the maximum and minimum of two numbers, which is approximately 28% faster then the processor without branch prediction.

From the preceding discussion, the advantage of this branch prediction technique is apparent, since a processor with branch prediction mechanisms would waste fewer clock cycles on average than a processor without them.

9.10 CHAPTER SUMMARY

In this chapter we have applied register-transfer synthesis techniques in designing general-purpose processors that are defined by their instruction sets. To do this, we discussed various types of instructions, with their fields and addressing modes, and demonstrated that there is a close relationship between instruction-set design and processor architecture. We also defined a processor design flow and demonstrated it by designing a 16-bit CISC processor and a 32-bit RISC processor.

For this demonstration, we introduced IS flowcharts and showed how to refine them into processor ASM charts from which we could derive a processor's architecture. Finally, we introduced the concepts of data forwarding and branch prediction, which are used to improve the performance of modern processors.

9.11 FURTHER READINGS

Hayes, J. P. *Computer Architecture and Organization*, 2nd ed. New York: McGraw-Hill, 1988.

Good overview of computer architecture, parallel processing, and design methodology.

Hennessy, J. L., and D. A. Patterson. *Computer Organization and Design: The Hardware/Software Interface.* San Mateo, CA: Morgan Kaufmann, 1993.

A detailed explanation of processor design based on the MIPS architecture, written by the pioneers of RISC technology, with excellent explanations for the reasons behind all design decisions.

Hwang, K. *Advanced Computer Architecture: Parallelism, Scalabilty, Programmability.* New York: McGraw-Hill, 1993.

A thorough overview of advanced computer architectures and their applications.

Kain, R. Y. *Computer Architecture: Software and Hardware,* Vols. I and II. Englewood Cliffs, NJ: Prentice Hall, 1989.

Provides an excellent explanation of software/hardware relationships in the design of computer systems.

Katevenis, M. G. H. *Reduced Instruction Set Computer Architecture for VLSI,* Boston: M.I.T. Press, 1985.

One of the first books discussing RISC architecture and design. It requires knowledge of VLSI technology and physical design.

Kogge, P. M. *The Architecture of Pipelined Computers.* New York: McGraw-Hill, 1989.

An excellent introductory text on datapath and control pipelining with emphasis on pipelining principles.

9.12 PROBLEMS

9.1 (Instruction formats) Write a sequence of instructions that will compute the value of $y = x^2 + 2x + 3$ for a given x using:

(a) Three-address instructions

(b) Two-address instructions

(c) One-address instructions

Assume that no register file is available in the processor except a single accumulator for part (c). Give the number of instructions and memory accesses for each case.

9.2 (Instruction formats) Do Problem 9.1 assuming the availability of a register file. For both register file and memory addresses use:

(a) One-address instructions

(b) Two-address instructions

(c) Three-address instructions

Minimize the number of memory addresses in each case.

9.3 (Instruction formats) Using three-address instructions, develop the instruction sequences for reading and writing:

(a) A push-down stack

(b) A FIFO queue

(c) A LIFO queue

9.4 (Addressing modes) Write procedures for reading from and writing to a FIFO queue, using a two-address format, in conjunction with:

(a) Direct addressing

(b) Indirect addressing

(c) Relative addressing

9.5 (Addressing modes) Write procedures for deleting and adding list elements. Assume that each list element uses two memory words, the first containing a data value and the second containing the address of the next element in the list. Use only three-address instructions, in conjunction with:

(a) Direct addressing

(b) Indirect addressing

9.6 (Addressing modes) Write a sequence of instructions that will compute $\sum_{i=1}^{100} a_i x_i$, where $A = [a_1, a_2, \ldots, a_{100}]$ and $X = [x_1, x_2, \ldots, x_{100}]$ represent arrays that are stored in the main memory. Use two-address instructions, in conjunction with:

(a) Direct addressing

(b) Relative addressing

(c) Indexed addressing with an auto-increment mode

9.7 (Instruction set design) Modify the instruction set presented in Figure 9.5 by extending the address field to 22 bits. This can be achieved by using only one register file address in the memory and control instructions and by assuming that the six most significant bits are in the *Src*1 and *Src*2 fields. Assume that the register $RF(0)$ always contains the base during its relative addressing mode.

9.8 (Instruction set design) Assume that the *PC* is register $RF(0)$. Show that *Call* and *Return* instructions are not needed since they can be implemented with a sequence of other instructions.

9.9 (IS flowchart) Assume that the *PC* occupies *RF*(0). Modify accordingly the IS flowchart shown in Figure 9.6 and the ASM chart shown in Figure 9.8.

9.10 (Instruction set) Add a dedicated base register (*BR*) to the 16-bit processor shown in Figure 9.10 and show the changes this requires in the instruction set and the processor schematic.

9.11 (Processor allocation) Using the same 16-bit processor, show the changes brought about in the ASM chart by allocating a dedicated:
  (a) Base register (*BR*)
  (b) Stack pointer (*SR*)

9.12 (Processor allocation) Using the same 16-bit processor, show the changes required in the ASM chart when memory access takes:
  (a) Two clock cycles
  (b) Three clock cycles
  (c) Four clock cycles

9.13 (Reduced instruction set) Using the instruction set presented in Figure 9.11, propose the changes that enable it to accommodate a register file with:
  (a) 16 registers
  (b) 32 registers
  (c) 64 registers
  (d) 256 registers

9.14 (Reduced instruction set) Propose changes in the instruction set presented in Figure 9.11 to increase the offset field.

9.15 (IS flowchart) Develop an IS flowchart for the reduced instruction set presented in Figure 9.11.

9.16 (ASM chart) Develop an ASM chart for the reduced instruction set presented in Figure 9.11.

9.17 (RISC processor) Write a program for the RISC processor shown in Figure 9.12, assuming that it computes $y = x^2 + 2x + 3$ for a given x. Assume also that the ALSU can perform multiplication in one clock cycle. Derive the timing diagram for this processor, using the one in Figure 9.13, as a model.

9.18 (Branch prediction) Write a program that computes absolute value for the RISC processor shown in Figure 9.12. Develop a timing diagram for this processor:
  (a) Without branch prediction
  (b) With branch prediction

9.19 (Data forwarding/branch prediction) Write an assembly language program that computes the square-root approximation (presented in Chapter 8) for a RISC processor:
  (a) Without data forwarding and without branch prediction
  (b) With data forwarding but without branch prediction
  (c) Without data forwarding but with branch prediction
  (d) With data forwarding and branch prediction

Appendix: Laboratory Experiments

In the previous chapters we learned how to design digital circuits on gate, register, and processor levels. After finishing the design on any of these levels, we must ensure that the designed circuits behave as intended in addition to satisfying the imposed constraints on some quality metrics. As we mentioned before, the best-known quality metrics are cost, performance, and power consumption.

Cost can be measured in the number of transistors, gates, registers, or processors used in the design. An alternative cost metric is the area of the microchip or printed-circuit board used to hold these components. The total cost is obtained by summing the number of transistors, gates, or registers in each component in the final schematic. On the other hand, the area metric is more difficult to estimate since it requires estimating the area used by wires as well as estimating the position or placement of each component on a microchip or a printed-circuit board.

The performance is measured differently on different levels of abstraction. On the transistor and gate levels, it is measured as the time needed to propagate (propagation delay) the input change to the output pins. On the register-transfer level, it is measured in number of clock cycles or number of states, while on the processor level it is measured in number of instructions per second or as execution time on selected benchmarks.

Power dissipation is equal to the product of average current and supply voltage. Since supply voltage is usually constant for the whole microchip or printed-circuit board, power dissipation is proportional to the average current being drawn from the power supply. In bipolar technology such as with the TTL family, the gate circuits draw a small current in the "off" state and a much larger current in the "on" state. Therefore, the power dissipation is proportional to the average number of gates in the "on" and "off" states. With MOS technology, on the other hand, gate circuits draw a current only in transition from 0 to 1 and 1 to 0. The power dissipation, thus, is proportional to the average number of gates changing their output value in a specific time interval. In either case, the number of gates toggling is dependent in a major way on the input data and in a minor way on circuit design. Thus, in order to measure power dissipation we must count the number of gates in the "on" state or the number of gates toggling for a large number of random data, compute the average count and then multiply it by the nominal gate current and supply voltage.

A.1 LABORATORY EQUIPMENT

As we explained in the previous section, we use the laboratory to check functionality and other quality metrics after the design is completed. The design functionality can be validated in several different ways.

A.1.1 Breadboarding

The most traditional way, called **breadboarding**, uses a **breadboard** containing several strips of sockets for mounting integrated circuits (ICs) containing a small number of gates, flip-flops or small register-transfer components such as 4-bit registers, counters, ALUs or 4-word register files. Several examples of such integrated circuits in the TTL family were shown in Figures 3.18 and 3.19. The rest of the circuits could be found in TTL and CMOS Data Books.

The breadboard also contains light-emitting-diode (LED) indicator lamps to show the output values, toggle switches to provide values 0 and 1 for input signals, and a power supply for integrated circuits. The other necessary equipment for breadboarding includes hookup wire and a pair of wire strippers for cutting and stripping the wires. During breadboarding, designers plug the necessary IC types into sockets, cut wires of proper length, and connect the ICs on the breadboard according to the schematic generated during the design phase. The toggle switches are connected to the circuit inputs so that circuit behavior for any combination of input values can be observed. In order to observe the output values, we must connect the LED lamps to the circuit outputs. The design validation is performed by observing the output values for every combination of input values. In other words, every row in the circuit's truth table is checked for correctness. Although checking each row in the truth table is possible for a small circuit with few inputs and few outputs, it cannot be done in a reasonable time for large circuits. In order to avoid a long and exhaustive testing phase, designers normally select a much smaller set of input patterns, called test vectors, such that each pattern toggles the output of at least one gate or flip-flop and that each gate or flip-flop output is toggled in at least one pattern.

This process of test pattern generation is not simple in cases when components are buried deep in the design and whose inputs are difficult to control and outputs to observe. In order for the gate or flip-flop to change the output value, we must be able to induce the change on some of its inputs. To induce this input change, we must find one or more paths that leads from the input pins of the circuit to the inputs of a particular gate or a flip-flop and create an input pattern that will propagate this input change to the input of the gate or flip-flop. Similarly, we must find the path from the output of the gate or the flip-flop under observation to the circuit output pins and create an input pattern that will propagate this output change to the circuit output pins where it can be observed through LED indicator lamps. Many times, particularly in the sequential circuits with complex internal feedback loops, finding such patterns is not possible.

In order to measure propagation delay, we need a pulse generator and a multiple-trace oscilloscope. The pulse generator is connected to one or more inputs that will allow propagation of the pulse sequence to a particular gate or flip-flop. The oscilloscope probes (one for each trace) are connected to the output of gates or flip-flops under observation. This way, we can compare input and output signals on the oscilloscope screen and measure delay between them.

Power estimation is more difficult to compute. For a small circuit we can find the state or switching frequencies of each gate from the truth table. Furthermore, if we assume that each input pattern will follow another input pattern with the same frequency, we can find the current for each gate and average it over all gates and all patterns to produce an average power dissipation. In the case of large circuits, we must select a representative set of input patterns and use CAD tools to measure gate and flip-flop status or switching frequencies and arrive at an average power. Note that the average power is dependent on the selected set of input patterns since some patterns may cause large changes in the circuit while some others may cause just a minimal change.

A.1.2 FPGA Boards

A **FPGA board** is similar to a breadboard with a difference being that the strips of sockets and small-scale ICs are replaced by one or more FPGAs. Each FPGA contains up to several thousand gates as described in Section 3.11 and Figure 3.23. The other important difference is that designers cannot connect the gates individually since they are encapsulated inside the FPGA package but they have to program the connections. For this reason we need a schematic capture tool which converts the schematic created by the designers on the computer screen to an internal format called netlist which contains all the connections, their sources, and destinations. Since the sources and destinations are gates or flip-flops, the netlist is equivalent to the captured schematic. However, it is not possible to regenerate the schematic from the netlist since the netlist does not contain any information about the position of the gates and other components on the screen. In order to regenerate a schematic from the netlist, we need placement and routing tools.

The second CAD tool needed for the FPGA board is a design implementation tool that maps (downloads) the captured schematic into the logic blocks of the FPGA architecture, determines an optimal placement of the logic blocks, and selects the routing channels that connect logic and I/O blocks.

For performance and power measurement, we can use, as in the case of breadboards, pulse generators and the oscilloscope to measure input-to-output propagation delay and switching activity.

A.1.3 Capture-and-Simulate Labs

Instead of breadboards or FPGA boards we can use **event driven simulators** for functionality and performance validation and **schematic capture** or **hardware-description languages** (HDLs) for specifying digital designs. Event-driven simulators compute the output value from input values for each gate, flip-flop, or any other digital component whose model is in the simulator library or specified by the designer. Simulators also assign time stamps to each output value indicating when the output signal will be assigned this precomputed output value. Each simulator also keeps track of the simulated time and schedules the assignment of new values to output signals, called events, according to the time stamps associated with each value. An event-driven simulator repeats the following four steps for each event.

1. It assigns new values to one or more output signals according to the schedule it maintains.
2. It computes a new output value for each component whose inputs have been changed by the assignment in (1).
3. Schedules the assignment of the new value (new event) computed in (2) to the output signal some time into the future according to the time stamp computed from the component model.
4. Advances the simulated time to the next scheduled event.

A simulator performing the four steps indicated above can be used for functional and performance/power validation. In addition to computing the proper output values for each output signal, a simulator also indicates when the output signal will reach this output value in relation to the changes in the input values. By counting all changes in output values for all components over some time interval, we can also compute power dissipation. As mentioned earlier in the section, each simulator requires a digital-circuit description which can be obtained through a schematic capture tool or HDL. A schematic capture tool captures this information graphically while a HDL does it textually. Writing a design description in a selected HDL, such as IEEE Standard VHDL or Verilog languages, is called **modeling**. The major advantage of HDLs is that they allow designers to describe digital circuits on different levels of abstraction. For example, we can design a digital circuit and describe it by specifying all the gates and flip-flops and their connections. On the other hand, we can describe it by using Boolean expressions for every flip-flop input, or by specifying all the register transfers in each clock cycle. At even higher levels of abstraction, we can describe a processor using its instruction set. In this case the model is an infinite loop containing a case statement whose case variable is the instruction type and opcode fields. In such a processor model, each iteration of the loop represents one instruction-execution cycle.

The advantage of modeling on a higher level of abstraction is shorter simulation-run times. Because of short run times an instruction-set model of the processor can be used for debugging of assemblers, compilers and operating systems software while the processor is being designed and manufactured.

A.1.4 Describe-and-synthesize Labs

Since use of HDLs allows designers to describe digital circuits on higher abstraction levels, we can take advantage of these shorter, more efficient, and readable descriptions and automatically synthesize lower level designs using different synthesis tools.

For example, logic synthesis tools will convert Boolean expressions into gates and optimize the gate level design for a particular cost, performance, power and gate library using methods similar to those explained in Chapter 4. Furthermore, sequential synthesis tools perform state minimization and encoding for sequential logic and generate Boolean expressions from FSM and ASM descriptions, as explained in Chapter 6. On the other hand, behavioral synthesis tools perform register transfer-synthesis, including storage sharing, functional unit sharing, bus sharing, and scheduling as explained in Chapter 8.

A.2 LABORATORY TYPES

The equipment and the tools described in the previous section allows for creation of different design labs, shown in Table A.1, in which each lab is suited for one or more specific tasks in the design process.

The most traditional is the **breadboarding lab** in which students design digital circuits, connect gates, flip-flops, and small medium-scale components. In this lab they verify the functionality of combinatorial and sequential components. (This material was covered in Chapters 5 and 7.) In order to measure performance, we can upgrade the breadboarding lab with pulse generators and oscilloscopes, so that students can observe different signal waveforms and measure delay and power.

TABLE A.1

Laboratory Types

LAB NAME	BREAD-BOARD	FPGA BOARD	GEN. & SCOPE	SCHEMATIC CAPTURE	SIMULATOR	HDL	LOGIC/SEQ. SYNTHESIS	BEHAVIORAL SYNTHESIS
Breadboarding lab	×							
Perf. oriented breadboarding	×		×					
FPGA lab		×		×				
Perf. oriented FPGA lab		×	×	×				
Simulation lab				×	×			
Modeling lab					×	×		
Logic synthesis lab					×	×	×	
Behav. synthesis lab					×	×	×	×
Typical design lab		×	×	×	×	×		

A more modern lab would be a **FPGA lab** that would replace breadboards with FPGA boards and additional software for downloading the design schematic into FPGA, which is usually supplied by the

FPGA manufacturers. This lab can also be used for performance and power measurements if upgraded with pulse generators and oscilloscopes.

We can also practice designing digital components by using simulator tools which can easily accommodate larger designs than breadboarding. A **simulation lab** would have at least a schematic capture tool connected to a simulator. For teaching HDL and modeling practices, we would use a **modeling lab** in which students would learn how to describe different components on different levels of abstraction and how to write models to verify functionality, communication protocols, performance, power, and testability among others. Such a modeling lab would need a simulator tool with a standard language such as VHDL or Verilog as a front end.

In more advanced courses we may use synthesis tools for design of digital circuits. In a **logic synthesis lab** students would write higher level models and design digital circuits from written models. For comparison purposes each circuit can be designed first manually and then synthesized automatically. (This material was covered in Chapters 4 and 6.) In the **behavioral synthesis lab** students would do the same thing as in the logic synthesis lab except they would be able to work from instruction-sets to synthesize processors or from algorithmic descriptions to synthesize ASICs. (This material was covered in Chapters 8 and 9.)

In summary, a **typical design lab** that can be used for several courses would include a HDL-based simulator with a schematic capture tool for introductory courses and HDL input for modeling or advanced courses. It would also include FPGA boards with some generators and oscilloscopes for students to get a feel for real hardware and the manufacturing process. Logic and behavioral synthesis tools would be a useful add-on for schools with strong programs in design and manufacturing.

A.3 EXPERIMENTS FOR BREADBOARDING AND FPGA LABS

A.1 Design the full-adder and full-subtractor circuits given in Tables 2.3 and 2.4 using your own gate library. Breadboard/download the design and check that it works properly. Furthermore, find the worst-case input-to-output delay for each output.

A.2 Capture the 9-bit odd/even parity generator shown in Fig. 3.19 and find the worst-case input-to-output delay. Compute also the power dissipation for the library of your choice.

A.3 Redesign the 4-bit carry-look-ahead function from Example 4.10 using your own gate library while minimizing input-to-output delay. Check the design for functionality and find the critical path in the design by comparing all input-to-output delays.

A.4 Design the following combinatorial circuits using the gate library of your choice and determine the critical input-to-output delays.

(a) 4-bit ripple-carry adder (Section 5.1)

(b) 4-bit CLA generator (Section 5.2)

(c) 4-bit logic unit (Section 5.4)

(d) 4-bit ALU (Section 5.5)

(e) 3-to-8 decoder (Section 5.6)

(f) 8-to-1 selector (Section 5.7)

(g) 8-to-3 priority encoder (Section 5.9)

(h) 4-bit magnitude comparator (Section 5.10)

(i) 4-bit left/right shifter/rotator (Section 5.11)

(j) 8-bit left/right barrel shifter (Section 5.11)

A.5 Design the following storage elements using the gate library of your choice, verify their behavior and generate timing diagrams for each transition from one state to another.

(a) SR latch (Section 6.1)

(b) Gated SR latch (Section 6.2)

(c) Gated D latch (Section 6.3)

(d) Master-slave SR flip-flop (Section 6.4)

(e) Master-slave JK flip-flop (Section 6.4)

(f) Master-slave D flip-flop (Section 6.4)

(g) Master-slave T flip-flop (Section 6.4)

(h) Edge-triggered D flip-flop (Section 6.4)

(i) Master-slave D flip-flop with preset and clear (Section 6.5)

(j) Edge-triggered flip-flop with preset and clear (Section 6.5)

A.6 Design the traffic-light controller (Problem 6.22), check its behavior, and determine the worst-case input-to-output delay.

A.7 By using your own library, design the following sequential circuits, define their state diagrams, check their behavior, and determine the minimal clock period needed for their operation.

(a) 4-bit register (Section 7.1)

(b) 4-bit shift register (Section 7.2)

(c) 4-bit counter (Section 7.3)

(d) 4-bit up/down counter (Section 7.3)

(e) BCD counter (Section 7.4)

(f) 4-bit asynchronous counter (Section 7.5)

(g) 2 port register file (Section 7.6)

(h) 4×4 RAM (Section 7.7)

(i) 4-word push-down stack (Section 7.8, Figure 7.20)

(j) 4-word FIFO queue (Section 7.9, Figure 7.23)

(k) 8-bit datapath (Section 7.10, Figure 7.26)

A.8 Using combinatorial and sequential components designed in Experiments A.4, A.5, and A.7, design the following control units and determine the worst-case delay.

(a) Hardwired control (Figure 7.34(a))

(b) Control unit with a state register and a decoder (Figure 7.34(b))

(c) Control unit with a counter (Figure 7.34(c))

(d) Control unit with a push-down stack (Figure 7.34(d))

(e) Microprogrammed control unit (Figure 7.34(e))

A.9 Using your own library, redesign the one's counter from Example 7.1 and determine the smallest operational clock period (highest frequency clock period) for the following cases:

(a) Datapath (Figure 7.26) and control unit (Figure 7.34(a))

(b) Datapath (Figure 7.26) and (Figure 7.34(c))

(c) Datapath (Figure 7.26) and (Figure 7.34(e))

(d) Custom datapath and control unit (Figure 7.34(a))

(e) Custom datapath and control unit (Figure 7.34(c))

(f) Custom datapath and control unit (Figure 7.34(e))

A.10 Design a datapath and control unit for the field insertion algorithm described in Problem 7.20. Determine also the highest operational frequency for your design (the shortest possible clock period).

A.4 EXPERIMENTS FOR SIMULATION LAB

A.11–20 Repeat experiments from the previous section. Instead of breadboarding use a schematic capture tool to specify the design and an event-driven simulator to validate functionality, and determine delays, critical paths, worst-case input-to-output delays and highest operational frequency.

A.5 EXPERIMENTS FOR MODELING LAB

A.21 Develop behavioral (arithmetic expressions), logic (Boolean expressions), and structural (gate netlists) level models for the following components:

- **(a)** 8-bit ripple-carry adder (Section 5.1)
- **(b)** 8-bit CLA generator (Section 5.2)
- **(c)** 8-bit logic unit (Section 5.4)
- **(d)** 8-bit ALU (Section 5.5)
- **(e)** 3-to-8 decoder (Section 5.6)
- **(f)** 8-to-1 selector (Section 5.7)
- **(g)** 8-to-3 priority encoder (Section 5.9)
- **(h)** 8-bit magnitude comparator (Section 5.10)
- **(i)** 8-bit left/right shifter/rotator (Section 5.11)
- **(j)** 8-bit left/right barrel shifter (Section 5.11)

Develop a test bench and validate models for functionality and timing.

A.22 Develop behavioral, register-transfer (clock cycle), and structural gate level models for the following components:

- **(a)** SR latch (Section 6.1)
- **(b)** Gated SR latch (Section 6.2)
- **(c)** Gated D latch (Section 6.3)
- **(d)** Master-slave SR flip-flop (Section 6.4)
- **(e)** Master-slave JK flip-flop (Section 6.4)
- **(f)** Master-slave D flip-flop (Section 6.4)
- **(g)** Master-slave T flip-flop (Section 6.4)
- **(h)** Edge-triggered D flip-flop (Section 6.4)
- **(i)** Master-slave D flip-flop with preset and clear (Section 6.5)
- **(j)** Edge-triggered flip-flop with preset and clear (Section 6.5)

Develop a test bench and validate models with respect to functionality and timing.

A.23 Develop model generators by extending models developed in the previous two experiments to work for any number of bits from 1 to 64. In other words, the number of bits n is a parameter to the model generator which generates the proper model with the number of bits specified by the parameter n. Verify your generator for 4, 7, 14, 29, and 60 bits.

A.24 Develop behavioral and structural models for:

- **(a)** Pushdown stack with shift registers (Figure 7.20)
- **(b)** Pushdown stack with memory (Figure 7.21)
- **(c)** FIFO queue with shift registers (Figure 7.23)
- **(d)** FIFO queue with memory (Figure 7.24)

(Hint: The behavioral model describes the function of the stack or queue but not its components, while the structural model consists of all the interconnected components with each component described by their behavioral or structural models developed in Experiments A.21 or A.22.)

A.25 Develop behavioral and structural models for the one's counter shown in Figure 7.31.

(Hint: The structural model consists of the control unit and the datapath components which have their own behavioral and structural models. The control unit behavior model consists of case statement and assignments to next-state and control vectors, while the structural model contains flip-flops and Boolean expressions for each flip-flop input or each control signal output. Similarly, the datapath behavioral model consists of several case statements while the structural model contains five different components, namely selector, register file, ALU, shifter and bus driver. Each component in turn is defined by their own behavioral or structural models.

A.26 Develop the model for the custom design of the one's counter (Figure 8.6) from its ASM chart and compare it to the model developed from its implementation (Figure 8.8).

A.27 Develop the behavioral, register-transfer (ASM chart), and structural models for the Black-Jack machine described in Problem 8.6.

A.28 Develop instruction-set (Instruction-set flowchart in Figure 9.6) and register-transfer (ASM chart in Figure 9.8) models for the CISC processor defined by its instruction set in Figure 9.5. Develop also the above two models for the RISC processor defined by its instruction set in Figure 9.11 and compare their models.

A.29 Develop structural models of the CISC (Figure 9.9) and RISC (Figure 9.12) processors and test them with benchmark code given in Figures 9.13, 9.14, 9.15, and 9.16. Compare execution times of each benchmark running on CISC and RISC processors.

A.6 EXPERIMENTS FOR LOGIC AND BEHAVIORAL SYNTHESIS LABS

A.30 Use logic (Boolean expression) models developed in Experiment A.21 for combinatorial components and synthesize each component with logic synthesis tools. Compare the results of logic synthesis with designs from Chapter 5 for:

   (a) 4-bit ripple-carry adder (Section 5.1)
   (b) 4-bit CLA generator (Section 5.2)
   (c) 4-bit logic unit (Section 5.4)
   (d) 4-bit ALU (Section 5.5)
   (e) 3-to-8 decoder (Section 5.6)
   (f) 8-to-1 selector (Section 5.7)
   (g) 8-to-3 priority encoder (Section 5.9)
   (h) 4-bit magnitude comparator (Section 5.10)
   (i) 4-bit left/right shifter/rotator (Section 5.11)
   (j) 8-bit left/right barrel shifter (Section 5.11)

A.31 Using the register-transfer (clock-cycle) models developed in Experiment A.22 for sequential components, synthesize each component with sequential synthesis tools. Compare the results with manual designs for:

   (a) 4-bit register (Section 7.1)
   (b) 4-bit shift register (Section 7.2)
   (c) 4-bit counter (Section 7.3)
   (d) 4-bit up/down counter (Section 7.3)
   (e) BCD counter (Section 7.4)
   (f) 4-bit asynchronous counter (Section 7.5)
   (g) 2 port register file (Section 7.6)
   (h) 4×4 RAM (Section 7.7)
   (i) 4-word push-down stack (Section 7.8, Figure 7.20)
   (j) 4-word FIFO queue (Section 7.9, Figure 7.23)
   (k) 8-bit datapath (Section 7.10, Figure 7.26)

A.32 Synthesize state-based and input-based versions of one's counter from their register-transfer models (ASM charts) given in Figure 8.6.

A.33 Synthesize one's counter state-based and input-based versions from their behavioral models. (Hint: Behavioral models do not have clock variables.)

A.34 Synthesize Black-Jack machine from its behavioral, register-transfer and structural models developed in Experiment A.27 using behavioral synthesis, sequential synthesis and logic synthesis tools.

A.35 Synthesize the square-root-approximation algorithm (Figure 8.9) from its behavioral and register-transfer (ASM chart) models. Repeat the synthesis for the (a) simple library in Figure 8.11, and (b) complex library in Figure 8.20.

A.7 FURTHER READINGS

The TTL Data Base, Dallas, Texas: Texas Instruments, 1988.

CMOS Logic Data Book, Dallas, Texas: Texas Instruments, 1990.

The Programmable Logic Data Book, San Jose, CA: Xilinx, Inc., 1995.

J. Duckworth, *Workview Office: Student Edition*, Upper Saddle River, New Jersey: Prentice Hall, 1997.

Index